BRIGHT RADICAL STAR

BRIGHT RADICAL STAR

Black Freedom and White Supremacy on the Hawkeye Frontier

Robert R. Dykstra

HARVARD UNIVERSITY PRESS
Cambridge, Massachusetts
London, England
1993

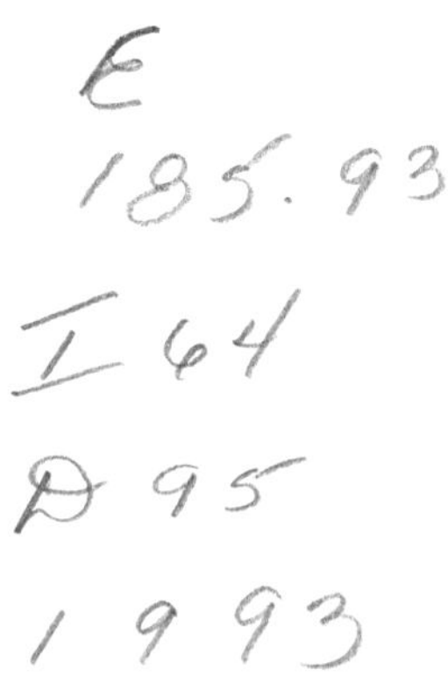

Printed in the United States of America
10 9 8 7 6 5 4 3 2 1

This book is printed on acid-free paper, and its binding materials have been chosen for strength and durability.

Library of Congress Cataloging-in-Publication Data

Dykstra, Robert R., 1930–
Bright radical star : black freedom and white supremacy on the Hawkeye frontier / Robert R. Dykstra,
p. cm.
Includes index.
ISBN 0-674-08180-3
1. Iowa—Race relations. 2. Racism—Iowa—History—19th century. 3. Afro-Americans—Iowa—History—19th century. I. Title.
E185.93.I64D95 1993
977.7'00496073—dc20 92-15672
CIP

FOR
JO ANN MANFRA

Preface

This book is about "life at the extremity of a culture," as V. S. Naipaul skillfully characterizes the American frontier. It is a study of white racism on the notoriously racist Middle Border between the years 1833 and 1880. In that important half-century every state and territory in the Union, whether initially free or slave, whether embracing large or small numbers of African-Americans, whether located in the North or the West or the South itself, had to confront the ultimate likelihood of black civil equality, of African-American equality before the law. This account tells how a pioneering people, advancing westward for nearly half a century, their long southern flank originally exposed to slavery, persistently responded to that egalitarian prospect—the central issue imposed upon them by the nation's great sectional controversy, by the Civil War, and by the aftermath of the war.

These women and men were not Iowans in the twentieth-century sense. They were New Englanders and New Yorkers, Pennsylvanians and Ohioans, southerners from Maryland and Virginia and North Carolina, immigrant Irish, Britons and Scots, Germans, Scandinavians. Their racial attitudes, we may suppose, had been shaped by the various cultural dispositions they brought with them. But once west of the Mississippi River the white adult males among them—that is, the politically empowered—had to devise a *common* polity that, however initially abstract the reality of a black presence, arranged the terms for interracial association. These terms themselves became increasingly salient political questions as small gatherings of black and white activists, occasionally prodded by abolitionist emissaries from the East, provoked debates over such tangible issues as integrated public schooling, equal access to welfare benefits and to the courts, interracial marriage, fugitive slave rendition, and—most extraordinarily—black voting and office-holding.

Iowa's early African-American community never grew as large as many continued to predict. In 1840, seven years after the territory had been legally opened to settlement, there were only 188 black Iowans—a mere 0.4 percent of its pioneers. By 1850 the number had risen to 333. On the eve of the Civil War it stood at 1,069. In 1870 black Iowans totaled 5,762, and in 1880 they were 9,516 in number—still just 0.6 percent of all residents of the Hawkeye State. How, one might ask, could they have been an issue?

The answer is that the rights and privileges of blacks—like slavery itself—prove to have been issues in every "free" jurisdiction in America by the Civil War era, even though the black presence everywhere outside the South was almost nil. In no northern state save New Jersey, for example, did nonwhites make up so much as 3 percent of the population in either 1860 or 1870. Yet white racial bigotry often has nothing much to do with first-hand interaction with blacks.

Frontier Iowans, like midwesterners in general, reacted not to the *fact* of a black presence but to the *prospect* of it. By the 1850s white Iowans disturbed by the likelihood need only look across their southern border, where lived some 115,000 slaves. The largest concentrations of these African-Americans—in about the same proportion to whites as in western Kentucky or on Maryland's Eastern Shore—lay scattered the width of Missouri within thirty to fifty miles of the Hawkeye line. A ceaseless theme of Iowa's conservative editors and politicians, both before and after emancipation, was that the immediate consequence of legislating racial equality in any form would be an overwhelming inrush from Missouri's nearby "black belt." That it never happened is almost beside the point.

The advantages offered to the historian by pioneer Iowans' collective experience are two. First, Iowa's early population was small enough to permit an uncommon intimacy with specific grass-roots reformers and racists, yielding an important human dimension too often absent from state-level studies of national issues. Second, three popular referendums punctuated Iowans' encounter with equal rights. These occasions invited them to register their attitudes toward blacks, and many thousands did so—once shortly before the Civil War, once just afterward, and once again at the close of Reconstruction. With respect to the last decades, of course, this book's narrative line necessarily narrows to the state's most important middle-level and top leadership. Quantitative analyses of these three great referendums, however, allow the reader to discern with some degree of precision how various population groups regarded black civil equality at three strategic moments in the nation's history, as well as over time.

It was the historian Mary R. Dearing who inadvertently thrust this topic on me—an Iowan-in-residence at the time—by mentioning something called the "Union Anti-Negro Suffrage Party" in her fine monograph on the Grand Army of the Republic. What followed, of course, was entirely self-inflicted, although I gladly acknowledge the honorable complicity of many other scholars and several institutions.

Harlan Hahn collaborated with me in composing and publishing the professional literature's first computer-aided analysis of a civil rights referendum. James C. Mohr then offered me the opportunity to expand that material into an essay on the larger aspects of Iowa's postwar political experience. Armed with Thomas B. Alexander's useful methodological criticism of the original, I accepted. Allan G. Bogue's compliment about the resulting piece, together with remarkably generous praise accorded it in book reviews by Michael Les Benedict, LaWanda Cox, James L. Crouthamel, Leonard P. Curry, Tilden Edelstein, and John V. Mering, nudged me irrevocably toward a full-length study.

The thoroughly professional staff of the State Historical Society of Iowa, at both its Des Moines and Iowa City centers, always proved unfailingly hospitable and helpful. Financial support from the University of Iowa and the Charles Warren Center of Harvard University allowed me the leisure to begin piecing together the antebellum chapters of the enterprise. A memorable one-on-one luncheon with David Herbert Donald at the Harvard Faculty Club rapidly focused my perceptions about what I thought I was up to.

In Worcester, Massachusetts, the truly incredible breadth of the American Antiquarian Society's holdings in nineteenth-century state and local history, plus an exceptionally user-friendly staff, permitted me to continue my Iowa research a thousand miles east of the Mississippi. A National Endowment for the Humanities fellowship (for which I suspect I have mainly LaWanda Cox to thank), supplemented by funding from the State University of New York at Albany, allowed me to spend a genuinely congenial year as an AAS associate. My colleagues there, especially Paul E. Johnson and Alden Vaughan, provided cautious encouragement, wise counsel, and good fellowship.

An unanticipated note from J. Morgan Kousser regarding an early published version of chapter 2 assured me that I was "right on all the major issues." Other friends tendered more specialized help. Peter S. Onuf gave expert advice on constitutional aspects of chapter 3. Jo Ann Manfra answered endless questions about legal procedure for chapter 5. Ronald F. Matthias generously lent his materials on the Iowa Know Nothings for chapter 7. Malcolm J. Rohrbough remained my occasional lifeline to unmicrofilmed Iowa newspapers for chapters 7 and 10. Hubert H. Wubben graciously let me publish a companion piece to his *Annals of Iowa* essay on the events of 1865–1868.

As indicated above, chapter 2 appeared earlier in somewhat different form as "White Men, Black Laws," *Annals of Iowa* 46 (1982): 403–440;

copyright © 1982 by the State Historical Society of Iowa (SHSI). A part of chapter 10 appeared as "The Issue Squarely Met," ibid. 47 (1984): 430–450; copyright © 1984 by SHSI. And a version of chapter 1 appeared as "Dr. Emerson's Sam: Black Iowans before the Civil War," *Palimpsest* 63 (1982): 66–82; copyright © 1982 by SHSI. I am grateful for the publisher's permission to incorporate that material here.

Although a few of my graduate students at Iowa—most notably Mary K. Fredericksen, Julia Mears, William Silag, and Lowell J. Soike—became "hands-on" adepts in my behalf, only a historian who has frequently depended on the kindness of computer-literate strangers will appreciate my encounter with quantitative methods. But sustained aid came at last. Richard Jensen's summer seminar at Yale University pleasantly refurbished my general methodological sophistication. John R. Reynolds, with unbelievable patience and amiability, guided me in restructuring an enormous and unwieldy data base badly scrambled in transit from Iowa City to Albany. Allan Johannesen, James P. Hanlan, and Gerald Zahavi helped reshape the date into a form usable by the desktop computer that Jo Ann Manfra made available. In the end, however, I braved the controversial mysteries of ecological regression quite alone, and no one but myself is responsible for the results.

On several formal occasions—at Brandeis University's history colloquium, the American Antiquarian Society's seminar in social and political history, the City University of New York's symposium on emancipation and its aftermath, the Schomburg Center's seminar in black history and culture, the annual meeting of the Social Science History Association, and public lectures at Iowa State University and Worcester Polytechnic Institute—skeptical Americanists of many persuasions heard, affably criticized, and guardedly applauded (or remained ominously silent about) successive drafts of what ultimately became chapter 12. C. Vann Woodward's kind words following one such encounter greatly heartened me, and immediately serviceable ideas for revision came from Dale Baum, Paul Johnson, Jo Ann Manfra, and Benjamin B. Ringer. Baum, Les Benedict, LaWanda Cox, Phyllis F. Field, Eric Foner, Morgan Kousser, and Peyton McCrary read and commented on one version or another of that concluding material and helped inspire its final form.

Cynthia Miller offered unexpected encouragement at a decisive moment. Bill Silag read and approved a draft of the entire manuscript. Aïda D. Donald and two readers for the Harvard University Press offered perceptive editorial suggestions, while Anita Safran rescued me from a fondness for stylistic excess. The Iowa Department of Transportation welcomed use of its official 1991 state road map as the base for the cartographic illustrations. Robert L. Frost constructed preliminary versions of the chart and maps that Anne E. Gibson painstakingly tailored for publication.

But the scholar to whom this book is gratefully dedicated did more than simply bring her enormously formidable critical talents to bear on its every paragraph. She also made real life worth living through all the years of its maturation.

Contents

Illustrations

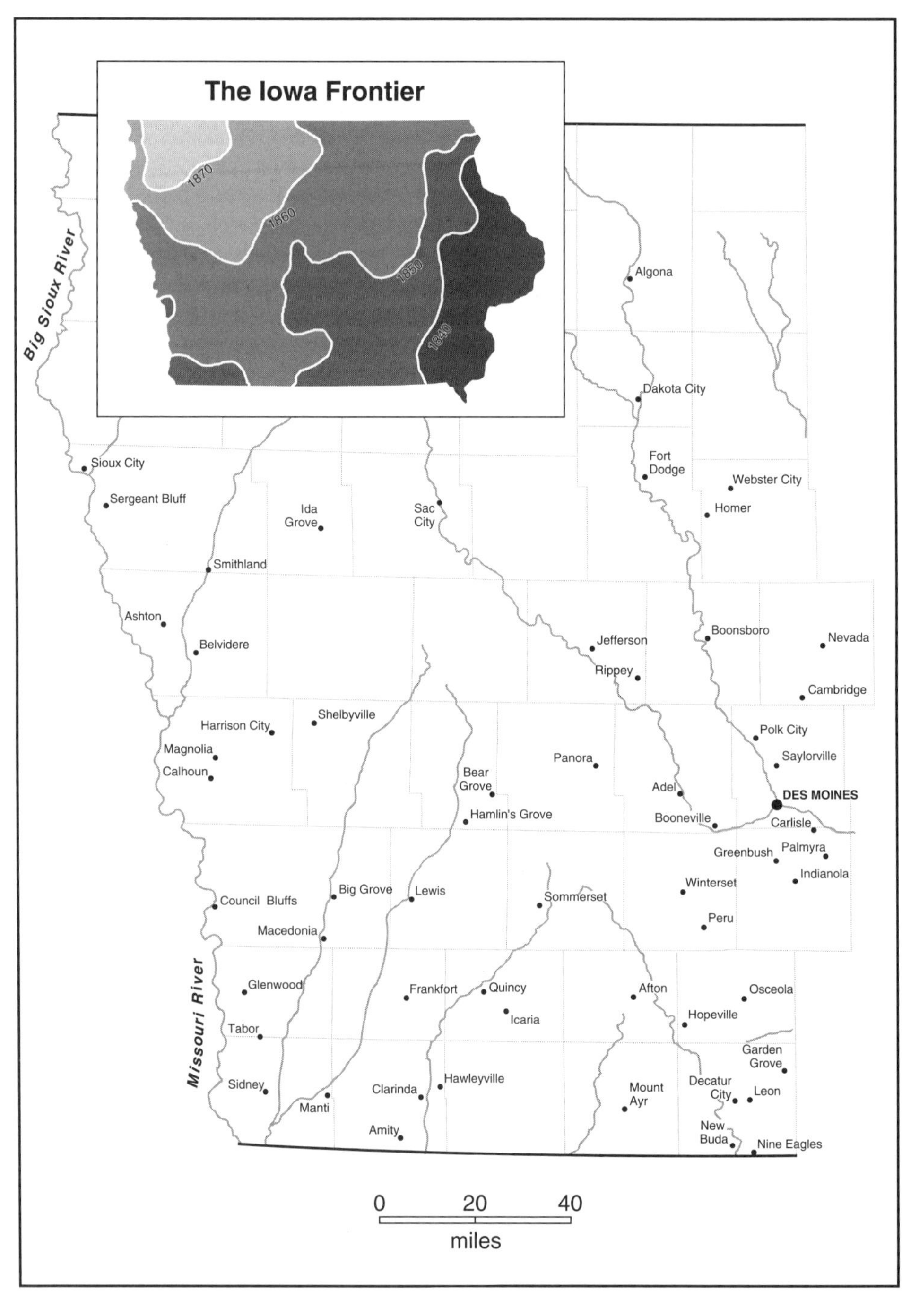
The Iowa Frontier
1870
1860
1850
1840
Big Sioux River
Missouri River
Algona
Dakota City
Fort Dodge
Webster City
Homer
Sioux City
Sergeant Bluff
Ida Grove
Sac City
Smithland
Ashton
Belvidere
Jefferson
Rippey
Boonsboro
Nevada
Cambridge
Shelbyville
Harrison City
Magnolia
Calhoun
Bear Grove
Hamlin's Grove
Panora
Adel
Booneville
Polk City
Saylorville
DES MOINES
Carlisle
Greenbush
Palmyra
Indianola
Winterset
Peru
Council Bluffs
Big Grove
Lewis
Macedonia
Sommerset
Glenwood
Frankfort
Quincy
Icaria
Afton
Osceola
Hopeville
Tabor
Garden Grove
Sidney
Manti
Clarinda
Hawleyville
Mount Ayr
Decatur City
Leon
Amity
New Buda
Nine Eagles
0
20
40
miles

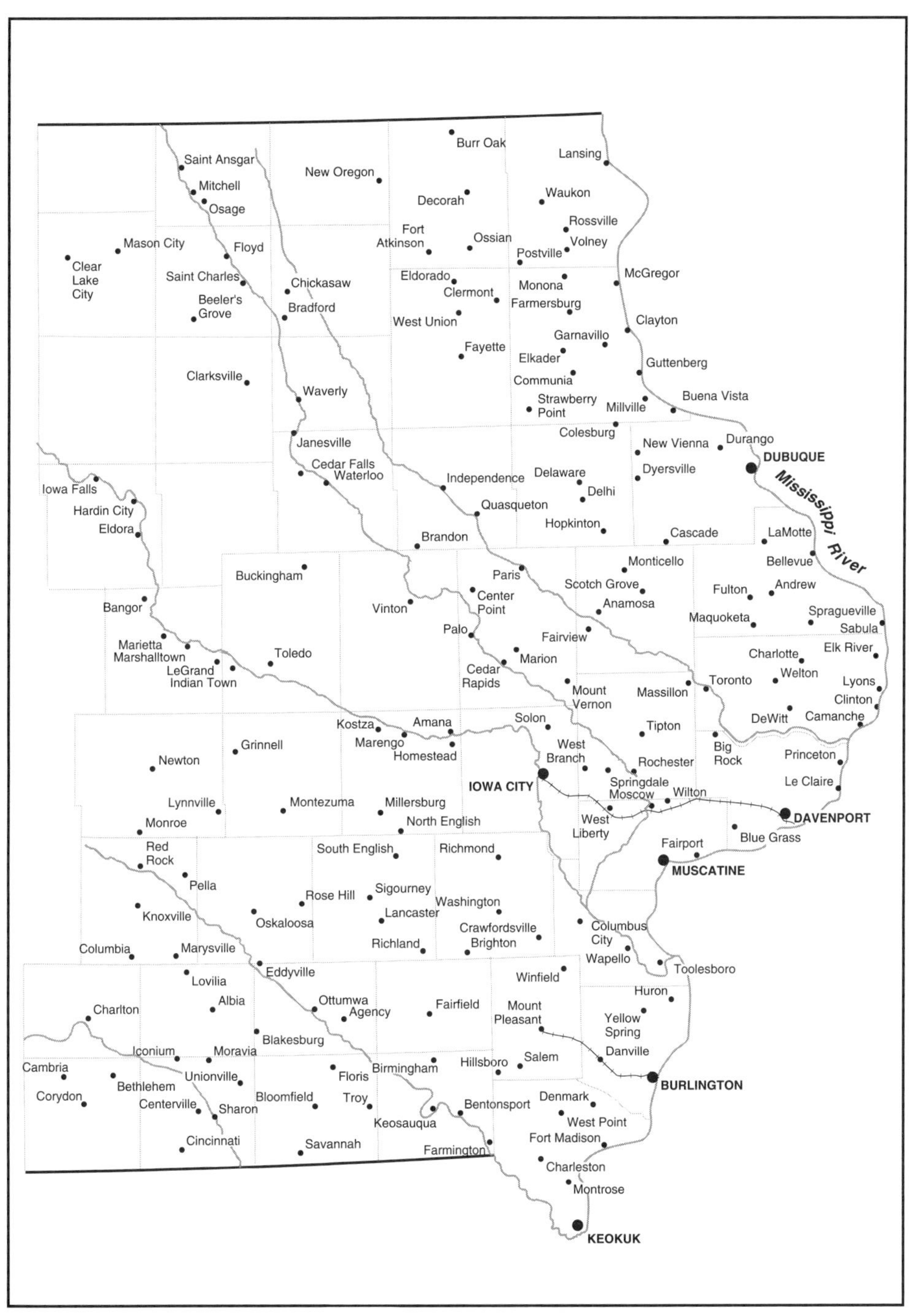

Map 1.1 Iowa in the mid-1850's.

ANTEBELLUM

I

Dr. Emerson's Sam

1

In the second decade of the nineteenth century two young slaves, Samuel Turner's Nat and Peter Blow's Sam, both of them slight in build and coal-black in color, approached adolescence in Southampton County, Virginia, a low, heavily wooded rural backwater abutting the North Carolina line. Both lads, in separate acts of rebellion against the world the slaveholders had made, created for themselves historic roles in the events leading to civil war.

One hot midsummer night in 1831 Nat, the elder of the two, now a moody Baptist preacher much given to visions and revelations, unleashed his personal apocalypse on the neighborhood of his birth. Twenty-four hours later he and his black companions had coolly butchered nearly sixty whites, mostly women and children, in the bloodiest slave uprising in American history. The slaughter electrified the entire white South, stimulating an increasingly furious political defense of slavery against its critics and one last doomed effort to reform it as a way of life more bearable to blacks. The dogs of war, let slip in southern Virginia, ultimately led America to Harpers Ferry and Sumter and Bull Run.[1]

The other young man, Sam Blow, would partake of neither the Nat Turner Rebellion nor its equally grim aftermath. He had gone west in his master's entourage to the Alabama frontier. A mecca for failed Virginia planters in the agriculturally depressed years following the War of 1812, Alabama unfortunately proved to be no promised land for the Blows. In 1820, after four seasons of hard-scrabble farming, Peter Blow, his family, and his slaves moved once again, locating this time in the burgeoning western city of Saint Louis. Here Peter Blow died, leaving many debts. To meet creditors' claims against the estate "the Blow boy Sam," the frailest of the late proprietor's bondsmen, found himself sold at public auction, fetching less than a third of what slaves his age normally brought. The successful bidder in Sam's case was a graduate of the University of Pennsylvania medical school, a struggling young Saint Louis physician named John Emerson. After acquiring a commission as an army medical officer, Dr. Emerson took his wife, his daughter, and his new black manservant along with him when reporting for duty as post surgeon at Fort Armstrong, Illinois, in the winter of 1833–34.[2]

Fort Armstrong commanded strategic Rock Island at the rapids of the upper Mississippi River, where during the War of 1812 a British cannon, three gunners, and the local Sauk and Mesquakie Indians had ambushed an American flotilla under Zachary Taylor. For Dr. Emerson as for Major Taylor before him, Rock Island turned out to be more than he'd bargained for, especially when subzero gales out of Canada hurtled down the frozen, snow-swept expanse of the great river. Pleading ill health, Emerson petitioned his superiors and his political friends for transfer to some more salubrious post. The surgery back at the Saint Louis arsenal would do nicely, he suggested, but to no avail. Spring came at last, the timber-shrouded riverbanks and islands greening in the bright April sun. As Emerson impatiently considered alternatives to Fort Armstrong, other members of the garrison drew his attention to the promising entrepreneurial prospects in real estate just across the river on the Iowa shore.[3]

Two years earlier a rebellious faction of the Sauk had been decisively crushed in the Black Hawk War. Their kinsmen, the largely uninvolved Mesquakie (whom the government referred to as the Fox), had been forced to surrender an enormous swath of the Iowa country, a cession that included the site of Chief Poweshiek's village opposite Fort Armstrong. In the summer of 1833, six months before Emerson's arrival, Poweshiek's people had peaceably vacated the crescent-shaped flood plain below the bluffs, joining the general Indian exodus into the interior. But before leaving they had insisted that the ground on which their village stood be granted as a gift to Antoine LeClaire, their interpreter. The government honored this demand. Other whites, however, began moving across the river as squatters in the wake of the Mesquakie retreat. They built log shanties and cleared small corn patches in the cane and underbrush, hoping to establish claims that would qualify them, in due time, to buy prime riverfront land at the minimum government price. And so it was that Dr. Emerson preempted 640 acres of shoreline a few miles upstream from LeClaire's reserve. Years later oldtimers professed to remember that the good doctor's slave, a diminutive black man, occupied the claim on his master's behalf.[4]

In the spring of 1836, however, War Department orders closed Fort Armstrong and sent Dr. Emerson north to Fort Snelling, in Wisconsin Territory. Sam went with him, never to return to Iowa. Emerson himself did. The army's medical corps suffered a cutback in strength at the close of the Seminole War, and Emerson found himself without a job. Pending reinstatement, he returned to the old site of Poweshiek's village, now a flourishing young city called Davenport. While once again attending personally to his land claim, Emerson offered himself as physician to the local folk. Late in 1843 he died rather suddenly, possibly from a sexually transmitted disease. Emerson's wife, who inherited the bulk of his estate, returned to Saint Louis, where three years later the slave she had known as Sam insisted that she sell him his freedom. Mrs. Emerson refused. Sam thereupon brought suit against her, his attorneys arguing that Sam's onetime residence in the State of Illinois and the Territory of Wisconsin—both off-limits to slavery—had nullified their client's status as a slave.

By this date Sam also insisted on answering to the name Dred Scott, and for the next several years the litigation over his freedom drew increasing national attention as it slowly worked its way up toward a judgment, ultimately, from the highest court in the land.[5]

I

Meanwhile, men and women who had set themselves to pioneer a new land crossed the great river, fashioned tiny urban enclaves along the Mississippi shore, and began to scatter inland, following the northwestward inclination of rivers into the southern Iowa drift plain, a country of flat lowlands, timbered slopes, and grassy upland divides. From the level crests of these ridges land-lookers gazing westward could imagine that the ancient, pre-alluvial contour of the earth's surface had somehow reconstituted itself, stretching ahead of them like some calm midwestern seascape beneath the big pale sky. Upriver, above the Raccoon forks of the Des Moines, the north bend of the Iowa, and the rapids of the Cedar and Wapsipinicon, the streambeds finally opened out, their enclosing landforms giving way to the gentler roll of the great prairie. Here the land rose more authentically to an uncluttered skyline, its sweep suggesting the awesome infinity of space. It was, its settlers were to discover, the most uniformly rich agricultural region of its size anywhere on earth.[6]

Some of these first pioneers were black. One such individual, a tall, very dark frontiersman called "Mogawk" by the Indians, was reported to be living at Poweshiek's village on the Iowa River in 1838. Other blacks, their precise numbers unknown, came as slaves. In the early thirties Isaac Campbell's slave John, his owner a prosperous Indian trader and merchant at Keokuk, the newly founded settlement at the mouth of the Des Moines, was "hiring out his own time," the phrase universally applied to slaves whose owners allowed them to work for wages and keep all or part of the proceeds. In 1834 a slave woman came to the Iowa country with the household of the famous army officer Stephen Watts Kearney. The first recorded death at the town of Bentonsport, founded on the lower Des Moines in 1839, was that of Shapley Ross's slave "Aunt Mornin." Forty miles upriver at the new Sauk and Fox Indian agency, two female slaves cooked meals for the construction crew putting up government buildings. Two others, purchased in Missouri, belonged to a white trader and his Indian wife. The agent himself owned several slaves; all were freed at his death in 1840.[7]

Iowa's achievement of separate territorial status in 1838—under a constitutional instrument that specifically forbade slavery—did not entirely suppress the tendency of owners to bring slaves with them from southern states. For a few years such transgressors included the two top officials in the territorial government. Ex-Congressman John Chambers of Kentucky, appointed governor of the Territory of Iowa by Pres. William Henry Harrison, disembarked at Burlington in 1841 accompanied, wrote an eyewitness, by "a small troop" of slaves. The territorial secretaryship, also a presidential appointment, fell to O. H. W. Stull of Maryland. A visiting Illinoisan was shocked to learn that the Burlington quarters of the two federal officials contained "seven or eight colored people" who were flogged, otherwise mistreated, "and kept in profound ignorance of the fact that when they touched the soil of Iowa they were *free*."

Since Chambers objected to the remoteness of the raw new territorial capital, Iowa City, both he and Stull sojourned there only during legislative sessions. During such visits the governor would be elaborately attended by his black bodyservant, "Uncle Cassius," and Stull decided that he, too, should display a style appropriate to high office while among the legislators. Luckily, he found a slaveowner willing to sell. The household of Richard Chaney, a suburban Iowa City sawmill operator from Virginia, included a mulatto boy less than ten years of age whom Stull purchased for $250, sealing the bargain in the lobby of a local hotel. When Stull was dismissed from office in a patronage dispute in 1843, he sold his slave to a brother-in-law, a fellow Marylander, who promptly took the lad south. When Chambers's own term of office ended two years later, at least two of his slaves, Cassius and a young woman named Carey Bennett, claimed their freedom and remained in Iowa.[8]

By this date slaveholding was fast becoming as socially unacceptable in most parts of the territory as it was illegal. As early as 1837 the Keokuk merchant and slaveholder, Isaac Campbell, responded to criticism by moving to the right bank of the Des Moines River from where, safe on Missouri soil, he continued to direct his many Iowa business ventures. A few years later Shapley Ross angrily decamped to Texas after some of his Bentonsport neighbors interfered with his attempt to recapture a runaway slave. Other Iowa slaveholders simply dissembled. The territorial census takers counted 188 black Iowans in the summer of 1840, but less than

10 percent of them went into the record as slaves. Many owners, such as Chaney the sawmiller, mislabeled their chattels, for the benefit of the enumerators, as "free colored." Ten years later the census marshals recorded no slaves at all in Iowa, although it is known that new settlers crossing the Missouri line occasionally carried blacks with them. In the early fifties, for example, an alcoholic farmer from North Carolina, a music-lover named L. P. ("Tune") Allen, brought into Ringgold County two teenaged slaves, a male and a female. He worked them a year before taking them south for sale. In adjoining Decatur County a middle-aged black man named George, owned by John McDaniel's family since boyhood, was held to service for some dozen years. In 1852 his owner formally freed him and lit out for the Oregon country.[9]

II

Only at Dubuque could blacks be said to have constituted a community in Iowa's earliest years. Here a booming frontier village had risen amid the weathered debris of an enormous cornfield where, as Iowa's first commercial farmers, enterprising Mesquakie women had raised thousands of bushels of maize for upriver sale to the white traders at Prairie du Chien. It was not the site's agricultural prospects, but rather the rich deposits of top-grade lead ore on the encircling bluffs that beckoned irresistibly to frontier entrepreneurs. A French-Canadian trader, from whom the town took its name, had been permitted to mine lead there from 1788 until his death, after which the area was closed to outsiders. Adventuresome newcomers extracted ore from the site as early as 1830, only to be twice driven out as illegal squatters by the army. Settlement resumed in 1833, swelling the town to some five hundred souls, many of them tough Irish immigrants and hardbitten veterans of the southern Missouri diggings. Such men, often drunk on corn liquor or cheap brandy, sometimes well-armed, made early Dubuque a kind of prototype of the legendary mining camps of the American West.[10]

In June 1834 Dubuquers organized a vigilante court and tried, sentenced, and ceremoniously hanged a quarrelsome Irishman for putting five slugs into the chest of a friend. Three days later the town's Methodists sought to elevate the spiritual tone of the place, undertaking the erection of the territory's first church. At least six local blacks, some of them said to have been slaves, pledged modest sums to the Methodist building fund and had their names dutifully inscribed on a circulating subscription paper: "Uncle Tom" (50¢), Caroline Brady (12½¢), Walton Baker (25¢), Sam Welsh (25¢), Nathaniel Morgan (50¢), and Tilda (25¢). A black woman, Charlotte Morgan, wife to Nathaniel, was one of the seven charter members of the interracial congregation. Six years later Dubuque's blacks numbered seventy-two, probably about 5 percent of the town's population but enough to constitute the largest aggregation in the territory.[11]

In only two instances, both of them unusual, does history record the specific circumstances of blacks' coming to Dubuque. One case was that of Jordan Montgomery's Ralph. Born in Virginia in about 1795, Ralph had been reared in Kentucky until he moved with a new master to northeastern Missouri in 1832. Two years later, presumably employed as a farm hand, he encountered a white man just returned from the Dubuque diggings whose tales of boundless wealth to be acquired there inspired Ralph to make his owner a proposition that the cash-poor Montgomery found hard to refuse. In a written agreement Ralph promised that in return for his freedom, within one year he would pay Montgomery $550 plus interest. With Montgomery's permission, Ralph then set off to the Dubuque mines, intent on striking it rich. But by the spring of 1839 luck still eluded him and the note was long overdue. Ralph's contract with Montgomery was evidently no secret at the diggings. Two Virginians, viewing the slave's predicament as more than just a good joke, wrote to Montgomery, offering to return the defaulting black to Missouri for a hundred-dollar fee. Montgomery, by no means inclined to write Ralph off as a bad debt, accepted the offer.

The Virginians swore out an affidavit that Ralph was a fugitive slave, then presented the document to a local justice of the peace, who obligingly ordered the black man's arrest and extradition. Accompanied by the sheriff, the Virginians surprised Ralph at his mineral claim southwest of town, clapped him in handcuffs, and lifted him into a wagon. Thinking it best to avoid Dubuque, they took the road for nearby Bellevue, where they delivered him to the captain of a riverboat for transport south. But a Dubuque businessman, Alexander Butterworth, while plowing a field on his suburban farm, happened to witness Ralph's arrest. Armed with a writ of *habeas corpus* hastily obtained from Judge Thomas S. Wilson, and accompanied by the reanimated sheriff, Butterworth galloped to the rescue. He and the officer reached dockside just in time and forced the captain to return Ralph to Dubuque for a hearing before Judge Wilson. Recognizing the far-reaching implications of the case, Wilson urged its immediate transfer to the newly organized Iowa supreme court at Burlington, on which he himself—at a precocious twenty-four years of age—happened to sit. All parties agreed.[12]

In re Ralph (1839) became the second piece of litigation to come before the Iowa court. Representing the alleged runaway was David Rorer, a Virginia-born former slaveowner from Arkansas, a short, barrel-chested individual who nine months earlier had put a fatal pistol ball through the body of a political foe. Rorer also happened to be one of the brightest legal lights in the territory. Lawyerly talent, however, proved in this instance to be less important than that Ralph had a very strong case: American jurisprudence offered ample precedent for the freedom of a slave whose master intended to make free territory the slave's place of residence either by carrying him or her there or permitting the slave to locate there on his or her own. The supreme court of Missouri, in no less than a dozen cases, had been particularly zealous in applying this doctrine to freedom suits resulting from slave residence in Illinois. The facts of one such case, *Ralph v. Duncan* (1833), were similar to the Iowa case in more ways than just the name of the slave: the earlier Ralph had won freedom on grounds that his Missouri master, in return for a promissory note, had allowed him to hire his own time at the Shawneetown salt works and the Galena mines.[13]

Rorer's most powerful argument was to remind the court that the famous Missouri Compromise, wherein Congress granted Missourians statehood in 1821, had also specified that in the lands of the Louisiana Purchase north and west of Missouri's boundaries "slavery and involuntary servitude, otherwise than in the punishment of crimes, . . . shall be, and is hereby, forever prohibited." The color of legality had been given Ralph's arrest by a supplementary clause providing that "any person escaping into the same [free territory], from whom labour or service is lawfully claimed, . . . may be lawfully reclaimed and conveyed to the person claiming his or her labour or service as aforesaid." But by no stretch of the imagination, Rorer noted, had Ralph been a fugitive.[14]

The court's gaunt and melancholy chief justice, Charles Mason, had a decade earlier graduated at the top of his class at West Point, just above the brilliant Robert E. Lee. He now tendered the court's decision that Ralph was neither fugitive nor slave. Once permitted by his owner to establish a residence on Iowa soil he had become free, automatically emancipated by the Missouri Enabling Act. That Ralph had not paid Montgomery a lawful debt was certainly true, but the courts could not reduce a man to slavery for that, at least not in Iowa. Having issued their verdict, the justices adjourned, appropriately enough, on Independence Day. Ralph Montgomery, as he henceforth preferred to be known, went forth a free man.[15]

One fine spring morning, more or less on the anniversary of the famous arrest, Dubuque's Judge Wilson discovered the former slave at work in the garden behind Wilson's house. Asked to explain himself, Ralph obliged. It was his way of saying thanks. "I ain't paying you for what you done for me," he said. That, both he and the judge knew, would have been improper. "But I want to work for you one day every spring to show you that I never forget you." And he was as good as his word. As Wilson recalled half a century later, Ralph Montgomery "afterwards struck a big lode, but gambled [the proceeds] away, and died with the small-pox." Not, however, before gaining a modest immortality in the history of freedom litigation in the trans-Mississippi West.[16]

A far less pleasant fate awaited a second Dubuque black man a year after Ralph's case had been heard. Nathaniel Morgan and his wife Charlotte had come to the diggings from Galena, the Illinois mining town that was the immediate place of origin of many early Dubuquers. In 1833 a Dubuque boarding house owner offered them both employment. The Morgans accepted and, as already noted, played small roles in organizing Dubuque's first church congregation and funding its edifice. By 1840 they were among the community's oldest residents. Nat was in his early thirties, Charlotte a few years older. They shared their house with a boarder, a free black man. Nat now worked as a cook and waiter in a local hotel, Charlotte as a laundress. Some said that Nat occasionally pilfered cigars and other small items from the hotel's guests. Others later denied this, but by then it no longer mattered.[17]

One day in early September 1840 Nat had just cooked dinner and was carrying it to the guests when a group of angry men burst into the hotel, seized him, and accused him of stealing a trunk full of clothes. Nat denied knowledge of the theft, but a mob gathered, growing in size as the excitement emptied the bars. Col. Paul Cain, a New York-born miner and commander of the local militia, took charge. He and the crowd rushed Nat down to the riverfront, where they secured him to a post and bared his back. To make him confess they prescribed the southern slaveholders' biblically licensed "forty stripes save one."[18]

At first Nat screamed his innocence, then his guilt. He confessed, according to an eyewitness, several times, saying whatever his tormentors seemed to want him to say but thereby contradicting himself, which brought renewed applications of the whip. Finally Cain demanded that Nat lead them to the stolen trunk. Nat agreed, as he now agreed to everything, and they cut him down and dragged him to the confessed hiding place. No trunk was to be found. Thirty-nine more lashes fell upon Nat's lacerated back. Had he possibly hidden the trunk at his house? Nat cried yes. They dragged him there, where Charlotte's sobs no doubt accompanied the choreography of the mob. Once again the quest proved fruitless. Again the lash. Nat no longer cried out, but now, in a whisper, he named a place up on the bluff. He would show them the spot, he said, if they would just let him rest a moment. That was denied.

Our eyewitness may have been Dr. Ambrose Crane, who warned that further punishment would kill the victim, only to be told by the mob to back off unless he wanted some of the same. In any event, the eyewitness stayed behind as the mob half-led, half-dragged Nat Morgan into the woods. When they brought him home again he was dead, testified the eyewitness, "his *back broken, and his ribs and sides all stove in!*" The trunk was never found.[19]

The authorities charged Cain and several others with murder. The killers stood trial, but were acquitted on the ground that their *intent* to commit so gross a crime had not been proved. They went free.[20] And any attempt to reconcile the Dubuque that championed Ralph's freedom in 1839 with the Dubuque that in 1840 took Nat Morgan's life confronts a dilemma: which incident provides the truer insights into the town's underlying racial attitudes?

Lucius Langworthy, one of the brothers usually considered the founding fathers of Dubuque, once commented publicly on both Ralph's case and the lynching. Given Langworthy's standing in the town's business and professional elite and the deference due him as one of the community's oldest residents, and given also that he spoke to a local audience, his words would appear to possess a special authority. In a prepared address published many years later Langworthy first discussed the incident involving Ralph, praising the black man's rescuers as "liberty-loving citizens" who did not allow "the fear of being called abolitionists" deter them from their humane and historic task. Dubuquers were reminded to be proud of them. About the lynching, his message was that Nat Morgan's killers were not bad men—only misguided. Implying that the victim may in fact have been guilty of the theft of which he had been accused, Langworthy proved extravagantly judicious in his censure of the mob, whose savagery was simply "a mistaken zeal, and with entire ignorance, perhaps, of the injury they were inflicting. . . . No doubt," he added, "the men who inflicted this wrong, regretted their rashness and folly when too late." His concluding moral was that there was simply no accounting for man's inhumanity to blacks, beasts of burden, and females: "some men consider negroes, oxen, women and mules of like endurance and fit subjects for the cruel master's lash."[21]

Langworthy, in short, tempts one to discount Ralph's rescue as something of a fluke rather than typical of Dubuque, and to see Ralph's liberators as not only good men but, given the peculiarly virulent racism that must have infected the community by the late 1830s, as men of reckless heroism. Two additional items of evidence from the year 1840 support this interpretation.

First, Iowa's territorial assembly passed an act incorporating Dubuque, thereby providing for its civil reorganization. The customary clause setting the rules for the town's first election, however, did not specify voter eligibility in the language usual to such acts. Instead, presumably at the behest of Dubuquers themselves, the act asserted—much more stridently than necessary—that only "free white" males would vote. A small case in point, but ominous. Second, only in and around Dubuque lived Iowans callous enough in 1840 to identify to the federal census takers the servile status of their household blacks. Elsewhere, slaveholding Iowans at least had the grace to lie: Dubuquers nonchalantly called a slave a slave. Eleven of them headed households containing ten female and six male slaves.[22]

Evidently the largest slaveholder in town was none other than George Wallace Jones, one of Iowa Territory's two delegates to the United States Congress. Back in 1837, in eagerly assuring Sen. John C. Calhoun that Iowans were not, as a rule, abolitionists, Jones had told the white South's most powerful advocate that he himself owned ten or a dozen slaves. That may have been stretching things a bit for the beetle-browed South Carolinian. Three and a half years later Jones's Dubuque household included only three female slaves, one of them a child, as well as a free colored adult male.[23]

A second prominent Dubuquer, the Virginia-born receiver of the local United States land office, had a slave couple in residence in addition to a free black male. The household of a prosperous merchant included a young male slave. And so on. Most appear to have been employed as domestic servants, as was probably also the case of the fifteen free blacks residing in white households, since they are distributed singly or in pairs suggestive of live-in help.

The ill-fated Nat Morgan headed one of the ten free black households in the summer of 1840. Such household heads, their families, and their lodgers totaled forty-one, or nearly 60 percent of Dubuque's black population. The degree of cohesiveness within this black assemblage—free and slave—is of course difficult to judge. Of distinctly black institutions at this time virtually nothing is known; although an African Baptist society had formed by the late 1840s, Dubuque's first independent black church edifice would not materialize until after the Civil War.[24] Neither is there evidence of a black leadership structure. A case might be made that the relative value of contributions to the Methodist building fund indicates some gradation of status and seniority among black Dubuquers in 1834. That notion would, not implausibly, place Nat Morgan and Uncle Tom at the top of the local black hierarchy—the one a cook whose services were in demand by whites, the other a presumably venerable figure about whom nothing else is known. If this was true, Morgan's lynching takes on another tragic dimension, since it deprived the African-American community of an important leader.

What is suggested by the absence of record is a black community beset by fragmentation and disarray, on which the frightful lynching must have had a profound impact. That infamous episode, or the general decline of lead mining in the early forties, or both, probably had some relationship to the dispersal of the black Dubuquers of 1840. Of the ten free colored household heads in the census of that year, only two can be identified as still there in 1850: Aaron Baptiste, a Kentucky-born laborer, and Charlotte Morgan, Nat's widow, who at fifty years of age was the housekeeper for two immigrant miners, a Briton and a Scot.

Not only had the number of Dubuque blacks declined by well over half in the 1840s, but the twenty-nine survivors showed little evidence of a collective well-being. A fourth of them lived in white homes. The "nuclear" household—that is, father and mother and children (if any)—predominated among blacks over the "augmented" household—a nuclear household plus lodgers. But this is best interpreted as evidence not of socioeconomic health, but simply of an out-migration of blacks that had considerably eased the pressures on available housing. No black child had attended school in the 1849–50 academic year. All eight of the black adult males claimed occupations: a carpenter, a miner, a barber, two servants, and three laborers. But only three of them owned any real property. Thomas C. Brown, the black barber, claimed eleven hundred dollars' worth of land; a laborer, Anthony Arthur, claimed one thousand dollars' worth; and Aaron Baptiste reported six hundred dollars' worth.[25]

That the climate of race relations in Dubuque had improved much since the lynching is questionable. On election day in August 1856 a respectable Dubuque businessman made so bold as to remark publicly that he considered a black person to be as good as himself, "or as an Irishman, if he behaved himself." Infuriated onlookers knocked him to the sidewalk, seriously injuring him, and would doubtless have killed him, it is said, had the unfortunate man not been rescued by the police.[26]

III

In 1840, 42 percent of all black Iowans lived in Dubuque. Ten years later that percentage had dropped to 9. The new capital of African-American Iowa in 1850 was Muscatine, a Mississippi River settlement some eighty miles to the south.

Originally a small trading post at a site convenient for landing waterborne supplies for the Sauk and Mesquakie of the interior, Muscatine had been platted as a townsite in 1836 and early became an important stopping place for general steamboat traffic. In the 1840s it became, like Dubuque, a leading lumber-milling center fed by the vast pineries of northwestern Wisconsin. Young Mark Twain, who worked there for a few months in his brother's newspaper office, remembered Muscatine for its fabulous summer sunsets.[27]

In 1840 the census taker counted twenty-five blacks in Muscatine, a figure amounting to perhaps 5 percent of the total village population. All lived in households headed by whites. But in the following decade local blacks doubled in number, although their proportion of the town's total population shrank to less than 2 percent. They also had been relatively successful in establishing residential independence from whites. In 1850, with the exception of two hotel boarders and a mulatto child evidently living with her white kinfolk, only one of the town's sixty-two blacks lived with a Caucasian family. Independent living, it may be imagined, was indispensable to the development of a true black community possessing its own institutions and leadership structure.[28]

The Mathews kin group constituted an important part of that community. Its acknowledged leader, Benjamin J. Mathews, had been brought to town in 1837 by David Warfield and his two cousins, who in that year purchased a preemption claim on Mad Creek for a dam and sawmill. The Mathewses had been slaves belonging to the Warfield family back in Maryland, but had been freed, probably with the understanding that they become the cousins' work force out on the labor-scarce frontier. In 1840 young Warfield's interracial household included four black couples and their children, amounting to fifteen persons in all. By 1850 the Warfields had sold the mill and turned to farming, and the Mathews clan, minus one of its original families, now occupied three separate cottages. The clan matriarch, Ellen ("Aunt Nellie") Anderson, lived separately with her husband, "Uncle Daniel" Anderson, a whitewasher and lay preacher. Ellen's sons, Benjamin and Edmund Mathews, the former a teamster and the latter apparently without a regular occupation, maintained their own houses elsewhere in town. When Daniel Anderson died in 1856 after a long illness, a newspaper editor testified that "his scrupulous integrity and Christian faith and fortitude will long be remembered." Of the entire extended family a local antiquarian years later recalled that "they were all hard working and industrious colored citizens."[29]

A Maryland-born barber, Thomas C. Motts, ranked as another black notable. He had arrived in Muscatine at about the same time as the Mathewses, but whether he shared the circumstances of their migration from Maryland is unknown. By 1846 he operated the City Barbering Saloon on Second Street, several years later transferring his business to quarters in a popular Muscatine hotel. As an apparently lucrative sideline Motts also sold and delivered coal from his own coalyard. By 1850, at age forty-one, he was the town's wealthiest African-American, having acquired real estate worth six thousand dollars. He was also a new father: his second wife, Mahala, a native of Delaware, had just given birth to their son Job. Six-year-old Jo Ann Motts, possibly a daughter by his deceased first wife, lived next door with the Cook family, and two unmarried women named Motts, possibly Thomas's sisters, lived in a separate cottage nearby.[30]

But it was Alexander Clark who was to become frontier Iowa's most prominent black citizen. Light-skinned (three of his great-grandparents were white), with closely cropped hair, a commanding gaze, a long aquiline nose, and a tuft of chin-whiskers, Clark had been born in southwestern Pennsylvania in 1826, the son of emancipated slaves. At age thirteen he sought his fortune in Cincinnati and briefly attended grammar school while living with an uncle who taught him the barbering trade. Two years later he served a stretch on the Ohio as a riverboat bartender. One spring day in 1842 the sixteen-year-old Alex Clark stepped off the boat at Muscatine and made it his home for the next forty years. Resuming work as a barber, he soon managed to purchase a house, in later years speculated widely in real estate, and held profitable contracts for the supply of firewood to various steamboat lines. By his mid-twenties he had married a Virginia-born woman, had fathered a daughter, and with twelve hundred dollars' worth of property was the second most prosperous black in town.[31]

A youthful member of the Mathews clan, ten-year-old Charles, boarded with the Clarks, a hospitable arrangement by which the overflow from one black household might be accommodated by another. That Muscatine's black families remained cramped for space is suggested by this sharing of homes. Of the fifteen dwellings inhabited by black folk in 1850, ten housed at least one person whose surname differed from that of the household head. Yet the average number of occupants per dwelling was only four, an indication of the small size of housing available to families of modest means. The so-called augmented household, emblematic of a black community experiencing population growth, predominated. No house contained more than one married couple, however, and no intergenerational "extended" households were in evidence. Even within the Mathews family, each couple, as already noted, maintained a household of its own.

In 1850 the black community included eighteen children of school age (that is, five through fifteen years), a third of whom had attended classes the previous winter. Black parents must have sponsored a private grammar school, inasmuch as a Kentucky-born black woman identified herself as a teacher. Muscatine's black adult males constituted a work force similar to Dubuque's. It included a blacksmith, three cooks, four barbers, two teamsters, a house painter, and a day laborer. A relatively higher proportion (eight of twenty) reported no occupations, however, something usually taken to imply unemployment. Any plausible comparison of property holdings among the blacks of the two towns seems precluded by T. C. Motts's enormous realty valuation. Indeed, any very specific economic or demographic comparisons between Muscatine and Dubuque blacks, or between either group and its associated white community, would be naive; the numbers involved are simply too small for sophisticated use. But it can probably be said that in terms of general socioeconomic configuration the blacks of Dubuque and Muscatine did not differ appreciably from urban African-Americans elsewhere in the antebellum North.[32]

Unlike the Dubuque blacks of the late 1840s, Muscatine's blacks were able to make the transition to an authentic community, and an important event of 1848 reflected their coherence and social maturation. In June of that year they organized a Methodist Episcopal (African) Educational and Church Society, their next order of business being the purchase of a lot on which they intended building a church. The following summer, on August 1, they held a fair as a means of raising money from Muscatine's white community for their building fund. "It was attended by the beautiful and fashionable ladies of the town," reported a local editor, "who made quite an imposing display. They enjoyed themselves to their hearts' content." Two months later the newly organized African Methodist Episcopal Church accepted ownership of the lot, and in 1851 supervised the construction thereon of one of the trans-Mississippi West's first AME edifices.[33]

The ostensible purpose of Muscatine's "colored fair" of August 1, 1849, may have been fund-raising, but it also demonstrated a solidarity with free black communities all across the northern United States. That August date—the anniversary of slavery's abolition in the British West Indies—increasingly served as an African-American substitute for the Fourth of July, a kind of measured civic insubordination by which America's free blacks reminded themselves (and white bystanders) of the painfully ironic contrast between the egalitarian words of the Declaration of Independence and the sustained reality of American slavery. By the mid-1850s the local black community's early August celebration had become an annual event that very much conformed to a standard national model. Certainly that of 1857 appears typical.[34]

Out-of-town black guests, as well as the white community at large, had been invited. For many of them it was no doubt their first opportunity to meet Rev. Richard H. Cain, the local black community's new pastor, whose background appears to have been remarkably similar to that of his most prominent layman, Alex Clark. Of virtually the same age, both had been free-born, both reached manhood in Cincinnati, and each served on the river before finding his true vocation.[35]

At midmorning on August 3 the black participants formed up behind Muscatine's African Brass Band for a parade into the countryside to Hoops's Grove, where, no doubt from a stand specially erected for the occasion, the Rev. Mr. Cain offered a formal oration, followed by music from the band. At noon the members of the committee on arrangements served dinner, presumably from trestle tables laden with chicken, ham, and other substantial fare. More band music followed, and then Alex Clark (in later years widely praised for his oratorical skills) addressed the crowd, as did a prominent black visitor from Mount Pleasant. More music, after which all paraded back to town, heard a few remarks by Cain "on the subject of education," and dispersed. The more youthful and high-spirited reassembled that evening at Hare's Hall for an Emancipation Ball, all admission fees being earmarked for support of the pastor. Once again whites were invited to attend, for it was "from this class," explained an editor, "that the main patronage of the festival is expected."[36]

Nine months before Muscatine's blacks began to celebrate West Indian emancipation day, a Muscatine version of the *Ralph* case, *In re Jim* (1848), served to emphasize the relatively benign racial ambiance of their town. Dr. Samuel H. Merry was a Saint Louis physician who in 1833 had helped his good friend and colleague, Dr. John Emerson, obtain an army appointment. A decade later, now in his early sixties, Merry followed Emerson's example and retired to Iowa, locating in rural Muscatine County. Before leaving Missouri, perhaps to avoid the kind of trouble Emerson's heirs soon would have with the Dred Scott litigation, Merry agreed with his wife Catherine's decision to transfer ownership of her young slave, Jim, to her married daughter in Saint Louis. But Jim, as Catherine Merry later testified, could not be controlled by anyone but herself. Hired out to work on a steamboat on the lower Mississippi, the lad suffered a severe head injury in a brawl with the boat's steward, whereupon Mrs. Merry escorted him north to Iowa for a medically supervised convalescence in the fresh country air.

But Jim could no longer be managed very well even by Catherine Merry. He proved so impudent a patient that the exasperated Dr. Merry ordered him off the premises. Jim readily obliged. He trudged the dozen miles to Muscatine, where he asked for and received a job at a local hotel, the American House.[37]

Although Merry had washed his hands of the obstreperous young man, the daughter and her husband insisted that he return to Saint Louis to be made available for sale. Jim refused. In October 1848 the couple dispatched a Saint Louis detective named Horace Freeman to bring him home. Freeman put up at the American House, and after a day or two paid his bill, collared Jim in the hotel kitchen, and wrestled him toward the door. But the hotel proprietor intervened, demanding that Freeman get a proper arrest warrant. Freeman drew a pistol, and at that the screams of the kitchen maids brought others to the scene who overpowered the detective. While Jim took refuge at Alex Clark's house, the hotel proprietor had Freeman arrested for assault and battery. The detective, in turn, had Jim arrested as a fugitive slave. Both cases came before David C. Cloud, a local justice of the peace.

Cloud first heard the case against Freeman, but reserved his decision until after hearing the evidence as to whether or not Jim was a fugitive slave. That procedure consumed three days. Partisans for both sides daily jammed Cloud's small office, and during midday and evening adjournments pestered him with unwanted advice. ("Sah, that nigger is as much property as a *hoss,*" insisted one late-night visitor, "and I hope you will not deprive the owner of his property.") When, during closing arguments, one of Freeman's lawyers almost came to blows with Dr. C. P. Hastings, an excited supporter of Jim's freedom, only the press of the onlookers kept them apart.[38]

The sole precedent cited by Jim's lawyers was *In re Ralph,* which Cloud took as decisive. He discharged Jim and held Freeman guilty, assessing him twenty dollars plus costs. But the angry detective refused to give up. He concocted a scheme to have Jim kidnapped, only to be outwitted by Alex Clark. He then tried another tack. He obtained a precept for Jim's arrest from John J. Dyer, the federal judge for the District of Iowa, then resident at Dubuque, intending that the subsequent hearing be held in an atmosphere much less protective toward blacks. But no sooner was Jim rearrested than his supporters—on the alert for further trouble from Freeman—filed for a writ of *habeas corpus,* stalling the prisoner's removal to Dubuque. S. Clinton Hastings, a Muscatine judge (and Dr. Hastings's brother) who served as acting chief justice of the Iowa supreme court, granted the writ, obliging Freeman to appear before him to justify Jim's arrest. After learned counsel had argued the pros and cons, Hastings ruled that the arrest had been improper, since Judge Dyer's court was a court of concurrent jurisdiction, according to the United States code of procedures, with that of Justice Cloud, and could not therefore entertain the case once it had been disposed of by Cloud. Judge Hastings also refused to force Cloud to grant an appeal, thereby quashing further litigation in the matter.

Later, on the front steps of the American House, Dr. Hastings dramatically placed his hand on Jim's arm. "Gentlemen," he announced to a knot of interested bystanders, "here is a free man."[39]

IV

In mid-century another numerically important black community settled on the frontier northwest of Dubuque. In central Fayette County, fifty miles from the Minnesota line, a rural enclave known as the "colored settlement" constituted, by 1854, the third largest aggregation of blacks in the state.

A light-skinned people of mixed ancestry, they were understood never to have been slaves. Their original patriarch, Sion Bass the elder, had been born in Virginia in the early 1780s. He and his wife crossed into the somewhat freer environment of North Carolina in the 1790s—either as fugitives or, more likely, as manumitted slaves induced to leave a commonwealth increasingly hostile to freed men and women. Sion Bass the younger was thus of North Carolina birth, as was Sion the younger's son, T. R. Bass. In the 1820s two households of Basses came north, probably under the auspices of a Quaker program for resettlement of North Carolina's free blacks, and spent the 1830s in Indiana before crossing into Illinois in the mid-forties. There, in the countryside south of Kankakee, they made up a community of some eighty persons of color.[40]

During their Indiana residency one of the Bass women, Melinda, married Joel J. Epps, a young freedman from Georgia. The Eppses thereafter joined the Basses in forming the community's nucleus: by 1850 six of the colony's twelve cottages contained household members surnamed Bass or Epps. Dwellings averaged seven residents each, rather more crowded than among Muscatine's blacks that same year, although here as in Muscatine the multi-generational household had been successfully resisted. Sion Bass the elder, for instance, maintained a separate dwelling, as did Sion the younger and T. R. Bass. The augmented household predominated, as in Muscatine. Seven of the settlement's dwellings contained occupants whose surnames were not that of the household head. Only two houses appear to have sheltered more than one married couple each.

Although precise family relationships are difficult to extract from the 1850 census manuscripts, it is likely that family size was the most important demographic difference between the blacks of the Illinois colony and those of Muscatine. We do know that Melinda Bass, for example, married at age twenty-one, gave birth at twenty-two, and averaged a child every 2.6 years through the first thirty-seven years of her marriage to Joel. And therein lay probably the colony's most important problem. In 1850 fourteen of the settlement's children were in the ten-to-nineteen age bracket. As potential candidates for matrimony within a culture that apparently cherished the independent family farm as an ideal, they would soon need land, if possible nearby, so as not to sever their ties with the community's kin network. In fact, a lack of sufficient farmland already troubled the colony. Twenty male members called themselves farmers or farm laborers in 1850; only six of them owned land. Those who reported real estate valuations to the Illinois census enumerator averaged thirty-eight years of age, while nonowners proved to be substantially younger, averaging twenty-seven. A potentially dangerous fissure had appeared that could only get worse as a rising generation of young people married within the group. The best solution for the colony, or at least a substantial portion of it, was to move to a region in which land was both abundant and cheap.[41]

A frontier preacher, David Watrous, a middle-aged New Englander of the strongly antislavery United Brethren faith, provided the catalyst.

Although a white man, "Father" Watrous had once ministered to the Illinois colony and knew of its pressing need. In Iowa he glimpsed the magnificent prairie stretching northwestward from the heavily timbered left bank of the Volga River, and he wrote immediately to his former flock about the local availability of high-quality government land. In response, Sion Bass the younger, his son T. R. Bass, and a third member of the community, Ben Anderson, traveled west in 1852 to view the possibilities. They liked what they saw and each staked out a claim before returning home. The following spring Joel Epps and a young friend, Seymour Wilson, toured Fayette County. Epps at once entered a claim, and both men, as the county's historian puts it, "wrote back for all to come along as soon as possible."

At seventy years of age, Sion Bass the elder evidently felt himself too old to migrate once again, but he gave his blessing to the new exodus. Nearly half the Illinois colony moved west. Except for T. R. Bass, none of the migrating adult males had owned property in Illinois. Within three years Fayette County's colored settlement sheltered fifty-nine souls, most of them having come directly from the Illinois colony but with a sprinkling from Indiana and other parts of Illinois. All but one of the men were farmers, as in Illinois; the only nonfarmer among them was Sion Bass, the new settlement's blacksmith. In their household arrangements one married couple per dwelling was now the norm as well as the ideal. The nuclear household predominated: only three of the settlement's dwellings contained occupants with surnames different from those of the household heads.[42]

Fayette County's black settlers made up a small minority—less than 4 percent—of Westfield Township's population in 1856. Nevertheless, they soon encountered race prejudice. Strongly averse to slavery their white neighbors might be: they would, in fact, cast 75 percent of their ballots for the Republican party's first presidential candidate in 1856. But, testifies the local historian, "the coming among them of these colored people was not looked upon with favor, and there were, at times, various consultations among the [white] settlers to see what had best be done about it." When Seymour Wilson died in a well cave-in, his body was not welcomed at any Westfield Township cemetery. His mourners laid him to rest on his own claim. Thereafter a wooded knoll on Joel Epps's property became Pleasant Hill Cemetery, the settlement's burying ground, in a self-segregating initiative that helped defuse local racism.

The high value placed by the settlement's adults on the education of their young also helped lessen tensions. Back in Illinois less than half the colony's adults could read and write, and only four of their twenty-four children of school age had attended classes in 1849–50. Now Westfield Township's School No. 4, a stone structure standing just down the road from the cemetery, was built, apparently designed by tacit public consent for the exclusive use of the settlement. It thereafter functioned as its school, its church, and the center of its social life.[43]

V

In the meantime Dred Scott's case finally came before the United States Supreme Court. In March 1857—some twenty years after Dr. Emerson's Sam had dwelt on the brushy flats opposite Rock Island—the justices announced their decision: Dred Scott was still a slave. And since the Founding Fathers had not intended that blacks qualify for American citizenship, Dred had never been entitled to sue for his freedom in the first place. But while his fate was important in and of itself, the high court's real bombshell was its opinion that the Founders had never granted Congress the right to prohibit slavery in Wisconsin Territory or any other portion of the federal domain. In the words of the elderly Chief Justice Roger B. Taney, the only power conferred on Congress in the matter of slavery in the territories was "the power coupled with the duty of guarding and protecting the owner in his rights."

As the political reverberations spread across the nation, most Democratic party spokesmen lauded this "solution" to the divisive issue of slavery in the West. Republicans reviled it as another instance in which the South displayed its commanding influence within the federal government. "Have you [seen] the decision of the Supreme Court of the U.S. in the Dred Scott case?" inquired Iowa's Samuel J. Kirkwood of another Republican loyalist, state senator Aaron Brown. "*It is infamous,*" Kirkwood added, his pen furiously underscoring the words. He himself took comfort only in a kind of grim conviction that he passed along to Brown: "Well thank God there is a better day coming."[44]

Had Kirkwood been clairvoyant, he might have phrased the thought differently while still holding to the truth of it. Within five years he himself, as governor, would lead Iowans through the appalling first years of the Civil War. His correspondent, Aaron Brown, would be the third man from his county to offer himself to the Union army, and he rose to command the gallant 3d Iowa Infantry Regiment, leading it into the heart of his native state, Mississippi, until he fell, his thigh torn by a gunshot wound from which he never fully recovered, in the great sacrificial charge of Lauman's Brigade into the massed rebel guns defending Jackson. But Aaron Brown's rendezvous with destiny, like Kirkwood's, lay ahead of him. For the moment a southern-born, Ohio-bred physician-turned-realtor approaching middle age, he dwelt comfortably with his wife and three children in the village of Fayette, within two miles of Westfield Township's colored settlement. Among the neighbors Colonel Brown would ride south to represent in the bloody struggle to reform the Union were, fittingly enough, the descendants of Sion Bass.[45]

The citizenship of African-Americans—what the high court had denied in the *Dred Scott* case and what all too many white Americans collectively denied again and again—the individual conscience could not always deny, even when it tried. In a township just west of Fayette County lived one Andrew Felt, a local lawyer, justice of the peace, and militant Democrat. A year in the Confederate death camp at Andersonville, Georgia, would ultimately bring a change in him, and dramatically so, it was said. But in the late 1850s he remained an outspoken southern apologist who strongly defended the *Dred Scott* decision, frequently quoting Justice Taney's infamous opinion that blacks "had no rights which the white man was bound to respect."

It seems that a black man living in the village of Bradford had his watch stolen by a white neighbor, and he therefore commenced a suit of replevin before Judge Felt to recover the watch. It was a clear-cut case, but counsel for the defense, a lawyer named David Babcock, cleverly moved for a dismissal on grounds that the plaintiff was black and the Supreme Court had ruled that blacks had no rights a white man was bound to respect.

Andy Felt thought that over for a moment or two, then turned to Babcock. "Look here, Dave, that may be good politics," he said, "but Dred Scott decision or *no* Dred Scott decision, this nigger's going to have his watch."[46]

Landscape with Black Code

2

In October 1838 on a downtown street in Burlington, temporary capital of the newly created Territory of Iowa, the prominent young lawyer David Rorer, of slave-state nativity and education, exchanged gunshots with the United States district attorney for Iowa, one Cyrus Jacobs, an officer remembered as "a Southerner by birth and instinct" despite his having been born a Pennsylvanian. Jacobs's violent demise cut short a promising political career, for he had just been elected to the first territorial assembly.

A few weeks later Iowa's charter lawmakers (minus Jacobs) gathered expectantly in Burlington's most capacious edifice, an unfinished Methodist church. In welcoming them, the newly arrived territorial governor, Robert Lucas, his erect military bearing, collar-length hair, and severe features lending him an uncanny resemblance to Andrew Jackson, his political hero, took occasion to deplore the prevailing custom of carrying concealed weapons and referred disapprovingly to the recent encounter that had deprived the legislative assembly of one of its members-elect.[1]

As it happened, Lucas, by birth a Virginian, was himself one of the so-called southern element that lent such an unruly ambience to Iowa's early frontier. In 1838 native southerners dominated the first legislature. Over half its thirty-nine members had been born in states where slavery would persist until the Civil War. Nine were Virginians, with a tenth, the session's eldest lawmaker, of free-state birth but, in the recollection of a colleague, "a dignified Virginia gentleman" who "had been many years in the Virginia legislature." Eight other transplanted southerners hailed from Kentucky, two from North Carolina, and one each from Maryland and Tennessee. Little differentiated Whigs from Democrats: over half of each legislative party was southern-born, their median ages were virtually identical, and most within each party identified themselves as farmers.[2]

Rep. Hawkins Taylor recalled that a more hardworking group of legislators never met in all his years as an observer of such bodies politic. "A new code of laws had to be formed, and there were few amusements and no dining out to divert members; there were few citizens of Burlington then that entertained outsiders."[3] One most important piece of business: devising a set of statutes to protect white Iowans from a numerically important in-migration of free blacks. Unhappily, as historians have come to know, frontier enthusiasm for such laws was by no means limited to the southern-born and bred.

I

The precedents for Iowa's racist legislation date to the close of the American Revolution, when the citizens of the northern states were well on their way to wholesale emancipation, immediately or gradually, of their slaves. But lest social control over persons of color be entirely sacrificed, specially devised laws carefully ensured against their general rise to civil equality with whites. By the time Iowa's first assemblymen mustered at Burlington just four northern states—all in New England—allowed wholly impartial male suffrage, and in New York blacks could vote only if they met certain property and residence requirements not asked of whites. In Connecticut, New Jersey, and Pennsylvania blacks had been disfranchised after having once enjoyed voting rights. With respect to the courts, many northern states had proved no more egalitarian than their southern counterparts. None accepted African-Americans as jurors, and nonwhites' testimony against whites had been barred by Indiana Territory as early as 1803, a constraint later imposed in Ohio and Illinois. Although black soldiers and sailors had fought and died in both the Revolution and the War of 1812, for a decade no state had allowed black service in the militia: the thought of an armed and militarily trained black underclass produced considerable unease north as well as south. Statute or custom mandated segregated schools in nearly every northern community, and northern states in which interracial marriage had been forbidden included Maine, Massachusetts, Indiana, Michigan, and Illinois.

Designed for the social discipline of nonwhites, such "black codes," as they came to be called, also were thought to be of good effect in discouraging northern migration of newly freed slaves. In the opening decades of the nineteenth century, however, those seeking a more comprehensive legal barrier to black ingress came to rest their hopes on statutes expressly forbidding it. First devised by the legislators of New Jersey and Massachusetts in the 1780s, so-called exclusion laws barred residence by colored migrants. But article IV, section 2, of the United States Constitution gave exclusionists pause. Many authorities regarded this, the controversial "privileges and immunities" clause, as ruling out restraints on the interstate movement of free persons, white or black. In 1823 a justice of the U.S. Supreme Court, on circuit, held that the clause expressed the right "of a citizen of one State to pass through, or to reside in any other State, for purposes of trade, agriculture, professional pursuits, or otherwise." But the full Court never so ruled, and whether free blacks were to be considered "citizens" would remain in doubt until the decision in *Dred Scott*. Meanwhile, boldly phrased exclusionary laws flatly forbidding entry to African-Americans became the general mode in the South, where whites particularly dreaded freedmen as fomenters of slave revolts. Legislators north of the Ohio River, rather more sensitive to the constitutional issue, sought the same result more subtly.[4]

In the 1790s the Commonwealth of Virginia set in motion a series of events that culminated in the Middle West's first efforts to repel black migration. The Old Dominion's lawmakers, animated by the fact that their state contained some 40 percent of the entire nation's nonwhite population, liberalized the procedure for individual manumission of slaves. At the same time, prominent Virginians such as Thomas Jefferson began urging a federal program for relocating freedmen on the western frontier. When Jefferson's own presidency passed without institution of any such scheme, however, Virginians acted unilaterally to thin out their black population. In 1806, in what historian Winthrop D. Jordan calls a great turning point in the evolution of the nation's attitudes toward African-Americans, the Virginia general assembly mandated that every ex-slave leave the state within a year of his or her manumission.

The trans-Appalachian West, however, did not propose to become the land of the freed. The lawmakers of Kentucky and Louisiana territories promptly enacted exclusion laws. Ohioans grew as fearful as Virginia's other neighbors about a possible influx of new freedmen. In 1804 Ohio assemblymen had acted to identify fugitive slaves within the state's borders by requiring of each black resident "a certificate of his or her actual freedom," such "free papers," as they were called, to be filed with a local county clerk. Now, in their 1806/07 session, they amended the registration law to require additionally that each incoming black post bond "with two or more freehold sureties" in the amount of $500 within twenty days of entry, to be forfeit should the newcomer prove an expense to local taxpayers by becoming a pauper or a thief. Any Ohioan employing or harboring an unbonded black could suffer a monetary penalty stiffer than that for aiding a fugitive slave.[5]

The Ohioans' 1807 regulatory statute was not an innovation. In requiring a penal bond as an assurance of self-support from a migrant who would otherwise be "warned out" as a bad risk, Ohioans merely introduced into midwestern law a precedent from Colonial New England, and their requirement of security for good behavior was simply a well-known species of preventive justice known as "surety of the peace." But in singling out blacks for such blanket treatment, the Buckeye State contributed to the codification of American racism by introducing slave-state practices into a vast region that had never known much of chattel slavery itself.[6]

The Missouri statehood controversy brought exclusionary legislation to national attention. In 1820 Missourians petitioned for acceptance into the Union under a proposed constitution that required a future Missouri legislature "to prevent free negroes and mulattoes from coming to and settling in this State under any pretext whatsoever." It was on this issue, rather than on its legalization of bondage, that the fledgling antislavery bloc in Congress chose to focus in seeking to frustrate admission of yet another slave state. In the end Congress could do no more than force from Missourians a pledge not to pass an exclusion law, a promise cynically broken within four years. Neither the courts nor the White House seemed disposed to challenge Missouri's defiance of the national legislature, although whether Congress would again treat a similar case so leniently remained to be seen.[7]

Within this context Iowa's first legislators proceeded to the task of framing their black code. Without apparent controversy they approved a school bill that limited public education to "every class of white citizens," a bill on elections that barred anyone "not a free white male citizen" from voting, a militia bill that required enrollment only of "free white male persons," and a bill regulating judicial practice, one specification of which mandated that "a negro, mulatto, or Indian, shall not be a witness in any court or in any case against a white person." All passed without recorded votes. Governor Lucas, whose Jacksonian penchant for the executive veto had brought him into fierce conflict with the legislature, in these instances signed the measures into law. Only the matter of interracial matrimony had been overlooked by the busy assemblymen; a year later an act repaired this oversight by asserting that "all marriages of white persons with negroes or mulattoes are declared to be illegal and void." So much for the routine foundations of white supremacy.[8]

House File 97, a nonwhite regulatory bill, occasioned at least some dispute in that first assembly. The speaker of the house, a young northern-born Whig, charged a committee with preparing a measure "concerning free negroes, mulattoes, servants, and slaves." His message employed the title of an Illinois regulatory act of 1819, but that law had in fact been superseded. The committee did possess three extant midwestern examples on which to model a regulatory law for Iowa. It rejected the most severe—the revised Illinois act of 1829—and devised a composite of the rather more humane Michigan territorial statute of 1827 and the Indiana law of 1831.[9]

The Iowa bill's original title, An Act to Regulate Blacks and Mulattoes and to Punish the Kidnapping of such Persons, was taken from Michigan's law, although Indiana's provided most of its substance. Borrowed from the latter was a requirement for $500 bonds "with good and sufficient security," a requirement that could be met (as it probably was in most cases) through the paternalism of a white cosigner. Violation could lead to arrest and hiring out for six months "for the best price in cash that can be had," and the penalty for employing or harboring was a maximum $100. Any sheriff or jailer who imprisoned a nonwhite illegally could be fined, although the Iowans lowered the maximum penalty from $500 to $100. Finally, they included the Indiana "sojourners' provision," a clause guaranteeing the right of visiting slaveholders to bring their bondservants into free territory for short periods of time.

From Michigan's regulatory law the committee extracted a requirement for court-certified free papers, as well as its generous provision for recovery of suspected runaways by owners. As originally reported by the drafting committee, the bill included a clause modeled on the Michigan law that made kidnapping a free black with an intention of carrying him or her into slavery punishable by hard labor. Iowa's house majority apparently found this far too onerous and sent the bill back to committee for amendment, deleting the phrase "and to Punish the Kidnapping of such Persons" from its title. The assemblymen instead followed Indiana's lead in making kidnapping and its penalties part of a general statute on crimes and punishments. The regulatory bill passed the house without a roll call vote.[10]

In the legislative council Charles Whittlesey, one of the upper chamber's six Whigs, opposed H.F. 97. Whittlesey was, in Hawkins Taylor's recollection, "a Connecticut man, keen and active, . . . but less influential than if he had been from the Hoosier or Sucker state." His motion to postpone indefinitely resulted only in the bill's consignment to a committee headed by "a dignified Virginian" from Dubuque, and including Robert Ralston, an Ohio-born Democrat, and James M. Clark, a young New York-born Whig. From this committee H.F. 97 emerged the next day unscathed, although Ralston and Clark opposed the bill's passage, at least in its final form. They did so to no avail. Whittlesey absented himself from the roll call on the Act to Regulate Blacks and Mulattoes, and in addition to Ralston and Clark only one other councilman, a Democratic ex-mayor of Davenport, voted against it. Governor Lucas signed it within the week.

On January 25, 1839, conscious of having made history, Iowa's first lawmakers gaily called it quits. "Legislature adjourned in confusion," Lucas's private secretary primly confided to his diary. "All drunk with few exceptions."[11]

II

Within two years the territorial assembly would be obliged to defend the racist handiwork of its 1838/39 session, impelled to do so by constituency pressures from Iowa's early abolitionists, whose commitment to the eradication of American slavery required their vigorous protest of racial discrimination.

Before the 1830s concern for the civil liberties of free blacks was not a necessary component of antislavery activism. As in a kind of inexorable logic, the late eighteenth-century clash of proslavery self-interest and emancipationist republicanism had given birth to an apparent resolution in the prestigious American Colonization Society (1816). Of Appeal to slaveholders as well as northerners, the society's implicit aim was to encourage southern manumission through its explicit program: financing the voluntary removal of freed slaves to new homes in Africa.

Creation of the American Anti-Slavery Society (1833) liberated the movement from colonization. Its inspired doctrine of "immediate abolition" introduced the necessity of viewing the antislavery and civil liberties causes as two sides of the same coin. Black equality before the law was, above all else, a practical requirement of the fight against slavery. To rid the nation of the South's notorious labor system by means of colonization, abolitionists realized, demanded too much of American volunteerism. The plan asked that individuals and governmental bodies contribute the enormous funding required, that blacks accept deportation, that slaveholders cheerfully manumit. The wild impracticality of the scheme bordered on fraud. The implacable truth was that slavery's end would mean the addition of millions of blacks to *some* form of citizenship—just what so many white Americans, both north and south, passionately feared.

Those fears constituted one of the most dynamic components of slavery's defense. The antislavery cause, in consequence, required that white Americans be brought to the acceptance of freed blacks as fellow-citizens, an educational task distressingly impeded, among other things, by free-state discriminatory laws. Even if only sporadically enforced, these laws importantly served slavery by giving the imprimatur of the state to racism. Reason might dictate that color prejudice was illogical, conscience that it was un-Christian, but the laws of the land proclaimed its legitimacy. Clearly recognizing this, abolitionists urged black code repeal.[12]

Protests against Iowa's black laws first issued forth from its early centers of antislavery strength, a handful of tiny frontier settlements scattered across southeastern Iowa in a rough arc beyond Burlington. The village of Denmark still lies ten miles southwest of the city in Lee County. Founded in 1836 by a trio of adventurers from New Hampshire, within two years it consisted of three dwellings and a schoolhouse that doubled as a church, the nucleus of a rural community of dairy farmers of almost wholly Yankee stock. "You would suppose yourself again in New England amidst its granite hills," reported a visitor. "This people have emigrated *directly* from New England and have not sojourned as is usually the case in Ohio, Indiana or Illinois." In 1838 these migrants called to minister unto their spiritual needs the Rev. Asa Turner Jr., a remarkable man under whose direction the Denmark church was to become the cradle of Iowa Congregationalism.[13]

Turner, a Yale graduate from Massachusetts, had been one of the determined young clergymen sent west by the American Home Missionary Society to evangelize the frontier. Originally more concerned with temperance reform than abolition, he nevertheless helped found the Illinois Anti-Slavery Society, and the lynching in Illinois of the nation's first abolitionist martyr, Elijah Lovejoy, completed his radicalization. By 1837 he was an officer of the American Anti-Slavery Society. "Slavery," Turner was to confide to a parishioner shortly before the Civil War, "is a cancer eating out the life of our body politic. *There is no remedy for it but the knife.* . . . The nation may bleed to death, *but it is our only hope.*" In Denmark village Turner found a congregation already warmly opposed to liquor, card playing, dancing, and desecration of the Sabbath. To these moral intolerables he proposed to add slavery.

His flock regularly heard Father Turner sermonize on slavery, although even among these transplanted New Englanders there were those who resented the intrusion of abolition into matters religious. Undaunted, Turner persisted. On New Year's Day, 1840, two-thirds of the laymen remembered as the early pillars of the Denmark church joined their pastor in organizing Iowa Territory's first abolition association, the Denmark Anti-Slavery Society. They lifted articles 2 and 3 of their constitution from that of the American Anti-Slavery Society, phrases that had flowed from the pen of the famous William Lloyd Garrison six years before. The first pledged them to work for the "entire" and "immediate" abolition of slavery throughout the United States. The second specified that "this Society shall aim to elevate the character and condition of the people of color, by encouraging their intellectual, moral, and religious improvement; and by removing public prejudice; that they may, according to their intellectual and moral worth, share an equality with the whites, of civil and religious privileges." With these words, the thirty-three signatories took upon themselves the duty of voicing strenuous opposition to the territory's new black laws.[14]

Twenty miles northwest of Denmark, a second important antislavery population gathered in and around the village of Salem, a predominantly Quaker community in Henry County. This first settlement of Friends in the trans-Mississippi West dated from 1835 or 1836, when three Quaker frontiersmen preempted the site and laid it off into streets and blocks. Additional Quaker families followed, mainly from eastern Indiana. Within four years nearly two hundred coreligionists had settled the village and the prairies of surrounding townships, which soon took shape as four encircling satellite neighborhoods informally named Cedar Creek, East Grove, Chestnut Hill, and New Garden. In 1838 the village and its rural outliers organized a local church congregation (or "monthly meeting") under the ultimate aegis of their parent Indiana conference (or "yearly meeting") and put up a log house of worship at Salem of a size appropriate to some three or four hundred members. The Salem meeting rapidly became to Iowa's Quakerism what the Denmark church was to its Congregational faith.

Being "pastoral" Friends, common to Indiana, Salem's communicants elected Thomas Frazier as their first minister. Frazier had joined the great exodus of antislavery Quakers out of North Carolina to Indiana in the twenty years following the War of 1812. There, it was recalled of him, he developed his gifts as "a natural orator" by lecturing on the "evils of intemperance." In 1837 he came west to Salem. He and the Friends migrating with him brought to Iowa the antislavery radicalism that was at that very moment transforming Wayne County, Indiana, into a leading center of immediate abolitionism in the Middle West.[15]

The immediatist doctrine had jolted the Quakers much as it had other antislavery constituencies in New England and the Middle Atlantic states. Its crusading, uncompromising militancy contrasted sharply with the traditional gradualist Quaker witness against slavery. Conservative Friends responded to immediatism with alarm. They deemed Quaker entry into "the excitements of the day" as internally divisive, especially deploring Friends' participation in many state and local associations newly organized on the model of the American Anti-Slavery Society. In 1840 a conservative "advice" against Quaker participation in secular or interdenominational antislavery associations became an official article of discipline within Indiana Yearly Meeting, the nation's only Friends conference in which antislavery radicals had been numerous enough to cause true dissension. The Indiana radicals responded by formally urging the establishment of abolition associations composed exclusively of Friends.[16]

Three weeks later, in February 1841, a group of Iowa Quakers convened at the Salem meetinghouse to form the Salem Anti-Slavery Society. Its constitution, like that of the Denmark abolitionists, committed its signatories to the "universal and immediate . . . extinction of slavery throughout the world," and—since "the prejudice against color which exists in this country is sinful in the sight of God, and should be immediately repented of"—to the "elevation of our colored brethren to their proper rank as men." A year later, reassembled, the Salem abolitionists spelled out their deepening conviction that racism served slavery: "It is evidently the policy of the slaveholder to render the victims of his cupidity hated and despised, especially by the people of the nominally free States. . . . Prejudice against color [is] eminently calculated to strengthen the bonds that bind almost three millions of human beings in vilest slavery [and] forms one of the greatest barriers to the spreading of . . . anti-slavery principles."[17]

Twenty-five miles north of Salem, two frontier settlements formed a third abolitionist constituency. As at Denmark and Salem, a majority of its first families shared a common religious faith, in this case Associate Presbyterianism, originally an immigrant Scottish sect, its adherents usually referred to as Seceders. In 1811 the synod had officially declared the South's labor system an evil, urging southern members to manumit their slaves. Although it then equivocated in enforcing this discipline, in 1831 it flatly excommunicated all slaveholders, becoming by the 1840s one of the most consistently and radically antislavery religious bodies in America.[18]

Ignoring his pastor's warning that "no good will come of it . . . for the Gospel will never cross the Mississippi," an adventuresome church elder from western Illinois led a colony of Seceders into Washington County in 1836. Other Seceder families followed, hailing from both Illinois and New Athens, Ohio, the site of a Seceder community that was becoming a hotbed of antislavery Presbyterianism. In 1839 three migrants from New Athens laid off a townsite astride the new military road connecting Mount Pleasant and Iowa City, subsequently naming it Crawfordsville. A church edifice there became the nucleus of a Seceder parish that installed its first settled pastor in 1841.

Meanwhile, a territorial commission named to pick a central site for the county seat had founded the village of Washington ten miles northwest of Crawfordsville. Associate Presbyterianism claimed at least a plurality of its citizens from the start, a success owed in part to the efforts of James Dawson, Washington County's most influential Seceder layman. In 1841 Washington village already sheltered a small Methodist congregation but no pastor. Through Dawson's urging, a young Seceder missionary, the Rev. George C. Vincent, agreed to visit Washington to preach. The visit proved a triumph: the townspeople, irrespective of denominational preference, joined Dawson in a campaign to impel the pastor to relocate from Illinois. Vincent came to stay. A brilliant administrator and preacher, he was also, in the words of a local chronicler, "an active and prominent" abolitionist, "and nearly all the members of his church cheerfully and zealously followed his leadership in the anti-slavery cause." Although some local Methodists and Baptists also respected Vincent's abolitionist message, by no means did Washington village become so consistently antislavery as the territory's smaller, more religiously homogeneous centers of radical sentiment.[19]

Finally, back toward Burlington, a fourth abolitionist settlement materialized in Des Moines County, a dozen miles north of the capital city. Like Washington County's Seceders, the pioneers of this community for the most part adhered to Presbyterianism, but they proved neither so unequivocally abolitionist nor so doctrinally homogeneous as their upcountry coreligionists. Although members of the regular denomination, which had not yet shorn itself of religious communion with slaveholders, many of them had been in the thick of an intramural fight against slavery in Ohio while under the pastoral care of the Rev. James H. Dickey, one of mainstream Presbyterianism's earliest champions of denominational action against slavery. The great theological schism of 1837 split Presbyterians into New School and Old School adherents, but this had no evident impact on antislavery attitudes. The national leadership of both assemblies remained conservative, even as many of the rank and file of both grew increasingly radical.[20]

Presbyterianism had come to northern Des Moines County in 1835 with Thomas and David E. Blair, who purchased preemption claims at the edge of a stretch of meadowland called Round Prairie. Additional families arrived, and within four years the village of Yellow Spring had been laid out at the site. Local Presbyterians organized the Round Prairie (Old School) and Yellow Spring (New School) churches in 1839 and 1840, those from the Rev. Mr. Dickey's domain in Ohio forming the core of the first congregation, while families from Illinois and Indiana for the most part made up the Yellow Spring church. The Blair brothers split, however; David followed his wife into Round Prairie church, while Thomas and his wife became charter members at Yellow Spring.

Each congregation believed itself inherently more antislavery than the other. Yellow Spring spokesmen looked for justification to the national New School assembly, the theological liberalism of which had caused it to be less attractive in the South and thus, it was reasoned, potentially more antislavery than the Old School assembly. Indeed, animated by such men as William McClure, remembered as "firm in his religious convictions and dauntless in his opposition to intemperance and slavery," the Round Prairie church possessed, in the words of a local chronicler, "more and more radical" abolitionists than its nearby New School rival. Events were to bear this out.[21]

III

Iowa's abolitionists first expressed themselves as critics of the territorial black code, particularly the Act to Regulate Blacks and Mulattoes, at the legislative session of 1840/41. Two freshmen Whig representatives served as their instruments: Paton (pronounced "Peyton") Wilson, a middle-aged farmer living among Quaker neighbors near Salem, and Daniel F. Miller, a young, physically imposing antislavery lawyer of Fort Madison whose constituents included the Denmark Congregationalists and the Quakers of rural New Garden. Their joint attack on racist legislation stressed its failure to provide due process. Nonwhites, as Miller explained years later, "could not give testimony in a court of justice against a white man in a civil proceeding, and any white man could go before a justice of the peace and file an affidavit alleging that a certain colored man was his slave; and simply from that affidavit the justice was authorized by law to issue a writ to any constable to arrest the colored man and hand him over to the possession of his alleged master, not even giving the colored man the benefit of a court hearing." Representatives Miller and Wilson, as well as those constituents for whom they spoke, may well have had the recent *Ralph* case in mind, since only Alexander Butterworth's timely intervention had stayed the routine functioning of the law in exactly the manner Miller described.[22]

On January 4, 1841, Wilson laid before the house a petition signed by sixty-five Salem men, a list embracing every male of prominence in the village. The petitioners invoked the words of the Declaration of Independence that "all men are created equal; that they are endowed by their Creator with certain unalienable rights; that among these are life, liberty, and the pursuit of happiness." Iowa's regulatory law, they noted, "being a pointed contradiction of this declaration, and being unjust and oppressive in its nature, we therefore respectfully request you to repeal." The house speaker referred the document to a committee composed of a representative from each legislative district, five Democrats and four Whigs, including Wilson and Miller. Miller promptly produced a bill amending the law so as to provide jury trials for accused runaways. The Democratic majority allowed his bill to go the house floor, where Paton Wilson introduced it as House File 121.

A week later Miller presented a petition from Denmark praying for the bill's passage, and the clerk read H.F. 121 a first time. "I stirred up a hornet's nest of opposition all around me," Miller recalled, "but I would not yield to the clamor of friends to withdraw the bill, and I finally succeeded in forcing a vote on it." The assemblymen killed it by striking its enactment clause. Only Miller, Wilson, and two other Whigs voted to save it. As in 1839, most Whig legislators proved no more progressive on the civil liberties of blacks than the more predictably racist Democrats.

In another sense, however, the vote on H.F. 121 suggested a trend toward Whig support for such measures. House Whigs had split four to seven on the bill, rather than solidly opposing it. And one of the bill's

Whig friends, Asbury Porter, had served on the drafting committee that originally had devised the regulatory act. Now, newly sensitive to his Salem constituents—he, like Paton Wilson, represented Henry County—Porter came decisively over to the progressives. And in young Daniel Miller the episode helped produce a radical civil rights activist. Southern-born but Ohio-bred in an antislavery household, three years a lawyer, two years an Iowan, one year a Whig, Miller would always remember that week in the assembly of 1840/41 "when it cost a great deal of nerve to stand up for the cause of the colored man, and to brave the prejudices and insults of the white community." He would not again sit in an Iowa legislature, but as one of the Hawkeye State's most distinguished criminal lawyers he would wage a lifelong war against racism in its courts.[23]

Defeat of the Miller bill left the territory's civil rights activists determined to try again. In the summer of 1841 the Salem Anti-Slavery Society resolved that its members would oppose any candidate for the forthcoming legislative session "who was not favorable to abolition and temperance." The association appointed a committee "to attend the county conventions of the two political parties, and inform them of our resolution," and to threaten that if neither convention nominated such men "we would bring out candidates of our own." Henry County's dominant Whigs, seeing nothing to be gained from specific pledges, received the Salem committee with thinly disguised disdain. The antislavery society therefore voted to back the more receptive Democratic candidates, who then lost the election. The county's Whig delegation to the next legislature again contained, as in every previous session, at least one overt racist.[24]

Legislative petitioning now seemed the only available option. In November, on the eve of the 1841/42 session, Rev. Asa Turner, accompanied by the president and one of the managers of the Denmark Anti-Slavery Society, attended the second annual meeting of Iowa's Congregational Association and persuaded the assembled pastors and laymen to adopt the organization's first formal political resolution:

> WHEREAS: The laws in relation to blacks and mulattoes are in our opinion a violation of the principles of justice and of the laws of God; oppressive in their operations on colored persons, and forbidding us arts of humanity; therefore,
>
> RESOLVED: That we invite our churches to unite with us in petitioning for their repeal.[25]

The legislature received at least three religiously inspired petitions that winter. The first, presented to the council on January 7, 1842, originated with twenty-five Congregationalists of Brighton, a Washington County community. The councilmen briskly shunted the document to their judiciary committee, which recommended that "it would be impolitic and inexpedient to grant the prayer of said petitioners." That same day Paton Wilson presented the other two repeal petitions to his colleagues in the house. Similar in wording, they displayed the signatures of 245 Salem men and 41 Quakers from adjoining Jefferson County. The representatives tabled the documents without comment. The house subsequently entertained identically worded petitions from Lee and Henry counties, carrying 311 signatures, that urged *retention* of the regulatory law on grounds that repeal "would have a tendency to flood our Territory with a colored population." These, together with the two tabled petitions, went to committee for recommendation.

Having already spoken on the issue, the members of the legislative council now chose to remain entirely aloof from it. They tabled a petition from Washington village opposing regulatory law repeal and passage of any bill that would make colored persons competent witnesses in trials involving whites. The petition, penned by a Whig lawyer serving as clerk of the Washington County board of commissioners, warned that such legislative action would "Change this Spring time of Our Territory to the *Yellowness* of Autumn and the *Blackness* & *darkness* of Winter would forever blight the *Fair* prospects of our youthful Country & shroud it in a veil of *Brown*." The forty signatories comprised perhaps half the residents of the village. They included the county assessor, the sheriff, the district court clerk, the postmaster, two of the town's three physicians, two liquor dealers, at least four merchants, and Alex Lee, building contractor, stockman, and merchant, a Kentucky-born Whig described by Washington County's historian as the individual who, "during much of his stay in this county, was the most prominent man in it." The conservative neighbors of the Rev. Mr. Vincent's Seceders had spoken forcefully. They would soon do so again.[26]

Meanwhile, the outnumbered legislative friends of racial justice had more than they could handle. In an attempt to modify a house bill on poor relief that excluded nonwhites from welfare benefits, Asbury Porter moved to strike the clause specifying that "nothing in this act shall be so construed as to enable any black or mulatto person to gain a legal settlement in this Territory." Only Paton Wilson and William Patterson, a Virginia-born Democrat, no doubt in deference to his Denmark constituents, supported him. Seven of the body's nine Whigs voted with the majority to tighten the grip of the territorial black code. So did Yellow Spring's David E. Blair, serving as an assemblyman, despite his strongly antislavery attitudes.[27]

Finally, on February 9, the house judiciary committee issued its report on regulatory law repeal. It proved far from encouraging. The committee, three Democrats and two Whigs, recommended against repeal in a report that conceded nothing to racial equality. The 1839 law was, it said, "essential to the protection of the white population, against an influx of runaway slaves and out-cast blacks, from adjoining States. . . . So far, then, from recommending an alteration in our law on this subject, giving still greater liberty and protection to blacks and mulattoes, your Committee think that an amendment to the law, prohibiting, positively, their settlement among us, would approach more nearly the true policy of our Territory."

With this statement Iowa's legislative racists introduced what would become a standard tactic throughout the antebellum years: when too closely pressed on matters of equal rights they invariably retaliated by threatening to throw caution to the winds and bring forth an exclusion law. In thus expressing themselves wholly unterrified of the larger constitutional issue, they served notice that the price of any serious discussion of black code liberalization might prove unpleasant indeed. For the moment, however, they thought a word to the wise sufficient. As the report delicately put it, exclusionary legislation was something "your Committee do not now feel themselves fully instructed to recommend."

And so the less said the better: "Your Committee refrain from any discussion of this subject as it is one which has already created a dangerous excitement throughout the States of the Union; and your committee . . . deem it most prudent to meet the first outbursts of the spirit of fanaticism among us, with a respectful silence, rather than run the risk of increasing its fury by discussion and formal opposition." A few days later the assembly adjourned, apparently thankful to have escaped a substantive discussion of the regulatory law.[28]

In June 1842 the Seceders of Washington village played host to an antislavery convention, most probably called to organize the county's first abolition society. The antislavery Congregational minister from nearby Brighton, Rev. Charles Burnham, and Samuel L. Howe, abolitionist schoolmaster from Mount Pleasant, came as featured speakers. No sooner had Burnham begun talking than a mob, headed by the town's leading physician and including, a resident recalled, "quite a number of our prominent and influential citizens," burst through the door and manhandled the minister out of the building. Only the intervention of James Dawson and the Rev. Mr. Vincent's husky brother-in-law prevented a bare-knuckle brawl, and the meeting reconvened elsewhere. In the end abolition won considerable public sympathy by this conservative attack on free speech. The converts may have included David Bunker, a prominent farmer who that autumn won a seat in the territorial house of representatives.[29]

The 1842/43 legislative assembly avoided reconsidering the regulatory law almost as successfully as its predecessor. The session's opening found the territory's Whigs with their healthiest representation yet, being one member short of an assembly majority. Nothing came of this, however, in terms of civil rights legislation. David Bunker introduced a petition from his constituents asking "the repeal of all acts regulating blacks and mulattoes," which died in committee, and he never forgot, as a biographer later phrased it, "the amount of courage required to even present such a petition." Paton Wilson fared no better. His Salem constituents' prayer urged repeal of that section of the Act to Regulate Blacks and Mulattoes making it a crime to employ or harbor an unbonded colored person. A hostile committee promptly buried the document. "The [black] laws here, as every where in the West are oppressive," conceded a disappointed activist at Salem, referring particularly to the regulatory statute. "But this with all other oppressive laws of the kind," he said, "we hope will be short lived. At least, we intend, through the help of Him who hath all power, to keep battling against them, until they are repealed."[30]

In that year of 1843 the winds of religious schism swept America. Evangelical abolitionists throughout the North sought to incite their various denominations to declare slavery a heinous sin, to excommunicate slaveholders, and to endorse antislavery activism as a Christian endeavor. Conservatives and their moderate allies everywhere resisted, most dramatically within denominations with large southern constituencies; thus the Methodists and Baptists teetered on the brink of outright separation into northern and southern wings. The issues reverberated all the way out to Iowa, affecting even the relatively homogeneous Congregationalists. In September 1843 Rev. Asa Turner induced the annual meeting of Iowa's Congregational association to withdraw Christian fellowship from slaveowners, but the majority of his ministerial colleagues did so with great misgiving and refused to allow the resolution's publication in the newspapers. Meanwhile, the same controversy finally split western Quakerism in 1843, with very important consequences for Salem's abolitionists and, through them, the entire course of Iowa's antislavery enterprise.[31]

Petitioning state legislatures for the repeal of black codes had been specifically urged by Indiana Yearly Meeting since 1840, and civil rights petitions to Iowa's legislature had enlisted virtually the whole Salem community. The village also maintained a conventional Quaker witness against slavery. In 1841, for example, having learned that the newly appointed Governor Chambers had brought household slaves with him to Burlington, Salem's Friends sent a delegation to visit that officer, presenting him copies of an antislavery pamphlet and "an address on civil government." Yet continuing advices from Indiana forced the Quaker majority at Salem to view with growing concern the activities of the local antislavery society: it had become increasingly evident that the parent body remained as hostile to "modern abolition societies" composed entirely of Friends as it had been to mixed societies. The climax came at the 1842 annual convention in Indiana. Conservatives and radicals at last confronted one another openly, resulting in the purge of eight abolitionists—including Rev. Thomas Frazier, Salem's pastor—from the governing committee of the yearly meeting.[32]

In February 1843 the Indiana assembly's abolitionists formally seceded from Indiana Yearly Meeting and founded a duplicate conference, designating themselves the Anti-Slavery Friends. In Iowa some thirty families of Salem and vicinity, embracing perhaps fifty of the settlement's most vigorous Quakers, withdrew into this new communion and raised their own meetinghouse in the village, becoming one of the alternative conference's four regional assemblies. Thomas Frazier joined the rebels, as did the original meeting's two leading laymen: Henderson Lewelling, the town's most prosperous businessman, and Aaron Street Jr., son of Salem's principal founder and an indefatigable antislavery spokesman. In March 1843 the regular body, on advice from Indiana, began excommunicating the separatists for "neglecting the attendance of our religious meetings and for detraction," as well as other charges tailored to individual cases.[33]

Not all of Iowa's strongly antislavery Quakers seceded, but the most passionate did. Thus freed from restraints hitherto imposed by higher authority, they promptly moved toward organizing a common front with Iowa's other antislavery radicals, an action leading to formation of the first territorial antislavery society in the trans-Mississippi West.

IV

In April 1843 Aaron Street Jr. informed the editor of Chicago's abolitionist weekly that he and his colleagues had begun talking about "a convention of the friends of the cause throughout the Territory, to be held sometime in the fore part of next summer, to consider the propriety of forming a Territorial Society." Within the next month Street got in touch with, among others, James G. Birney, the former slaveholder turned abolitionist, now a resident of Michigan, who had already been named the antislavery Liberty party's candidate for President in 1844. For Birney's convenience the Iowans scheduled their convention for the end of October in Yellow Spring, the easternmost of the territory's abolitionist settlements, and Birney tentatively promised to be on hand. In the meantime, Salem's activists organized a local Liberty ticket for the forthcoming legislative election. This first Liberty party appearance in Iowa offered as nominees Samuel L. Howe, the Mount Pleasant educator, by religious belief a Congregationalist, and Joel Garretson, a farmer living near Salem who had been reared a Quaker but never actually affiliated with the local Friends. That autumn the pair ran last, as expected, but an important start had been made.[34]

The association of Liberty party activism with the scheduled antislavery convention encountered some political disapproval within Iowa's original antislavery centers, all of which remained stoutly Whiggish. The advertised appearance of James G. Birney as keynoter evidently unsettled Yellow Spring's New School Presbyterians, but on denominational rather than political grounds. For the past three years Birney had been particularly harsh in criticizing the New School's reluctance to excommunicate its relatively few slaveholders; its Presbyterians seemed "more earnest to equal the Old School in numbers," Birney charged, "than to outstrip it in righteousness."

As it turned out, the Liberty party candidate finally felt obliged to cancel his western trip in favor of a campaign swing through Massachusetts. Iowa's New School Presbyterians nevertheless absented themselves from the convention. Their decision may have been influenced by the anticipated attendance of the Rev. William C. Rankin, their former pastor, whom the Yellow Spring majority had terminated, probably because it found him too ardent an abolitionist.[35] No representative from Washington County's Seceders put in an appearance, but the reason presumably had less to do with religion or politics than with illness or the effects of autumn's rains on the state of the roads.

On the chilly, overcast morning of October 31, 1843, sixty-four Iowans and nine eastern visitors gathered in Round Prairie church, a rude log structure in the woods two miles northeast of Yellow Spring village. They included Aaron Street Jr. and seven other Salem Anti-Slavery Friends, accompanied by William Beard, a prominent Indiana Quaker. A physician, Dr. George Shedd, a recently arrived New Hampshireman and Dartmouth graduate who was soon to become one of Iowa's leading activists, led a delegation of four Congregational laymen from Denmark. Asa Turner himself had to remain behind to expedite ordination for the famous Iowa Band of home missionaries, just come from Massachusetts. But two of Turner's ministerial brethren, Revs. Reuben Gaylord and Charles Burnham, represented the Congregational clergy, the latter having hiked the thirty-five miles from his Brighton parish. Finally, of the major groups represented, nearly forty local Presbyterians made their appearance. The antislavery but racist David E. Blair was not one of them. Neither was David's wife, but his sister-in-law Margaret was one of the few New School members present and took an active role in the deliberations. John Waddle and William McClure, the ruling elders of Round Prairie church, together with William's father John, were the convention's most prominent Presbyterian lay delegates.[36]

The participation of three distinguished visitors from east of the Mississippi lent a special drama to the proceedings, almost making up for Birney's absence. Of this trio, the Rev. James H. Dickey, now in his mid-sixties, stood first in seniority in both age and antislavery commitment. A native South Carolinian who had moved north in order to free his slaves, he had then transformed Ohio's Chillicothe Presbytery into one of the Midwest's most thoroughly abolitionized religious conferences. He now held a pastorate in Illinois. The names of former Ohio parishioners appended to the announcement of the Iowa convention had prompted his appearance, and his reunion with them provided a touching moment. All present deferred to Father Dickey as one of Presbyterianism's most prominent antislavery pioneers.[37]

The other distinguished guests, the Rev. William T. Allan and Augustus Wattles, had both been converted to immediate abolition by that towering figure within the western antislavery movement, Theodore Dwight Weld. The two had followed Weld to Presbyterian-affiliated Lane Theological Seminary near Cincinnati, and had been, with Weld, leading members of the famous Lane Rebels, forty abolitionist students who in 1834 had resigned to protest the school trustees' ban on antislavery activism. Since their days at Lane, both Allan and Wattles had worked tirelessly for the cause. Allan, a professional antislavery lecturer, now served as chief agent of the Illinois Anti-Slavery Society. Wattles, an Ohioan, had never been ordained, having for the past decade devoted himself to the education, vocational training, and job placement of free blacks. He had been drawn from Ohio to the Iowa convention, perhaps, through a recent correspondence with Aaron Street Jr. on the employment prospects at Salem for a few black artisans from racially troubled Cincinnati.[38]

Dickey represented the older generation of midwestern evangelical activists. Allan and Wattles represented something less familiar: both nourished more Garrisonian attitudes than were usually encountered on the banks of the Mississippi. For the past five years eastern abolitionism had been fragmenting over the wisdom of William Lloyd Garrison's leadership, two important issues being Garrison's insistence on viewing organized religion in America as hopelessly proslavery and his abrasive hostility to Liberty party activism. The result, as historian Lawrence J. Friedman makes clear, was the emergence of two distinct non-Garrison immediatist nuclei, New York City's Lewis Tappan circle of church-centered abolitionists, and the Liberty party "voluntarists" under the leadership of upstate New York's Gerrit Smith.

The intramural wrangling did not extend much beyond Ohio, but, if forced to choose, most midwesterners obviously felt a bit more comfortable with Garrison's enemies than with his friends. In Iowa, for example, the Salem Anti-Slavery Society subscribed not to the Garrisonians' *Liberator* or *National Anti-Slavery Standard* but to the opposition's *Emancipator*. And the Society's acceptance of women as members on an equal basis with men, although a novelty outside Garrison circles, was not to be construed, said its president, as implying a Garrisonian allegiance. But it would be wrong to put too fine a point on it: in the eclectic atmosphere of the upper Mississippi Valley Garrison's followers were deemed eccentrics, not heretics.[39]

Back in Ohio a Garrisonian like Wattles might surround himself with like-minded friends, but finding himself ideologically isolated in Illinois, Allan increasingly played the role of a one-man loyal opposition within the movement. "The abolition of this State is of the Liberty party stamp," Allan finally complained of Illinois to Garrison himself. "There are a *few* of us who have not taken that course. . . . The greatest obstacle, however, is the prevalent religion. The community are drugged with the notion that universal and impartial love is not essential to Christianity. When called on to take sides with God against oppression . . . they cry—'That's abolition, and not religion.' And they are bolstered up in the cruel and ruinous position by a multitude of professed ministers of Christ." Such was his feeling shortly after Aaron Street Jr.'s announcement of the Yellow Spring convention.

Allan came straight to Iowa from an Illinois Anti-Slavery Society meeting where, as one of that gathering's most prestigious participants, he had offered a resolution asserting "the duty of all abolitionists to come out from the Episcopalian, Baptist, Methodist, and Presbyterian churches, on the ground that those denominations are fully committed to the system of slavery." The embarrassed Illinoisans spared Brother Allan's feelings by tabling his proposition rather than decisively voting it down. Now, a week later, Allan may have viewed Iowans' rudimentary Liberty party loyalties and recent intramural religious conflicts as offering him a more congenial reception.[40]

The Rev. Mr. Rankin gaveled the meeting to order, after which the convention called on Aaron Street Jr. to preside. Following the reading of a biblical verse, a moment of silent meditation, and a prayer by Allan, those assembled got down to work. A committee of ten men and women prepared resolutions, a second committee devised a constitution for an Iowa Anti-Slavery Society, and Rankin addressed the delegates. Only the first resolution had been discussed and approved before a break for dinner, after which Dickey and Allan offered the session's keynote speeches.

Next morning the delegates reassembled and unanimously approved a proposed constitution, a preamble, and a declaration of sentiments for the new territorial association. Although participation in its affairs was to be open to women as well as men, the charter officers proved exclusively male: Street as president, William McClure and the Rev. Mr. Burnham as vice-presidents, with other offices distributed equally among the men of Salem, Denmark, and Yellow Spring.

Of the fourteen resolutions proposed by the business committee, only Allan's condemnation of organized religion, in the apparently watered-down version in which it finally reached the floor, provoked serious division. Those assembled agreed (resolution 1) "that pure and undefiled religion makes thorough and active anti-slavery men and women," and (resolution 5) "that it is the especial duty of teachers of religion . . . 'to plead the cause of the oppressed,' and if they fail to do so, they preach not the whole gospel of Christ," and even (resolution 6) "that the American church, by having slaveholders in her communion, and holding fellowship with them, is the main bulwark of American slavery." But at nightfall they finally recoiled from resolution 9: "that no consistent abolitionist can support a church or ministry that is not found in active opposition to slavery."

"The point of debate was the 'sin of schism,'" Allan later reported, "i.e. the duty or not of forsaking a manstealing church. It was contended on the one hand that we should 'come out,' and on the other, that we should wait till we are 'cast out.'" Wattles joined Allan in strongly urging passage of the resolution; the two old Lane Rebels termed organized religion "a cage of unclean birds" and exhorted the antislavery faithful to "come out of her and not be partakers in her iniquities." But the venerable Father Dickey argued just as vehemently that religious schism could be a sin "more damning than that of slavery," and he himself, he said, would remain a loyal Presbyterian until they thrust him out or killed him. On Dickey's motion the delegates tabled the measure.[41]

The only other inherently controversial issue—the propriety of antislavery political action—provoked no open debate. But, significantly, the only resolution primarily championed by an Iowan, in this case Denmark's George Shedd, was resolution 3: "the anti-slavery doctrines and measures of the present day are no new doctrines and measures; they are taught in the Declaration of American Independence, and recognized in the Constitution of the United States, and were carried out in action by Congress, in the [Northwest] ordinance of 1787, and were subscribed to by all the worthies of the Revolution."

This assertion of what historian William M. Wiecek has termed "moderate antislavery constitutionalism" had been developing among Ohio's political abolitionists and was well on its way to becoming a guiding doctrine of the national Liberty party. In this formulation both Gerrit Smith's and William Lloyd Garrison's positions on the federal Constitution stood rebuked. Smith held the document to be profoundly antislavery, permitting Congress, if it wished, to legislate the abolition of slavery everywhere in the land. Garrison, on the other hand, stridently proclaimed the Constitution an ironclad proslavery document that denied the practicability of affecting slavery by working within the system.

Taking a middle ground, the new Liberty party view conceded that slavery existed legally within the various states by virtue of state law; the Founding Fathers had not attempted to abolish it because they lacked the authority to do so. But they had intended that the libertarian principles of the Declaration of Independence and the Constitution ideologically override this concession. As Ohio's Salmon P. Chase phrased it, the Founders meant to "keep the action of the national government free from all connection with [slavery]; to discountenance and discourage it in the states; and to favour the abolition of it by state authority—a result then generally expected; and, finally, to provide against its further extension by confining the power to acquire new territory . . . to the General Government." In time this doctrine would become the antislavery component of the Free Soil and Republican parties.

Resolution 3 provoked Allan, Wattles, or both, to offer the Garrisonian line, calling the Constitution a "covenant with death and an agreement with hell." They argued in vain. With at least two abstentions, presumably, the assembly "unanimously" approved resolution 3.

That evening, having rejected Allan's "come-outer" plank on religion, the convention—at Father Dickey's urging—approved an identical *political* proposition (resolution 10) requiring that members abandon both Whig and Democratic parties: "No consistent abolitionist can support a political party, or vote for a man to any office, [that] is not found in active opposition to slavery." And Iowans adopted the Chicago *Western Citizen*, a Liberty party sheet, as their official organ. The most important inferences pointed in one direction: toward third-party politics.

In other resolutions the delegates formally approved immediate abolition, pledged themselves to disobey the federal Fugitive Slave Law ("the law of love requires us to protect and aid the fugitive in his escape from slavery"), and censured the proposed entry into the Union of Texas, a potential slave state. And Iowa's black code did not escape their scrutiny. Resolution 4 argued that "the principle of equality . . . gives the colored people an equal right with ourselves to a residence in this country, together with the possession of all its privileges." The thirteenth was even more specific, stating that "the laws of this Territory, making a distinction on account of color, are wrong, and a stigma upon our statute books, and . . . we urgently recommend the circulating [of] petitions in every county and neighborhood of the Territory, to present to our next legislature, praying for their immediate repeal."[42]

V

Late in the evening of November 1, 1843, the convention adjourned, thereby completing the abolitionists' first five years' encounter with white supremacy in what would become the Hawkeye State. Two days later, back home in Salem, Aaron Street's brief recapitulation of the event stressed the emotional impact of the muster at Yellow Spring. "Although a considerable number of us had no previous personal acquaintance with each other, and were of different religious denominations," he wrote, "we met and felt as brethren . . . and we parted with the bonds of union much strengthened. The Anti-Slavery platform is large enough for all men to meet and labor together upon."

Street's use of the political term "platform" is significant, since the Salem abolitionists had already plunged boldly into third-party activism and would soon carry Iowa's other abolitionists with them. But compared with their counterparts in Illinois—to whom they would continue to look for inspiration, and whose state antislavery organization dated from 1837—the Iowans might consider themselves six years behind the times. Indeed, since early 1842 Illinois abolitionism had been, in the words of its historian, "a political rather than a moral agitation, and the Illinois Antislavery Society . . . only an adjunct of the State Liberty party." By the time a comparable statement could be made of the Iowa movement it would be 1847—again a gap of nearly six years.[43]

Still, organization of the Iowa Anti-Slavery Society fittingly closed the first phase of the struggle. The issues had been joined. Iowa's black code had been confronted. The majority Democrats had been exposed as militant racists, for the most part, and the Whigs as weak civil libertarians at best. Constituent pressures on legislators had demonstrated good effect in forcing racially progressive behavior, especially from Whig legislators, and perhaps the fielding of Liberty candidates among heavily Whiggish voting constituencies would be the most effective pressure of all. At the same time, the imperfections in their movement had become clearer. The racist vote of Yellow Spring's David Blair in the 1841/42 assembly emphasized the depressing fact that antislavery attitudes and a concern for the civil liberties of blacks did not always coincide, while the recent convention boycott by New School Presbyterians revealed the vulnerability of antislavery unity to religious sensitivities. Finally, racists' resistance to the civil rights movement was not to be underestimated in any tactical calculation. Black exclusion would be their ultimate political weapon, and within the next decade the Iowa general assembly would indeed pass the nineteenth century's second free-state exclusionary law.

For Iowa's activists the worst was yet to come.

The Ghost of Justice Story

3

Faded free papers and dusty penal bonds executed under the terms of the Act to Regulate Blacks and Mulattoes sometimes turn up in the tall-windowed courthouses of southeast Iowa. Thus we learn that in 1849 Jefferson County's Widow Mosely, lately of Kentucky, officially certified the freedom of her maidservant Caroline, "a mulatto girl now aged thirty-nine years, about four feet three inches high, [with] stout, bony frame, but not corpulent, large face, strongly marked features, hazel eyes, . . . of neat habits; rather intelligent and cheerful, and free of speech, with hair turning gray on close inspection, but otherwise black." And in 1841, Walter Butler, presumably white, cosigned a bond with Francis Reno and his wife Maria, a "free colored" couple, as surety that they should "not at any time become chargeable to the said County of Johnson nor to any other County in this Territory, and shall at all times conduct and behave themselves in an Orderly and Lawful manner."[1]

The Reno case may well have been an instance of coercive employment of the 1839 statute, although only two specific episodes of such action have come down to us. One involved Charles Forrester, a slave brought to Iowa Territory by the Sauk and Mesquakie Indian agent, and freed by that officer's will in 1840. Three years later Forrester moved to the nearby town of Fairfield and opened a barber shop. He did not post bond as required by the regulatory law, something noted by local critics who demanded that Jefferson County's officers take action. The county attorney dutifully looked into the case but recommended against prosecution, on the charming but legally dubious grounds that Forrester had been brought to Iowa by a federal employee and that his residency predated that of his persecutors. Forrester remained an Iowan, bond or no bond.

Fifty miles to the west a more dramatic test of the regulatory law stirred the first families of Marion County. Rose Ann McGregor, a handsome, high-spirited black woman, had come from Illinois with her white husband, Thomas, who preempted a claim and set himself to raising a crop. Alerted by the neighbors, a constable brought the McGregors into court for violating the territory's law against interracial marriage. But the unrepentant couple promptly obtained a change of venue to Oskaloosa, a village with a growing Quaker population, where a grand jury quashed the case. Marion's county commissioners then agreed to intervene on the basis of the Act to Regulate Blacks and Mulattoes, ordering Rose Ann to produce her free papers and post bond on or before January 29, 1846, or "be sold to the highest bidder." The McGregors ignored this command and the county fathers ordered out the sheriff.

One winter day when Tom McGregor was to be away on business, the lawman and a volunteer deputy rode out to the McGregor claim, intent on an arrest. The wary Rose Ann barred the door and refused their demand for entry. Heeding gossip that the woman was armed, was a crack shot, and was—in the words of a local raconteur—"*some* in a bear fight," the two officers first tried persuasion. That failed, and as evening closed in on them, their exasperation moved them to a frontal assault. They shattered the cabin door with an old sledge tongue, disarmed Rose Ann just as she raised her heavily charged muzzleloader to fire, bound her, mounted her on the deputy's horse, and began the trek back to Knoxville. A mile or two down the road, however, the captive abruptly heeled her horse to a gallop and disappeared into the night.

The next day Rose Ann and Tom McGregor presented themselves at the courthouse and posted her bond, but it is said that after a season they sold their claim to some newcomer and moved on west.[2]

Was Iowa's black code more symbol than substance? Its haphazard enforcement suggests the chiefly psychological importance of such legislation. As an issue, it appears to have polarized only a minority of frontier Iowans. Historians may have erred in viewing the civil liberties of blacks in the antebellum North as a two-sided issue, egalitarians against racists. In fact, if the actions of Iowa's first constitutional convention can be taken as typical, the northern civil rights movement was part of a three-cornered fight: abolitionists versus conservatives versus a moderate center, the embattled members of which considered themselves a bulwark of rationality between two excitable, politically dangerous extremes.

I

For reasons not clear, pioneer Iowans yearned only modestly for statehood. Thrice their territorial governor urged them to approve a convention to write a state constitution on the basis of which an enabling act might be requested from Congress. In 1844, at long last, the voters did as they were told.

That autumn seventy-two delegates gathered in Iowa City to devise an organic instrument for the proposed Hawkeye State. Opposite the half-finished Greek Revival capitol in which they met, their voices echoing in the freshly plastered but carpetless house chamber, the oaks on the bluffs above the Iowa River offered a splendid deployment of color against the tall western sky. But it was politics, more than October's bright blue weather, that stirred the delegates' blood. To the south and east of them the nation's voters were preparing to cast ballots in a presidential election. Having changed his mind once again on the burning issue of the day—Texas annexation—the Whig nominee, Henry Clay, appeared to be in trouble vis-à-vis the colorless but straightforwardly annexationist Democrat, James K. Polk. Both were slaveholders, not incidentally, and James G. Birney's Liberty party candidacy, a forlorn hope in itself, increasingly seemed capable only of helping Polk by inducing antislavery Whigs to desert Clay. And so it proved.

Not yet qualified to vote for President but nevertheless energized by the national campaign, Iowans had gone heavily Democratic in the selection of constitutional convention delegates. Democrats dominated the gathering by a hefty 71 percent. Observers sensitive to portents on the matter of racial justice might have detected that, in comparison to the 1838/39 legislature that devised Iowa's black code, the 1844 delegates reflected a subtle demographic shift. No longer did Democrats of slave-state nativity predominate. While the raw numbers of Whigs and southern-born Democrats had changed hardly at all, northern-born Jacksonians had increased threefold, now commanding a plurality. And whereas the northern-born Democrats of 1838/39 had been precisely divided among natives of New England, the Middle Atlantic states, and the Old Northwest, in 1844 most of the free-state natives had come from the Middle states. The northern-born Democrats of 1844 were, however, less experienced legislators than their colleagues. Only 12 percent had ever served in the territorial assembly as against 39 percent of the other Democrats and 19 percent of the Whigs. What was chiefly new, then, was the pronounced increase in Democrats of northern nativity who were relatively fresh to lawmaking but who in all other respects very much resembled the convention membership at large.[3]

Would the responsibilities of impending statehood impel an abandonment of Iowa's discriminatory laws? The prognosis was not good. As territorial legislators, six delegates—five Democrats, one Whig—had already voted negatively on questions of civil rights, half of them on more than one occasion. At the same time, moreover, none who had voted positively in such roll calls now sat in the convention. The only apparent spokesmen for racial equality were two Whigs, Joseph D. Hoag and George Hobson, both Salem village Friends. The former was a Vermont-born farmer and "approved minister" who had served the East Grove meeting since early the previous year; the latter, a native North Carolinian, had lived at Salem since 1839. Neither had withdrawn from the regular Quaker body to join Salem's Anti-Slavery Friends, and, shying from certain excommunication, neither was active in local or territorial abolition societies. Still, the antislavery commitments of both seem clear: Hoag would become one of the most vigorous members of the "underground railroad" at Salem, while Hobson had twice signed legislative petitions urging repeal of the Act to Regulate Blacks and Mulattoes. Although the political circumstances of their election as delegates are lost, it is possible that Henry County's Whig leadership had welcomed them to the ballot to forestall troublesome Liberty party nominations from Salem.[4]

In any case, Iowa's abolitionists prepared themselves to influence the convention delegates about equal rights. On October 8, 1844, the same day the convention began business in earnest, the second annual meeting of the Iowa Anti-Slavery Society (IASS) convened in Washington village. The territory's association of Congregational ministers adjourned at nearby Brighton on the morning of October 7, allowing the Rev. Asa Turner and his colleagues ample time to reach the antislavery gathering the next day. Washington County's Seceders had been Iowa's only major abolitionist constituency unrepresented at the founding of the society the previous year. Now they had been invited to host the first anniversary meeting.

Of over sixty men and women who gathered at Washington village, John McClure alone represented Des Moines County's antislavery Presbyterians, while the Rev. Mr. Turner was the sole representative of the Denmark abolitionists. But as in 1843, Salem's Anti-Slavery Friends dispatched a substantial delegation consisting of Aaron Street Jr. and at least four others. Local Seceders composed the meeting's majority. Besides the Rev. George C. Vincent, their pastor, they included James Dawson, the county seat's prominent layman, as well as several of the Crawfordsville faithful, among them Dr. Isaac Crawford, the settlement's leading citizen, two of his sons, and a daughter-in-law. Only a disappointing four of the Congregational clergymen from the recent ministerial conference put in an appearance. Because a conservative backlash against outspoken abolition pronouncements had dominated that meeting, only Asa Turner, Charles Burnham, and two missionaries whose homeward routes took them through Washington village braved the prospect of additional controversy over religious fellowship with slaveholders. Thomas Neal, a founder of

Crawfordsville, and Samuel B. Jagger of Danville represented the territory's Congregational laity. The Rev. Hiram Burnett, the Baptist minister at Mount Pleasant, contributed importantly to the ecumenical character of the gathering. An Indiana Quaker appears to have been the single eastern emissary present.

The Rev. William Salter, who left the sole record of the IASS convention, paused only to note that "there seemed to be the prospect of a harmonious and serviceable meeting" before pushing on. We know of only one item of business accomplished. Addressing a memorial to "the Delegates assembled in Convention for the purpose of forming a State Constitution for the Territory of Iowa," those gathered forcefully drew their lawmakers' attention to the matter of civil inequities based on race.[5]

Writes William M. Wiecek: "Abolitionists made a distinction between civil rights, in the nineteenth-century sense of that phrase, and political rights. They insisted that immediatism required that blacks be given civil rights as part of emancipation, but they were indifferent about voting power for freedmen." Abolitionists elsewhere, perhaps, but not those of Iowa Territory in 1844. Their petition embraced the expansive, twentieth-century definition of civil rights, all of which they claimed for Iowans of African descent:

> WHEREAS, all men are created free and equal, invested by the Author of their being with the same inalienable rights, and by the principles of our government, possessed of the same rights and privileges,
>
> AND WHEREAS, some of these rights and privileges such as the right of voting and of a trial by jury, and the like, have by the laws of this Territory heretofore been withheld from people of color,
>
> THEREFORE, we the undersigned citizens of the Territory of Iowa, do respectfully petition your honorable body, that in presenting to the people of this Territory a Constitution for their acceptance, you would so frame it as to secure to people of color all such rights and privileges, civil, social, moral and educational, under the same circumstances and upon the same conditions as are secured to others.

Sixty-two men and women appended their signatures, and copies of the IASS petition also were carried home for circulation among local groups for signing and forwarding to the appropriate constitutional convention delegates.[6]

II

On October 11, four days into the Iowa City convention, the delegates first heard talk of race: their committee on suffrage and citizenship recommended that limitations on the franchise enacted by the 1838/39 legislature be placed into the new constitution—a suggestion that provoked more controversy by its denial of the ballot to immigrant aliens than by its denial to blacks. The next morning George Hobson loosed upon his colleagues the antislavery society's petition.

The IASS memorial caught the delegates by surprise, and they promptly split over how best to handle it. They rejected a motion simply to bury the document by tabling it, and instead entertained a proposal to place it in the hands of a bipartisan select committee that could issue a printed report recommending for or against action. A substantial minority of the delegates, however, objected to this as playing into the abolitionists' hands by giving them public exposure. What was the use, asked the Virginia-born William W. Chapman, "of sending reports to agitate the country?" Better to relegate the petition to the regular committee and let the matter come up, if it did, when the delegates, as a committee of the whole, responded to what was sure to be a draft on suffrage that limited the franchise to whites. There was, he repeated, "no use in printing reports to send abroad to excite discussion. We want to settle the matter without excitement." Another Whig, also an attorney, agreed with Chapman. The convention had not met, he cautioned the delegates, "for the purpose of sending reports to the world upon vexed questions."

Most of the convention's racial conservatives seem to have found this concern for shielding the public from controversy unnecessarily elitist. One Kentucky-born Democrat was not afraid to have a committee report "go to the people," whom he characterized as being as concerned as himself about the prospect of "negroes swarming among them." In the end, by a 19–51 roll call vote, a coalition of conservatives, moderates, and progressives defeated a motion embodying the Chapman option and accepted a lawyerly compromise offered by Jonathan C. Hall.[7]

Although a newcomer to the territory, J. C. Hall made a lasting impression on his colleagues as "the readiest debater in the Convention." A dozen years hence, with a kind of permanent scowl contorting his beefy face, his heavy jowls fringed by whiskers, his hair receding untidily, he resembled nothing so much as the belligerent, hard-drinking Irish immigrant caricatured in American political cartoons. But in 1844, at age thirty-six, with his "powerful frame and large red cheeks," he was deemed the convention's handsomest delegate. Good-natured and "convivial to a high degree," he proved popular with friend and foe alike. A "self-educated man," the Rev. Mr. Salter loftily described Hall, "of no religious character, [but] of high standing in his profession."

He had been born in Batavia, in upstate New York, the son of a pioneer farmer. He was eighteen years old when the disappearance and presumed murder of a local stonemason, a renegade member of the Masonic Order, brought to Batavia and its hinterlands a firestorm of social and political conflict, giving rise to the famous Antimasonry party and what modern scholars have come to see as the origins of "mass politics" in America. Entrepreneurial, middle-class, moralistic, and reformist, Antimasonry planted the seedbed out of which sprang the nation's Whig party and the political system that served America until the 1850s. But J. C. Hall's youthful experience with it only solidified his antagonism to Whiggery, and he did not reject his beloved Democracy until the Civil War. He would soon hang out his shingle in more lucrative Burlington, but for the moment Mount Pleasant was J. C. Hall's home and he represented the same constituency as delegates Hoag and Hobson. Unlike his Henry County colleagues, however, Hall was on record as a confirmed white supremacist, having signed a petition to the legislature urging retention of the Act to Regulate Blacks and Mulattoes.[8]

Hall politely expressed himself sensitive to the petitioners' prayer, arguing the political necessity of "candor and discretion" in the matter. As befits a man simultaneously counseling frankness and prudence, terms often thought contradictory when applied to matters politic, Hall began his lengthy career as spokesman of "responsible" racism for Iowa's Democratic party. To have the IASS petition dealt with by a select committee had been his suggestion, and he made it, as a reporter paraphrased his words, "for one reason, because he presumed its report would be adverse to the prayer of the petition," something that "would settle the whole matter without further trouble." The delegates approved Hall's plan, and the convention president named Hall himself to chair the new committee.

The petition, it will be recalled, singled out only two specific inequities demanding redress: the denial of jury trials for alleged fugitive slaves, and the territory's racial qualification for voting. In strict constitutional law, denial of trial by jury violated a fundamental civil right, while withholding the elective franchise involved only a political privilege, a civil liberty. Yet the Iowa convention majority, from the beginning, responded to the Washington village petition solely in terms of its prayer on behalf of equal suffrage. Two factors seem accountable.

First, the issue of jury trials for alleged fugitive slaves had recently been put beyond redress by local legislative bodies. The federal Fugitive Slave Law of 1793 mandated summary ministerial hearings in which the testimony of slaveholders alone was to be admitted into evidence; now a unanimous decision of the United States Supreme Court in *Prigg* v. *Pennsylvania* (1842) decisively barred states from modifying the established procedure. In addition, the implications of *Prigg* were rapidly becoming a heated national issue, and no delegate hoping for a prompt resolution in Congress of Iowa's pending statehood would have dared bring the matter to the convention floor. None did.

Second, and even more important, the convention majority viewed suffrage as the single most precious privilege it was theirs to grant. More exalted authorities might quibble over terms, but the contemporary *Webster's Dictionary* to which jurists and lawmakers frequently had recourse clearly defined a "citizen," in American usage, as "a person, native or naturalized, who has the privilege of exercising the elective franchise." As J. C. Hall explained years later, making unusually explicit the enormous importance racists invested in the right to vote, "suffrage is a delegation of political power. In our [form of] government it is more than a mere badge of equality of rights. It is a guarantee of social, political and personal equality."[9]

This explains the narrow focus of the conservative response, and also the abnormally strong backlash the IASS petition provoked from many delegates. Although historians of civil rights have not been persuaded to draw distinctions between "routine" and "extraordinary" legal discriminations against African-Americans, exclusion laws raising barriers against black immigration and residence were obviously extraordinary. And it was pressure on lawmakers for liberalization of conventional black codes that frequently served as the immediate catalyst of exclusionary proposals. Such had been the case in passage of the nation's first northern exclusion laws, and Iowa's 1844 constitutional convention again offered a particularly clear example of the exclusionary proposal as an ultra conservative reflex to agitation in behalf of equal rights.[10]

Following their approval of Hall's motion, the busy delegates moved on to other matters. As a long Saturday afternoon session deliberated the interminable question of state boundaries, delegate William H. Galbraith, a young attorney who had come to Iowa from Cincinnati, a city long troubled by racial strife, bided his time. The boundary debate at last suspended, the chair announced the names of those appointed to J. C. Hall's committee. Galbraith now rose to move that the committee members "be instructed to inquire into the expediency of excluding from the State all persons of color, or of admitting them under severe restrictions, and report their opinion upon the subject to this Convention." The delegates' response to the Galbraith motion prompted historian Eugene F. Berwanger, 123 years later, to observe that "Iowa reanimated the idea of excluding free Negroes by means of a constitutional provision."

This is not, strictly speaking, the case. The 1820–21 Missouri statehood controversy in Congress had indeed been the most recent instance of national notoriety. But in 1835, evidently responding to the growth of Detroit's black community, the delegates to Michigan Territory's constitutional convention briefly considered an exclusion clause. In 1837, in response to race riots in Philadelphia, a convention called to revise Pennsylvania's organic document did the same. But true enough, the Iowa convention delegates did grant constitutional exclusion its most hospitable hearing yet in the nineteenth-century North.[11]

As the last words of Galbraith's motion echoed in the legislative chamber, ex-governor Robert Lucas, who had interrupted a bucolic retirement to serve as a delegate, rose to lecture young Galbraith on the folly of any such proposal. "Missouri," he sternly observed, "was nearly kept out of the Union by inserting such a provision in her constitution." But the territory's senior statesman won few colleagues to his motion to table, and Galbraith's resolution passed handily. And when, after a weekend recess, a Whig delegate from Washington County suggested an amendment specifying that "free emigration to and from this State shall never be prohibited," the delegates peremptorily voted him down.[12]

The next day Hall's committee issued its report on both the IASS petition and the Galbraith resolution. A document of some fourteen hundred words in length, it is the first extended formal discussion, however intellectually untidy, of nonwhite citizenship produced by a free-state lawmaking body that has come down to us intact. Hall apparently wrote it himself; a dozen years later he would proudly bring it again to the attention of a constitution-writing body. A few terms at Wyoming Academy back in western New York, a two-year legal apprenticeship, and fourteen years' law practice had better equipped him for courtroom argument than for constitutional exegesis. His essay owed nothing at all to the tenets of "scientific" racism, which were only then being produced by scholars. Nor did it look to the authority of positive law and social usage, which characterized a growing body of learned opinion against black equality. Instead, Hall's appeal, though bare of specific citation, was to fundamental political theory, on the one hand, and to social hypothesis on the other.[13]

The petition displayed two essential errors, said Hall. The first was its presumption that "the negro has a *natural* right to be admitted as an equal citizen." To refute this postulate he invoked one of the great products of Western thought, the theory of the "social compact." In one of the most commonly known formulations, John Locke explained the structure of society and government by inferring the existence of a prehistoric assembly ("that great town-meeting of the human race," a critic derisively termed it) in which groups of individuals had voluntarily bound themselves together into a formal community. Thus had human society been created. But a second compact (only implicit in Locke) was just as plausibly a contemporary as a primordial event. By its means government had been formed, defining the terms by which a society agreed to be ruled.

Through such agreements, then, civilized individuals had relinquished some of the independence previously enjoyed in the state of nature in order to gain a more perfect protection of themselves and their possessions, submitting to majority rule and delegating power to government so that they might better enjoy the life, liberty, and property that remained theirs—inherently and inalienably—by virtue of God-given "natural law." America's intellectuals of the Revolutionary generation employed compact theory to describe the actual creation of new polities, by which federal and state governments were validated through the "consent of the governed." By the fourth decade of the nineteenth century compact theory had become part of the familiar vocabulary of the nation's lawyers, if not most educated Americans.[14]

James H. Kettner observes that before 1820 one of the "central aspects of the concept of citizenship . . . was the assumption that citizenship was a status without gradations of rank; that is, whatever the social practice, the law in principle would not envision a hierarchy of fundamental privileges separating citizenship into categories of 'first class,' 'second class,' and the like." Thus American polity admitted of only three mutually exclusive civic conditions: *citizen* (a possessor of both civil and political rights), *alien* (a possessor of only civil rights), and *slave*. "But," adds Kettner, "once Americans seriously began to consider the legal status of the [free] black population, [these] working categories . . . operated as constraints, limiting the alternatives available to men who wished to exclude the Negro within the framework of law." What the Founding Fathers had not provided, racists must now invent. Ancient Roman usage tendered one precedent for a graduated citizenship, prompting Pennsylvania's Judge John Fox to suggest that a free black man "may, perhaps, be considered as a citizen of inferior grade, incapable of political power or dignities, but equal *in civil rights* to [members of] the white race." Compact theory offered a far more comprehensive justification for distinctions, however. Another Pennsylvania jurist explained the inferior citizenship of his state's African-Americans with the simple maxim that "no coloured race was party to our social compact." Lacking citizenship (or at least "full" citizenship), America's free blacks could be categorized as residents who had not been invited, or whose ancestors had not been invited, into the compact at its formation.[15]

"That all men are created equal, and are endowed by their Creator with equal unalienable rights," read J. C. Hall's report, "your committee are free to admit; that, so far as nature is concerned, those rights are as sacred to the black man as the white man, and should be so regarded." At the outset, then, in viewing Thomas Jefferson's famous Preamble to the Declaration of Independence as racially impartial, Hall conceded vastly more to the abolitionist position than many conservatives. But, he explained, total civil equality "is a mere abstract proposition, and although strictly true, when applied to man in a state of nature, yet it becomes very much modified when man is considered in an artificial state in which government places him." In the civilized world legitimate civic inequality *did* exist, the best example being the denial of political privileges—"the elective franchise, holding office, &c."—to minors and women. "No one thinks of sympathizing with them in their deprivations. The philanthropist has never had occasion to commiserate their fate, still it is in those respects the same as the *citizen of color*."[16]

Hall silently appropriated Sir William Blackstone's distinction between "absolute" (or natural) rights and "relative" (civil and political) rights, briskly maneuvering it into support of his text.[17] The antislavery petitioners, he said, had confused those natural rights belonging to all humans—life, liberty, and the pursuit of happiness—with the "artificial" rights of citizenship arbitrarily conferred on whomever they chose by those originally forming a social compact. The civic entity resulting from any such compact was, furthermore, an expedient, and thus legitimately exclusive. "It is made for those who are to be benefitted by it," he emphasized, "and is not bound to unbar its doors and receive every vagrant who may take refuge in it"—that is, it is not required to confer citizenship on all who happen to inhabit its domain. Those for whom such discrimination proved intolerable possessed the absolute right to locate elsewhere.

At this point Hall moved from abstraction into the reality of Iowa in 1844—but without abandoning compact-theory terminology. The admission of black Iowans to citizenship, he said, "should be properly treated as a question of policy or contract, where self-interest is just as properly consulted as in the promotion of a commercial treaty or a private contract. It is the *white* population who are about to form a government for themselves. No negro is represented in this convention, and no [such person] proposes to become a member of the compact." The conclusion was inescapable: "The negro, not being a party to the government, has no right to partake of its privileges." African-Americans could yet be granted citizenship as a gift from those who *were* party to the social compact, but then the context shifted from political science to sociology.

What would be the effect of black citizenship on Iowa's inner community of adult white males? "Would the admission of the negro, as a citizen, tend in the least to lessen, endanger or impair the enjoyment of our governmental institutions? . . . If it would, we should be unwise to admit them; if it would not, then it would be wanton and wrong to exclude them."

This brought Hall to the second proposition implicit in the IASS petition: "That the negroes are a desirable, or, at least, a harmless population." In refuting it Hall's greatest debt was to the long-nourished slave-state fantasy that American society literally could not survive as an egalitarian, biracial culture, but that the mass emancipation of slaves would result, sooner or later, in a blood bath. In the 1780s Thomas Jefferson had given enormous respectability to this prediction. As he put it in a frequently quoted passage from his *Notes on the State of Virginia:*

"Deep rooted prejudices entertained by the whites; ten thousand recollections, by the blacks, of the injuries they have sustained; new provocations; the real distinctions which nature has made; and many other circumstances, will divide us into parties, and produce convulsions which will probably never end but in the extermination of the one or the other race."

Endlessly articulated—its adherents included even the brilliant French observer of American society, Alexis de Tocqueville—the frightful image of a racial *Götterdämmerung* received perhaps its most authoritative expression in James Kirke Paulding's *Slavery in the United States.* A celebrated New York novelist and playwright, Paulding produced a defense of the South's peculiar institution based largely on the social evils of emancipation he envisaged. Should immediate abolition be followed by investing blacks with full civil liberties, warned Paulding, "there can be no doubt that the first struggle would be for ascendancy in political power. Elections would become battles; and blood, not ballots, would decide the mastery." In short order, he added, "the body politic would be rent asunder . . . and a deadly war of extermination be the end of this woeful experiment of philanthropy." Emancipate slaves *without* political rights, however, and the ultimate outcome would be no less cataclysmic. Free but shiftless, "this rabble of newly created freemen could [never] endure the plenty of the white man [without] attempting to wrest from him a part, if not the whole, of his property. . . . And thus would be engendered the seeds of a civil, carrying with it all the attributes of a servile war, which could only end in the subjection, exile, or extermination of one or other of the parties."[18]

A second sociological projection to which Hall's treatise may be considered indebted was the universal southern belief that emancipation would inevitably produce an orgy of interracial sex, only slavery itself allegedly holding in check the otherwise unrestrainable appetite for white women shared by black males. Once again, Jefferson had endowed this hoary folk-belief with intellectual respectability when, immediately following his passage on interracial war, he wrote of the superior beauty of the white race as impelling miscegenation by virtue of blacks' "own judgment in favour of the whites, declared by their [sexual] preference of them." Jefferson and other spokesmen of Caucasian purity shrank from the prospect of a large mulatto population on aesthetic, religious, and patriotic grounds. It remained for Paulding, in anticipation of the strictures by biological scientists in the 1850s, to warn that in the occurrence of such "unnatural" amalgamation of black and white blood "the result has always been the same, namely, the production of an inferior race."[19]

Adroitly converting these nightmares into an ominous premonition of an inundating black migration north, J. C. Hall conjured up a scenario of appalling social import:

> However your committee may commiserate with the degraded condition of the negro . . . and feel for his fate, yet they can never consent to open the doors of our beautiful State, and invite him to settle our lands. The policy of other States would drive the whole black population of the Union upon us. The ballot-box would fall into their hands, and a train of evils would follow, that, in the opinion of your committee, would be incalculable. The rights of persons would be less secure, and private property materially impaired. The injustice to the white population would be beyond computation.
>
> There are strong reasons to induce the belief that the two races could not exist in the same government upon an equality without discord and violence, that might eventuate in insurrection, bloodshed and final extermination of one of the two races. No one can doubt that a degraded prostitution of moral feeling would ensue; a tendency to amalgamate the two races would be superinduced; a degraded and reckless population would follow; idleness, crime and misery would come in their train, and government itself fall into anarchy or despotism.

It hardly seemed necessary to add, as Hall did, that his select committee deemed it "inexpedient" to grant the prayer of the IASS petitioners. But the anticlimax came in its pronouncement on the Galbraith motion. The committee—if its report's repeated metaphors of physical entry may be seen as perfectly consistent with its final apocalyptic paragraph—had produced one of the most eloquent briefs for black exclusionary legislation ever presented to a body of free-state lawmakers. Yet it now deferred to Governor Lucas, its most distinguished member. Seemingly despite its own better judgment, it recommended *against* including a black exclusionary clause in the new constitution.

The delegates, some of them no doubt stunned by the disjuncture between rhetoric and recommendation, ordered the report printed, then tabled it without debate, evidently prompted by a desire to forestall further agitation of an issue best shunned.[20]

III

Col. Jesse Williams wholeheartedly agreed with that wish. Over the weekend his Iowa City newspaper, the *Capital Reporter,* carried the text of the Hall committee report. In another column the editor, a young spoilsman taking a fling at journalism while servicing the convention printing contract, offered a few remarks of his own on abolitionism. He guardedly applauded the report's recommendation against full black citizenship, echoed its suggestion that to grant civil liberties to nonwhites would amount to reverse discrimination, and closed on a note that betrayed the anxiety underlying his normal editorial silence on the topic. "We hope,"

Williams confided to his readers, "that this black subject will now rest in Iowa forever."[21]

Such was not to be the case, of course, but the newspaper's attitude reflected the mood of America's Democratic party elite. In Iowa Territory no less than elsewhere, behind all the stormy Jacksonian rhetoric about business monopoly, financial aristocracy, and corporate privilege lurked the issues associated with slavery, so menacing in their potential to tear apart the party—and indeed the Union—that avoidance offered the only psychological relief.[22]

Nationally, true enough, Whigs as well as Democrats constituted a party made up of northern and southern men, a political coalition apt to collapse should sectional issues stemming from slavery take precedence. But Whigs proved less assiduous in maintaining an embargo on antislavery politics than did Democrats. As historian Leonard L. Richards notes, "Democrats marched shoulder to shoulder on the race question," while "the Whigs were never united on [it], and a few [national] Whig leaders clearly sympathized with the plight of the dark-skinned." In addition, sheer political advantage constituted an important factor. In Iowa as elsewhere Whigs remained a minority party, and as such proved alert to issues with which to confront the incumbents. Northern Whigs were not above making common cause with abolition when they could do so without compromising their ideological distance from it. They might maintain an outward disapproval of antislavery "agitators," for example, yet stand foursquare for free speech—to the political discomfort of Democratic leaders sponsoring gag rules against abolitionist petitions to Congress, condoning the refusal of southern postmasters to deliver antislavery tracts, or regarding with only faint condemnation the use of terror and lynch law to silence abolitionist lecturers and editors. It was on the constitutional right of freedom of expression, not on the divisive issues of slavery and equal rights, that voters were to be won from the Democrats.[23]

But in October 1844 an element of Iowa's Democracy, not its Whigs, shouldered the responsibility for refusing to let "this black subject" rest in peace. Finding the egalitarian urgings of the IASS an unbearable provocation, ultra conservative Democrats viewed bipartisan rejection of full black citizenship an insufficient rebuke to civil rights radicalism. Although the select committee had already recommended against it, they demanded the ultimate racist disapproval: a constitutional barrier to further nonwhite entry into the proposed state.

By the time Colonel Williams's cautionary editorial hit the streets it was already too late: the convention's most forceful champion of black exclusion had spoken. Dubuque's Edward Langworthy, a mining capitalist of the same age as J. C. Hall and, like Hall, a New York-born Democrat, was without doubt the wealthiest convention delegate. He had been a minority voice in the Hall committee's deliberations, and he now bluntly defied Governor Lucas's insistence on political prudence when it came to exclusion. He moved, in phrases reminiscent of Missouri's once-beleaguered organic instrument, that a future Iowa general assembly "at as early a day as practicable, pass laws to prevent the settlement of Blacks and Mulattoes in this State." Those assembled approved his motion in a 32–21 vote, with a dozen cross-pressured delegates abstaining. The proposed amendment then went for consideration, as did all such successful motions, to the revision committee.[24]

The following week, as a committee report pended, rhetorical hostilities between the territory's abolitionists and the convention exclusionists flared once again. A Whig delegate from Washington County produced a petition identical in wording to the IASS memorial signed by thirty-nine Crawfordsville Seceders and Congregationalists. The convention majority tabled it with dispatch, and no other such document reached the convention floor. The next day Ed Langworthy's Democratic colleague from Dubuque, Francis Gehon, a Tennessean, moved that the delegates impose on future state legislatures a permanent gag rule against "petitions in regard to negro suffrage."

Governor Lucas rose to say he was "sorry to see resolutions introduced here about negroes." The question of suffrage, he said, would be fully treated by the new constitution. He could see "no occasion for introducing such propositions into the Convention" and deeply regretted "that gentlemen would bring them forward." Gehon replied that he was not so much against blacks as against abolitionist petitioning, which in Congress over the past eight years "had come nearer severing the Union than any other thing." He would not venture to say that African-Americans were "better or worse than the white man," though he himself was "not disposed to recognize them here as equals," and, for example, he would not sit at table with a black. Gehon closed, according to a newspaper report, by presuming that "the negro was entitled to as much freedom as the white man, . . . but he did not want the State he lived in agitated with petitions to give negroes the right of voting. He considered it an evil, and wanted to choke it off." The delegates tabled his motion without debate.[25]

Four days later the revision committee recommended disapproval of the Langworthy amendment, provoking a strong rejoinder by its author. His constituents, Langworthy insisted, had instructed him that something be put into the new constitution to bar free persons of color from entry into the new state. Their attitude, as an alert journalist captured his words, amounted to this: "Slave, or no negro." The citizens of Dubuque County could tolerate slavery easily enough, Langworthy was saying, but they would not abide the presence of free blacks. No proslavery apologist, North or South, would ever encapsulate better than this the case for

African-American bondage as a social form with which great numbers of northern whites were not really uncomfortable.

Langworthy went on to express his disdain for the spineless caution of those who feared congressional disapproval of Iowa statehood; simply let the delegates phrase an exclusionary clause as cleverly as the Missourians had done. Iowa was, he said, "upon the borders of a slave state, and if we had not something to keep them out, we should have all the broken-down negroes of Missouri overrunning us."

Governor Lucas rebutted, offering his most forceful reference yet to constitutional theory. The Langworthy amendment was "in direct contravention of the Constitution of the United States. The States regulated the rights of citizenship, each for itself, and the Federal Constitution guaranteed to the citizens of each State the rights of citizens of the several States. If evil should arise by emigration of blacks, as had been anticipated, the [Iowa] Legislature could make the necessary provision against it. This Convention should say nothing about it."

A moment later the chairman of the revision committee, James Grant, a Democrat, attorney, and University of North Carolina honor graduate whose "business ability, experience, eloquence, quick perception, . . . active mental and physical habits, and zealous regard to his official duties" had earned him a reputation as "the most noticeable and popular man in the Convention," rose to defend his committee's report. Grant admitted having originally voted for the Langworthy amendment, but since then Lucas had put into his hands a copy of the congressional debates on Missouri statehood, and had directed him to material in which the late U.S. Supreme Court Justice Joseph Story had expressed his opinion of the privileges and immunities clause. Grant conceded that he was "as anxious as anyone to keep negroes out of the State," but he now had no doubt that if Iowans tried to obtain statehood with an organic law containing the Langworthy amendment, "it would endanger our admission into the Union."[26]

What opinion of the great Justice Story's Grant referred to is not made clear. The note on the privileges and immunities clause in Story's imposing *Commentaries on the Constitution* does no more than to assert that every citizen of a state also holds a federal citizenship. A few years later, however, Story explicitly invoked this assertion in a matter of interstate travel. It is probable that Lucas directed Grant to the eleventh volume of *Peters's Reports* and the case of *Mayor of New York* v. *Miln* (1837). The high court's decision in that case upheld a state law requiring ships entering New York harbor to furnish information on passengers, the court majority deeming this a legitimate use of police power. But Story, in the first of his important dissents from the jurisprudential drift of the Taney court, insisted that the statute infringed on the exclusive power of Congress to regulate interstate trade. In so arguing, Story disapprovingly emphasized that one section of the law allowed *"a citizen of the United States"* to be denied entry to New York State, and that it authorized "the removal of passengers under certain circumstances out of the state . . . and this, though they are citizens of the United States, and were brought from other states."[27]

Reviewed in conjunction with the Missouri debates, then, Story's *Mayor* dissent lent considerable support, in retrospect, to Congressmen who had viewed exclusionary legislation as unconstitutional. The logic now flowed in this manner: (1) all who hold state citizenship (however defined) also hold United States citizenship; (2) the privileges and immunities clause of the U.S. Constitution guarantees freedom of interstate migration to all U.S. citizens; (3) some free blacks—as in New York and New England—possess the elective franchise, and are thus *indisputably* state citizens and therefore also U.S. citizens; (4) any law barring entry of free blacks into a state is unconstitutional by virtue of its violation of the rights of such U.S. citizens who happen to be black. To Lucas and Grant it must have seemed that the most respected constitutional scholar of the era had definitively rejected the legality of exclusionary laws.

Langworthy's response to Grant reinforces this interpretation. He moved an amendment to his own motion, specifying that exclusion would apply only to those black migrants "who are not citizens of other States." This escape clause, modeled on that contained in Missouri's exclusionary law, probably changed few minds. To expedite matters the delegates agreed to Langworthy's amendment of his amendment, then voted on striking the provision altogether. We cannot know who, besides Grant, had reversed himself on exclusion in the week and a half since passage of Langworthy's motion. We can guess that few had; most likely, the dozen previously undecided delegates moved decisively into the antiexclusion camp. Grant and Lucas—and Justice Story—carried the day, therefore, but just barely. What would have become the nation's only extant free-state black exclusionary measure lost by two votes, 35–33.[28]

IV

Despite the decision against Langworthy, the constitutional convention of 1844 could hardly have been called a success for equal rights. As it finally emerged, the organic document of the proposed State of Iowa outlawed slavery, but also asserted that only a "white male citizen" could vote. It limited general assembly membership to "free white male citizens." It specified that only "white inhabitants" would be enumerated in state censuses. It required militia service only of "white male persons." In addition, all territorial laws not deemed repugnant to the new constitution remained on the books as Iowa passed into statehood, providing renewed authority for the 1839 regulatory law and other racist legislation.

Congressional approval of Iowa's statehood, as it happened, hinged only on how the admission of a new nonslave state into the Union might affect the balance of power between free- and slave-state Senators. Congress passed and the President signed an enabling act offering Iowa and Florida to the Union simultaneously—the latter, interestingly enough, with a black exclusion clause in its constitution despite a furious attack on it by the New England delegations of both houses. Senatorial sectional parity had been preserved, but in Iowa's case the national legislators had erred politically in imposing more restricted boundaries on the future state than its residents were prepared to accept. Twice in 1845 Iowans narrowly rejected statehood under the constitution of 1844, as revised by Congress, forcing the territorial assembly of 1845/46 to mandate elections for yet another constitutional convention.[29]

In the same legislature a revived exclusion impulse emerged—once again—in response to IASS pressure. Spurred by the emergence of an abolitionist movement among Methodists and Presbyterians willing to face the extraordinarily conservative atmosphere of the territorial capital, the IASS convened in Iowa City in December 1845, the better to influence the coinciding session of the territorial assembly. The abolitionists met in the basement of the town's Methodist chapel; those present included small delegations from Salem and Washington village, although the association's president and its recording secretary proved unable to attend. As in 1843, the peripatetic Rev. William T. Allan rode in from Illinois to serve as featured speaker, offering a fiery Garrisonian denunciation of the U.S. Constitution the first night, followed by a similar fulmination the second night against America's Presbyterian, Methodist, Baptist, and Episcopal denominations.

The meeting's eight resolutions, however, proved to be "considerably shaved down from the positions assumed by the speakers," noted an onlooker. Its only call to action, resolution 6, declared once again that "the laws of this Territory in relation to blacks and mulattoes are anti-democratic, and oppressive, and opposed to the rights of humanity, and ought to be repealed." It pledged the society's members to "petition the Legislature now in session, to repeal all laws making a distinction on account of color."

The gathering adjourned on December 12, and that very day a plucky first-term Whig legislator from Henry County, Norton Munger, presented a memorial signed by the IASS convention's twenty-nine delegates "praying for the repeal of the laws making a distinction on account of color in our inhabitants." He then moved that the petition be submitted to the house judiciary committee "with instruction that [it] report by bill or otherwise, as to the constitutionality of the law that requires blacks to give security for their good behavior." The tactical thrust of Munger's motion is clear enough: after a lapse of three years the territory's abolitionists had resumed their assault specifically on the Act to Regulate Blacks and Mulattoes, again stressing its violation of rights guaranteed by the U.S. Constitution.

Munger's legislative colleagues obligingly approved his motion, but its only positive result was to impel conservatives to rise to the occasion and flaunt their contempt for political discretion. Introduced by David S. Wilson of Dubuque, brother of Judge Wilson of the *Ralph* case, House File 82 apparently would have transformed the 1839 regulatory law into an exclusionary measure. The judiciary committee speedily reported H.F. 82, and in January 1846 it passed the house, with only four Whigs and three Democrats opposed. Iowa's incomplete statehood, however, continued to exert a restraining influence. The Wilson bill's opponents included such legislative veterans as the speaker of the house. Leery of its political effect, they somehow convinced two Democratic and the two Whig supporters of H.F. 82 to change their minds. The next morning they obtained the bill's reconsideration and unceremoniously killed it.[30]

No debate of black exclusion disturbed the deliberations of the freshly elected delegates who gathered in Iowa City in May 1846 to devise a second Iowa constitution. Democrats again dominated by a comfortable margin. With respect to the rights and liberties of blacks the new convention—a quarter of whose members had served in the 1844 body—simply reproduced the wording of the earlier document. In August 1846 Congress, the White House, and grass-roots Iowans all approved statehood under the new instrument, the chief issue having been its incredibly Jacksonian prohibition of banks. Four months later Iowa became the twenty-ninth state of the Union.[31]

No sooner had the cheering stopped than Iowa's antislavery activists, meeting at Denmark, renewed their assault on the 1839 regulatory law. Members of the Hawkeye State's first general assembly presented no less than eight repeal petitions from Henry, Washington, Des Moines, and perhaps other counties, with signatures of probably five to six hundred Iowans attached.

Thus goaded, the assembly's white supremacists once again sought to tighten the provisions of the 1839 act in such a way as to convert it into an exclusion law. This time, however, they found themselves hampered by the results of a startling Whig upsurge. By virtue of a fusion of Whigs and dissident Democrats in Lee County, the Whigs controlled the house of representatives. Here, in February 1847, seven Democrats and sixteen Whigs—including Yellow Spring's antislavery racist David E. Blair—handily turned back House File 120 with only one Whig defection to the conservatives. In the state senate, however, the friends of civil liberties suffered defeat. Only four Whigs—whose constituencies embraced Denmark, Salem, Washington, and Yellow Spring—voted to wring a repeal measure from the upper chamber's committee on federal relations. The other Whigs joined their Democratic colleagues in opposing it.[32]

V

The furor over black exclusion would not reappear in an Iowa legislature for four years. Its disappearance coincided, significantly enough, with the abrupt waning of equal rights petitioning, as the state's abolitionists abandoned the Iowa Anti-Slavery Society and shifted decisively into the Liberty and Free Soil movements. From their own foreshortened perspective, it may have seemed that the six-year campaign to influence Iowa lawmakers against *de jure* racism had accomplished little. And so it had in terms of legislation. But politically it proves to have possessed considerable importance: it had incited radical white supremacists to press for black exclusion, which in turn had forced "ordinary" racists to define themselves to the left of their truly reactionary colleagues.

Iowa's legislators and constitution writers submitted to few roll call votes on matters of race between 1838 and 1847, but the message of the seven that occurred is unmistakable. The importance of the distinction between routine discriminatory legislation, on the one hand, and exclusionary legislation on the other is empirically verified by the voting records of thirteen lawmakers who participated in roll calls on both. All but one had supported ordinary racist legislation, but these twelve then divided 5–7 when it came to exclusion (table 3.1).[33]

All five men who supported both ordinary black laws and black exclusion turn out to have been Democrats, while the seven antiexclusionists

Table 3.1 Exclusionists versus "ordinary" racists, 1839–1847

	Favored exclusion	Opposed exclusion
Favored ordinary black laws	5 Democrats	3 Democrats 4 Whigs
Opposed ordinary black laws		1 Democrat

Sources: Iowa Council Journal (1838/39), 164; *Iowa House Journal* (1840/41), 258; ibid. (1841/42), 159; ibid. (1845/46), 179; ibid. (1846/47), 353; *Iowa Senate Journal* (1846/47), 194; Jesse Williams, ed., *Journal of the Convention for the Formation of a Constitution for the State of Iowa* (Iowa City, 1845), 165; T. D. Eagal and R. H. Sylvester, eds., *The Iowa State Almanac and Statistical Register for 1860* (Davenport, 1860), 16–21.

Table 3.2 Roll calls involving equal rights, 1839–1847 (egalitarian positions italicized)

	Democrats	Whigs
Nonwhite regulatory law (1839)		
For	5	4
Against	2	1
Jury trials for alleged fugitive slaves (1841)		
For	0	4
Against	12	7
Racially impartial welfare system (1842)		
For	1	2
Against	13	7
EXCLUSION (1844)		
For	30	3
Against	19	16
EXCLUSION (1846)		
For	7	1
Against	6	6
Nonwhite regulatory law repeal (1847)		
For	0	4
Against	9	4
EXCLUSION (1847)		
For	8	1
Against	7	16

Sources: See Table 3.1.

break down as three Democrats and four Whigs. This suggests that black exclusion impelled Whigs—even racist Whigs—to coalesce in opposition, while it caused racist Democrats to split. Such interpretation wins support from the configuration of party divisions on all seven roll calls involving race (table 3.2). With respect to routine discriminatory measures, Iowa's Whigs could be counted on to fragment into racist and egalitarian factions. Outright exclusion, however, repeatedly drew them toward unanimity. The effect on Democrats was just the opposite. Wonderfully united against black equality in routine civil rights roll calls, Jacksonians split in response to exclusion. Proposals to bar free black immigration, in short, brought Whigs together on the race issue at the same time as they divided the Democrats.

Black exclusion was not the only divisive issue, though the legislative parties polarized less frequently than might have been expected. In the 1844 constitutional convention, for example, hotly debated issues included banking, a proposal to open convention sessions with prayer, the poll tax, a motion to grant suffrage to aliens, a proposed two-year gubernatorial term (a test of attitudes toward rotation in office), and capital punishment. With respect to only one of these—daily prayer—do party divisions possess statistical significance. As to the others, the banking and alien suffrage questions resembled black exclusion in dividing Democrats while solidifying Whigs.[34]

The political import is obvious. It would be a coalition of Whigs, ex-Democrats, and Free Soilers, mustering on an issue of race, that a decade hence would spawn the state's Republican party. Exclusion, while not the instrument of death for the antebellum party system in Iowa, was at least one harbinger of its doom, though the writing on the wall might be as yet too faint to read. Of the 112 lawmakers who participated in exclusion roll calls in the 1840s, the post-1856 party affiliations of nearly 20 percent are known. Of this sample, composed of the least anonymous, over half the opponents of black exclusion later turned Republican; fewer than a fifth of the exclusionists did so (table 3.3).

It would be wrong to grant too much explanatory power to these data. After all, of the eight antiexclusionists who ultimately joined the party of Frémont and Lincoln, all but one had been Whigs, and three-fourths of the Democrats—exclusion and antiexclusion alike—retained their original affiliations. The data further suggest that even most of the Democrats who had registered as racial moderates would refuse to defect. More than black exclusion moved the Iowa lawmakers of the forties toward their ultimate political fates.[35]

For most opponents of black exclusion neither the death of slavery nor a racially impartial citizenship, we may guess, was yet a part of their vision of the state and national future: only one antiexclusionist, George Hobson, would become an identifiable Free Soil radical after 1848.[36] But

Table 3.3 Post-1856 party affiliations of exclusionists and antiexclusionists

	Remained Democrats	Became Republicans
Favored exclusion	10	3 Democrats 1 Whig
Opposed exclusion	5	1 Democrat 7 Whigs

Sources: Eagal and Sylvester, *Iowa State Almanac,* and miscellaneous.

the continuing political conflict of abolitionist petitioners and legislative exclusionists removed the easy middle ground of conventional racial discrimination on which most moderates unreflectingly stood. If nothing else, pondering the matter of exclusion's unconstitutionality exposed them to the novel idea that free blacks might hold a citizenship vested in them by the highest law of the land, a notion that once admitted, as southern slaveholders well knew, could prove the entering wedge of a deep reassessment of racial justice in America. But for the most part, no doubt, moderates simply read black exclusion as unconstitutional—and therefore, in the political language of a later era, "un-American."

As a Jacksonian strategy for removing the African-American from Iowa's internal politics, exclusion was an influential mistake. Its main effect was, in fact, enormously political. It helped push most Whigs and many Democrats toward—if not into—the embrace of equal rights, endowing black citizenship with a public respectability it had not hitherto enjoyed. Exclusion, the most powerful political expression of "the race question" in America short of slavery itself, and sharply differentiated from other civil liberties issues by its penumbra of unconstitutionality, would come up again, and again help impel Hawkeye voters toward the dramatic transformation of their political scene.

Fires of Liberty

4

"Here, Sir, is our hope for the final extermination of slavery," Henry B. Stanton, a young Massachusetts abolitionist, argued at the 1839 convention of the American Anti-Slavery Society in New York City. "Six or eight large States shall yet march into the Union with free banners floating in the breeze. Already are those young sovereigns Wisconsin and Iowa preparing to take their seats at the council board of the nation."[1]

The first legislative assembly of the Territory of Iowa had adjourned three months earlier. Were its new session laws available to Stanton, their racist content might have dampened such optimism about the progressive electoral influence of the frontier. At any rate, the AASS was already beginning to split over the alleged incompatibility between voting or office-seeking and the ideological purity of abolitionism. People like Stanton, dedicated to overthrowing slavery at the ballot box, withdrew from the AASS to found the nation's Liberty party in 1840. They continued to view Iowa's impending statehood as a benign potentiality, while their ideological opponents, the "old organization" constituents of William Lloyd Garrison, coolly discounted it.

Thus the Garrisonians' New York City newspaper, the *National Anti-Slavery Standard,* seized on a rumor that Iowa's 1844 constitutional convention had produced an organic instrument mandating black exclusion. While therefore urging a petition campaign to frustrate congressional approval of Iowa statehood, its editor nonetheless glumly predicted admission to the Union of yet another "proslavery" state. One of the political abolitionists' most important spokesmen, the editor of the Cincinnati *Herald and Philanthropist,* on the other hand, took pleasure in refuting this false report. He observed that "such a clause would be strangely out of place" among the document's "liberal and enlightened provisions," its "ridiculous as well as invidious and oppressive" routine restrictions on black civil liberties being no worse than those of many other states.[2]

Iowa briefly captured the attention of eastern antislavery circles a year later, when a delegation of prominent British Quakers arrived in the United States to mediate the schism within Indiana Yearly Meeting, hoping to bring the secessionists back into the fold by initially approaching them where they appeared to be the most psychologically vulnerable—at their isolated outpost far out on the Iowa frontier. Salem's Anti-Slavery Friends stoutly rebuffed the visiting Britons, however, an act that earned them the warm congratulations of Garrison's Massachusetts Anti-Slavery Society. But the tenor of old-organization attitudes remained essentially negative. A "friend in Iowa" finally wrote the Boston *Liberator* to assure Garrison that the antislavery prospect west of the Mississippi was much less gloomy than frequently assumed: "Abolitionists—thorough, brave, hearty—are numerous in this State, and speak and act as openly and decidedly as I have been accustomed to see them in the East. . . . We in Northern Iowa are mostly from Northern States, and, of course, we bring the leaven of anti-slavery with us." And later that year the political abolitionists' *Liberty Almanac* offered the first complete report of Iowa voting returns for Liberty party candidates, a tiny but allegedly significant 182 ballots in 1846.[3]

Eastern abolitionists may be forgiven their incomplete impressions. Only readers of the Chicago *Western Citizen*, the official publication of the Illinois Anti-Slavery Society, or of the Newport *Free Labor Advocate*, organ of the Indiana Anti-Slavery Friends, acquired anything resembling sustained intelligence on the movement's progress in the trans-Mississippi West. Reports from the Iowa frontier, moreover, appeared irregularly, depending as they did on official minutes of infrequent major meetings and an occasional correspondence from particularly well-spoken activists such as Aaron Street Jr. Otherwise, the Midwest's antislavery editors seem to have been not much better informed than those to the east. As late as 1845, for example, the *Western Citizen* printed the canard that Iowa's proposed state constitution contained an exclusionary clause.[4]

For contemporaries the information flow improved considerably after Iowa's political abolitionists launched their own newspaper in 1848. But a century and a quarter later evidence of the early movement remains extremely sparse: less than 10 percent of its official newspapers, and a mere handful of letters to and from participants, have survived. And for all their attention to the state's two-party electoral warfare of the 1850s, three generations of political historians have produced little on the antislavery antecedents of Iowa's Republican party. Until the 1960s, when Ward Robert Barnes painstakingly pieced together an unpublished account of the Iowa movement, scholars had made no advance at all over

Theodore Clark Smith's 1897 study of the midwestern Liberty and Free Soil parties. Richard H. Sewell's distinguished reinterpretation of the national movement relies wholly on Smith in its infrequent references to Iowa in the forties.[5]

I

While the emergence of Iowa's Liberty and Free Soil parties awaits sustained analysis, the larger context is now well known, if by no means less complicated than it has always been. The advent of organized antislavery politics in the 1840s transformed the nature of the fight against slavery in the northern United States, supplementing the ranks of the abolitionists—that is, those determined to rid the nation of slavery as expeditiously as possible—with a much larger contingent of activists willing to oppose slavery's spread into the West. Henceforth the term "antislavery" would embrace both constituencies for purposes of general political discourse, although the enormously important ideological difference between them would persist, constituting a tactical problem of some complexity for those who would have them politically act as one.

In the late forties circumstances encouraged such a coalescence. Key events included the decision of a Democratic presidential administration to fight the Mexican War (1846–1848), assertions by critics that the war was being fought mainly to acquire new lands in which slavery could flourish, and a consequent dispute in Congress over the Wilmot Proviso of 1846 that proposed to bar the introduction of slavery into any new territory annexed as a result of the conflict. The national controversy over "slavery extension," as it was termed, increasingly energized free-state Whigs. In Iowa, as elsewhere, they rose to the political occasion by demanding congressional passage of Wilmot.[6]

The extension controversy, however ultimately useful to the fight against slavery, importantly complicated the effort to organize an Iowa Liberty party. In 1843, as we have seen, Salem's abolitionists had begun fielding local Liberty tickets, and those of Yellow Spring, Denmark, Iowa City, and Davenport subsequently offered similar slates of nominees. In the spring of 1846 petitions signed by fifty activists from Salem, Iowa City, and Davenport urged the calling of a midwestern Liberty convention in Chicago, although no Iowan attended the gathering. A November 1846 meeting of the IASS endorsed a plan for convening early in 1847 to form a state Liberty party. But implementation faltered, abruptly undermined by the pro-Wilmot posture of the state's Whig leadership. Iowa's voting abolitionists, most of them still Whigs, now hoped that the antiextension stance of their venerable party would preclude their having to abandon it for something new. At the same time, and by no means incidentally, the robust rejection of Wilmot by Iowa's reactionary Democrats enhanced the attractiveness of Whiggish antislavery initiatives and in the same measure weakened the abolitionist appetite for third-party action.

A month after Congress's initial rejection of the Wilmot Proviso despite almost unanimous northern Whig support, Iowa's Whigs proclaimed that "in the name of christianity, civilization and common humanity, [we] solemnly protest against the farther extension of involuntary servitude in what now is, or hereafter may become a portion of our Republic." Four months later, in the 1846/47 general assembly, the Whig-controlled house resolved that "in case of any acquisition of Territory by the United States . . . it is earnestly recommended that the evil of slavery . . . be forever prohibited within the limits of said acquired Territory." A Democratic majority in the upper chamber buried this resolution, but in the early months of 1847 the state's Whig editors produced a drumfire of antiextension rhetoric. In February a Whig state convention asserted that the Wilmot Proviso "meets with our marked approbation and deserves the thanks of every friend of human progress, civilization and Christianity."[7]

Iowa's Whigs, in short, were doing what northern Whigs everywhere were doing: challenging the Democrats to a showdown where they seemed especially vulnerable. At the same time, the Whigs hoped to keep their own antislavery enthusiasts within the fold, avoiding the defections to the Liberty party that had cost them the White House in 1844. Thus, in the first half of 1847, resolutions against slavery extension passed the Whig-controlled legislatures of seven northern states (Maine, New Hampshire, Vermont, Massachusetts, Rhode Island, New York, and Ohio) and even the Democratic-controlled legislatures of two states (New Jersey and Pennsylvania). Similar Whig-initiated efforts failed in Michigan, Indiana, and Illinois by varying margins. In Iowa, given Whig fervor throughout the North, it seemed an unrewarding moment in which to organize a Liberty party, and no local Liberty tickets took the field in summer's elections.

By autumn, however, the political winds had shifted just enough for new optimism on the part of Liberty men everywhere. It increasingly appeared that war hero Zachary Taylor, a Louisiana slaveholder, would be tendered the Whig presidential nomination in 1848, the party's national strategists counting on the general's modest disbelief in the executive veto to persuade antislavery Whigs that a Taylor presidency would not endanger congressional passage of Wilmot. This Whig hypocrisy tempted many important Liberty men to ponder a merger with discontented antiextensionists from both major parties. By 1847 most of these figures had decided that "the One Idea"—strict abolitionism—was an idea whose time had gone. "The real question for the Liberty party was not whether One Idea should be modified," notes William M. Wiecek, "but whether it should be diluted or supplemented. Radicals wanted to supplement it with broad, universal-reform planks, while [the moderates] hoped to dilute it as part of an appeal to nonabolitionist Democrats and Whigs. This determination suddenly hardened as moderates perceived the widespread popularity of the Wilmot Proviso," the most significant public judgment against slavery, they reckoned, since the Missouri Compromise.

By October 1847 all three parties had spawned separatist factions. Those from the major parties, Conscience Whigs and Barnburner Democrats, appeared hospitable to fusion with Liberty moderates in making slavery extension the leading issue in the upcoming 1848 presidential campaign, leaving the radical rump of the Liberty party, the universal-reform Liberty League, to its own fate. Liberty party moderates nominated for President a pro-Wilmot Democrat, John P. Hale of New Hampshire, but Hale thereafter held himself in readiness to vacate the nomination in favor of a candidate offered by an expected "free soil" political fusion.

Officially, the national Liberty party remained as unswerving from its abolition principles as ever; its 1847 national platform, for example, proved virtually as outspoken as its progressive political statement of four years before. But its leaders had begun soft-pedaling their views, downplaying, for example, their party's strong 1844 and 1847 platform commitments to the civil liberties of free blacks. In this instance they deferred to the straightforward racism of many—perhaps most—Barnburner Democrats, for whom the Wilmot Proviso seemed less appealing for keeping the West free of slavery than for keeping it free of blacks.[8]

So things stood late in 1847. Iowa's Whig press, in response to the swelling national popularity of a Taylor candidacy, had fallen silent on the slavery extension issue. Prompted by the appearance of the Rev. Alanson St. Clair, the state's abolitionists consequently deployed themselves to form what would be the last state Liberty party organized in America.

II

St. Clair's trans-Mississippi sojourn turned out to be brief but very important, bringing to Iowa's eleventh-hour Liberty movement the same kind of vicarious contact with the eastern antislavery establishment that William T. Allan's visit had given Iowa abolitionism four years before. Just as the Rev. Mr. Allan had symbolically enriched the IASS's founding, so the Rev. Mr. St. Clair now sparked the translation of that organization into a political party.

Once a major figure within eastern abolitionism, St. Clair had rubbed shoulders—and crossed swords—with its giants. One of William Lloyd Garrison's confidants characterized St. Clair as "a *saucy brawler.*" Another described him as "getting as fat [and] always as saucy, as Jack

Falstaff." His religious vocation resembled that of many within the Lewis Tappan network of churchly abolitionists. Maine-born, the young St. Clair had embraced liberal religion—Universalism—but had returned to Congregational orthodoxy at age thirty-six, becoming an ordained minister of that faith. In 1838 he won appointment as "travelling agent" for the Garrisonians' Massachusetts Anti-Slavery Society, and for six years thereafter had made his living on the abolition lecture circuit in Massachusetts, New Hampshire, and Vermont.

As one of three principal conspirators against Garrison's increasingly anticlerical leadership of the northeastern movement, however, St. Clair became anathema in old organization circles, and persistent rumors about his personal opportunism and his expense accounts brought his official usefulness to the Liberty cause in New England to an end. In 1845 he moved west and purchased rural property near Chicago, intending to settle down to the life of a middle-aged gentleman farmer.[9]

Spell-binding lecturers and experienced fundraisers being in short supply in the West, political abolitionism beckoned once again to St. Clair. Ever the enthusiastic activist, he accepted an assignment in August 1847 as financial agent and corresponding secretary of the Liberty party of northeastern Illinois. In October he served as featured speaker at the first antislavery convention ever held in heavily conservative downstate Illinois, where in a single speech he convinced one initially skeptical member of the audience to abandon a twenty-year allegiance to colonization. In November—"on his own hook," surmised Chicago's antislavery editor—he abruptly appeared in Iowa, offering a series of public lectures on abolition at Burlington. Then, on December 14 and 15 at nearby Yellow Spring, he helped preside over the birth of Iowa's Liberty party.[10]

The Liberty convention, evidently by design, coincided with the fifth annual meeting of the IASS, at which, according to the Rev. Asa Turner's report, "a part of the afternoon and the evening sessions of each day were devoted to the friends of Liberty friendly to political action, for the purpose of . . . organizing a Liberty party." No minutes of this last IASS convention ever appeared: its only transacted business that we know of was its employment of St. Clair to lecture in Iowa through the winter. A number of IASS veterans evidently agreed that the society's usefulness had been superseded by political abolition. Half its officers elected in 1846—Denmark's Asa Turner and George Shedd, as well as Salem's Aaron Street Jr., William Lewelling, and Elwood Ozbun—already had gone on record as Liberty men. Of the twenty Iowans taking the most visible roles at the Liberty meeting, at least a quarter had been IASS activists. Indeed, four of them—Turner, Shedd, William McClure of Yellow Spring, and Samuel L. Howe of Mount Pleasant—had served as IASS officers. A fifth, Salem's Eli Jessup, had participated in the society's 1844 and 1845 conventions. And all of Iowa's staunch abolition constituencies, with the exception of the Washington County Seceders, proved well represented at the Liberty convention. No more disposed to travel to Yellow Spring for organizational purposes in 1847 than in 1843, the Seceders' absence was not a matter of ideology.

"Mr. A. St. Clair, so long and well known as an agent and lecturer in the Eastern States, was present," reported Turner, "and added not a little to the interest and efficiency of our meetings." Most important, the distinguished visitor offered a workable plan for starting an antislavery newspaper, an idea the last two IASS conventions had discussed but not implemented. St. Clair drew on his experience as one of the four founders in Boston of the *Massachusetts Abolitionist,* organ of the short-lived Tappanite antislavery society in the Bay State, and cofounder of the Concord *People's Advocate,* the official weekly of the New Hampshire Liberty party. In both cases his contribution had been primarily one of fundraising rather than editorial management. Named chairman of the Iowans' newspaper committee, St. Clair reported a plan for raising $1,000 in forty shares of $25 each, the shareholders "to locate the paper, select and employ its editor and printer, and superintend its general concerns." Those present approved this recommendation, and various delegates pledged themselves to installment purchases of half the shares. They charged St. Clair himself with obtaining subscribers for the remainder during his winter's speaking tour.[11]

St. Clair also appears to have strongly influenced the assembled Iowans' ideological stance. Dr. George Shedd, instrumental in forming the IASS platform four years earlier, headed the present convention's committee on resolutions, while his brother James chaired a committee responsible for producing a declaration of sentiments. Neither set of statements strayed much from the recently approved national Liberty platform. The Iowans hewed loyally to its One Idea emphasis and, in fact, embraced a number of the national platform's resolutions in their declaration.

It was in their own resolutions that the Iowans primarily expressed their individuality. The convention call, issued from Fort Madison, had urged the attendance at Yellow Spring of "all those who are opposed to the *further extension of Slavery on this continent. . . .* Come, men of all parties, to the meeting!" Now, on the evening of December 14, at least a few conventioneers found the mood less ecumenical than expected. Resolution 1 proved noncontroversial enough: "We believe in the spirit and letter of the Declaration of Independence, that all men are created equal, and are alike entitled to life, liberty, and the pursuit of happiness." That passed without opposition. But those assembled approved the next platform statements only, reported Asa Turner, "after a full and lucid discussion from Mr. St. Clair and others."

Resolution 2 pledged the party not only against slavery extension but to further the system's total eradication ("it is the direct antagonist of liberty and must be destroyed"), while resolution 3 reasserted the doctrine that "the Constitution furnishes no guarantee to perpetuate slavery." The time limits imposed by the Constitution on U.S. toleration of the international slave trade, and the Northwest Ordinance excluding slavery from territory lying above the Ohio River, were both "evidence conclusive that the framers of those instruments and their contemporary patriots, intended . . . to inflict upon the system a moral consumption that would ere long work its utter destruction." Therefore, "the institution of slavery in all the Territories of the United States where it exists, and in all the *nine* slave States not of the number of the original six, [is] contrary to the spirit and intent of those instruments and ought to be immediately abolished."

Either resolution might have discomfited any Whig or Democratic anti-extensionist present at Yellow Spring, none of whom would have agreed that slavery in the states south of Georgia and west of the Appalachians was unconstitutional or legitimately subject to federal action. But resolution 3 also defied the "coalitionist" faction that had recently assumed effective control of the Liberty party in the Middle West.

Led by Ohio's Salmon P. Chase, the westerners saw the victory of political abolition coming in a pro-Wilmot fusion of Liberty men with antiextension Democrats and Whigs. Meanwhile, the easterners, for whom New York's Gerrit Smith was a major voice, urged that the party continue to pursue an independent course, uncorrupted by extramural associations. But ideology as well as strategy divided the Chase and Smith factions. By late 1847 they agreed on only two essentials. Both rejected the Garrisonian view of the United States Constitution as totally without value as an instrument of reform, and both held that slavery did not lawfully exist in territories still under federal control. But the westerners believed slavery to exist unconstitutionally *only* in exclusively federal jurisdictions (the District of Columbia and the territories), while the easterners just as resolutely held slavery to be unconstitutional *everywhere.*[12]

Alanson St. Clair appears to have played a major role in the Iowans' rejection of Chase. In October he had specifically repudiated the Wilmot Proviso as a fair expression of abolitionism, no doubt repeating its doctrinal insufficiency at Yellow Spring. Yet resolution 3 adhered no more to Gerrit Smith's perspective than it did to Chase's. Although remote from the centers of intraparty conflict, the Iowans did their bit toward trying to heal the ideological fracture. They accepted the westerners' contention that slavery was entirely constitutional where it continued to exist in the "old thirteen states," the former British colonies that had first formed the Union. But they also endorsed the Smith circle's contention that slavery was unconstitutional in all the "new" states—those fashioned from the federal domain and admitted to the Union since 1789. Thus the spirit of compromise inspired the calculated wording of resolution 3.

The second session of the conference on the fifteenth proceeded without incident. The remaining resolutions passed "with much zeal and unanimity," according to Turner, "and with but little discussion." In one very important way the Iowans had retreated not an ideological inch in the four years since the Iowa Anti-Slavery Society's founding:

> 6. *Resolved,* That the Black Laws of our State, which forbid to the free man of color a settlement within our borders, to breathe the free air of our prairies and cultivate our soil without free papers and $500 bonds [as] security against crime and pauperism in our State, while they make no such discrimination of any other race of people; . . . are but the legitimate, though monstrous offspring of slavery in our country; are anti-republican and anti-christian, the antipode of the spirit of the age, and ought no longer to be permitted to blot the pages of our Statute Books—[and] against which we declare unceasing warfare.

Before adjourning the Iowans entertained two motions from the floor and approved both. The first appointed George Shedd as Iowa's Liberty party national committeeman, the second approved the presidential nomination of John P. Hale and promised to "use all fair and honorable means" in helping secure his election.[13]

III

By mid-February 1848, Alanson St. Clair had roamed Iowa for three months, and already had been "mobbed" three times, he claimed, by hostile audiences. "I found in it many warm hearted friends of the slave," he wrote of the Hawkeye State to his sister-in-law back in Boston, "and many supple doughfaces, ready to follow any popular current, and many—very many—negro haters, willing & ready to trample on any human being 'guilty of a skin not colored like their own.'" St. Clair's family had been temporarily ensconced at Denmark, designated as Liberty party headquarters for the coming year, where Alanson worked with George Shedd to establish the movement's newspaper. He had agreed to be its editor only until April, wishing to return home to Illinois as soon as possible.

St. Clair visited Chicago in February, and saw to the production of a "specimen number" of the new publication in the offices of the Chicago *Western Citizen*. Back in Iowa again he and the stockholders contracted for regular publication with the editors of the Fort Madison *Statesman*, a weekly that would be Iowa's only Democratic paper to support the Wilmot Proviso. The first issue of the *Iowa Freeman*—named after such contemporary Liberty party organs as Vermont's *Green Mountain Freeman* and Wisconsin's *American Freeman*—appeared on March 4, 1848. St. Clair agreed to stay on through the summer pending employment of a permanent editor and regularly spent three days a week in Fort Madison seeing to the publication and mailing of the paper, commuting the ten miles from Denmark by buggy.[14]

Within the month St. Clair helped galvanize the state's Liberty men to action by printing and circulating in several southeastern counties Liberty party tickets naming abolitionist Samuel L. Howe for state superintendent of public instruction. It was a botched effort, done hastily and without proper coordination, but a combination of Democratic chicanery in canvassing the ballots and Howe's thirty-five Liberty party votes proved enough to deny the election to its legitimate winner—the Whig candidate—and give it instead to the Democrat. "The *Iowa Freeman,*" observed an uncomfortable Whig editor, "rejoices in the prospect that the abolitionists hold the balance of power in this State."[15]

On May 11 Iowa's Whigs met in convention to name presidential electors and candidates for state office. The delegates refused to commit themselves to General Taylor's nomination and, for the third year in a row, resolved that "we are in favor of the application of the principle contained in the Wilmot proviso (so called) to all territory to be incorporated into this Union, and are utterly opposed to the farther extension of slave territory." It was, true enough, the shortest of the convention's fourteen resolutions, and readers found it buried halfway down the list, but it had been the most forceful Whig endorsement of Wilmot yet.

Outwardly unimpressed by the Whigs' performance, Iowa's Liberty men convened in Salem on May 24. Successful resolutions included one "denouncing the black laws." Another sustained Hale's presidential candidacy. The delegates also nominated three Liberty party newcomers—at least two of them former Whigs—for secretary of state, auditor, and treasurer. Samuel Howe and Washington's James Dawson, two antislavery veterans, accepted nominations for Congress. At a moment when many of the movement's national leaders had generated considerable enthusiasm for fusion with antiextension elements of the two major parties, little coalition sentiment appears to have characterized the Iowans' convention. An eyewitness, in fact, almost transformed it into a gathering of universal-reform Liberty Leaguers. "They are true to the *one idea,*" wrote a visitor from Illinois. "Yet they are not unwilling to partake of the fruit of different branches of the Tree of Liberty, when the glory of God, and the welfare of men require it." Their newspaper, he added, had been charged with attention to the subjects of "Popular Education, Temperance and Peace" as well as immediate abolition.[16]

IV

The next six weeks dramatically reordered the nation's political configuration, a shift to which the Iowans did not prove immune. Meeting May 22 through 26 in Baltimore, the Democratic national convention spurned its Barnburner delegates, nominated an anti-Wilmot Michigander, Lewis Cass, for President, and approved a platform that avoided the slavery extension issue altogether. Meeting June 7 through 9 in Philadelphia, the Whig national convention, as expected, nominated Taylor and also shunned a stand on extension. Less than two weeks later Ohio antiextensionists from all parties issued a call for a national Free Soil convention to be held in Buffalo in August. On June 22 New York's Barnburners met in Utica and nominated ex-President Martin Van Buren, a Wilmot champion, for President and adopted a vigorous antiextension platform. On June 28 a regional convention of Conscience Whigs at Worcester, Massachusetts, denounced Taylor's nomination and urged all "lovers of Freedom" to gather at Buffalo in August.[17]

Events in Iowa also hastened toward the 1848 presidential race. The state's Democratic convention dutifully ratified a strong endorsement of Cass, and, in its only reference to the extension issue, declared that "all efforts of the abolitionists or others, made to induce Congress to interfere with the question of slavery ought not to be countenanced." Antiextension sentiment thus found no official hospitality among Democrats; the consistent conservatism of Iowa's Jacksonians would continue to work to the disadvantage of the state's third-party politicians by making Iowa's Whigs appear, in contrast to the Democrats, so much more antislavery than realities warranted.

Yet as rumors of coalition filtered in from the East, Iowa's Liberty men fielded local tickets in several southeastern counties, and for the most part stood firm against Whig merger initiatives. In Yellow Spring, for example, Liberty men agreed to caucus with Burlington Whigs, reported Alanson St. Clair, "to unite in nominating and electing candidates opposed to the black laws of Iowa, and in favor of the Wilmot Proviso." But news of Taylor's nomination, arriving before the appointed date, shattered abolitionists' enthusiasm for fusion, and the meeting never occurred. Liberty men succumbed to Whig blandishments in Davenport, however. Conversely, Henry County's activists, as they had done before, mounted an opposition to locally dominant Whigs by coalescing with Democrats willing to pledge themselves to Wilmot. A convention called by "72 persons, without distinction of party," met under a Free Soil banner in Cedar County, evidently resulting in abolitionist support for the Whig congressional candidate. A Liberty activist from Crawfordsville wrote that "the glorious cause of Free Soil and Free Labor" had stirred "great excitement" in Iowa. In the forthcoming elections, he predicted, "the friends of the slave here will unite with the Barnburners."

Editor St. Clair strongly urged against all such political arrangements keyed to Free Soil. "Our only safety, and the only hope of the oppressed is," he cautioned, "that we shall prove true to our principles, stand by each other, [and] let all other questions go as they may, if need be, and consecrate our ballots to the liberty of the slave." But of course the more obvious advantage of political independence for the Liberty men also could not be overlooked: through autonomy, not fusion, the minority abolitionists might yet prove influential in Hawkeye politics by establishing and maintaining a regular balance of electoral power between the older parties.[18]

In July illness and overwork forced St. Clair's return to Illinois, and his departure proved permanent. August's elections nevertheless appeared to bear out his judgment. In the state's first congressional district, where Liberty voters were most in evidence, the Democratic nominee won by just 50 percent of the ballots. Had those cast for Samuel Howe—although a mere 2 percent of the total—gone instead to the Whig candidate, that nominee would have fallen only seventy-seven votes shy of victory. No other Liberty candidate did as well as the Mount Pleasant schoolmaster, but local election returns convinced the editor of the state's leading Whig sheet that Liberty votes had cost the Whigs control of Iowa's upper house. Whether the abolitionist turnout portended trouble for General Taylor in November remained to be seen, but the state's Liberty movement, despite its numerical weakness, had abruptly become a force to be reckoned with.[19]

The votes of August had not yet been counted when the grand Free Soil convention in Buffalo, New York, brought out one more permutation of 1848's antislavery politics. Dr. William H. Miller, a physician from the Van Buren County village of Birmingham, represented Iowa. As he was the only delegate from the trans-Mississippi frontier, Miller's presence was of considerable symbolic value to a gathering dedicated to saving the West from slavery. Dr. Miller cast Iowa's vote for Hale rather than for the convention favorite, Van Buren, but, like most of the gathering's Liberty men, he acquiesced as the majority effectively ended the life of the Liberty party and replaced it with the new Free Soil party and a watered-down antislavery platform. A week or two later the *Iowa Freeman,* praising the Buffalo meeting as "doubtless the largest, most intelligent, harmonious and glorious Convention ever held in this country," proudly endorsed Van Buren and the new party's shibboleth: "Free Soil, Free Speech, Free Labor, Free Men."

"Say to our Eastern friends," wrote an Iowan to the voting abolitionists' national organ in Washington, D.C., "that the prairies are on fire." The editorial staff of the *National Era*, seeking to underscore its wholehearted endorsement of August's turn of events, fancied the metaphor. "We had designed to note the progress of the Free Soil movement," wrote its publisher, "but for want of room we are unable to do so. We must content ourselves by saying that in all the free States, from Maine to Iowa, the fires of Liberty are burning brightly."[20]

V

Historians have emphasized that the chief casualty of the transformation of the One Idea into Free Soil was the abolitionists' formal commitment to racial equality: the new party's Buffalo platform was entirely silent on the subject, leaving it to the Liberty League remnant of the old party to restate its egalitarian principles. Scholars have disagreed, however, on the meaning of this silence. The most reasonable interpretation would seem to be this: abolitionist architects of the Free Soil coalition knew that Barnburner leaders could not be drawn into an antislavery political movement that asked them to rethink old Jacksonian antipathies to blacks. Less necessary for gaining the cooperation of leading Conscience Whigs, tactical silence on civil rights was an absolute imperative for winning that of the antiextension Democrats. Yet, abolitionists reasoned, there need be no easing of their commitment to racial equality at the state level, where fewer compromises with racism might prove necessary. Thus a chief engineer of the Buffalo fusion, Salmon P. Chase, returned home to Ohio to continue the war against discriminatory laws in that state. Other abolitionist delegates, consciences clear, followed suit.[21]

Iowa's Liberty men appear to have made the transition to Free Soil as calmly as Chase. Alanson St. Clair's retirement may have smoothed the way somewhat, although he too would ultimately become a Free Soil activist elsewhere. His replacement at the helm of the *Iowa Freeman* was David M. Kelsey. A transplanted New Englander, Kelsey had settled west of Chicago in the 1840s, where he taught school and for a year coedited a village newspaper. By 1847 he was a well known figure on the Illinois antislavery lecture circuit—"one of the best fellows I meet on the line," wrote St. Clair—and had become a more or less regular correspondent of the Chicago *Western Citizen*. He visited Iowa's Liberty convention in May 1848, and late July found him at his new editorial post in Fort Madison. One of his first important duties was to raise the Van Buren banner and issue the call for a Free Soil convention to be held at the state capitol on September 19 and 20, 1848.[22]

A Democratic editor left us our only first-hand account of the historic occasion in Iowa City. He estimated the crowd at about forty former Liberty men, a handful of Whigs, and a couple of Democrats. Two prominent Iowa Citians addressed the assembly. One of them, a Taylor presidential elector, sharply berated the delegates and urged them to support the true antiextension cause by voting for Taylor. But the second, lawyer William Penn Clarke, had changed his allegiance and thus represented a major Free Soil acquisition.

A Baltimore native, Clarke happened to be a devout Methodist despite the Quaker cast of his given names. A slender, dark-haired thirty-year-old with a boyish face and the thoughtful, somewhat aesthetic look of a man more at home with the fine arts than with politics, he had arrived from Ohio in 1844 and struck up a friendship with Gov. John Chambers, whose protégé he briefly became. For a year he edited the weekly *Iowa Standard* at the capital while also serving on the territory's Whig central committee, running unsuccessfully for the legislative council, and reading the law. The extant files of his newspaper make him out to be the quintessential progressive Whig: in favor of banks, tariffs, internal improvements, and business enterprise in general, and against war, capital punishment, liquor, and slavery.

The *Standard*'s running commentary on Clarke's native South dripped acid, its hero in 1845 was the notorious antislavery Kentucky Whig, Cassius M. Clay, and a reader of Clarke's fulminations might forget entirely that the South harbored thousands of Whig as well as Democratic slaveholders. And although Clarke silently distanced himself from northern abolitionism, Clay's antislavery belligerence finally moved him to a startling comment that then went the rounds of the antislavery press. "We confidently believe that the time will come," Clarke disclosed late in 1845, "when the people must not only *read,* but *act,* with reference to American Slavery, and the sooner they begin to prepare for the crisis, in our judgment, the *better.*" A few weeks later, however, Clarke visited the 1845 IASS convention, where the Rev. Mr. Allan's Garrisonian animadversions on the Constitution and organized religion cooled his antislavery ardor considerably. "Slavery may be an evil—we do not say that it is not—but admitting that it is," he cautioned, "we do not conceive that, for the eradication of one evil, we should . . . bring greater evils upon the people and nation."[23]

With respect to Clarke's racial attitudes, two independently written pieces invite close attention. News items from Kentucky, so much the focus of Clarke's interest that season, prompted both. The first angrily deplored mob violence against Lexington's free black community. The second noted the reward offered for a runaway slave who had been licensed to preach. "The crime for which he is advertised is two-fold—he is black and was born contrary to the Declaration of Independence," Clarke wrote. "Is not this a great country, where preachers of the everlasting gospel are advertised like stray cattle?"

In 1851 Clarke helped a free black family wishing to emigrate to Liberia to obtain aid from the American Colonization Society, although he was not himself evidently a member of that organization. Six years later, while repudiating the label "abolitionist," he offered remarks that again suggest the tenets of classical republicanism as his ideological scheme of things. His starting point was "that all men are created free and equal; that all men have the same natural rights." From this the full citizenship of free blacks could be inferred as given, entailing rights of residence, property ownership, access to public education and the courts, and other unchallengeable civic attributes. Color prejudice, since it took no account of individual character differences, he dismissed as irrational: "Man has made the distinction [of race], but the Great Father of all has never made any. He has given the negro the same mind, and the same moral faculties that He has to the white; and He holds him to the same accountability." With respect to such qualities as honesty and trustworthiness blacks did not differ from other human beings. "I was born where there were many of the negro race," he said, "and I know something about them, and I say that as a people they possess as strong integrity as any other class. . . . All men who have ever investigated this subject, concede that integrity is one of the traits of the negro character."

Clarke flatly discounted the legitimacy, however, of what a later age would call affirmative action: "I do not care three pins for the negro, as far as [special philanthropy] is concerned, and would not undertake to benefit him more than it is my duty to act for the benefit of all God's creatures." He opposed black suffrage for reasons that he did not make entirely clear. We may infer, for one thing, that Clarke drew the conventional distinction of his day between civil rights and civil liberties, the elective franchise being of the latter category rather than the former, which meant that it legitimately could be withheld from some classes of citizens if the majority so willed. We may also assume that a Whiggish elitism impelled him to oppose black voting for the same reason he opposed voting by aliens and new immigrants: the precious gift of political power should not be indiscriminately entrusted to the undereducated, the economically and socially underprivileged, and those not otherwise seasoned to exercise it with discretion, wisdom, and deference to their betters.[24]

Whether or not Clarke's moderately left-of-center attitudes had anything to do with it, the *Iowa Standard* did not prosper. Admitted to the bar in 1846, Clarke left journalism without regret, and after a period of vocational uncertainty advertised himself as an "attorney at law & solicitor in chancery." As his lawyerly stature rose at the state capital, his voice resounded within the highest Whig circles, urging the Wilmot Proviso on his cautious colleagues. At the 1848 Whig state convention he struggled heroically on behalf of a dynamic endorsement of Wilmot, but, as we have seen, with only modest success. A month later, with news of General Taylor's nomination, his patience ran out. Our eyewitness paraphrased Clarke's political confession at the Free Soil convention: "although he had been an ardent and consistent whig, ever since his eighteenth year, he felt constrained in duty to God, [to] his country, and to himself, to abandon [his old party] now."[25]

The delighted Free Soilers voted Penn Clarke to head their ticket of Van Buren electors. His defection to the Free Soilers represented their first important accession of a major nonabolitionist figure, the beginning of a political process that eventually gave life to Iowa's Republican party. Because of its larger significance, Clarke's presence tended to overshadow the rest of the proceedings. Of specific Liberty men at the gathering we know only of Salem's Joel Garretson and Eli Jessup, Denmark's George Shedd and/or his brother Curtis, and David Kelsey of the *Freeman*. Hoping to convince Iowans that the meeting was "not an abolition convention," delegates named no former IASS activist as a presidential elector, and instead nominated Clarke, Dr. Miller, and two absent Democrats rumored to harbor Free Soil leanings. But Samuel L. Howe and James Dawson were asked to serve with Clarke and others as a state central committee. Editor Kelsey, "who acquitted himself with tact as well as talent," took the occasion to review planks in the Buffalo platform other than the slavery extension issue: cheap postage, governmental retrenchment, river and harbor improvements, free land for western homesteaders, and payment of the federal debt by tariff revenues. Thus a broadened leadership and broadened appeal for votes underscored the new look in antislavery politics in Iowa as well as in the nation at large. How much local modulation of civil rights militancy would be asked of the movement's abolitionists remained to be seen.[26]

A day or two after the Free Soilers' adjournment, one of the Democrats named to their electoral ticket, a Muscatine physician, declined the honor. Another Muscatine medical man, Dr. John H. Dayton, cheerfully stepped forward to fill the vacancy. A New York-born surgeon, formerly a Democrat, the urbane and energetic Dayton promptly joined with Clarke and Kelsey to form an unofficial triumvirate that would guide the party through its next two years.[27]

VI

Election day in November came and went, and with it any illusion that a Free Soil conquest of the Hawkeye State would be the work of a season. Among themselves Iowa's antislavery campaigners had admitted as much. "With you," Dayton wrote to Clarke in October, "I have no hope of getting the State but we shall surely hold the rod *in terrorem* over both

Whigs & Locos [that is, the Democrats]. For instance, the Locos have a large majority in our Legislature & yet not one of them will dare to vote for any other than a Proviso man for Senator, ie if they ever hope or wish to get back [into office] again."

The returns indeed implied a Free Soil balance between the old parties. The canvassing commission threw out Pottawattamie County's returns as fraudulent, leaving Lewis Cass with 12,051 votes as against 10,537 for Taylor. Van Buren's 1,126 ballots, if cast for the latter, would not have given the edge to the Whigs, but the relatively large "scattering" of 1,241 ballots—that is, votes cast for men not actually on formal party tickets—was the key. As Kelsey later explained:

> We, at the time, believed a respectable majority [of these scattered returns] were intended for Free Soil, Free Speech, Free Labor, and Free Men. This inference was drawn from the fact that the supporters of Van Buren had, and still have, but one organ in the State, and even this has a very limited circulation in several counties; that the Free Soil Ticket was formed but a few weeks prior to the election, and that the electors had but little time to canvass the State, circulate intelligence and scatter tickets.
>
> Recent information has corroborated the truth of this presumption. We have seen and heard of numerous instances, where individuals and groups of friends uninformed of the Free Soil Electors, nominated a ticket of men known to them, and thus cast their suffrages for such irregular electors. Such was the case among our friends about Sugar Grove, in Lynn Co., where about twenty votes were cast either in this manner or directly for Van Buren. . . . The same thing occurred in some parts of Lee, Jackson, Muscatine, Cedar, Jones and other counties.

Had Iowa's Free Soil ballots *and* its scattered votes been credited to Taylor, the general would have carried the state by a majority of 853.[28]

Computer-aided analysis of the returns supports this logic by suggesting that the scattering of November 1848 consisted wholly of ballots cast by men who had voted Whig in August's congressional election. These Whigs thus appear to have been as much defectors from the Taylor ticket as their less numerous colleagues who cast unimpeachable Van Buren ballots. The overall damage done to Iowa's Whiggery by the Free Soilers is clear. Despite a strong turnout—approximately 95 percent of the Whigs of August voted again in November—less than half supported Taylor.[29]

Taylor won the presidency without Iowa's electoral votes, but an acknowledgment of the Democrats' undiminished local strength and the Free Soil balance of power tempered Whig celebrating in the Hawkeye State. November's effect was to move Whigs and Free Soilers toward political reconciliation. Eighteen-forty-nine was to be the year of antislavery coalition throughout the northern United States, but with the exceptions of Michigan and Iowa, the collaboration was between Free Soilers and Democrats, who had been usefully chastened by the slavery extension issue. In

Michigan, Cass wielded sufficient authority to keep his state party from flirting seriously with Free Soilers. In Iowa, in contrast, the Democratic leadership simply proved itself so grossly reactionary as to forestall any honorable Free Soil alliance. Thus the Democratic majority in Iowa's 1848/49 general assembly briskly returned two arch-conservatives to the United States Senate. Then, with rough contempt, it again rejected an effort to influence congressional support of the Wilmot Proviso, shrugging off the awesome indignation of the eastern Whig and antislavery press—and Iowa's new reputation as the single free state whose legislature had not instructed its Senators to support Wilmot. Only one Democratic editor dared endorse the Proviso, and, led by diehard delegations from Dubuque and Burlington, the 1849 Democratic convention peremptorily suppressed discussion of slavery extension. Iowa's Free Soilers, taking a cue from their Ohio colleagues, technically renamed themselves Free Democrats and their paper, now edited at Mount Pleasant, as the *Iowa Free Democrat,* but earnest negotiations with the state's Jacksonians never materialized.[30]

Iowa's Whigs, in contrast, scrambled to assert their affinity for Wilmot in the legislature and in the columns of their papers. The Free Soilers got the message. Eager to test the potency of their balance of power, they nominated John Dayton for the top political position at issue in 1849, the presidency of the state board of public works, and a young abolitionist Whig, William M. Allison, for board secretary. Ten days later the Whigs cooperated by also nominating Allison and issuing a resolution closely echoing the two major antislavery planks of the Buffalo platform: no extension of slavery into the western territories, and its abolition in the federally controlled District of Columbia. Leading Whigs then made overtures to the Free Soilers' guiding triumvirate, but a formal Whig/Free Soil alliance foundered, possibly because Dayton, who was cool to a merger, refused to withdraw his candidacy in favor of the Whig nominee, Thomas McKean. Although the two parties went into the election belabored by Iowa's Democracy for having formed a "disgusting coalition," in fact it was merely "understood in many counties," as a Whig postmortem explained, "that the Free Soil party would vote with the whigs."[31]

The election returns, however, pleased only the Democrats, who captured both offices. Whigs and Free Soilers blamed each other for their mutual defeat, the former charging that Free Soilers had not supported McKean, Free Soilers retorting that hundreds of Whigs had scratched Allison's name from their ballots and voted Democratic. Analysis of the returns validates neither accusation. Most Free Soilers had indeed supported Dayton; virtually all Whigs had voted for Allison as scheduled. But the most important truth about the election could be seen in the simple statewide tallies: had Whigs and Free Soilers coalesced perfectly, they still would have fallen some 150 votes shy of triumph.[32]

Penn Clarke, who had favored a formal alliance with the Whigs, responded to the debacle by seeking to bring the two parties into closer collaboration in 1850, certain that a combined ticket could carry the forthcoming state and congressional elections. But this time it was the Whigs' turn to play hard to get, and the softening of the Whig position on slavery extension repelled many Free Soilers. The latter nevertheless endorsed Clarke's overtures to his old political friends by nominating him for governor, but the Whigs proved unresponsive, and for the third year in a row the Free Soil ticket flopped. With partisan positions well drawn, few voters switched parties. While about half the nonvoters of 1849 turned out in 1850, they did so only to vote Democrat or Whig. With the Whig turnout substantially down, Penn Clarke's 575 votes did not come close to constituting an electoral balance of power. The Democrats won handily.[33]

In retrospect 1849 and 1850 offered little encouragement about the Iowa movement's prospects. Liberty party strength in the 1848 congressional elections had been 488 votes, Dayton had won 564 votes a year later, and Clarke got 575 votes in 1850. These figures amounted to between l and 2 percent of the state's estimated eligible voters. The rewards of Free Soil, so far, had been the permanent accession of only about a hundred followers to the movement's original abolitionist constituency—a meager harvest indeed.

But with some 85 percent of Iowa's Free Soilers consisting of old antislavery men, little defeatism surfaced. Instead, as they had done for the past decade, the state's activists simply soldiered on, displaying "an elasticity under defeat, and a persistence in organization," as historian T. C. Smith aptly concluded, "quite different from the complete depression into which the party fell in every other State except Ohio. The reason for this elasticity lay in the fact that the Iowa Free Soilers were practically all abolitionists." Their lack of success over the past two years now served as a unique source of strength; with little peripheral voting support to melt away in response to adversity, the hard-core center held, encouraged, as always, by the smaller evidences of progress. "Our party has increased 30 votes since '48," wrote a Washington County Free Soiler to Penn Clarke, adding that the local Whig increase was only seven and that the Democratic vote had declined by fourteen. "We are all full of hope & determined to ever strive for the ascendancy over all opposing principles." In Iowa the fires of Liberty burned low but resolutely.[34]

Virtually as abolitionist in 1850 as it had been in 1848, therefore, Iowa's Free Soil party appears to have made no concessions at all to racism. Late in 1848 David Kelsey and other civil rights activists challenged Iowa's Democratic superintendent of public instruction on the propriety of forcing black taxpayers to support the state's lily-white school system. The official, a Dubuque schoolmaster, angrily admitted the justice of their argument, later including a proposal for tax relief for black Iowans in his legislative recommendations. The 1849 Free Soil platform, the only one extant for this period, condemned the recent general assembly for not instructing the state's U.S. Senators to support Wilmot, to support suppression of the slave trade, and to support abolition of slavery in the District of Columbia. But it also chastised the legislators for "refusing to repeal all laws in this State, making distinctions on account of color—which laws are a dead letter upon our statute book."

In July 1850 a Free Soil candidate for state representative, a Henry County Quaker, stated his personal political code as embracing a full endorsement of the Buffalo platform, a belief in the need for legislation allowing banks in Iowa, and a commitment to racial equality. "The Black Laws of our State," he wrote, "I consider oppressive and unjust, prohibiting a portion of our fellow beings from the enjoyment of citizenship in our State, depriving their offspring of the blessings of a good education, and [forcing them to] feel, though in the midst of freedom, that they are ground down by the iron heel of political oppression." And late that year the Free Soilers' editor reminded readers that the general assembly had convened: "If the people have any petitions to prefer, on peace, the Black laws, the land reform [question] or any other subject, now is the time to forward them."[35]

Racial equality had not been so much soft-pedaled by Iowa's Free Soilers as merely required to assume a place among a number of reforms on which their party had staked its political fate.

The Salem Nineteen

5

By the 1840s, excepting only the Virginia panhandle opposite Pittsburgh, the top four tiers of counties in the State of Missouri constituted the northernmost area of the United States lawfully open to slavery. In the Civil War it would prove as fiercely Confederate as any part of Dixie. Frontier Iowans, caught up in the expansive, free-market ambience of the nineteenth-century Middle West, may have been tempted to forget that they shared a 225-mile border with a slave state. But legal actions involving alleged runaways occasionally forced them to confront the disquieting relationship of themselves and their political culture to all aspects of their regional and national coexistence with slavery.

The unsuccessful attempts to recover Ralph and Jim, as we have seen, did nothing to deny the legality of slaveowners' interstate pursuit of bona fide human properties. The United States Constitution itself mandated that "a person held to service or labour in one State . . . escaping into another, shall . . . be delivered up on claim of the party to whom such service or labour may be due." The Fugitive Slave Law of 1793 further provided that whenever a slave fled to free territory the slave's owner, or the owner's agent, might search out and seize the fugitive, hale him or her before a federal judge or local magistrate, and by oral testimony or affidavit prove title. It thereupon became the duty of the judge or magistrate to provide a certificate entitling the petitioner to remove the slave. The act contained no provision for alleged runaways to offer evidence in their own behalf, although this did not prevent captives from doing so if presiding officials chose to permit it. Finally, the act also provided criminal penalties, in addition to any civil action the owner might have under state law, for obstructing the capture and for rescuing, harboring, aiding, or secreting a fugitive slave.

The decision of the U.S. Supreme Court in *Prigg* v. *Pennsylvania* brought renewed attention to the rendition process. The court upheld the constitutionality of the Fugitive Slave Law, it declared unconstitutional any free-state statute interfering with the prompt return of runaways to owners, and it affirmed that slaveowners engaged in recapturing fugitives need not even follow the judicial procedure outlined in the federal law, but instead could simply seize an escaped slave in free territory and return home without a legal proceeding of any kind—so long as recapture had been accomplished "without any breach of the peace, or illegal violence." The only good thing about *Prigg* that abolitionists could see was its opinion that, since the interstate rendition of fugitive slaves was a federal matter, state magistrates need not enforce the act, especially where forbidden by state law to do so—an opinion soon misconstrued in some northern courts to mean that state officials lacked any jurisdiction whatever in rendition cases.[1]

From the beginning, however, Iowa's statutes had supplemented the Fugitive Slave Law in two ways. First, the state's Act to Regulate Blacks and Mulattoes "empowered and required" judges and magistrates to make the services of local law-enforcement officers available to claimants. Second, the statute disallowing courtroom testimony by blacks against whites insured that in Iowa no rendition hearing would be needlessly complicated by an alleged slave's own story.[2]

Civil libertarians, as historian Thomas D. Morris has noted, campaigned against the Fugitive Slave Law for the same reason they fought slavery extension: to contain the "extraterritoriality" of the peculiar institution, hoping to confine it to its original geographic base as a first step in destroying it. But more than just ideology and political strategy became involved here. All states bordering slavery, from New Jersey out to Iowa, harbored free black populations. The lack of due process therefore posed wonderful opportunities for unscrupulous bounty-hunters who were not above kidnapping the occasional free black likely to fetch a good price somewhere south. In response to this possibility several states, including Iowa, had enacted kidnapping laws. But disallowing the court testimony of alleged fugitives themselves sharply undercut their effect. The only sure protection of free blacks from false claimants, said activists, lay in introducing conventional due process into rendition proceedings. In Iowa's 1840/41 legislature, as we have seen, proposed abrogation of the law against black testimony had inaugurated abolitionists' long campaign for black code repeal. When the *Prigg* decision then appeared to render this line of argument a dead end, the 1839 regulatory statute, the imposing centerpiece of Iowa's array of racist laws, became the focus of their energies.[3]

I

No case involving fugitive slaves offered Iowans a better lesson in the unavoidable realities of coexistence with slavery than that of *Ruel Daggs* v. *Elihu Frazier et al.* (1850), a lawsuit originating at Salem.

Salem's Quakers became the first Iowans to traffic with any degree of regularity in escaped slaves. As early as 1838 Winston and Henry, two resourceful young runaways from central Missouri, made it all the way to a Mesquakie village in Iowa's Washington County. The Indians seized the pair, however, and traded them for nine bottles of whiskey to a settler who had them work off their purchase price, then turned them loose. The two lived among local whites through the winter, thinking themselves safe, only to be recaptured in the spring by their owner. The returning search party, unwisely enough, stopped for the night at a house near Salem, where Winston and Henry, in the words of their irate owner, "run away or were stolen. . . . It is supposed that said runaways will be assisted to escape by some particular white men."[4]

Soon the Quaker settlement, only eighteen miles above the state line, had earned a notorious reputation among the slaveholders of northeast Missouri, and defiance of the federal Fugitive Slave Law by the bolder spirits among them had begun to divide the community itself. In 1841 a formal complaint was brought against Reuben Joy in the Salem meeting "for going in company with others who encouraged a prisoner to make his escape, and expressing his gratification that he was gone, and for making contradictory statements about the same." When Joy proved unrepentant after four months' persuasion, the meeting excommunicated him. There was also talk about resisting slavecatchers with force: the meeting proscribed two additional members for justifying "defensive war" (one of them had reportedly purchased a pistol). Although it seems certain that the proper community posture toward fugitive slaves, in the judgment of historian Louis Thomas Jones, "was frequently the subject of guarded discussion" in the local meeting, "still on the records no written reference to the subject is to be found."[5]

All along the great border between slavery and freedom the fugitive slave question vexed Quakers much more than they chose to admit, since it blurred the distinction between offering traditional Christian hospitality to black strangers and criminally aiding and abetting them. In the voluminous accusations and rebuttals associated with the schism in Indiana Yearly Meeting, neither side chose to make the question a central issue in the dispute, although a hint of its role indeed entered the record. Soon after the split Aaron Street Jr. explained the position of Salem's Anti-Slavery Friends. Contrary to rumor, he insisted, they did not enter Missouri "to run off slaves; but when the slaves were on their way to a land of freedom, and called on us, we believed it right to take them in and feed them, and give them such directions and assistance, as we ourselves would wish bestowed on us, were we in their situation."[6]

Later that year, with both Street and Reuben Joy present at Yellow Spring, this credo became a part of the Iowa Anti-Slavery Society's charter, but precisely when representatives of Iowa's other abolitionist centers joined in defying the Fugitive Slave Law cannot be ascertained. Much that was irregular and unplanned came to be retrospectively systematized under the sinister rubric "underground railroad," and in Iowa, no less than elsewhere, the metaphor should not be taken too seriously. But by 1844 Salem activists had begun carrying occasional black fugitives to Galesburg, Illinois, known far and wide as an abolition town, where tradition later persisted that black refugees brought there for transport to Canada by way of Chicago "were from Missouri, and most of them would first stop at a Quaker settlement in southeastern Iowa, where friends would keep them and bring them on at night to Galesburg." Within two or three years, it appears, a few Yellow Spring abolitionists had transported fugitives to Galesburg, perhaps serving as a link between that place and Salem. The earliest certain instance of Denmark's participation in such activities, however, was its supporting role in the drama leading to *Daggs* v. *Frazier*.[7]

II

In May 1848 an official committee of Indiana Friends arrived in Salem village to inaugurate a new quarterly meeting and to help dedicate the regular body's new brick meetinghouse. A few days later abolitionists gathered in Salem for the Iowa Liberty party's second annual convention. A week after that the most exciting moment in the town's history began to unfold: thirty miles to the south a party of nine slaves made a break for freedom.[8]

Ruel Daggs, a Delaware-born Virginia planter, had migrated to northeast Missouri with his family and slaves in the late 1830s, settling near the village of Luray, one son taking up a nearby farm, another establishing himself in an adjoining county. Daggs was neither the largest slaveholder in Clark County nor, at nearly seventy-five years of age, its most influential.[9]

On or about the first of April 1848, one of his slaves, apparently young John Walker, had fled Missouri and taken refuge at Salem, joining the small number of blacks occasionally sheltered there by the Quakers. Two months later, obviously encouraged and aided by certain abolitionist Friends, Walker slipped back across the border to rescue his wife and child and any other Daggs slaves who wished to escape to freedom.[10]

In the late evening hours of Thursday, June 1, 1848, the fugitives set forth, making up a party of nine: Sam Fulcher, a large, dignified man in his late forties; Fulcher's wife Dorcas; Walker and his wife Mary; Julia, a teenager; three children under ten years of age and a babe in arms. It seems that they first made for the isolated farmstead of one Richard Liggon, an eccentric ex-Virginian whose household included a free mulatto woman, four small colored children, and an adult male slave. The fugitives laid over Friday while a welcome downpour hindered pursuit, and that night Liggon drove them to the Des Moines River below Farmington, which with some difficulty they crossed on a makeshift raft. The slaves then hid themselves on the Iowa shore, waiting out a cool, rainy Saturday for promised transportation that would carry them the rest of the way to Salem.[11]

Daggs, meanwhile, had sent for sons William and George, who instituted a search and strongly suspected refuge at Salem to be the fugitives' goal. On Saturday afternoon Will's party, consisting of himself and neighbor James McClure, had crossed into Iowa. They encountered a local Lee County farmer, Samuel Slaughter, a native Virginian who had lived in the area for nearly a decade. In return for a share of the reward posted by Ruel Daggs, Slaughter agreed to lead McClure on a scout of the countryside toward Salem. Feeling the job was in capable hands, Will Daggs rode home.

Slaughter and McClure stayed the night in or near Farmington, escaping another furious rainstorm. The next morning they discovered a fresh wagon track leading over the prairie toward Salem. They started in pursuit. Three or four miles south of the Quaker settlement they sighted a horse-drawn covered wagon that increased its speed as they gave chase. Spurring ahead, Slaughter was gaining on the wagon when, a half-mile from town, it abruptly swung into a brushy, densely wooded area adjoining Little Cedar Creek and was momentarily hidden from view. When he caught up with the wagon, the three young white men in it claimed to be returning from a fishing trip to the Des Moines. Slaughter, in turn, disguised his mission as a search for two strayed horses. He accompanied the wagon into town, where McClure joined him. The two spent Sunday afternoon looking for some evidence of the fugitives, but with no success. They put up for the night at the local hotel.[12]

As the two slavecatchers sauntered about Salem that outwardly calm Sabbath, news of their quest spread among the villagers, whose reactions varied. Aaron Street Jr. had once confessed that "our community is not clear of prejudice against color," and a residual racism no doubt remained. As a village of perhaps five hundred souls, Salem had also lost some of its original religious homogeneity; its denizens now included persons openly proslavery in sentiment. The Quakers themselves, on the other hand, had begun closing ranks. Although still divided into regular and antislavery meetings, the seceders no longer held a monopoly on deeply felt abolitionism: four of the six men against whom the *Daggs* jury would find judgment held membership in the regular body.[13]

One of those four, John H. Pickering, was an antislavery activist; his brother Jonathan a staunch conservative. Both were present Sunday afternoon, as others guardedly discussed the presence of runaways in the vicinity. John Comer noted that slavecatchers were in town. So did John Pickering, who proceeded to remark that he had lent his team to Eli Jessup to take a Methodist preacher to Farmington. The horses had left town in mid-week hitched to a light carriage, John added, but had not been returned until just that day—at which time they were pulling a wagon. The indignant Jonathan Pickering accused his brother of having had something to do with the fugitives, which John airily denied. Comer backed John up, asserted that the runaways had not come in the wagon and, as Jonathan later described it, "sniggered in his sleeve and seemed to know where they were."[14]

On Monday, returning to the spot where they had overtaken the covered wagon, Slaughter and McClure flushed Sam Fulcher's party from the underbrush. Only Walker resisted, but he was quickly subdued and tied onto one of the mounts. All were escorted out to the Salem road, where Slaughter left McClure in charge while he himself rode back into town to hire a couple of additional men for the journey south. Upon returning he found his partner and the nine blacks surrounded on the road by perhaps a dozen local men who appeared intent on keeping the captives from being carried off. Thomas Clarkson Frazier and his brother Elihu presented themselves as spokesmen. One of the two asserted that Slaughter's party would have to appear before a magistrate before it could lawfully remove the blacks. The other, with equal determination, remarked that he would "wade in Missouri blood" before he would see the captives peremptorily taken away. The second brother's threat legitimized the demand of the first, since no do-it-yourself recapture could legally proceed under conditions of a disturbed peace. After fifteen or twenty minutes, during which time the group grew considerably larger, Slaughter agreed to submit himself and his charges to the jurisdiction of Nelson Gibbs, Salem Township's justice of the peace.

On the quarter-mile trek back to the village Slaughter lost control of the situation. Fearing that Walker would attempt to escape, Slaughter dismounted him and, himself on foot, held the young black by the arm. But a farmer named Johnson pulled Walker out of Slaughter's grasp, advising the slave to punch Slaughter if he touched him again. Slaughter kept his distance, and in a moment or two Walker darted away into the accompanying crowd. Then, after one of the black women complained of fatigue, Sam Fulcher persuaded Slaughter to let the women and children stop to rest, pledging that if he himself returned to Missouri so would the others. Slaughter, jostled by the increasingly demonstrative citizens, plodded on, now in direct charge only of Fulcher and Fulcher's three-year-old son. As the throng, numbering some fifty to one hundred, flowed past the village academy, its young schoolmaster dismissed class and mounted a pile of boards, urging everyone to act peaceably. The office of the justice of the peace in the Henderson Lewelling house proved much too small for the overflow crowd, so Gibbs ordered an adjournment to the Anti-Slavery Friends meetinghouse two blocks away.[15]

It was now noon, and the legal proceedings consumed scarcely half the villagers' lunch hour. Aaron Street Jr. and Albert Button, a local attorney, offered themselves as counsel for the blacks. They and the slavecatchers huddled with Gibbs on the meetinghouse dais, Fulcher and his son sat quietly on the front bench, villagers filled the other benches and stood in the aisle and along the walls. As historian Paul Finkelman observes, an antislavery magistrate had three options when faced with a fugitive slave case: "he could accept jurisdiction and decide the case on its merits according to the federal law; he could accept jurisdiction and free the alleged slave on the basis of natural law; or the judge could invoke the *dictum* of *Prigg* that he was not obligated to hear the case." Gibbs prepared to choose the third option by conducting an informal inquiry as to whether, in his estimate, his court held jurisdiction.

Slaughter did the talking for himself and McClure. He explained that the captives were Missouri slaves he and McClure had been hired to recover. Button asked Slaughter to prove that the captives were slaves, and, indeed, that slavery existed in Missouri. Slaughter replied that McClure could so testify. Button then asked if either man possessed written authority to act as Daggs's agent. Slaughter admitted that they did not. Button produced a leatherbound book, probably the *Revised Statutes of the Territory of Iowa* (1843), the most recent compilation of Iowa law, from which he apparently quoted the section on kidnapping and its penalties: "If any person or persons shall forcibly steal, take, or arrest any man, woman or child in this Territory . . . with a design to take him or her out of this Territory without having legally established his, her or their claim according to the laws of this Territory, or of the United States, shall upon conviction thereof, be punished by a fine not exceeding one thousand dollars and by imprisonment in the penitentiary at hard labor not exceeding ten years."

Nobody advised Slaughter, a simple farmer, that the Supreme Court's ruling in *Prigg* had rendered this measure unconstitutional, and he evidently pondered its strictures. Somebody, presumably Gibbs, stated that he and McClure might have time to go get written proof of agency from Daggs, as well as a certificate from a Missouri clerk of court, properly sealed, as proof of Daggs's ownership of the blacks, during which time

Gibbs could have them officially detained. But Slaughter declined, having become convinced that he and McClure had acted unlawfully and now wishing only to extricate himself as expeditiously as possible. Button then asked Gibbs to discharge the blacks from custody, to which the justice replied that he could not, having decided that his court held no jurisdiction in the case. Button then asked Gibbs to declare Fulcher and his companions free. The magistrate merely replied that they were already as free as himself, for ought he knew.[16]

The spectators cheered as Fulcher and the child rose from their seats and moved toward the door; the crowd jamming the aisle parted to let them pass. Henry Brown, a local layabout whom Slaughter had recruited that morning, shouted, "I'll shoot that damned son-of-a-bitch." He began drawing a handgun from his pocket, but subsided when threatened with arrest. Outside, Fulcher received verbal instructions from John Pickering. He then walked to a waiting horse, mounted, was handed his boy, and the two cantered off, led by a local character named Paul Way, who whimsically pretended to deny culpability by shouting, "Stop them niggers. Don't let them niggers follow me."

At that point Slaughter himself departed, withdrawing quietly, as he testified, "because I did not wish to embroil myself and was tired of the business." Somebody later told him that Jim McClure had been "run out of town."[17]

III

Keokuk's papers broke the news first. The town's Democratic editors pounced on the excitement at Salem as a welcome diversion from an eruption of smallpox in southeast Iowa. "THE SMALL POX CAST IN THE SHADE," read the headline in their June 8 edition. That same day Keokuk's Whig paper, its editors skeptical of the report, nevertheless carried the story as a "Riot at Salem." Both papers passed along the rumor—untrue, as it turned out—that McClure had been killed or seriously injured. South of the border editors also hastened into print. The June 9 issue of Saint Louis's leading newspaper broke the story under the heading "Abduction of Slaves—Their Recovery, and Rescue by a Mob." Thus the first accounts of the incident agreed in terming it a scandalous, criminal affair of which all Iowans should be ashamed. But nobody, then or later, suggested a causal connection between the Liberty party convention at Salem on May 24 and the Daggs slaves' flight to freedom on June 1—despite the surface plausibility of such a linkage. Only the initial report of Keokuk's Democratic sheet came close, in its fulminations against "man-stealing, and peace-destroying abolitionists." Its writers viewed the Salem incident as a powerful reason for Democrats to hold themselves unequivocally aloof from any thought of political collaboration with Liberty men.[18]

But more news was to come. One of the Keokuk stories had concluded on a decidedly ominous note: "The Missourians retreated with the threat of returning . . . with an additional force, and carrying their point, at all hazards." Indeed, accounts of the Salem encounter, carried south by Jim McClure, threw the entire slaveholding community of Clark County into "an unpleasant state of excitement," according to a correspondent at the scene. On Wednesday morning citizens gathered "for the purpose of devising measures to recover the negroes, and, if possible, to guard against such occurrences for the future. . . . If this state of things should continue, negroes will be useless property here." And that afternoon, exactly as promised, a small army of Ruel Daggs's friends and neighbors crossed the Iowa border, picking up additional recruits at Farmington, eventually making up a mounted force variously estimated at from sixty to a hundred men. It came well armed. According to local legend, the Missourians even brought with them a small field gun.[19]

In mid-afternoon the raiders descended on Salem, effectively sealing the village with roadblocks at every exit. Guided by Salem's belligerent Henry Brown, they fanned out in a house-to-house search for the missing blacks. The raiders searched no house without permission, and when forbidden entrance, as they were in a few cases, they resorted mainly to rough language. "In one instance one of the Missourians snapped a pistol at an old crippled man," according to eyewitnesses. "Several of the citizens were most grossly attacked, and guns were presented at them frequently and the most provoking threats were uttered for their not telling where the negroes had gone." A committee of Salem conservatives later verified that only a few of the raiders "behaved with apparent becoming civility.—And but for the restraining influence of those few over the rabble, there is no telling to what extent the rioters would have carried their threats into execution."[20]

In any event, they came up empty-handed. The Missourians thereupon proceeded to arrest local men identified by Brown as having been important participants in Monday's events, employing for this purpose a number of blank warrants issued by a justice of the peace from another township and served by a constable from another county. By sundown they had placed Elihu Frazier, Clarkson Frazier, John Pickering, John Comer, and five or six others under arrest and confined them at the hotel.[21]

That night somebody slipped through the raiders' cordon and rode to Mount Pleasant to alert the sheriff, a Virginia-born racist with little sympathy for Salem's abolition attitudes. On Thursday morning he nevertheless hustled the eight miles to the Quaker village and, choosing to believe that the inhabitants' peace had not been illegally disturbed, negotiated a settlement. The Missourians released their prisoners, but only after each had signed a recognizance to appear at the next term of the federal district court "to answer unto an indictment then and there to be found for *wickedly* and *maliciously*, and with force and arms," robbing Slaughter and McClure of the recaptured slaves. The raiders then withdrew, some of them threatening, however, that if the fugitives were not soon surrendered they would return, set fire to the town, and hang its leading abolitionists. A number of them indeed lingered at the village of Hillsboro, six miles distant, where they reportedly "drank up all the liquor they could find" and continued to talk tough. In response, some of Salem's menfolk armed themselves—as Clarkson Frazier and John Comer admitted later—while Elihu Frazier galloped the twenty miles to Denmark for help. Late Thursday afternoon some forty armed Denmarkers arrived in Salem to aid in repelling any returning raiders, but all the Missourians had finally gone home.[22]

What happened to the fugitives during the excitement is unclear. Local legend speaks only of Sam Fulcher and his son, who are said to have been secreted in the countryside east of town until Thursday night, when they were taken to Denmark by returning members of the would-be rescue party. John and Mary Walker and the baby also permanently eluded recapture. But the others—Dorcas Fulcher, Julia, and two of the children—soon were returned to Daggs, evidently betrayed by some unsympathetic person interested in the offered reward. The five successful escapees are said to have been carried east by way of Yellow Spring, and in July none other than the editor of the Chicago *Western Citizen* certified that the Missourians "did not succeed in their efforts [at recovery] as we have the best reason to know. They will have to travel as far as Canada to accomplish their object, and then go back with fleas in their ears."[23]

IV

That autumn Ruel Daggs's attorneys filed suit in the U.S. district court for the District of Iowa against Elihu Frazier, Clarkson Frazier, John Comer, Paul Way, John Pickering, William Johnson, and thirteen other citizens of Salem and vicinity "for the purpose of recovering compensation for the services of nine slaves who escaped into Iowa from Missouri, and were afterwards assisted to elude the control and custody of plaintiff's agents, by the defendants or some of them."[24]

The case of the Salem nineteen came before Judge John J. Dyer, on circuit, in January 1849 at the capitol in Iowa City. A University of Virginia graduate, Dyer had practiced law in his native Shenandoah Valley before migrating west, eventually settling at Dubuque, and being appointed the new state's first federal judge.

A battery of three attorneys, two of them Iowans, presented Daggs's case, an action at trover and conversion requiring the legal fiction that plaintiff had "casually lost the said goods and chattels out of his possession," that they had come into the possession of the defendants "by finding," and that the defendants had not yet returned them "although often requested to do so," and had instead "converted and disposed of the said goods and chattels to their and each of their own use." Implicitly concealing the recovery of four of the runaways, the suit asked $10,000 in actual damages—the claimed cash value of all nine slaves—plus consequential damages to cover funds expended for their recapture, the value of their lost services and the crops they would have produced, and so forth.[25]

Jonathan C. Hall and John T. Morton, both of Mount Pleasant but otherwise a seemingly ill-matched pair in light of the case at hand, appeared for the defense. Hall, it will be remembered, chaired the constitutional convention committee that in 1844 had rejected, on thoroughly racist grounds, the civil rights petition signed by leading Salem abolitionists. Hall's young colleague, on the other hand, was a strongly antislavery Whig. In response to Daggs's declaration they filed a demurrer that asked the court to dismiss the lawsuit on several grounds, the most important being that in the Hawkeye State persons may not be property, and therefore "the action of trover will not lie to recover the value of human beings."

In a pretrial hearing, Judge Dyer entertained oral arguments on the demurrer. Hall and Morton first urged, as William Penn Clarke summarized their words, "that the subject matter of trover must be property in the strictest and most technical sense of the term, not only capable of conversion, but such in its character as to raise the presumption that the defendants knew the right of ownership to it was vested in others than themselves." But since slavery was not tolerated in Iowa, the presumption was that African-Americans were not slaves until proved otherwise. The status of the nine blacks had not been decided when the defendants encountered them, and they consequently invited such treatment as was conventionally extended to *free* blacks. For their part, counsel for Daggs appealed to the doctrine of interstate comity in a conflict of laws, urging the court to consider Daggs's right to an action at trover for human property in Missouri as also binding Iowa. They did so in vain. "The averments in the declaration are not sufficient to support the action," Dyer ruled. "Trover will not lie in this state to recover the value of slaves. . . . Demurrer sustained."[26]

First round thus went to the defendants, although Dyer allowed Daggs's attorneys to amend their client's declaration in light of his ruling, continuing the case at the costs of plaintiff. Daggs fired his lawyers, who had indeed erred badly in not bringing suit under the terms of the Fugitive Slave Law, and replaced them with a pair of Keosauqua attorneys, one of whom was Augustus Hall, J. C. Hall's younger brother, remembered as "superior [to Jonathan] in eloquence, dramatic power and scholarly attainments." A courtroom test of this proposition was not to be, however. Augustus and his partner evidently did not give satisfaction, the suit being continued from term to term for cause shown, until the exasperated plaintiff finally dismissed his second attorneys and hired as his sole counsel probably the most expensive legal talent in Iowa, the prestigious Burlington attorney—and successful advocate of Ralph's freedom in 1839—David Rorer. In pitting Rorer for the slaveholder against J. C. Hall for the abolitionists, explicit ironies multiplied.[27]

V

In the twenty-four months between the excitement at Salem and the plaintiff's long-awaited day in court, the fugitive slave question had become an increasingly volatile national issue. The effort to keep slavery from taking root in the West remained the foremost sectional issue of the late forties, but the failure of northern states enthusiastically to enforce the Fugitive Slave Law ran a close second. Did not the Constitution, southerners asked, specifically mandate interstate rendition of escaped chattels? And had not the law of 1793 been sustained as constitutional? The answers were yes, and by the autumn of 1849 southern hotspurs clamored for the translation of these guarantees into a new federal statute tough enough to override all antislavery resistance in the North. Southern secession from the Union seemed the alternative many slave-state militants deemed entirely thinkable. Early in 1850 a responsive Congress began to consider measures to amend the old Fugitive Slave Law, the dominant congressional mood—evidently reflecting the attitudes of most northerners—being a willingness to compromise for the sake of national unity.

Other provisions of what would become known as the Compromise of 1850 helped sweeten the pill. In return for a greatly strengthened federal statute governing interstate rendition, the South agreed to a series of measures insuring a West free of slavery. The word from Washington therefore was that the two most delicate issues tending toward national disintegration—fugitive slaves and slavery extension—were at last being comprehensively dealt with; grass-roots agitation of either issue not only would do more harm than good but was in fact dangerously against the national interest. In no state was that message taken more seriously than in Iowa. Yet in June 1850 congressional action still pended and disunion hung like a cloud over the land.[28]

Two years to the very week since the inception of the case, Judge Dyer, on circuit in Burlington, presided a second time over *Daggs* v. *Frazier*. Despite a cholera scare that gripped the city that spring, the trial opened on a warm, rainy Thursday to a courtroom packed with spectators. Fascination with the proceedings owed as much to the excitement engendered by the national controversy over slave rendition, in the opinion of the *Hawk-Eye*'s editor, as it did to the eminence of the opposing attorneys or attitudes toward abolition. It would be, as Paul Finkelman has noted, "one of the last cases [in America] argued solely on the basis of the Fugitive Slave Act of 1793."[29]

The plaintiff's suit had now been recast as a trespass on the case, a form of action at common law adapted to the recovery of damages for some injury resulting from another's wrongful act. The claimed injury remained the same, but now the alleged act was the defendants' violation of section 4 of the Fugitive Slave Law. Plaintiff's declaration contained six counts. The first two charged that following the capture of Daggs's runaways by Slaughter and McClure, "defendants after having [received] notice that said negroes or persons were fugitives from labor and that said agents had a right to reclaim and arrest said fugitives, rescued, aided and assisted said fugitives in making their escape to some place beyond the reach of the plaintiff and his agents." A third count alleged that the defendants "concealed said slaves from said agents," the fourth that they had "harbored and concealed said slaves." Counts five and six alleged that the defendants had "obstructed and hindered" the arrest of the fugitives. Although Daggs now admitted the later recovery of four of his slaves, and had scaled down the value of the five still at large, he continued to estimate his total loss at $10,000, again demanding that amount as damages.

The defendants pleaded not guilty. Dyer immediately boosted their prospects by ruling that because of technical irregularities the plaintiff's depositions—written testimony from McClure and Will Daggs—would not be allowed as evidence. Rorer then entered a *nolle prosequi* as to several of the defendants, and promptly subpoenaed them as witnesses to supply the excluded evidence.

Rorer offered five witnesses: Ruel's son George, Sam Slaughter, and three Salem residents, the conservative Jonathan Pickering and two men—attorney Albert Button and a local farmer—who had been defendants but whom Rorer decided to employ as witnesses. While Pickering's evidence proved valuable to the plaintiff, Button and the farmer were of no help whatsoever in implicating the others. Following the direct examination of these five, and their cross-examination by the defense, Rorer asked the court for time to procure another witness. Hall objected, Dyer sustained the objection, and Rorer abruptly rested plaintiff's case.

Says Finkelman: "Unlike most fugitive slave cases, in this case the defendants did not challenge the constitutionality of the 1793 act." J. C. Hall simply presented as witnesses six men who had been present at Squire Gibbs's inquiry. None had seen the slavecatchers coerced or the captives encouraged to run away, and all withstood Rorer's cross-examination without yielding ground. Hall then presented, as his last witness, Jonathan Frazier, the younger brother of the two leading defendants. Young Frazier's testimony, intended to dissociate the defendants from the fugitives' original flight to Salem, actually stripped much of the credibility from their claims to innocence. Frazier admitted having driven the wagon chased down by Slaughter that fateful Sunday two years before. The young men accompanying him, he said, were one Hamilton and another whose name he could not recall. No blacks had been in the wagon.

Rorer cross-examined. After eliciting an admission that the horses pulling the wagon belonged to John Pickering and the wagon itself to Elihu or Clarkson Frazier, Rorer's questions encountered in the witness a very poor memory indeed: "Had been to Farmington. Drove down with the same men. Don't know where they lived. Can't say what their business was. First saw them when I was about starting for Farmington, in the neighborhood of Salem. Think it was at my house. Don't know what they came there for. Saw them in Salem after I returned. They were there some days. Saw them in the streets of Salem. Can't tell what day. Don't know where they boarded. It was not at the hotel." At this juncture Hall heatedly objected to Rorer's next question. The objection was sustained; Rorer then said he had no more questions, whereupon Hall rested the defense. Concluding arguments by Rorer and Morton occupied the whole of the afternoon.[30]

Hall resumed the next morning, summarizing the defense version of the events of June 5, 1848. He maintained that the slavehunters had made their arrest unhindered by any defendant, they had been peacefully persuaded to submit themselves to Gibbs, and after Gibbs refused to take cognizance of the case the captives had departed without the aid of anyone. There had been no "rescue" either before or after the pretrial proceeding. One of the defendants, William Johnson, had not even been in town on the day in question. "The balance charged," said Hall, "stand free from all evidence, unless you adopt the advice of the plaintiff's counsel and make *residence at Salem* conclusive evidence of the defendants' guilt."

In his final comments Hall boldly asserted that plaintiff was relying on the pressure of national events for a finding against his clients. Daggs would never have brought suit "had he not counted upon prejudice—had he not sought in the signs of the times, for a feeling in your bosoms which would predispose you to convict the defendants." Hall then invited the jurors to imagine the immensity of a popular bias against the accused: "The Union is at stake—agitation is covering the land; rebuke the one and sustain the other. You are called upon for a victim. My clients are demanded for a sacrifice."

Rorer rose to deliver the plaintiff's closing argument. He devoted attention to the issue of Slaughter and McClure's agency, but added that, in any event, the charges of harboring and concealing could be sustained irrespective of agency. He then dwelt at some length on the circumstantial evidence so important to the plaintiff's case. "Here are men who have established a law of their own," he said of the defendants. "They affirm that they may aid in the escape of persons held to service under the Constitutions of other States, though by so doing they violate the laws of the Union. If you find fugitives from service secreted among such a people, what is the presumption? Can it be anything else than that they aided and assisted in their escape, or assisted to secrete them?"

Two independent items of evidence pointed toward the same conclusion, said Rorer. The first was Jonathan Pickering's testimony that on the day *before* the confrontation between slavecatchers and citizens at least some abolitionists—certainly John Comer, probably John Pickering as well—had knowledge that runaways were hidden in the neighborhood. The second was the obvious dissembling of Jonathan Frazier on the stand, and the unwillingness of the defense to allow a "wide-open" cross-examination. The conclusion to be drawn was that the defendants, or some of them, were guilty of harboring and concealing on Sunday, June 4, in addition to whatever they may have been guilty of the following day.

Rorer closed on much the note Hall had concluded:

> The very subject upon which you are called to decide is now agitating our country from Washington to the most distant borders. It has been a source of contention and distrust among the people of both North and South—of slave-holding and non-slave-holding States. Your verdict will show whether there is just ground for this suspicion, as to us. Whether fanaticism is to be encouraged among us of the North, or the wild and maniac cry of disunion in the South. . . . Above all, the law should be vindicated—its supremacy confirmed. The idea that any man or society of men, may be permitted to trample upon the plain letter of the law and Constitution, should be severely rebuked, and the offenders convinced that the impunity they have enjoyed in other places, will never be found in Iowa.[31]

Dyer read aloud that part of the federal statute under which Daggs had brought suit and instructed the jurors as to what each count demanded by way of proof, generalizing from some thirty years' weighty judicial precedent that, in its most recent official publication, had made the footnotes to the 1793 Fugitive Slave Law more than twice as lengthy as the statute itself. To find the defendants guilty of rescuing the fugitives it must be proved, he said, "that the defendants possessed the knowledge, no matter how obtained, that the negroes owed service to the plaintiff, either by the confession of the negroes, or by a written or verbal notice, and that they knew at the same time, that Slaughter and McClure were the agents of plaintiff." To find them guilty of harboring and concealing, however, it was only necessary to prove that the defendants had been aware that the blacks were fugitives, whom they then hid "with the intention to defeat the means of the claimant" to recover them. Finally, with respect to the charge that the defendants hindered or prevented the fugitives' arrest, said Dyer, "if the evidence is that an arrest was made by Slaughter and McClure before any of the defendants interfered, they cannot be found guilty under this count."

It took the jurors less than two hours to reach a verdict. They found six defendants—Elihu and Clarkson Frazier, John Comer, Paul Way, John Pickering, and William Johnson—guilty on the first four counts—that is, of rescuing, aiding and assisting to escape, harboring, and concealing the fugitives. They allowed the plaintiff damages of $2,900, a sum representing the upper estimates of the claimed market value of Fulcher and Walker ($1,000 each) and of Mary Walker ($700), plus $100 each for the two missing children.[32]

Hall and Morton moved that the court grant a new trial "because the verdict was against the evidence as to some of the defendants, and upon no evidence as to others." Opposing counsel discussed this motion at some length, after which Rorer entered a *nolle prosequi* as to Johnson. Dyer then exercised a rarely utilized judicial option by overruling most of the jury's findings. The verdict, he said, had been bad—that is, contrary to the evidence—with respect to counts one through three, but was good on the fourth. The two Fraziers, Comer, Way, and Pickering stood properly convicted only of harboring and concealing. But one count was enough. Dyer overruled the defense motion for a new trial, and held it to be ordered, adjudged, and decreed that plaintiff recover $2,900 in damages plus costs of nearly $1,000 more.[33]

Hall and Morton asked for time to file a bill of exceptions with the intention of appealing the case to the United States Supreme Court. Since Rorer raised no objection, Dyer granted the request. *Daggs,* however, never reached the highest tribunal in the land, and it is not known whether the plaintiff ever succeeded in collecting judgment. Prior to the trial, it is said, the defendants "had put their property out of their hands," presumably by distributing it to kin. This rendered the judgment worthless, a fact Daggs discovered or would have discovered when he had the sheriff seize and sell the defendants' movable goods and lands. Iowa's population and agricultural census manuscripts for 1850 support this contention, indicating that none of the defendants but Paul Way claimed real or personal property of any value whatever—even though Elihu Frazier, for example, actually held farmland worth $800 and Pickering an acreage valued at $3,000.

It may have been their clients' determination to "beat 'em on the execution," otherwise known as intent to defraud a creditor, that discouraged Hall and Morton from appealing the case further.[34]

VI

The *Daggs* court had underscored for Iowans' benefit the hazards of defying the federal protection of slavery, and for most of the state's editors the judgment in the case spoke for itself. But two of southeastern Iowa's leading Whig journalists could not resist comment. The editor of Keokuk's *Valley Whig and Register* heartily applauded the result: "The verdict will be a warning to meddlers." A preliminary report of the trial carried by the Burlington *Hawk-Eye* the same day included a similar, if somewhat less pointed, sentiment: "It may be proper to add that the verdict has given universal satisfaction, both to those who were in attendance, and the public." But nearly a month's reflection, together with the reading of a partial transcript of the proceedings, brought the paper's senior editor, who had not attended the trial, to a more profound judgment. "The Trial.—South should be satisfied," read the title of his editorial. "It may be somewhat puzzling to the readers of the evidence as it has been to us," he wrote, "how a jury could find . . . in favor of the plaintiff." In its larger significance, the verdict "certainly shows a disposition to give to the South all they can possibly claim; and all this clamor about the necessity of more stringent laws to catch runaway slaves, as far as Iowa is concerned, is all a humbug."[35]

Six weeks later Iowa's Augustus Caesar Dodge rose in the United States Senate to emphasize Iowa's compliance. He had not intended to speak on the controversial fugitive slave question to which the assembled gentlemen had been devoting their attention. But the Senator from Florida had uttered generalizations about "abolitionist" northern opinion that implicitly embraced Dodge's constituents. Eager to assure southerners of Iowans' inhospitality to runaways, Dodge read aloud the state's 1839 Act to Regulate Blacks and Mulattoes. In judiciously skipping only section 3, which specified punishment of careless sheriffs and jailers for false imprisonment, he sought to emphasize how neatly Iowa's regulatory statute interfaced with the Fugitive Slave Law of 1793. "Negroes have often escaped [into Iowa] from the State of Missouri," he added, "and never, in a single instance, in which the parties to whom they belonged have brought suit, have the courts and juries of Iowa failed to give damages against those who have harbored or secreted them; and in a recent case a very large verdict, amounting to $2,900, was given against parties who were charged with harboring fugitive slaves." To Senator Dodge the meaning was obvious. "The great body of the people of the North are entirely sound upon this subject," he said, "and determined to discharge their constitutional duties. So far as my State is concerned, its laws and its conduct speak a language . . . that cannot be misunderstood."[36]

In the end, however, Dodge and his Iowa senatorial colleague, George Wallace Jones, capitulated to southern anxieties in much the same measure that the *Daggs* jury and Iowa's editorial fraternity had similarly capitulated. Dodge and Jones—and one other free-state Senator—threw their support to a new federal statute that substantially eased the rigors of slave recapture in the North. And once again Iowa stood alone—the only free state in the Union whose U.S. Senators had both voted for the notorious Fugitive Slave Law of 1850.[37]

Whatever Happened to Billy G. Haun's Law?

6

The Compromise of 1850 renewed most Iowans' faith in the two-party system and the ability of the nation's Whig and Democratic leaders to arbitrate all issues pertaining to slavery. Its political magic worked wonderfully through the winter of 1850–51. Even the most controversial provisions of its component Fugitive Slave Law—the special commissioners to try all rendition cases, a fee system that rewarded commissioners more generously if a fugitive were returned to an owner than if he or she went free, its edict forcing citizens to help prevent fugitive escapes—proved incapable of provoking alarm.

October's Free Soil convention gravely condemned the measure, but few Iowans seemed concerned. In December the state's outgoing governor lectured its citizens on the civic duty of unquestioning compliance with the rendition law, remarks echoed by the incoming chief executive. The 1850/51 general assembly similarly urged the patriotic necessity of obedience to the Constitution and to all new measures mandated by the Compromise. "I tell you," Denmark's Dr. George Shedd confided to William Penn Clarke, "the prospect for the cause of right looks dark to me, not only in this State but through[out] the North. The cause of Liberty has never seemed to me much weaker than now. Many that I had supposed were at heart her fast & faithful friends & would prove themselves such in any emergency, are favoring & shaking hands with the enemy, with Slavery."[1]

Defections from Free Soil had returned Iowa's voting configurations to politics as usual, and Whig and Democratic editors vied in offering elaborate praise of the congressional settlement. Only two Iowa journalists, in fact, ventured sustained criticism of the new Fugitive Slave Law. And both suffered punishment for speaking out. James G. Edwards, the highly respected founder and editor of the Burlington *Hawk-Eye,* by all accounts

Iowa's most distinguished Whig journal, deemed the measure bipartisan and thus fair game for independent judgment. His words reflected a deep disillusionment about the signs of the times. In "a boasted age of progress," Edwards wanly observed, "no progress has been made in blotting out the curse of slavery." Nothing bespoke that truth more convincingly, he thought, than the new rendition law: "Were it only a reenactment of its prototype of 1793, the friends of progressive liberty would not have so much to complain of; but when we see the features of that law so marred as to compel freemen to become slave catchers, and to create new officers and offer them rewards for hunting up poor fugitives . . . and drag[ging] them back to slavery, the bright hope that this curse will ever be removed grows fainter and fainter every day."

Angry conservatives organized efforts to curtail the *Hawk-Eye*'s circulation and threatened to fund an alternate Whig organ. In stepping down from his lengthy editorship six months later, Edwards hinted that the powerfully negative response to his mildly advanced stand on rendition had played no small part in his retirement.[2]

The Free Soilers' *Iowa True Democrat* similarly took strong exception to the new law—with similar consequences. In the spring of 1850 David M. Kelsey had resigned its editorship and left for California, relinquishing the paper to the more pugnacious management of his coeditor, the Mount Pleasant schoolmaster Samuel L. Howe. Howe's exceptionally outspoken attitude toward the new rendition law apparently provoked as much consternation among Wilmot Proviso moderates as among conservatives. In November, consequently, two Mount Pleasant Whigs lured away Howe's publisher and founded a rival newspaper that espoused a pro-Wilmot posture on slavery extension together with a carefully modulated call for amending the new Fugitive Slave Law "so as to render it more in harmony with the most enlightened views of correct principles and justice."[3]

Howe, beside himself with rage, struck back. Within weeks his cross-town feud had escalated to such heights of personal acrimony as to cost him readers. "Mr. Howe has been a prominent man among us," noted George Shedd, "but is losing ground in this part of the State by the course he has taken in his paper. . . . Many complaints have been made to me & much feeling manifested, darkening the prospects of the paper for support & usefulness." Finally, with the *True Democrat* $800 in debt and its subscribers down to only a few hundred, Howe sold his farm to keep the newspaper afloat; a year later he had to mortgage the rest of his property to the same end. "A settled, chilling, blighting stupor seems to have come over the Free Soil mind in Iowa," he complained, and in truth his personal editorial style was only partly to blame.[4]

The managers of the Fort Madison *Statesman* underscored the ideological distance even pro-Wilmot publicists insisted on putting between themselves and anything resembling an incitement to civil disobedience. That journal had been Iowa's only Democratic organ to have endorsed the Proviso. Now its editors nevertheless applauded Iowans' calm response to passage of the new rendition law:

> However much the citizens of our State deprecate the evils of Slavery, they are determined to give to their brethren of the South the rights guaranteed to them by the compact which the founders of our independence entered into. . . . May this bright star in the west—IOWA—remain steadfast in her integrity, in this matter, and while the waves of fanaticism and dis-union are spreading over other portions, we trust that the bright waters of freedom will here flow on, uninterrupted by fanaticism of whatever name or grade it may be.

Some Iowans interpreted the stiffly conservative mood of the moment as a strategic opportunity. In December 1850 one of them offered formal notice of an intent to introduce into the legislature "a bill for an act to prevent free negroes and fugitive slaves from entering the state."[5]

I

In 1844, as we have seen, Iowa's constitutional convention narrowly rejected Ed Langworthy's proposal for excluding free persons of color from the future Hawkeye State. This well-publicized racist gambit, followed by the 1845 admission of Florida into the Union with an exclusionary article in its constitution, appears to have revived northern interest in accomplishing black exclusion by organic law. Conventions called to write or revise constitutions met in a number of free states and territories between 1847 and 1850. In Illinois convention delegates passed a separate black exclusion clause that went to voters as a referendum proposal. Although a majority of those casting ballots approved the proposition, by 1850 Illinois legislators had not yet passed the necessary statutory provisions. A similar measure won delegate approval in Indiana late that same year.

Conventions held in Ohio and California, however, strongly rejected exclusion clauses. Three other important political bodies also considered black exclusion. In the U.S. Senate a proposed ban on slave trading within the District of Columbia—part of the Compromise of 1850—provoked a slave-state Senator to move, unsuccessfully, a ban on free-black entry into the federal district. Meanwhile, the California general assembly rejected its governor's call for black exclusion, while the legislature of Oregon Territory enacted what became the nineteenth century's first new northern exclusionary law.[6]

This midcentury flurry of reactionary activism, initiated by Iowans as a response to abolitionist militancy, came full circle in the Iowa assembly of 1850/51. The session convened with a Democratic majority of 83 percent, strongest since the inception of Iowa's separate political existence twelve years before. Responding to vigorous currents of legal reform stirring the northeastern states, the legislators' top priority was a new state code that would consolidate and revise "all the statutes of a general nature" so as to make them more intellectually accessible to nonlawyers sitting as state legislators and local justices of the peace, to law-enforcement officers, and to the public at large. A veteran of that session many years later vividly recalled the great question of the moment: "We talked code in the morning at breakfast and talked code at noon and talked code at night; everybody talked code."[7]

Three years' hard work by a special code commission structured the assembly's deliberations. Charles Mason, first chief justice of Iowa's supreme court, now retired to private practice, chaired. Stephen Hempstead of Dubuque, whose commission service closed with his 1850 election as governor, and William G. Woodward of Muscatine, the commission's only Whig, also served. Although the three men divided the work among them, it was later generally understood that Mason, the trio's legal scholar, had performed the lion's share. Judge Mason took great professional pride in supervising an Iowa codification that would win national admiration and stand the test of time.[8]

Mason composed the famous *Ralph* decision in 1839, but he was at heart a conservative Democrat in whom the Civil War would unleash a violent bias against blacks. That lay ahead, however, and whatever racial animus lurked in Charles Mason in the late forties evidently faded before his lofty perfectionist sense that no model code of laws would complicate itself with special color distinctions. As laid before the legislature in December 1850, the document silently revoked all, or virtually all, Iowa's black laws save those embedded in its constitution. Gone was the state's ban on interracial marriage, its embargo of black testimony in court cases involving whites, its exclusion of blacks from public schooling, its notorious 1839 regulatory law.[9]

An alert Democrat from Dubuque, an 1844 exclusionist, noticed that Mason had provided for a racially integrated militia in violation of Iowa's organic law; the assemblymen hastily rectified that error. Other legislators discovered Mason's rewrite of the clause on the competence of witnesses. After considerable discussion in both chambers, they amended it by specifying that "an Indian, a negro, a mulatto, or black person shall not be allowed to give testimony in any cause wherein a white person is a party." With respect to public education, the assemblymen reinstated the exclusion of black children by adding to the new state code the previously codified body of school laws. And whether or not part of the commissioners' original draft, the final version of the 1851 code also limited "legal settlements" (and thus welfare benefits) to whites, and insured that none but white males might qualify to practice law.[10]

The commissioners' discard of the old Act to Regulate Blacks and Mulattoes seemed to some of singularly grave concern, and a representative sitting on the house code committee moved to replace the 1839 statute with a comprehensive black exclusion law. He was a new face on the Iowa political scene, Kentucky-born William G. Haun. Proprietor of a grist mill, a distillery, and a backwoods townsite speculation, Haun had come from Saint Louis to the wilds of upcountry Clinton County in 1846. The product of his distillery, nine barrels per day, was mainly retailed up in the Wisconsin pineries, according to a local historian, "and as the reputation of Elk River whiskey was not yet fully established, it was customary to brand the barrels 'Old Rectified Whisky, from B. J. Moore & Co., Cincinnati, Ohio.'" Virtually unknown in east-central Iowa in 1850—a stagecoach driver mistakenly identified him to a journalist as a Whig—Billy G. Haun promptly became one of the assembly's most active and vocal Democrats.[11]

Introduced in January 1851, Haun's House File 66 straightforwardly forbade the settlement of blacks and mulattoes in the state. Colored intruders would be notified to leave Iowa within twenty-four hours or suffer fines of ten dollars per day plus costs. Arrest could be made either by law officers or private citizens, and the local magistrate concerned would be sole judge of a prisoner's racial makeup. Any certifiably free persons of color already in residence would be permitted to remain "and enjoy such property as they may now possess," but as an inducement to their outmigration all such property as they might thereafter acquire was to be confiscated to support the state's all-white public school system. Haun's original draft appears to have been the product of his own fancy, although the property-confiscation clause may have been suggested to him by the recent Indiana constitutional convention's consideration of a ban on colored newcomers' ownership of land.[12]

That Haun had struck a responsive chord became apparent with the immediate endorsement of H.F. 66—sight unseen—by Iowa City's Democratic editor. And the legislative reception given it was in part predictable, since fully a quarter of the 1850/51 general assembly—nine Democrats, four Whigs—had legislative records on civil rights. Of the Democrats, one had helped pass the nonwhite regulatory law in 1839, one had rejected jury trials for alleged fugitive slaves, two had helped vote down a racially impartial welfare system, five had supported exclusion, and one had opposed repealing the regulatory law. Only five assemblymen, in contrast, were documented racial progressives. Three of them happened to be Henry County Whigs: Paton Wilson of Salem, the veteran legislative foe of Iowa's black code; Abraham Updegraff, who had voted against exclusion in the 1846/47 house; and John T. Morton, the young lawyer who had helped defend the Salem abolitionists in the *Daggs* case, who had opposed the 1847 exclusionary legislation, and who had more recently begun to coedit the new Mount Pleasant newspaper that so agitated Professor Howe. Also representing a heavily antislavery constituency was David Bunker of Washington County, who had courageously sought repeal of the nonwhite regulatory law in the 1842/43 assembly. Finally, Democrat John Thompson, a farmer from Denmark, had opposed Ed Langworthy's motion in 1844.[13]

In the final roll calls on H.F. 66 all thirteen recidivists cast votes consistent with their records. That this polarization involved considerable settled conviction is not surprising. Nor does the comparative demography of Whigs and Democrats differ appreciably from 1838 and 1844, except for a notable lack of southern-born Whigs that may be merely an artifact of the unusually small number of Whigs elected in 1850.[14] What *does* appear to have changed significantly since the last extensive discussion of black exclusion is the character of the debate. In 1844 the antiexclusionists' sharpest weapons had been a pragmatic concern for congressional disapproval and a subliminal fear that passage of an exclusion clause might reflect on Iowans' patriotism: Langworthy's antagonists were at their most dynamic on the subject of Justice Story's application of the privileges and immunities clause. Six years later, however, the most active of Billy G. Haun's critics relied most heavily on sarcasm and other expressions of contempt. In Iowa, at least, black exclusion was no longer an issue about which opposing gentlemen might reason together.

Haun's house colleagues referred H.F. 66 to a committee composed of two exclusionists, two antiexclusionists, and a swing man who favored exclusion but objected to the confiscation clause. The deadlocked committee finally reported H.F. 66 without recommendation. The legislators threw out the offending clause, but all attempts to bury the measure failed, and its enemies had no option but to join the more responsible exclusionists in making it a bit less harsh. At their instigation those present struck the citizen's arrest provision, probably because it would encourage kidnapping; they reduced the daily fine to two dollars; they increased the grace period for offenders to three days; and they insured the safety of all property colored Iowans might acquire. The majority then approved H.F. 66 by a 20–15 vote, after which an angry Whig moved to change its title to "An act . . . declaring inoperative in certain cases, so much of the constitution of this state as reads, 'all men are by nature free and independent and have certain unalienable rights, among which are those of enjoying and defending life and liberty, acquiring, possessing and protecting property and pursuing and obtaining safety and happiness.' "[15]

With the failure of that bitter flourish, the hopes of antiexclusionists centered on defeating Haun in the upper chamber. On January 31 the senators heard H.F. 66 read for the first and second times, after which John Morton moved to amend the bill so that it would "take effect, and be in force, by publication in the *Iowa True Democrat,* a weekly newspaper published in Mount Pleasant." His motive for doing so is unclear. He would later say that, as an attorney of some experience, he was well aware that the Haun bill would become law once published in the new volume of session laws whether Howe's Free Soil paper printed it or not. It is most likely that Morton offered his motion merely to mock Haun's proposal and annoy its supporters. But, caught off guard by the word "Democrat" in the Free Soil weekly's title (and, incidentally, demonstrating how little its message carried beyond an immediate readership), the exclusionists approved Morton's rider, thereby granting to a radical abolitionist an apparent veto of the bill.

The majority then tabled the measure in order to consider a message from the governor—and three days later had not yet cottoned to the joke. H.F. 66 passed the senate by a 9–7 vote. Once again—as in 1844, 1846, and 1847—black exclusion fractured the ranks of the Democrats while tending to solidify the Whigs, who for the first time gave it not a single roll call ballot (table 6.1).[16]

Later in the day of the senate vote the house majority concurred in Morton's facetious amendment to their previously approved "Act to prohibit the immigration of free niggers into this State," as the clerk pronounced the title. That eleven of its critics voted with them instead of against them must have given Haun and his exclusionist colleagues pause, but by the time one of them caught on it was too late. The assembly adjourned the next day, and Governor Hempstead—who had voted for the nonwhite regulatory law in 1839 and supported Langworthy in

Table 6.1 Roll calls involving equal rights in the 1850s (egalitarian positions italicized)

	Democrats	Whigs	Anti-Nebraskans
The Haun exclusion bill (1851)			
For	29	0	
Against	13	9	
Motion to table Clark antiexclusion petition (1855)			
For	26	6	7
Against	1	1	24

Sources: Iowa Senate Journal (1850/51), 295; *Iowa House Journal* (1850/51), 299; ibid. (1854/55), 319; T. D. Eagal and R. H. Sylvester, eds., *The Iowa State Almanac and Statistical Register for 1860* (Davenport, 1860), 21–22.

1844—signed H.F. 66 into law, evidently confident that an obscure editorial veto would have no binding effect.[17]

Howe's reaction of course proved negative. He scathingly censured the legislature for a measure that, in his eyes, transformed Iowa into "a slave holding State. . . . When we take into consideration this new law . . . we think our legislature serves the Devil . . . with more alacrity than even their slave holding lords could desire." And in an era characterized by scanty coverage of legislative news, the enactment touched off a small flurry of editorial response.

One of the Iowa Democracy's leading spokesmen applauded an enactment that would, he hoped, "make gentlemen of color shun our shores hereafter." Edwards of the *Hawk-Eye* dryly termed Morton's rider "The Best Joke of the Season," and he hoped that a veto by Howe would render the act a nullity. The editors of Fort Madison's *Iowa Statesman,* having celebrated Iowans' reception of the new Fugitive Slave Law, now saw nothing to be proud of in the Haun bill. "Rather Funny" was their editorial's title, meaning odd rather than amusing. "We have always been taught to believe," asserted its writer, "and it is hard for us to forget it, 'that all men are created equal.' But according to modern ethics the quotation should read 'that all men (*except niggers*) are created equal.' " The legislative correspondent of Keokuk's Whig paper brusquely summed it all up: "A 'black law' (as it is called) has been passed, and a *black* thing it is. It is a disgrace to our State, and I am satisfied that it will meet with no favor."[18]

II

Six months after editor Kelsey had joined the California gold rush, Dr. John H. Dayton died, leaving Penn Clarke as the sole surviving member of the Free Soil party's informal directorate. In 1851, with only the state superintendency of public instruction at issue and with his Iowa City law practice at last beginning to flourish, Clarke counseled the rank and file simply to support the Whig nominee. The following summer Clarke allowed his second district colleagues to offer his name as a congressional candidate, only to suffer the humiliation of winning but 135 votes. Perhaps understandably, he allowed his party role to fade, and leadership reverted to such veteran political abolitionists as Samuel Howe and the Rev. Asa Turner. In 1852 these two led Iowa's delegation to the national Free Democratic convention in Pittsburgh, which nominated John P. Hale of New Hampshire as the antislavery candidate for the forthcoming presidential race.[19]

In November's balloting Iowa became the only nonslave state in the Union to increase its official third-party presidential vote over that cast in

1848—though by a minuscule 486 ballots. The more substantive good news, which some grass-roots Free Soilers had sensed and which modern regression analyses confirm, was that in Iowa—as elsewhere—Whigs had begun to drift from their party moorings. A quarter of them cast no votes at all, evidently disheartened by a national platform that, in its pledged fealty to the 1850 Fugitive Slave Law, proved virtually indistinguishable from the Democratic party line. Only half of them loyally voted for Gen. Winfield Scott, their party's nominee. The remaining quarter divided fairly evenly between Hale and Franklin Pierce, the Democrat, whose main appeal was to conservatives of both parties. But these beginnings of Whig disintegration, while heartening, gave no very dramatic boost to Iowa's Free Soil strength. The third party's main support still lay in various strongly abolitionist rural neighborhoods and villages of southeast Iowa. Moreover, the state's Democrats continued to stand fast against Free Soil: the minority that defected from Pierce strongly gravitated not to Hale but to Scott.

The principal result of the Iowa Whigs' disarray was that, as in 1848, the antislavery candidates fell just short—by some three hundred votes—of obtaining a balance of power between the two closely matched major parties. Small though it was, a third party had once again shown its strength, and to many Free Soilers it seemed only a matter of time before the Whigs would agree to combine forces. An aborted effort to arrange a fusion may have occurred in 1853, when neither Free Soilers nor Whigs initially offered nominees for the only major office to be filled that season. Early in 1854 the Whigs finally succumbed to the political bait dangled by the Free Soilers—but only after it had been sweetened with a second powerful advocacy, in addition to opposing slavery extension, on which the two parties could agree.[20]

Liquor prohibition—or "temperance," as it was still usually referred to in the 1850s—represented the effort to save millions of antebellum Americans from their most morally destructive drug of choice. Prohibitionists sought to ban the manufacture, sale, and consumption of alcohol for recreational purposes. A New England idea that most dramatically expressed itself in the dazzlingly reformist Burned-Over District of western New York State, prohibition for a generation had been considered too hot a potato for either major political party to handle, since the "wets" and "drys" in each were sure to be strongly alienated should their party take a stand—one way or another—on drink. Although many, if not most, political abolitionists probably registered as strongly antiliquor as they were antislavery, they too generally respected the political boycott on temperance reform. In 1850, however, the apparent resolution of the slavery extension issue by the celebrated Compromise seems to have suggested to thousands of antiliquor activists that prohibition was now an idea whose political time had come.[21]

In a number of states Whig politicians welcomed prohibition merely to forestall voter apathy. But more than just the lapse of slavery issues enlivened the sudden antiliquor crusade. In many northeastern states it played into growing ethnocultural antagonisms. Old-stock evangelical Protestants provided the temperance reformers; Catholics and immigrants, especially the Irish and Germans who began to arrive in such vast numbers in the 1840s, were the strongest resisters. And it was at just this moment that America's Catholic hierarchy chose to become militantly involved in disputes over the Protestantized character of public education in many locales. Consequently, an anti-Catholic nativism that would restrict office-holding by Catholics and lengthen the five-year residency required for citizenship (thus delaying immigrant voting) became the other side of the temperance coin.[22]

Iowa's experience resembles that of several other states. Just as the conjunction of Pennsylvania's and Michigan's ethnocultural conflicts and temperance movements in these years can be seen to best advantage in Pittsburgh and Detroit, Iowa's is best glimpsed in the city of Muscatine, where the attempt to keep saloons from being licensed generated political conflict with German-born residents, and where Iowa's only chapter of the nativist United Sons of America appeared. But in the state as a whole the antiliquor crusade seems to have proceeded on its own momentum. A Sons of Temperance organization, with some eighty local chapters, mounted the state's first concerted petition campaign in an unsuccessful attempt to wrest a prohibitory law from the 1850/51 assembly. Passage of model legislation in Maine in 1851, copied by the Massachusetts legislature in 1852, galvanized temperance men and women throughout the land. Iowans flooded their 1852/53 legislature with an even larger volume of antiliquor petitions. The assembly adjourned early in 1853 without satisfying these demands, but not before Iowa's Free Soilers had boldly endorsed local passage of a Maine Law, an endorsement they repeated in November.[23]

Thereafter, events moved swiftly. In December 1853, with Chief Justice Joseph Williams of the Iowa supreme court presiding over their deliberations, the state's temperance activists—emulating those of Maryland, Pennsylvania, Michigan, and elsewhere—threatened to field their own political party unless either the Whigs or the Democrats made Maine Law passage a platform plank for 1854. At the same time, the slavery extension issue, dormant for almost four years, abruptly came to life again in January, as Congress began debating the Nebraska bill. If passed, that measure would establish to the west of Iowa and Missouri a Territory of Nebraska whose own citizens would decide whether or not to permit slavery on their soil—a formula whereby a considerable area of the trans-Missouri West, formerly closed to slavery under the terms of the old Missouri Compromise, would now be at risk. Iowa's Democrats, initially oblivious to the implications of the bill, met to urge the "speedy organization of the Nebraska Territory." Two days later the Free Soilers set in motion the mechanisms by which a Whig/Free Soil fusion finally fell into place.[24]

That only a miracle could have brought Whigs and Free Soilers together, given the record of mutual betrayal that so bitterly divided them, is suggested by those who took leading roles in the merger. Fittingly, they were three Congregational clergymen from New England. The Rev. Simeon Waters had just been dismissed or had resigned (possibly because of ill health) from his seven years' pastorate at Mount Pleasant. The Rev. George F. Magoun, currently reading law in Burlington, was a relative newcomer to Iowa whose father, the wealthy mayor of Bath, Maine, had coauthored the famous Maine Law. The third member of this clerical trio was Denmark's venerable Rev. Asa Turner, Iowa's original abolitionist. Perhaps only three such men of the cloth, with their technical status as embodiments of good works and elevated purpose, could have brought it off.[25]

At a state Free Soil convention at Washington village the Rev. Mr. Waters, in his very first role as a third-party activist, accepted nomination to the top of the ticket as candidate for governor—a nomination made "not with any hope of electing him," recalled Turner, "but [simply] to show our strength." Waters then did the unexpected. A month after accepting his Free Soil gubernatorial nomination, he audaciously took his seat as a delegate to the Whig state convention in Iowa City. Meanwhile, the Rev. Mr. Magoun had suggested to an influential delegate that the Whigs nominate James W. Grimes for governor and, as Magoun later recalled his own remarks, that if the respected Burlington lawyer "would take up the cause of slavery restriction and the Maine law, possibly (with his influence in the state and the votes of temperance and anti-slavery men and new settlers from the East) he might be elected." In Iowa City the Whigs not only nominated Grimes, strongly denounced the Nebraska bill, and endorsed liquor prohibition, but they also nominated Waters (described to the delegates as a "sound and reliable Whig" who had "always voted with the Whig party") as their candidate for secretary of state—the second most important office at stake. Waters then addressed the delegates, pledging to withdraw from the Free Soil ticket in the interests of bipartisan unity on Grimes.[26]

A week later Waters also graciously declined his latest nomination on the ground that his earlier Free Soil candidacy might discredit Grimes with conservative Whigs. The unemployed clergyman nevertheless followed through on his pledge, helping persuade the Free Soilers to meet once again. Waters, Magoun, and Turner all attended this second third-party gathering, which convened at Crawfordsville. Magoun acted as Grimes's agent, having brought with him a manuscript copy of the Whig nominee's forthcoming campaign pamphlet. Waters withdrew as the Free Soil gubernatorial candidate in favor of Grimes. Turner, at Magoun's urging, then composed a brief platform pledging support for a Maine Law, opposition to the Nebraska bill, and support for Grimes.

Few at the convention, including Turner, knew much of either Grimes or his thoughts on slavery. That proved to be an obstacle until the candidate's manuscript had been read aloud. Its characterization of the Nebraska bill as an "infamous attempt to nationalize slavery" and its promise to "*war and war continually* against the abandonment to slavery of a single foot of soil now consecrated to freedom" brought the assembled Free Soilers around. They approved a fusion with the Whig ticket and abandoned their original slate of nominees. The Whig candidate for treasurer had, like Waters, declined nomination, and the convention concluded by offering two of their own for these positions, thereby completing the makeup of a Whig/Free Soil slate—or Anti-Nebraska ticket, as such coalitions everywhere were coming to be called.[27]

Four months later, on August 7, 1854, Grimes won an astonishing victory, taking not only the gubernatorial race but carrying with him one of Iowa's two congressional seats, the state auditor's office, and a majority of the seats in the general assembly and thus (in those days before the direct election of senators) the U.S. Senate seat that came with legislative dominance. For their part, having played John the Baptist to Grimes's messiah, the Rev. Messrs. Waters, Magoun, and Turner promptly disappeared from politics. Now, God help them, it would be up to the politicians.

III

In the four years since its passage Billy G. Haun's law had also vanished from politics. Shortly after the close of the 1850/51 session Eliphalet Price, one of the measure's most strident legislative critics, suggested to Penn Clarke an implausible strategic use for it: "I have not seen any of our [Democratic] freesoilers since I returned," Price reported, "but have written to a number of them. . . . I tell them that the Negro Law was only a preliminary step to the passage of a law to prohibit freesoilers from coming into the State, which will . . . in all probability be enacted at the next session."

Price exaggerated, of course. The 1852/53 Iowa assembly considered no such legislation. But, less expectedly, its five recidivist Haun opponents—including David Bunker and one other Washington County Whig—mounted no effort to repeal the law. Some normally antiexclusionist legislators, in this and subsequent general assemblies, must have believed that Professor Howe's furious refusal to publish had indeed aborted

Haun's brainchild. They could point to the law's omission from the 1851 Iowa code, which understandably left many—progressives and conservatives alike—with the impression that it was not on the books. Only this can explain why racists continued to petition Iowa's legislature for passage of exclusionary legislation, why the law was never enforced until the Civil War, and why civil libertarians made no sustained effort to obtain its repeal.[28]

But whatever the Haun Act's statutory reality, many racial progressives seem to have been quietly persuaded that it would be best to let well enough alone. The deplorable measure was not likely to be enforced, and legislative efforts to repeal it might backfire by resolving all ambiguity about its status. This argument shrewdly comprehended that the measure was chiefly of symbolic rather than substantive value. As an unequivocating endorsement of white supremacy, it offered ultra conservatives complete psychological protection from blacks even if it did not represent actual public policy.

Iowa's Free Soilers seem to have been among those who succumbed to the notion that the Haun bill had never become law. Their 1851 state convention condemned the measure, after which they let it slip from their collective consciousness as other issues clamored for attention. Initially their civil rights concerns were preempted by the most pressing item of the moment—drawing public attention to the iniquities of the new Fugitive Slave Law. Then came the Maine Law excitement. The Nebraska bill brought them back to slavery and equal rights. Late in 1854 a Free Soil gathering at Marion produced petitions signed by seventy-seven citizens "on the subject of the Fugitive Slave Law; laws making distinctions on account of color; African slavery, etc." Whether or not these documents made specific reference to existing statutory exclusion is questionable; the smooth response to them in both houses of the 1854/55 legislature—the Democrats did not bother with attempts to postpone them indefinitely—suggests that they did not.[29]

But another group of Iowans had not forgotten Billy G. Haun's legacy, and for the first time, so far as is known, they formally spoke up for themselves. Obviously emboldened by the Anti-Nebraskans' electoral triumph and feeling "duty bound" to try to gain something from it, thirty-three "Colored citizens of Muscatine County" petitioned the 1854/55 legislators to repeal the 1851 exclusion law. "We your petitioners deem it onnessary to say anything about the injustus of the Law, or its oppresstive influences upon us," they declared, "but we will submit it to the honest consideration of your Honorable body ever hoping that the god of heaven may gide and direct your acts in favor of Justus and opprest humanity." Alexander Clark, Iowa's most influential black spokesman, had evidently instigated the document. Its signatories included Thomas C. Motts, the black community's most prosperous businessman, the Rev. William C. Trevan, pastor of its African Methodist Episcopal church, the Rev. Daniel Anderson, its venerable lay preacher, the assorted cooks, teamsters, and laborers comprising the community's male rank and file, and ten of its women, including the local matriarch, "Aunt Nellie" Anderson. Well over a third of them—eight men, five women—showed how they had been denied education by signing X's beside others' renditions of their names.[30]

Clark's petition reached the floor of the house on January 17, 1855—a singularly unpropitious day. The previous evening legislators, officials, and interested citizens had gathered at the state house to hear an address by the Rev. Henry Clay Dean, an eccentric Methodist preacher of legendary oratorical power who had just been appointed an agent of the American Colonization Society. Dean eloquently portrayed the abject conditions of the nation's blacks, both free and slave. An onlooker summarized the crux of his argument: "How, he asked, is the hopeless condition of the unfortunate African in this country to be ameliorated? Not by granting him the same privileges which we possess, for that is repugnant to our very natures and cannot ever be effected." Colonization, Dean insisted, was "the only plausible" option, and following his talk those in attendance formed an ACS chapter with Judge Joseph Williams, now retired from Iowa's supreme bench, as president.[31]

Alex Clark's attempt the next afternoon to reopen the matter of Billy Haun's law was not favorably received, and the encounter reveals several important aspects of the state's politics of white supremacy in the 1850s. Twenty-seven Democrats, thirty-one Anti-Nebraskans, and seven old-line "national" Whigs (who refused, at least initially, to consider themselves members of the Whig/Free Soil coalition), sat in the lower chamber that day.[32] Although six of them had served in a constitutional convention or in a previous legislature, none of them, significantly enough, had participated in the Haun bill's passage. Only one—Samuel H. McCrory, a diehard Whig who had opposed exclusion in 1844—had voted on a matter involving equal rights. Now McCrory, exemplifying the antiexclusionist but also antiblack attitude of "ordinary" racists, joined the 39–26 majority in tabling the Clark petition. A Crawfordsville Anti-Nebraskan later moved to retrieve the petition and refer it to committee. The majority instead voted to adjourn.

The following day the document's friends withdrew it, but subtly responded to its prayer by submitting House File 156, "an act to repeal Chapter 72 of the Laws of 1851"—that is, to overturn the Haun Act. The disguise was to no avail. Ben M. Samuels, a Virginia-born Dubuque lawyer whose motion had scuttled Clark's petition, now deftly did the same for H.F. 156, successfully moving that its consideration be indefinitely postponed.[33]

The vote to bury the petition virtually unified the house Democrats and had the same effect on the Whigs (table 6.1). But it split the Anti-Nebraskans, a quarter of whom joined the conservative majority in refusing even to discuss Alex Clark's appeal. For some reason—perhaps because many of its auditors misinterpreted Clark's prayer as a request for dismantling Iowa's entire black code, or because the petitioners had been identified as black, or both—the episode seemed charged with special meaning for both conservatives and progressives, summoning forth a roll call polarization of a type all too rare in the legislative record of Iowa's antebellum era. The exclusion roll calls of 1844–1851 admirably separated ultra conservatives from a mixture of progressives and moderates like Samuel McCrory. But the 1855 roll call—as in 1841, 1842, and 1847, though for the first time involving sufficient numbers to permit much analysis—appears to have isolated the progressives as a distinct legislative faction. This happenstance invites comparison of the 1855 progressives with their closest identifiable polar opposites—the Haun bill supporters of 1851 (table 6.2).

Political affiliation is clearly the most important variable separating the extremes. Democratic lawmakers monopolized the ultra conservative position, their partisan opponents the progressive roles. Birthplace offers much less predictability: although over half the ultras were slave-state natives and nearly half the progressives had been born in the Middle Atlantic states, the two birthplace groups do not polarize to such an extent that one could accurately predict that southerners invariably would prove to be ultras or that Middle states natives would be progressives. As for occupation, there are only small percentage differences between the two groups. Nor is some combination of birthplace and occupation significant. About half the farmers of each faction were natives of that faction's predominant place of birth, for example, so that southern-born farmers and farmers of Middle Atlantic nativity did not polarize on black equality. That the progressives were collectively a bit younger than their opposites does suggest some generational conflict over equal rights, although party affiliation remains the only demographic datum that usefully distinguishes the two groups.

To remove the influence of party in order to glimpse possible independent effects of biographical variables is also possible. It is perhaps best accomplished in this case by *intra*party comparisons that in turn can be measured against one another. Table 6.3 embraces the entire Democratic contingent of 1851 (not just exclusionists) and the entire Anti-Nebraska faction of 1855 (not just progressives). It indicates, by means of percentage-point differences, how Democratic ultra conservatives differed from their opponents within their own party, and does the same for the Anti-Nebraska progressives.

Table 6.2 Personal characteristics of lawmakers holding polar positions on equal rights in the 1850s (percentages)

	Ultra conservatives in 1851 (N = 29)	Progressives in 1855 (N = 26)
Party affiliation		
Democrat	100	4
Non-Democrat	0	96
	100	100
Birthplace		
New England	17	8
Middle states	17	42
Old Northwest	10	23
Slave states (1860)	52	19
Europe	3	8
	99	100
Occupation		
Farmer	55	42
Lawyer	21	15
Physician	0	12
Merchant	10	19
Miscellaneous	14	12
	100	100
Median age (in years)	39.0	36.5

Sources: For political affiliations and voting divisions see Table 6.1; 1851 demographic data from previous or subsequent legislative biographical listings, the U.S. census of 1850, or the Iowa census of 1856; 1855 demographic data from *Iowa Senate Journal* (1854/55), appendix, 246–248.

The small number of Anti-Nebraska conservatives dictates that any conclusions be considered very tentative. Yet the birthplace distinctions noted in the previous analysis now appear much sharper. Democratic ultras, virtually all slave-state natives, lacked party colleagues of Middle-states birth; conversely, the Anti-Nebraska progressives were mainly Middle-states natives. The sharply contrasting nature of these findings makes them compelling despite the small numbers involved. By the 1850s the strongly white supremacist culture of the South, as opposed to the less consistently racist New York or Pennsylvania, appeared to make an important difference in adult behavior toward blacks—which is just what Iowa's abolitionists and Liberty party men and Free Soilers, in stressing the political significance of immigration from the Northeast, had been saying for years.

Table 6.3 Intraparty differences among the Democrats and the Anti-Nebraskans in the 1850s (expressed as percentage point differences)

	Democrats in 1851: ultra conservatives from others (N = 41)	Anti-Nebraskans in 1855: progressives from others (N = 31)
Birthplace		
New England	− 8	− 6
Middle states	−25	+23
Old Northwest	+ 2	+11
Slave states (1860)	+27	−36
Europe	+ 3	+ 8
Occupation		
Farmer	+22	−30
Lawyer	+ 4	+17
Physician	−17	− 2
Merchant	+10	+17
Miscellaneous	−20	− 2
Median age (in years)	+ 2.0	− 8.5

Sources: See table 6.2.

Farmers seem proportionally much more important among Democratic ultras than among Anti-Nebraska progressives, although (unlike with nativity) no single occupation gains or loses in compensation. Instead, lawyers and physicians, as well as some of the "miscellaneous" occupations, are in short supply among the ultras and oversupplied to the progressives. The virtually identical surplus of merchants in each group, however, keeps this from resembling a clear rural-urban dichotomy that in turn might be interpreted as a contrast between a cosmopolitan attitude (egalitarianism) and a provincial prejudice (white supremacy). But is a *class* distinction expressing itself here? The evidence from the miscellaneous occupations is inconclusive but interesting. The Democratic ultras in this category consisted of three artisans (a brickmason, a carpenter, and a tailor) and only one businessman, a miller—Billy G. Haun himself. Their Democratic opposites, in contrast, were all middle-class entrepreneurs (a hotel keeper, an iron manufacturer, a millwright, and an engineer). The same small hint of class distinction appears within the Anti-Nebraskans of miscellaneous occupation. The single conservative listed himself as a brickmason; the progressives were a blacksmith, a newspaper editor, and a surveyor.[34]

Finally, the ultras were older than their intraparty opponents, and the

Anti-Nebraska progressives dramatically younger, supporting the earlier suggestion of generational differences over race. If this was in fact the case, then it seems significant that youth was on the side of equal rights rather than otherwise. The period 1825–1840 had introduced an emphatic change in the tenor of reformist attitudes in the Northeast, and many thousands who came of age in or after the 1830s acquired what John L. Hammond terms a "revivalist political ethos" that their seniors may never have shared—a morality that could not tolerate the notion of a permanent, institutionally mandated black underclass in America.[35] Of the 1854/55 Anti-Nebraska conservatives, in any event, only two (33 percent) had come of age in the mid-1830s; of the progressives, in contrast, the comparable number is seventeen (71 percent).

But obviously even more important than age was place of upbringing, the reformist or nonreformist ambience of the community within which men matured. The best nurturer of reformers, scholars have long been aware, was a village of first- or second-generation New Englanders—Asa Turner's Denmark being the prime Iowa exhibit. But the Hawkeye State's nineteenth-century legislators did not often leave to posterity the names of the communities in which they came of age, and generalizing about a reformist ambience at anything larger than the township level is dangerous. An instructive case in point is that no less than four 1854/55 house members had been born in Washington County, Pennsylvania, in the early 1820s. Two of these men became Democratic ultra conservatives, one was a Whig ultra conservative, the fourth was an Anti-Nebraska progressive. Again, five New York-born assemblymen are known to have come from the famous Burned-Over District, their birthdates ranging from 1815 to 1828. Two were Democratic ultra conservatives, one was an Anti-Nebraska ultra conservative, and two became Anti-Nebraska progressives.[36]

It is more to the point that of the four Pennsylvanians mentioned above, two of the ultras were religiously unaffiliated, while the third was an Old School Presbyterian. The progressive was also a Presbyterian, but apparently of New School allegiance. Similarly, the three Burned-Over District racists included the house's only Episcopalian, one of its three Disciples of Christ, and one of its Methodists. As historian Whitney R. Cross observed of the celebrated region, groups yielding consistent opposition to its reform crusades included religious skeptics, Old School Presbyterians, most Episcopalians, and many Disciples. New School and other revivalist Presbyterians, on the other hand, "stood foremost in all the activist benevolences." Methodists initially took neither extreme, but finally split, the majority expressing the reform point of view. These religious attitudes toward social reform in antebellum western New York, in other words, also characterized racial behaviors among Iowa legislators in 1855. That racial progressives were social reformers, and ultras nonreformers, gains additional credence from the fact that all three progressives cited above favored liquor prohibition while, with only one exception, all six ultras registered as wets.[37]

We may test, for the entire 1854/55 house, this apparent causal link between religion and behavior toward blacks by pitting the Clark petition vote against members' religious affiliations and also against the lower chamber's roll call on prohibition, again controlling for the important question of party preference (table 6.4). Although the resulting aggregates are so small as to trivialize any employment of percentages, they conform remarkably to John R. McKivigan's characterizations of specific denominations' antislavery attitudes, as well as to Cross's description of the unchurched.[38]

The three largest groups in the Iowa house—the Methodists, the unchurched, and the Presbyterians—each divided on equal rights. Methodists polarized very sharply. The Democrats among them registered as ultra

Table 6.4 Equal rights, party, religion, and temperance in 1855

	Democrats		Whigs		Anti-Nebraskans	
	conservative	progressive	conservative	progressive	conservative	progressive
Religious affiliation						
Methodist	8				1	9
Unchurched[a]	6	1	3		3	3
Presbyterian[b]	2		1	1		6
"Protestant"	4				1	
Quaker					1	3
Disciples of Christ	2		1			
Unitarian	3					
Universalist	1		1			1
Baptist						1
Episcopalian					1	
"Anti-Slavery"						1
Voting on liquor prohibition						
For (dry)	2		5	1	5	20
Against (wet)	24	1	1		2	3
Unknown						1

Sources: Iowa House Journal (1854/55), 229–230, 319; *Iowa Senate Journal* (1854/55), appendix, 246–248; Eagal and Sylvester, *Iowa State Almanac,* 22.

a. "None," "doubtful," or no entry.

b. Includes one Associate Reformed and three Old School; others not specified.

conservative, their Anti-Nebraska coreligionists (with a single exception) as progressive. The unchurched, while distributed among all three parties, were by a twelve-to-four margin predominately ultra. Presbyterians tended to be Anti-Nebraska progressives, except for the three Old School affiliates who were white supremacists. One of the chamber's four Quakers was an ultra conservative. As McKivigan observes, the Society of Friends "advanced [only] hesitantly toward an active abolitionist stance during the 1840s and 1850s." Moreover, as Salem's Anti-Slavery Friends would have testified, the denomination had not yet fully purged itself of racism.[39]

The three Disciples of Christ lawmakers reflected their denomination's social conservatism by registering as ultras. Thomas E. Turner was the rule-proving exception. He had been principal of a Disciples seminary in the Burned-Over District in the 1840s, but evidently rejected his church at about the time he became an abolitionist and subsequently listed his religion as Anti-Slavery. That the three Unitarians and two of the three Universalists registered as ultra conservative nicely reflects those denominations' hostility to aggressive social reform. The progressivism of the chamber's single Baptist likewise meshes with McKivigan's characterization of northern Baptists in the 1850s as "more antislavery than in earlier years."[40]

Roll call positions on temperance add another very important dimension to politics and racism in the 1854/55 house. Again, the great majority of the Democrats—regardless of religious affiliation—prove to have been *wet conservatives.* Old-line Whigs, as befitted the session's centrists, occupied a middle ground on activist benevolences and tended to be *dry conservatives.* Some two-thirds of the Anti-Nebraskans, finally, registered as *dry progressives*—thereby expressing the central tendency of antebellum social reform in America, an impulse strongly informed by evangelical religious belief to fuse varied programs of uplift into one grand strategy of universal emancipation. Among the many eminent antebellum reformers advancing quotable remarks to that effect, none did so with more engaging colloquial dispatch than a pseudononymous activist from conservative Dubuque. "Our objects," wrote he or she, "are the total abolition of all kinds of slavery . . . moral, mental or physical—of soul and body—political and social—and the unrestrained right of every son and daughter of Adam to pursue happiness and acquire property and reputation, and an equal footing with each other at home and abroad."[41]

Thus the fight against liquor, against the geographical spread of slavery, and against white supremacy came together in a natural confluence. But the 1854/55 Hawkeye legislature had offered only a foretaste of what lay ahead. Within the next three years *all* enfranchised Iowans would be asked to cast ballots on prohibition, on slavery extension, and—Billy G. Haun's law or no Billy G. Haun's law—on the civil liberties of blacks.

Present at the Creation

7

A former New Hampshire farm boy, the youngest child of prosperous second-generation Scots-Irish parents, the man who ended the long Democratic ascendancy in Iowa displayed the athletic figure and sensuous good looks once thought more appropriate to the footlights than the hustings. James W. Grimes also seems to have been a classic underachiever to whom ordinary success came with little strain. He entered Dartmouth College at a precocious age of sixteen only to drop out after five aimless semesters, impatient to get on with life. A year later, having mastered the law, he headed west. In 1836 he set foot in frontier Burlington, where he promptly won admission to the bar and for the next eighteen years practiced law, lucratively but indifferently, while speculating in lands and railroads—again lucratively—until, not yet forty, he retired to a suburban farm. There he was content to breed stock, pursue an interest in horticulture, and serve an occasional term in the legislature. But he had never run for a major political office until his 1854 gubernatorial nomination finally offered the challenge that had always eluded him.[1]

The first campaigner ever to stump Iowa from the Mississippi River all the way out to the Missouri, Grimes proved a brilliant politician. Until that moment he had been a fairly typical Whig virtually indistinguishable from, say, William Penn Clarke on all major policy issues, including slavery extension. He cast his first ballot at the 1848 Whig national convention for the antiextension candidate before acquiescing (unlike the more volatile Clarke) in the nomination of Taylor. But his three terms in the Iowa legislature left no record of attitudes toward either slavery or civil rights. Finally moved to outspoken criticism of the Fugitive Slave Law, he was yet able to deny, in the last days of the 1854 campaign, that he had ever urged repeal of the measure. He handled the difficult temperance issue with equal finesse: he silently allowed his reputation as a prohibition man win him the endorsement of the state's dry leadership. When campaigning in areas of heavy German population, he diverted attention away from liquor and toward slavery extension by playing on the alleged nativism of slave-state Congressmen and Senators in Washington.[2]

The efficacy of his efforts shows up in the results. Although virtually no Democrats came over to him, he nevertheless kept the Whigs magnificently in line. Without a third-party competitor on the ballot, Grimes captured a winning 35 percent of Iowa's estimated eligible voters in 1854 as against Scott's losing 32 percent two years before. Not that the state's Whigs proved very loyal members of the Anti-Nebraska coalition. Whig editors had ignored the Free Soil candidates on the fusion ticket, and in the balloting the rank and file followed suit: most Whigs who supported Grimes cast no ballots at all rather than vote for the Free Soiler running for treasurer.[3]

In his inaugural address Grimes urged that the general assembly strongly protest congressional repeal of the Missouri Compromise and help oppose the slave power "by every constitutional means." He also grew more forthright about his stand on drink. "I have no doubt that a prohibitory law may be enacted that will avoid all constitutional objections," he said, adding his conviction that the act would "meet the approval of a vast majority of the people of the State." A third issue very close to his heart involved removing the ban on banking from the Iowa constitution. Grimes believed that the public would agree: "There can be no question of a desire on the part of the people of the State that their constitution should be amended."

With the Democrats controlling the 1854/55 senate and old-line Whigs holding a balance of power in the house, Grimes privately assumed that little would come of his agenda. The assembly's immediate deadlock over election of a U.S. Senator, which would have much bearing on Iowa's part in national policy formation vis-à-vis slavery, forced him to overcome his inclination to stay above the fray. He intervened decisively, cajoling six of the assembly's nine Whigs into reluctant support of an active Free Soiler for associate justice of the Iowa supreme court, and seven of them into aiding the senatorial candidacy of James Harlan, a Mount Pleasant educator nominated by the Free Soilers of the Salem-Crawfordsville-Washington axis, whose venerable third-party tradition naturally carried considerable weight with the Anti-Nebraskans.

Although Whig refusal to cooperate in bringing forth a resolution on slavery extension ultimately nullified Grimes's call for legislative action on that issue, the Whigs did help in two other important respects, tipping the balance in favor of holding a Maine Law referendum and (along with most of the Democrats, as it turned out) supporting a similar referendum on constitutional revision. An unexpectedly successful Sunday observance law—for which even a majority of wet Democrats voted—also pleased Grimes. It "will prevent the dancing on the Sabbath," he reported to his wife Elizabeth, "that so much annoys us and our neighbors in the summer."[4]

Three months after the legislature had adjourned, a slavery-related issue captured the governor's attention and brought forth an expression of his personal attitudes. Involving some of the same dramatis personae and the same setting as *Daggs* v. *Frazier* five years earlier, the June 1855 incident led to what seems to have been the only case ever brought in Iowa under the terms of the new Fugitive Slave Law. It involved Dick, an armed black man apprehended by two free-lance slavecatchers while disembarking from the Burlington ferry. "How it will end no one knows," Grimes wrote from his home in Burlington to the vacationing Elizabeth. "I am sorry I am Governor of the State, for, although I can and shall prevent the State authorities and officers from interfering in aid of the marshal, yet, if not in office, I am inclined to think I should be a law-breaker." The following day, however, he "sent [word] to Denmark and Yellow Spring and Salem, and told my friends and the friends of the slave to be present at the trial." He and the members of a volunteer defense committee also summoned the area's district court judge from Keokuk that night, readying a writ of *habeas corpus* for use should the decision go against Dick.[5]

The hearing ended abruptly when the alleged owner's only witness, his son, testified that he'd never seen the prisoner before. "The negro is free, and is on his way to Canada," Grimes wrote Elizabeth. "I am satisfied that [he] would never have been taken into slavery from Burlington. . . . The State, the town, and the people, thank God, are saved from disgrace." He reflected how far Iowans had come since 1850. Back then he and perhaps five other Burlingtonians had been "the only men who dared express an opinion in opposition to the fugitive-slave law, and, because we did express such opinions, we were denounced like pickpockets. . . . How opinions change!" The contrast exemplified for him the sheer inevitability of universal emancipation. "It is a blessed thing that there is no ebb to the principles and progress of freedom: it is always a flood-tide."[6]

That summer the nation's attention increasingly focused on the trans-Missouri West. In his 1854 campaign address Grimes had emphasized the social and economic dangers to Iowa—already bounded on the south by a slave state—should another be organized to its immediate west. That threat had not materialized (Nebraska would ease into the Union as a free state), but now the anxieties of Grimes and the rest of the nation's Anti-Nebraskans shifted to Kansas, where events demonstrated the effect of the Missouri Compromise repeal and of "popular sovereignty" in practice.

By March 1855 antislavery settlers in Kansas outnumbered proslavery residents, although fraudulent ballots cast by some five thousand armed Missourians had resulted in a territorial legislature that not only voted to allow slavery but made proslavery sympathies a condition of holding office. In response, the territory's bona fide majority—many of them ex-Iowans—sponsored the organization of an alternate Free State government. When the territorial executive expressed himself more sympathetic to it than to the proslavery administration, Pres. Franklin Pierce fired him and replaced him with a staunch proslavery man. In November 1855 each side mobilized several hundred men in a dispute rising out of a murder. In the end no blood flowed, but the confrontation provided an ominous forewarning of the Bleeding Kansas of 1856. Northern hostility to Pierce and his administration escalated, increasing the pressure on all those disturbed by the western encroachment of slavery to coalesce in forming a new Republican party.

Meanwhile, given the Kansas crisis, many of the nation's leading Anti-Nebraskans—Grimes among them—could only view the burgeoning Know Nothing movement not as an opportunity to explore authentic new political issues but as an exasperating diversion; this nativist, anti-Catholic political crusade would serve only to delay a resolution of the pressing slavery extension question. During the 1854 campaign, whether by design or not, nativism had largely faded from Iowa politics. But after Grimes's election a number of politicians, including a reanimated Penn Clarke, took steps toward organizing local Know Nothing chapters and forming a state council of the order. By the end of the year, five Iowa newspapers editorially supported the movement. Ten more newspapers followed suit in early 1855. And Know Nothingism had begun to take a toll among Democrats as well as former Whigs, one alleged defector being the chairman of Iowa's Democratic central committee.[7]

In January 1855 the legislature's Anti-Nebraskans nominated candidates for spring's election, and—in the first formal appearance of nativism in Iowa politics—a state Know Nothing convention endorsed these same candidates. The subsequent voting returns reveal that Grimes's 1854 supporters proved more interested in liquor prohibition than in the fusion candidates—although, as any astute observer might have predicted, they favored both. The Democrats, in contrast, showed more interest in the election than in the referendum, but strongly rejected the fusion candidate and temperance. Both the coalition slate and the prohibitory law, in any event, won electoral majorities.[8]

Grimes read the results correctly when he saw Know Nothingism as opening the way for a new political movement. "It seems to me that it is time to thoroughly organize the Republican party," he wrote Salmon Chase a few days after the Iowa election, referring to events both at home and elsewhere. "The Know-Nothings have pretty well broken down the two old parties, and a new one, now organized, would draw largely from the foreign element that goes to make up those parties, while it will draw away one-half of the Know-Nothings, at least." A follow-up letter added his belief that "when new parties are constructed, as they shortly will be, ours will be uppermost, in my opinion."

In both his opposition to Know Nothingism and his enthusiasm for a new party Grimes found allies in the Free Soilers, whose loyalties already had served him so well. Toward the end of April 1855, in their last appearance as Free Democrats, delegates from some ten counties met in Washington village to condemn the Know Nothing effort as "anti-republican in form, false in principle, and dangerous to liberty," and to declare in favor of organizing a new third party. As a convention participant summed up Iowa's political situation at that moment: "A small portion of the Whigs . . . are inveterately Old Hunkerish [that is, slavery apologists]. The remainder are liberal on the Slavery question, but a large part of them absorbed by Know Nothingism. The Free Democrats supported Grimes for Governor, and are well satisfied with the result, and now hold themselves ready to unite with such as do not utter the shibboleths of Whiggery or Know Nothingism, to form a Republican party."[9]

Indeed, Penn Clarke seems to have been the only Iowa politician of any prominence for whom Free Soil, nativism, and the Republican impulse all managed to coexist comfortably. And in Clarke's case the linkage may have been expediency rather than ideology. In 1848 he had sacrificed his political career to lead Iowa's crusade against slavery extension, but the Anti-Nebraska fusion of 1854 had been organized and had triumphed without his aid and with no reward to his personal ambitions. He may have seen in Know Nothingism a chance for the antislavery coalition to consolidate its political success in a manner that would allow him to recapture its leadership from Grimes. But in attempting to work inside the Know Nothing movement so as to coopt it for Republicanism, Clarke was the exception. Ward Robert Barnes collected the names of 407 Iowans listed as Liberty party or Free Soil activists; Ronald F. Matthias similarly recovered the names of 318 confirmed or alleged Iowa Know Nothings. Clarke aside, only 5 of Barnes's activists appear in Matthias's biographical file. And for only 1 of the 5—an obscure Mount Pleasant Free Soiler who apparently ran for local office as a "Know Nothing fusionist"—is the identification at all plausible.[10]

Despite agreement on such important current issues as temperance (good), Roman Catholicism (bad), and reform of the election process (good), Iowa's antislavery and nativist movements in other respects had little use for each other. In the Hawkeye State as outside it, Free Soilers held the secrecy with which the Know Nothings shrouded their activities to be profoundly un-American, and they could not countenance any blanket criticism of immigrants that also applied to German-Americans, large numbers of whom were hostile to slavery. In return, many Iowa Know Nothings regarded the Free Soilers' civil libertarianism with scant enthusiasm, especially those living in culturally southern Missouri-border areas such as Davis County, Iowa's leading Know Nothing stronghold. Its nativists, asserted one resident, "can't swallow the nigger baby," a second writer adding that Davis "will never go the Nigger. My word for it." But whether nativists as a general rule were racist as well as anti-Catholic and anti-immigrant remains problematic. By 1855, for instance, 265 Iowans—16 of them apparent Know Nothings—had voted on civil liberties issues in legislatures or constitutional conventions. Far from being unanimous on black rights, however, the 16 prove to have been remarkably divided: 6 registered as racial conservatives, another 6 (having opposed black exclusion) as moderates, the remaining 4 as progressives.[11]

When the 1855 national Know Nothing convention in Philadelphia drafted a proslavery platform, Penn Clarke was dismayed but continued to entertain the idea of Anti-Nebraska/Know Nothing fusion at the national level for another eight months. Grimes, on the other hand, could not suppress his elation. "I have been afraid of that organization," he privately admitted. "I knew it would break down in a year or two, but I was fearful that before dissolution it would give a pro-slavery tinge to the sentiment of many of its members. It has gone overboard sooner than I expected, and I can see nothing now to obstruct a perfect anti-Nebraska and antislavery triumph. God speed the day!"

Local Republican conventions began to blossom in Iowa in midsummer, and the American party, as the Know Nothings now termed themselves, lost ground in August's elections. After that the Know Nothing press swung into line behind Republicanism. "I think that there can be no difficulty in combining all the opposition to the Nebraska swindle in this State," Grimes reported to Salmon Chase in November, "and arraying it under the Republican banner." Four days later, responding to the conciliatory attitude taken by Grimes and other leading Anti-Nebraskans, Iowa's Know Nothings convened to pass seven resolutions. Only one reflected the usual nativist concern with naturalization laws and public schools; the other six expressed hostility to slavery. The state's American party, in effect, had offered fusion.

The new year's political prospects beckoned irresistibly. On January 3, 1856, under the pseudonym "Many Citizens," Grimes addressed himself to the people of Iowa. He requested that all those "opposed to the political principles of the [Pierce] Administration, and to the introduction of slavery into territory now free," convene at the capital on George Washington's Birthday "for the purpose of organizing a Republican party, to make common cause with a similar party already formed in several of the other States of the Union."[12]

I

The editors of the nation's leading antislavery journal, the Washington (D.C.) *National Era,* had been uneasy about Hawkeye politics for several months. "We wish somebody who knows," they wrote in May 1855, "would instruct us into the real state of things in Iowa." Three reassuring replies did not fully satisfy them. "Iowa is in a position not clearly defined," they warned in October. "It has been wrested from the Administration by an apparent Anti-Nebraska majority, composed of Whigs, Free-Soilers, and Know Nothings; but which of these is the dominant section? What ideas are paramount with this majority? Is it prepared to organize as a Republican party, or is it controlled by Know Nothingism? The question ought to be answered practically, with as little delay as possible."[13]

The Iowans who crowded into the state capitol on February 22, 1856, indeed answered the question practically. There is no insider account of the Iowa City convention. Grimes felt obliged by his incumbency to remain aloof from any such partisan gathering, while Penn Clarke, in the belief that Anti-Nebraska fusion with Iowa's Know Nothings was well in hand, indulged himself in a larger political mission, attending both the Republican national convention in Pittsburgh and the American party's national gathering in Philadelphia.[14] A half-century later Louis Pelzer was able to recover the names of 290 individuals listed as delegates, convention committee members, presidential electors, and national convention delegate nominees. A closer look at these men discloses something of the underlying disposition of Iowa Republicanism at the moment of its creation.[15]

A precise measure of the Know Nothing influence is complicated by the often dubious identification of rank-and-file nativists in contemporary accounts. A handful of acknowledged Know Nothings and a larger number of alleged members of the order—forty-two men in all—appeared at the convention. Perhaps half of them actually merited the Know Nothing label, and the order's numerical strength therefore stood at between 7 and 15 percent of the conventioneers. While Davis County's racist Know Nothings were conspicuous by their absence, as were several men who (like Penn Clarke) had played key roles in the Iowa movement, the convention did draw all but one of the American party's state executive committee, on hand, we may presume, to help supervise the expected political merger.[16]

A similar assessment of the convention's ideological left wing—that is, its active antislavery component—is easier. In numbers it was roughly equal to the Know Nothing element. Twenty-three charter Republicans, or 8 percent of those listed, can be identified as former Liberty or Free Soil men.[17] Only one of them, Washington village's James Dawson, had ever run for state office on a third-party ticket, and none of Iowa's leading antislavery pioneers had come as delegates. Four men represented Denmark's abolitionists, true enough, but there were none from Yellow Spring or Salem. The inference to be drawn is that such figures as Rev. Asa Turner, Dr. George Shedd, Aaron Street Jr., and Samuel L. Howe had pretty much retired from the enterprise, content with Governor Grimes's triumph and the conversion of antislavery into a mainstream reform, more than happy to relinquish their roles to those with appetites for orthodox political endeavor.[18]

Indeed, the two most prominent Republican delegates associated with third-party activism were men whose commitment to it was not widely known. A native Marylander who had served a term in Congress from Iowa, Daniel F. Miller, a successful Fort Madison attorney, had twice sought abolitionist political support and had once actually been listed as a Liberty party man. This is not to disparage his radicalism: as described in chapter 2 of this book, Miller had fought valiantly for black rights in the 1840/41 territorial assembly. But he had not broken decisively with the Whigs until the Kansas crisis. Much the same could be said of Henry O'Connor, another former Whig. O'Connor was, on the face of it, a most unlikely radical. An Irish Catholic immigrant once apprenticed to a New York City tailor, he was now a busy Muscatine lawyer with a growing reputation as an orator of rare eloquence. More to the point, he was also (or shortly would become) a member of Muscatine's strongly abolitionist Congregational church.[19]

The ideological predispositions of the Republican conventioneers might be summarized as follows: about 10 percent Know Nothing, about 10 percent Free Soil, and about 80 percent former Whigs and Democrats not committed to either extreme. But the difference between the two polar factions, in the eyes of the majority, was all-important. The Americans, if not satisfactorily coopted, might yet frustrate a Republican political majority by hewing an independent course. The antislavery men, in contrast, seemed unlikely rebels at this stage of the game. In courting the Know Nothings the convention majority worried not about its radicals, but about the state's small but growing proportion of German-born voters. What Michael Fitzgibbon Holt has written of the Republican national convention held in Pittsburgh that same day also describes the Iowa City gathering: "The major problem debated by the delegates was what to do about the Americans (Know-Nothings) and still keep German backing."

Nativists and social reformers demanded a strong stand on prohibition enforcement, while German delegates urged forceful repudiation of suggested changes in the naturalization laws. The beleaguered convention majority simply proclaimed opposition to slavery extension and to the Pierce administration as the basis of Iowa Republicanism. Indeed, its bargain with the Know Nothings did not show up in its platform but, as Ronald Matthias has argued, in the convention nominations for four state offices to be disputed in August's election.[20]

The nominees appear to have been selected with an eye to their being acceptably anti-Catholic—although not too nativist (or prohibitionist) to alienate the Germans. As Iowa's most prominent broker between its incipient Republicans and its Know Nothings, Penn Clarke fully expected to be named to the state's first Republican ticket, probably as its candidate for attorney general. But he may have been deemed too visibly an antiliquor consorter with nativism, and his recent actions may have earned him the distrust of his old Free Soil comrades-in-arms. Moreover, he had made enemies within his own Johnson County delegation. Instead of Clarke, the convention nominated for attorney general a hitherto obscure young Oskaloosa lawyer with no evident Know Nothing ties—or any other claim to the office, for that matter.[21]

Before humiliating Clarke, however, the delegates gave the other Republican nominations to men with appropriately nativist credentials. For secretary of state they named Elijah Sells, an antislavery Whig with a reputation as a Know Nothing. For state treasurer they named the incumbent, a man who had been elected as a Democrat but who at the convention admitted his Know Nothing membership and afterward forthrightly termed himself an American-Republican. The nominee for auditor, also an incumbent, was later alleged to have a Know Nothing affiliation. A week later, in any case, the state convention of the American party promptly nominated the same individuals.[22]

In its other selections the Republican convention did not neglect the antislavery men, but it tended to acknowledge them at about the same frequency as it honored its nativists. It named Daniel Miller and Henry O'Connor as two of four presidential electors—but balanced them with Reuben Noble and William M. Stone, both plausibly identified Know Nothings. It allocated seats on its fifteen-member campaign committee to John P. Grantham, a Free Soiler, and to the veteran Liberty party activist William Leslie—but also filled at least one opening with a Know Nothing, John R. Needham. It selected the Free Soiler J. H. B. Armstrong as one of eight delegates to the forthcoming Republican presidential nominating convention—but similarly elevated Emmanuel Mayne, a Know Nothing.[23]

What portents for the civil liberties of African-Americans resided in these data? The relatively modest convention strength and equivocal influence of former Liberty men and Free Soilers has already implied one answer. Other evidence is supplied by the seventeen delegates who had served as Iowa lawmakers and had voted in roll calls on equal rights. Five (two ex-Democrats, three ex-Whigs) had been conservatives. Four (two ex-Democrats and two ex-Whigs), although not obliged to reveal their positions on ordinary racist legislation, had opposed black exclusion. The remaining eight had qualified as progressives. One was Daniel Miller. Another ex-Whig, Francis Springer, had voted to repeal the old 1839 Act to Regulate Blacks and Mulattoes. The rest had supported reception of the Alexander Clark petition in the most recent general assembly. It is perhaps significant that only a single conservative won a leadership position at the Republican convention, while two of the five antiexclusionists and six of the eight progressives were so honored. The antiexclusionist John A. Parvin, and the progressives Springer and Samuel McFarland, in fact, served in more than one such role.

To project the proportional divisions of attitudes among ex-lawmakers to the Republican convention at large would be stretching things: it is unlikely that a minimum of 47 percent of the delegates could have been racial progressives. But the compelling fact, whether merely fortuitous or not, is that Republicans holding at least moderate views on civil liberties issues outnumbered their ideological opponents when it came to convention prominence.[24]

It also seems worth noting that Elijah Sells, the nominee heading the Republican ticket, had twice opposed exclusionary legislation. Know Nothing he might be, but he was no ultra conservative. Similarly, presidential elector Reuben Noble, a probable nativist, had voted to receive the Clark petition, thus qualifying as a progressive. Of Noble's three fellow electors, Miller's credentials as a racial egalitarian cannot be disputed. O'Connor also proved to be a strong civil rights activist, later describing himself in the mid-1850s as "battling in my feeble boy way as much as I dared [for] negro equality." In 1857 he openly advocated granting the franchise to Iowa's blacks.[25] The fourth elector, ex-Democrat William M. Stone, opposed equal suffrage in 1857 but joined those who strongly advocated it in 1865. Of the new Republican party's first eight candidates, therefore, five either had opposed white supremacy or would do so within the next decade.

In contrast, the party's flirtation with nativism came to a more immediate resolution. Neither the national Know Nothings nor their Iowa counterparts, as it happened, permitted themselves to be coopted for free soil. When southern delegates maneuvered the American party's Philadelphia convention into refusing to condemn the Kansas-Nebraska Act and into giving its presidential nomination to ex-President Millard Fillmore, widely detested in the North for having enthusiastically signed the Fugitive Slave

Law, Penn Clarke joined the exodus of free-state delegates out of the convention. After that he had no more to do with Know Nothingism.

The local party similarly proved unreliable. Meeting in March, a majority of the forty-five delegates to Iowa's American party convention readily endorsed the fusion state ticket but balked at the Republican presidential electors, instead resolving in favor of Fillmore and the national American platform. Grimes expressed himself "disgusted with their proceedings—their want of good faith & their ignorance of all political arithmetic." He hoped that they might yet "rectify their foolishness," complaining to Salmon Chase that "the Fillmore nomination will damage us considerably in this State, and I fear will render the result doubtful."[26]

He need not have worried. The geopolitics of Bleeding Kansas would shortly impose on the slavery extension issue an immediacy for Iowans that minimized much else.

II

In May 1856 sparring between Free Staters and "border ruffians" in Kansas escalated alarmingly with the pillage of Lawrence by proslavery militiamen. This, coupled with the severe bludgeoning administered by a southern Congressman to Sen. Charles Sumner of Massachusetts as punishment for a speech on "The Crime against Kansas," provoked an unprecedented wave of northern indignation on which the Free State cause quickly capitalized. Col. James H. Lane, the flamboyant guerrilla chieftain, a Free State leader under federal indictment for treason, escaped from Kansas and embarked on a sensational lecture tour of the East. His tales of legalized robberies, property destruction, and murders in the territory, and of its "conquest" by armed bands of Missourians with the complicity of President Pierce, dramatically elevated the momentum of northern immigration to Kansas and financial aid for the cause.

Lane also revealed to a few confidants a bold plan to rescue the territory by establishing "a line of communication with Kansas, via Iowa & Nebraska, which shall be at all times open for passage of emigrants, transmission of supplies &c &c." Over this route he would then lead a paramilitary force of perhaps as many as one thousand volunteers. The federal troops deployed in Kansas as peacekeepers would refuse to fight him, Lane said, allowing him "to make a decided and firm stand against the Border Ruffians." If hard pressed by the enemy he would fall back into Iowa, inviting an incursion that would instantly mobilize "the whole power of that State . . . to repel the advance of an invading force of Missourians." Thus Kansas would be saved for freedom by shifting the war to the Iowa-Missouri border. Among the backers of this desperate strategy, it was said, was none other than Governor Grimes himself, who reportedly promised to "give it all practicable aid."

Grimes justified his support of Lane's scheme—as well as all his discreet actions in behalf of the Free State cause—on grounds that, as he later complained privately to President Pierce, emigrants from Iowa had been among those Kansas settlers robbed, terrorized, and killed by proslavery militia. Because they had been "virtually denied" Kansas citizenship, he argued, they remained Iowans. Having been forcibly disarmed, they could not defend themselves. The federal government "having failed to perform its duty by protecting" these expatriate Iowans, it became "manifestly the right" of the State of Iowa to protect them. And late in the year, when rumors began to describe how far Grimes had been willing to go in doing so, he reiterated this ingenious variation on the doctrine of state sovereignty, asserting "that it is the right and duty of the State to protect the rights of her former citizens in Kansas when the Federal Government fails to perform that duty."[27]

In June 1856 proslavery vigilantes closed the Missouri River to armed northerners bound for Kansas, and Lane's "line of communication" became a geographic necessity rather than an option. The attention of Free State support groups throughout the North now focused on Iowa as the only feasible lifeline to the beleaguered frontier. The tracks of the Mississippi & Missouri Railroad had reached Iowa City six months earlier and paused indefinitely, transforming Iowa's capital into the westernmost point north of slavery to be served by rail. And with Chicago as the new headquarters of the nation's Kansas support network, its farthest-flung commercial dependency, Iowa City, became the movement's principal rendezvous for Free State volunteers, arms, and supplies.

On June 7 Lane suddenly appeared in Iowa City. A hastily gathered audience crowded into the capitol for what a newspaper reporter termed "one of the most effective and withering [speeches] we have ever heard delivered." Grimes was at home in Burlington, but Lane conferred privately with a select group of local notables, including Penn Clarke. The upshot was the formation of the Kansas Central Committee of Iowa, chaired by Clarke and including in its membership the state treasurer, a partner in one of Iowa's leading banking houses, and the editor of the capital's Republican newspaper. On June 10 the committee declared that "we have here pledged *our lives, our fortunes and our sacred honors* to make Kansas a *free* State," and dispatched a delegation to establish Lane's overland line of communication across the nearly 250 miles (as the crow flies) of thinly populated prairie that lay between Iowa City and the extreme southwestern corner of the state. From that point Kansas would be accessible by a 50-mile dog-leg through Nebraska Territory. These agents were also to organize a local support group at each settlement along the route. The bulk of the Free State volunteers would walk or ride horseback. The more affluent could take the stagecoach, the committee having induced the Western Stage Company to extend its services out to Council Bluffs.[28]

Meanwhile, the members of "Jim Lane's army" had already begun to gather at Iowa City. "A very considerable company is here," reported the Iowa City *Republican* on June 12, "and additions are made to their number about every hour." Two days later Lane was back in town to coordinate the arrival of a large contingent of Chicagoans, and he again addressed the locals. "He is wild with excitement," noted a hostile spectator, "and exhibits a fury that strongly indicates insanity." The writer added that "quite a number" of the Free State volunteers "are encamped in the grove east of the city, and to-morrow, it is said, the arrivals will make the number 500 strong. They take cannon and arms, . . . *weapons of war,* and are, in fact, organized into regular military squads or companies. They are under pay, or in other words, they are aided by contributions from Chicago and other places."

Those other places included Massachusetts. Rev. Thomas Wentworth Higginson, the zestfully bellicose Unitarian minister of Worcester, had already organized and sent off one party of armed Free State volunteers and was in the midst of forming another. On June 21 he raised two thousand dollars from a somewhat lukewarm gathering of Boston merchants and that night, back in Worcester, received *"a telegraphic despatch from Chicago, imploring us to send that precise sum, for the relief of a large party of emigrants, detained at Iowa City for want of means."* Two weeks later Iowa's Kansas Central Committee, in a flyer circulated throughout the Midwest and the East, emphasized that the main need was indeed money rather than men, who continued to be in plentiful supply.

By June 25 the Iowa City committee's overland route had been surveyed, and an attendant network established as far west as the village of Quincy, which the committee mistakenly understood to be located on the Missouri River and where Lane therefore decided to fix his main arms depot, urging in a note to Penn Clarke that "as you *love me & the cause* hasten everything of that kind to that point [and] fail not in God['s] name." The backlog of young male volunteers at last began to move out, and none too soon for some Iowa Citians. Although no one could deny that Lane's enterprise had not been good for business ("I counted more men trading horses," one volunteer confided to his diary, "than I think I have ever seen before in my life"), others deplored the social costs. "While migratory bands of marauders, quartering in our midst, may go armed to the teeth with bowie-knives and revolvers, to intimidate honest peaceable, law-abiding citizens, and make them submit to insult and outrage," protested one local, the state law against carrying lethal weapons remained "a *dead letter*."[29]

New groups of volunteers detraining at the Iowa City railhead sought to be more discreet, but less because of local sensitivities than because national publicity about Lane's impending invasion of Kansas had dampened the enthusiasm of many eastern financial backers, whose pursestrings tightened at the thought of their dollars supporting anything that might initiate a shooting war between Free Staters and federal troops. In July the newly formed National Kansas Committee, meeting in Buffalo with Penn Clarke present as a delegate, rejected Lane's military strategy, and in one of its first actions dispatched both its president and one of its most prestigious members, Boston's Dr. Samuel Gridley Howe, out to Iowa to force Lane's resignation from the expedition's leadership. On their arrival at the emigrants' camp near Nebraska City, however, the two emissaries discovered that the leaders of the various companies—only a few of which had been raised by Lane's personal efforts—had already deposed him, fearing that his presence might provoke a preemptive assault by the proslavery federal military commander in northern Kansas or by some Missouri guerrilla unit masquerading as a federal posse.[30]

Behind the scenes, Governor Grimes also had been far from idle. Thirty years later the first professional historian to piece together a nonpartisan account of the Kansas conflict implicitly portrayed him as a grey eminence responsible for covertly arming Free State paramilitary forces with weapons from Iowa's state arsenal, and the memoirs of three participants confirm that allegation.[31] But no contemporary Iowan with knowledge of all the facts apparently ever committed them to paper. Why Grimes did as he did is obvious, given his intense commitment to a free Kansas. How it was accomplished has been something of a mystery.

In 1855 Congress had authorized the War Department to distribute firearms to the states for the use of their respective militias. A year later Washington informed Grimes that Iowa's current share of this bounty amounted to 1,918 muskets, a portion of which might be taken in an equivalency of other military hardware. Accordingly, in May 1856, Grimes requested that the War Department "furnish to the state fifty Colt's Revolvers and the residue of the quota due to the state in muskets." Washington in turn directed the Saint Louis arsenal to forward to Grimes the requested sidearms plus 1,790 percussion muskets.

In June came news that a large party of Free State volunteers, ignoring advice favoring the Iowa route, had foolishly attempted to slip through the Missouri River blockade and had been captured and disarmed. "It was claimed by the Missourians that the [confiscated] carbines were not the private property of the men," the Chicago *Tribune* editorialized, "but were taken from some State Arsenal. The idea was suggested by their own practices last winter in robbing the State Arsenal at Jefferson, Mo." A related item in a Saint Louis newspaper gave precise details: Missouri's Gov. Sterling Price, under the guise of distributing arms to militia units within the state, had *"sent twelve pieces of cannon and twenty two boxes of muskets"* to leaders of the proslavery forces *"for the conquest of Kansas."*

At this point, presumably, State Treasurer M. L. Morris of Iowa's Kansas Central Committee hand-carried to Grimes in Burlington an important message from Penn Clarke. Its contents are not known, but they must have called attention to what Governor Price had done for the proslavery cause and proposed that Grimes retaliate in kind with Iowa's quota of War Department arms. "Your note by Mr. Morris came duly to hand," Grimes quickly replied. "I made a requisition upon the govtm. for between 1700 & 1800 muskets & 50 Colts revolvers . . . two months ago. Col. Craig of the Ordinance Corps wrote me that they would be immediately forwarded from St Louis. Through some adverse influence, I presume, in or about St Louis, they have not reached me. I have directed them to be sent to Iowa City when they reach here."[32]

The consignment of weapons, ninety-four boxes in all, finally reached Iowa City by rail on June 30. And at high noon on July 1 the "Reverend General" Higginson's second contingent of Massachusetts volunteers, the thirty-two-man Stowell Company, also detrained at Iowa City. Grimes himself arrived in town on either July 1 or July 2 to be on hand for a special session of the legislature—and to participate in a conspiracy by which all but 290 of the newly arrived federal muskets would leave Iowa City with the Stowell party.

On July 3 the governor notified his lame-duck Democratic secretary of state, George W. McCleary (who also filled a secondary role as state adjutant general), that the arms shipment was at the local railroad depot, ordering McCleary to "receive and safely keep" them. And in his legislative address that same day he blandly asked for permission to distribute the 1,790 muskets and 50 revolvers. The handguns, he said, "are needed at the Penitentiary, and military companies in the State are anxious to obtain the muskets. There is no law under which they can be issued, and if it is the desire of the General Assembly that they should be distributed to such companies, an enactment to that effect is required. If they are not to be issued in that manner, then some provision should be made for their safe keeping." The legislators granted him the right to distribute the muskets, but solely to organized militia units—so as to avoid "the great danger . . . that some of the arms might fall into the hands of Kansas emigrants and thus be carried out of the State."[33]

At one point in this charade a young member of the Stowell party, Richard J. Hinton, met with Grimes in an encounter so sensitive that

Hinton could not bring himself to record it in his diary. But nearly a half-century later he described it this way: "At Iowa City, 1,500 United States guns were taken from the State arsenal, the key of which was conveniently left accessible to my hands on Governor (afterwards Senator) Grimes's desk." And several years later he again briefly described the incident, asserting that when Grimes "conveniently left the key of the state arsenal upon his desk and the executive chamber temporarily to the occupancy of a young free-state emigrant who, with others, was marching to Kansas, there should be no reason to wonder at the fact that some United States muskets found their way from the custody of Iowa into the service of Kansas freedom."[34]

The men of the Stowell Company, already equipped with Sharps rifles and Allen revolvers, had brought with them a cargo of fifteen hundred Springfield muskets acquired in New York City. These boxed weapons must have been put into storage in Iowa City for pick-up by a later group of volunteers, and the Massachusetts company's three covered wagons loaded instead with the fifteen hundred purloined arms. By late July, testifies Hinton, "the Iowa muskets, under charge of Pardee Butler, a Northern preacher who had been run out of Kansas by border ruffians at Atchison, had already got through in safety."[35]

But that was not the end of it. Grimes apparently placed restrictions on the muskets' use, possibly insisting that they be issued only to ex-Iowans. On August 7 Lane's expedition (minus its erstwhile commander) peaceably entered Kansas. Two days later Frank B. Sanborn detrained at Iowa City. A cultivated young Concord schoolmaster and friend to Henry David Thoreau, Sanborn was spending his summer vacation as agent for the Massachusetts Kansas Committee. Evidently at the behest of national headquarters, Sanborn proceeded to contact Secretary of State McCleary "with regard to some of the State muskets, which had been lent to settlers in Kansas for their protection against invaders from Missouri." His object, which concerned "the use of the State muskets in Kansas," must have been to obtain permission to distribute them among the Free State forces generally. McCleary sent the young activist on to Burlington to confer with Grimes himself. On August 10, pleased to learn that the governor had read law with Mrs. Sanborn's father, the young man "had an interesting interview with him in regard to Kansas and Iowa," then took tea with the Grimeses, accompanied them to a lecture, and stayed the night. The next day he proceeded west, carrying with him Grimes's decision (whatever it was) about the Iowa muskets.

With the Kansas fighting escalating once again, Free State volunteers continued to arrive at Iowa City and set off in parties for southwest Iowa, where a settlement of former Western Reserve abolitionists at Tabor became a base camp for emigrants rallying for the dash into Kansas and a place of deposit for a buildup of military and commissary stores. Also by this date the tracks of the Burlington & Missouri River Railroad had reached Mount Pleasant, furnishing a second Iowa railhead at which Free State emigrants might detrain. In late August, as a result of the railroad's having promised free passage for one thousand Kansas volunteers (and thus reducing to three dollars the fare from Chicago to the end of the tracks), another major expedition began to muster under the direction of Col. Shaler W. Eldridge, an important Kansas refugee who had persuaded the National Kansas Committee in Chicago to provide its funding. The Eldridge expedition became the climax of the Chicago committee's operations. Its support of this second major paramilitary effort was undertaken only after it had ascertained from a direct interview with President Pierce that he would not change his Kansas policy.

With the national committee paying the bills, the Eldridge column proved a far better organized and equipped project than Lane's had been. Eldrige purchased wagons, harness, tents, and camp fixtures in Chicago and had them shipped by rail to Mount Pleasant, where a regular military cantonment materialized. By late September 1856 his column was ready to move west. It consisted of a field gun and some twenty wagons loaded with small arms, edged weapons, munitions, tents, and provisions, escorted by about two hundred volunteers formally organized into artillery and rifle companies. Like Lane's army, it received a generous contribution from Grimes. Gossip about the Iowa muskets had not been lost on Robert Morrow, Eldridge's principal assistant. "While Colonel Eldridge was getting up the camp and wagons," Morrow recalled many years later, "I went to Iowa City to see Governor Grimes about getting some state arms. He said if I could get them without compromising him I could do so. I had letters to some good friends of Kansas; they got the keys to the arsenal, and in the night we loaded up three wagons with 200 stands of arms, and they were put into Colonel Eldridge's train and brought to Kansas."[36]

Grimes's role in furnishing seventeen hundred U.S. muskets to the Free State forces, an impressive statement of his fierce resolve to stem the westward spread of slavery, never did compromise him. The following winter, when a persistent Democratic legislator insisted on an accounting of federal arms furnished the state, the Republican majority buried serious discussion in an avalanche of jokes. Two years later Iowa's new Republican governor, in reply to a request from the legislature, asserted that there was no record of the exact number and disposition of weapons issued to the state. A committee of inquiry made no report. And Grimes himself, when closely pressed about having distributed firearms to Kansas emigrants, simply lied. "The gentlemen whose minds are exercised on the subject," he told a political colleague in 1858, "will have a jolly time proving any such charge against me. I never had the possession or custody of any portion of the State arms for one moment. . . . Some of them may [have been] taken to Kanzas or Nebraska, for ought that I know, but if so, I have no knowledge of it & had no instrumentality in their going."[37]

III

By the time Eldridge's column reached Kansas in October 1856, a newly appointed territorial governor, deploying the federal troops at his disposal in an impartial manner, had begun to neutralize the conflict. Arms and equipment forwarded by the National Kansas Committee and the independent Massachusetts Kansas Committee continued to arrive at Tabor, however, filling the village's every conceivable storage space to capacity. And back in Boston a conclave of the more warlike of the Northeast's important Free State supporters—including Higginson and Sanborn—toyed seriously with plans to raise a private army of ten thousand men and to station them in Iowa, ready for immediate action should the Missourians give further trouble. But the excitement was more or less over.

The impact of the conflict on Iowans' political behavior in 1856 appeared decisive to contemporaries. "Iowa is more deeply interested than any other State in saving Kansas from the grasp of the Slave power," Penn Clarke's Kansas Central Committee had declared on Independence Day, and the state's Republican governor, its Republican media, and its Republican campaign speakers all followed suit, emphasizing the necessity of victory in the forthcoming presidential election as the only certain means of accomplishing that transcendent task. Colonel Lane, by all accounts a spell-binder, took the stump seventy-two times during his midsummer trek across the Hawkeye State, eloquently urging the election of John C. Frémont, the new party's presidential nominee, in order to save Kansas for freedom. On July 22, from Lane's supply base at Quincy, Samuel Gridley Howe reported that the strategy was working. "The people of Iowa are all in a blaze of indignation," he wrote. Although too poor to help the Free State cause with money, "they will however go in for Fremont." The very next day Horace Greeley's New York *Tribune* confidently predicted that Iowa had been won for Republicanism: "As the State has been, and we think still is, hostile to the Nebraska policy, and is near enough to Kansas to feel the pulsations of the great struggle there proceeding, and as we believe there is no effort being made to throw away votes on Fillmore, we are confident it will go for Fremont in November by at least [a] 5,000 majority."

The Fillmore threat had indeed faded. Many Know Nothings moved quietly into the new party; others succumbed to the bipartisan appeal of county-level "people's" conventions that nominated Republican legislative candidates for August's state election. The result of that preliminary to the main event was a Republican sweep. Not only did the American-endorsed Republican nominees for office win good majorities, but for the first time ever Iowa's Democrats lost control of both legislative chambers. The jubilant editor of Burlington's Republican newspaper termed it "THE VERDICT OF IOWA UPON OUTRAGES IN KANSAS AND AT WASHINGTON." Salmon Chase, no less ecstatic, phrased it more elegantly. "Let me congratulate you on the redemption of Iowa," he wrote to Grimes. "Your election [in 1854] was the morning Star. The sun has arisen now."[38]

Nationally, the Democratic administration's neutralization of the Kansas fighting benefited the Democratic candidate, James Buchanan. But from their various vantage points the Republican party's national leaders, of whom Chase was among the most important, correctly intuited that the Hawkeye State's political transformation was complete. "In truth I find it will be very difficult to obtain speakers of eminence from abroad for our state," Senator Harlan complained to Penn Clarke. "They deem Iowa safe." Abraham Lincoln similarly declined Henry O'Connor's invitation to speak at an Iowa rally. "All thanks, all honor to Iowa!" he wrote. "But Iowa is out of all danger, and it is no time for us, when the battle still rages, to pay holy-day visits to Iowa. I am sure you will excuse me for remaining in Illinois, where much hard work is still to be done."

November's election fulfilled these expectations. Buchanan won nationally but lost Iowa by half again as many votes as Horace Greeley had predicted, capturing only some 34 percent of the state's total electorate as compared to Frémont's 43 percent. Fillmore placed a very poor third with 9 percent, winning not a single Iowa county. Buchanan's support, on close examination, proves to have been unremarkable. In addition to taking several sparsely populated frontier counties, he carried heavily ethnic Dubuque and its hinterland and most of the southern border of Iowa from Burlington and Keokuk all the way out to the Missouri River (map 7.1). His statewide proportion of the electorate was virtually what Pierce had won in 1852.[39]

But two things had changed dramatically since the previous presidential race. One was Iowa's voter turnout, a product of the difference between the voter apathy of '52 and the excitement of '56. Whereas some 70 percent of the Iowa electorate had voted in November 1852, turnout swelled to 85 percent four years later.[40] The second change was the enormous increase in new Iowans, and thus in newly enfranchised voters: only 49 percent of the 1856 electorate had been eligible four years earlier. While the 1852 nonvoters who now turned out divided their ballots fairly evenly between Frémont and Buchanan, the 1852 ineligibles who now voted favored Frémont by roughly a two-to-one margin. Much the same configuration characterized the 1854 electorate in 1856. Frémont carried

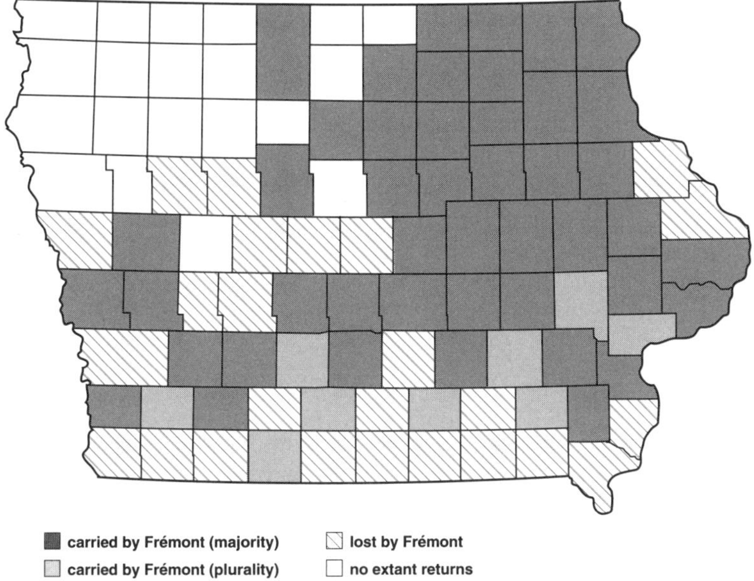

Map 7.1 The 1856 presidential election (for key to county names see map A.1, appendix A).

the Hawkeye State not by attracting any considerable proportion of normally Democratic voters (a feat managed only by Winfield Scott), but simply by winning strong majorities from the Whigs of 1852, from the Whig/Free Soil coalitionists of 1854, from the Anti-Nebraska/Know Nothing fusionists of 1855, and from those newcomers who turned out to vote.

Other important aspects of Iowa's 1856 presidential election are also apparent. Voters who had favored prohibition in the 1855 liquor referendum went strongly for Frémont, proving that the broad social-reform impulses of its Whig, Free Soil, Anti-Nebraska, and Know Nothing predecessors had transited smoothly into the ideological appeal of early Republicanism. No doubt a corollary to this was Frémont's weakness among Iowa's traditionally wet foreign-born voters. Virtually all the Irish supported Buchanan, and despite the endorsement of Frémont by three of Iowa's four German-language newspapers, he won the ballots of only about half the state's German-Americans. Among Iowa's larger European nativities only the dry-leaning Britons and Scots favored Frémont.[41]

American-born voters tended to replicate in Iowa Frémont's electoral strength in various states and regions of the United States. Thus nationwide Frémont carried New England, New York, and Ohio; in Iowa he won majorities among native Yankees, Yorkers, and Ohioans. Conversely, Buchanan carried the South, Pennsylvania, and Indiana, and in Iowa won a majority among southerners and pluralities among Pennsylvanians and Hoosiers. For Yankees, southerners, and perhaps New Yorkers the roots of group behavior may have been deeply ethnocultural—as for Irishmen or Germans. But Ohio, Pennsylvania, and Indiana are not usually thought to reflect discrete political subcultures. The relevant point, therefore, is that strong identification with their old homes distinguished Iowans of the antebellum generation. They tended to replicate the electoral behaviors of those original homes and to respect political messages transmitted from the East. It is probably no coincidence that Ohio, Pennsylvania, and Indiana happened to be diligently observed "October states"; their pre-presidential local elections were widely presumed to affect the outcome of the balloting in November.[42]

Information on Iowans' religious affiliations is far less precise than available birthplace data.[43] In general it comports with what historians have observed elsewhere: Presbyterians, Baptists, Congregationalists, Lutherans (mainly Scandinavian rather than German), and Quakers favored Frémont, while Catholics and Disciples of Christ voted Democratic. But Iowa's largest denomination, its Methodists, split. Members of the downstate Iowa Conference favored Buchanan, but also provided Fillmore's main strength, while Methodists of the northern Upper Iowa Conference went for Frémont—even though both conferences had officially spoken out against slavery.[44] William E. Gienapp is wholly correct in cautioning from the Methodist example that "to characterize evangelical voters as constituting anything approaching a voting bloc . . . badly distorts the political reality of the pre-Civil War years."[45]

With respect to the possible effect of economic and occupational differences among Iowa's voters, it appears that farmers, two-thirds of the work force, favored Buchanan. The farmers of agriculturally prosperous and middling counties yielded solid Democratic pluralities, while those of the state's poorer counties gave more ballots to Frémont than Buchanan. These less prosperous areas display a geographical configuration that suggests a clue to their behavior: from Allamakee County in the northeast corner of the state they stretch southwestward across Iowa's newly settled frontier to Carroll, Guthrie, Adair, and Clarke counties. But their lack of prosperity was strictly temporary; north-central and central Iowa would ultimately become the most agriculturally profitable region of the state. It may be that to these frontier farmers the Kansas question and other aspects of slavery's westward expansion spoke with a particular eloquence.[46]

In the case of nonfarmers the political differentiation is a little clearer. Only skilled artisans went strongly for Frémont, the business community granted a majority to Buchanan, and most of the state's unskilled laborers, predictably enough, did not bother with the election. This hint of a configuration along class lines lends statewide validity to Eugene F. Ware's recollection of late antebellum Burlington. Connecticut-born and reared in an abolitionist household, Ware later reminisced that the city's "wealthy people seemed to be Democratic in their tendencies, and to be proslavery. The principal merchants, the principal lawyers and the principal bankers gloried in being Democrats and opposed to abolitionism." In contrast, Burlington's artisans, such as the journeymen harnessmakers among whom young Ware worked at the end of the 1850s, most ardently articulated its grass-roots antisouthern attitudes, incessantly discussing slavery in terms of its powerful threat to the dignity and prosperity of free labor—"and what the African had been, was, or would be," Ware recalled, "was only collaterally considered."[47]

It would be wrong to overemphasize the influence of wealth and occupation at the expense of statistically more salient ethnocultural factors.[48] Yet one is strongly reminded of historian Eric Foner's portrait of the wealthy businessmen of Boston and New York, who "placed the preservation of the Union (and of their markets and business connections in the South) above agitation of the slavery question" and among whom, therefore, Republican rhetoric had little effect in the fifties. Even more relevant, Ware's comments about artisans mesh perfectly with Foner's characterization of "the free labor argument with its racist tinge" that formed, especially in the Middle West, the centerpiece of the Republican critique of the South. "Abolitionists had always had difficulty attracting northern labor to their cause," Foner writes, "and Republicans felt that by couching their appeal in terms of the effect of slavery upon labor, they stood a better chance of gaining these votes. . . . It was an appeal to the lowest common denominator of party ideology, allowing Republicans to sidestep both the problem of race and the effects of slavery upon the enslaved."[49]

IV

Even as Iowans prepared to respond to the various campaign messages of 1856, a lean and leathery man of cold gaze and grim demeanor, certain that the bloodletting begun in Kansas must continue, made his way across Iowa from west to east. Having escaped from the territory in early October, he had rested at Tabor, severely ill with dysentery, before retracing the route recently followed by so many Free State volunteers. He reached Iowa City late that month.

A hunted man, he tarried in Iowa's capital at his peril. Several miles onward the Quaker village of West Branch suggested sanctuary. Near this place, a year hence, he would convene his guerrilla fighters to train them for an exploit that would electrify the entire land. But on this first visit, unsure of his reception, he proceeded cautiously. Accompanied by one of his sons, looking weary and travel-stained, astride a Missouri mule liberated at the battle of Black Jack and leading a horse, he drew up at the settlement's only inn, dismounted, and identified himself to the waiting landlord.

"Have you ever heard of John Brown of Kansas notoriety?" he asked.[50]

Progress and Prejudice

8

Thomas C. Motts, Muscatine's black barber, coal dealer, and owner of a substantial six thousand dollars' worth of real estate, brought suit against Usher & Thayer, a white business partnership that managed a local hotel. Motts, who was no fool, employed the civil libertarian Henry O'Connor and his law partner, Iowa's attorney general, David C. Cloud, to represent him in court. As their key witness the defendants offered John Hinton, a black drayman. O'Connor and Cloud immediately objected. The 1851 Iowa code, they pointed out, specified that "an Indian, a negro, a mulatto, or black person shall not be allowed to give testimony in any cause wherein a white person is a party."

Defendants' counsel protested. Whatever its wording, they said, the cited provision had been designed for the benefit of Caucasian parties to lawsuits, not blacks. But the judge agreed with plaintiff, excluding Hinton's evidence. Motts won his suit. Defendants appealed to the Iowa supreme court. In April 1856 the justices, three newly minted Republicans, upheld judgment in favor of Motts.[1]

Four months later the electoral landslide of August 1856 carried one of Motts's lawyers into the first Republican-controlled Iowa general assembly. D. C. Cloud, like his partner O'Connor, was strictly a self-made man: while supporting his family as a carpenter, Cloud learned his law from a load of books received in payment for building the house of a Muscatine judge. In 1848, as a magistrate himself, Cloud freed the alleged fugitive slave Jim in Muscatine's version of the *Ralph* case, but he remained a loyal Jacksonian, successfully running as a political oddity in Iowa—an avowed Anti-Nebraska Democrat—for reelection as attorney general in 1854. Two years later, failing to win a nomination to succeed himself, he accepted a Republican invitation to stand for the legislature.

In December, a week into the 1856/57 session, Cloud revealed how far toward abolition and civil equality his antiextension attitudes threatened to carry him. In the debate of a resolution on Kansas, he gravely rebuked his old party for having become a proslavery organization whose very articles of faith relegated blacks to subhuman status. "Mr. Speaker, I maintain that the blacks have the rights of men in this country," he said, and he heatedly denied that Republicans favored, as their opponents would have it, some form of black supremacy. "Freedom of the black race implies more than this," he insisted. It promulgated no less than "the equal liberty of all."[2]

Across the hall in the senate chamber that same day George McCoy, a Kentucky-born farmer of the abolitionist Free Presbyterian faith, one of the early pioneer settlers of upstate Benton County, introduced Senate File 20, an act to repeal the nonwhite testimony clause of the Iowa code. An Anti-Nebraskan effort to this effect had gone nowhere in the previous legislature. But the ironic outcome of *Motts* v. *Usher* had lent fresh impetus to its repeal—and probably a misguided assumption that the effort now would attract bipartisan support. In somewhat altered form the McCoy bill easily carried the senate over the objections of its Democrats and a single Republican, and the majority beat back an attempt to change its title to "A bill for an act to equalize the white, the black, and the mongrel races." Introduced into the house, the bill survived desperate efforts to kill it. It passed by another virtual party-line vote, only one Republican and the chamber's single Know Nothing joining the Democrats in opposition.

The assembly's Republicans had proved remarkably unified on McCoy's bill, but once it became clear, as it did over the Christmas break, that the state's Democrats were making the new Act Relating to Evidence into one of that very frigid winter's hottest political issues, some Republicans—both within the legislature and without—entertained second thoughts. A Knoxville businessman described the moment when news of the McCoy bill's passage arrived in town. "The universal expression of opinion from all parties, without distinction," he said, "was that it would never do. The strongest Republicans in Marion county, those who stood front in the ranks of the party, were opposed to the bill, and said that such a measure would sink the Republican party into oblivion." As Ottumwa's Republican newspaper editor admitted, many of the faithful indeed had concluded that "it was impolitic in the Republican party in this early period of its existence to assume the responsibility of such an enactment."[3]

But Muscatine's rising black entrepreneur, Alexander Clark, viewed passage of the McCoy bill as a signal to urge the further dismantling of Iowa's black code. In December he and other local activists collected 122 signatures—of whites as well as blacks—on a petition praying repeal of Billy G. Haun's exclusion law. When the legislature reconvened in January

1857, D. C. Cloud introduced this document on the floor of the house, where it was shunted to committee. But the senate's McCoy responded to the petition by disclosing an intention to offer a bill repealing "chapter 72 of the session laws of 1851"—that is, the exclusion law. Somebody—most likely his party colleagues—dissuaded McCoy from doing so, perhaps on the theory that it was best to let sleeping dogs lie.[4]

African-Americans, meanwhile, interpreted the imminent muster of the new constitutional convention as a strategic moment for keeping up the pressure. On January 5, 1857, at least thirty-three delegates from various black communities of Iowa gathered in Muscatine's African Methodist Episcopal church in the state's first "colored convention." Besides resolving against colonization and applauding the movement of black Iowans into agriculture, they committed themselves, as an editor paraphrased their minutes, "to petition the Constitutional Convention to extend the right of the elective franchise to native born negroes and to bestow upon them all the rights and privileges of citizenship." The minutes also urged "the utility of pressing forward to obtain education over every opposition," as upon this "depends the moral and political elevation of the colored race." The delegates therefore appealed "for some aid from the school fund of the State, and very justly demur to being taxed for school purposes and at the same time being deprived from its benefits." Those in attendance then signed a petition demanding black suffrage and addressed it to the forthcoming convention.[5]

Democrats, meanwhile, also viewed the moment as strategic. Their party, confided one Jacksonian wheelhorse to another, must "join issue" with the Republicans "in every attempt they have made, or may make (in the Convention to amend the Constitution) to extend the rights of free negroes." If all went well, he said, the Republican delegates would totally discredit themselves in the eyes of "all except those miserable fanaticks for whom there [is] no hope."

In the third week of January the convention delegates descended on an Iowa City locked in the grip of a "New England winter," as a citizen phrased it, with morning temperatures hovering at minus twenty degrees day after day. Since the legislators had not yet disbanded, rooms were at a premium, as were accommodations in the capitol: the delegates crowded into the supreme court chamber. After organizing themselves they adjourned so that the Democrats among them could attend their state party convention scheduled for that afternoon. As expected, the assembled Jacksonians paused only to chide the legislature for failing to repeal the prohibitory law before turning their guns on the Act Relating to Evidence. Linking the new law to the assembly's endorsement of relatively restrictive immigration and naturalization measures, they saw it as reflecting a Republican determination to elevate African-Americans at the expense of the

European-born. They implored the constitutional convention to seek "a provision confining the rights of citizenship in this State to the white population, and to the exclusion of Negroes and Mulattoes."

In reply two days later the Republican state convention ignored the liquor issue but reaffirmed the party's position on immigration, in the same breath defending the McCoy Act as a measure no Iowan need fear. And before adjourning the Republicans appointed a state central committee consisting of Henry O'Connor, William Penn Clarke, and two others. Clarke had been elected a constitutional convention delegate, and his new party appointment—no doubt a reward for his indispensable role in the Kansas aid movement—would lend him considerable authority as a Republican spokesman within the gathering.[6]

News then stirred the legislature that one or more constitutional convention delegates planned to introduce petitions from Iowa's blacks—and perhaps from some of its white civil libertarians as well—urging the creation of a racially impartial suffrage and a school system open to all. On January 24 Thomas Hardie, a Dubuque Democrat, offered a resolution designed to head them off:

> WHEREAS, A portion of our citizens are in favor of, and advocate the *striking out* of the word *'white'* from the Constitution as used to define the right of citizenship, in order to place negroes and mulattoes upon an equal footing with the white race, therefore,
>
> *Be it Resolved,* That in the opinion of this House [the suffrage clause] as it now stands, is right and proper, and that it would be inexpedient to strike out the word white therefrom.

On D. C. Cloud's initiative the majority struck the clause disparaging reformers' motives, but that proved the end of Republican unity. The largest Republican bloc, twenty moderates, sought to avoid a vote on the resolution by tabling it or sending it to committee, but in the end did not oppose its passage. Only six Republicans voted against the resolution. Eight others—including Cloud—straightforwardly supported it. So much for "the equal liberty of all."

Things went little better for civil equality in the other chamber that day. The Republican president of the senate stepped down from his chair to offer an amendment to a bill reorganizing Iowa's educational system. A Dubuque County farmer, he deemed the pending measure incomplete without a clause specifying that "colored children shall not be admitted into any of the public schools of this state, without the unanimous consent of the householders of the district." Only George McCoy, six other Republicans, and one Democratic maverick opposed the amendment, though the main body of the Republicans rallied to reject a proposal transforming the clause into an absolute mandate of all-white schools.[7]

The 1856/57 general assembly adjourned before either measure had an opportunity for passage, but both had served to mark the limits of Republican political courage. The often intricate relationships between free-soil commitments, antislavery impulses, pressures from Iowa's suddenly vocal black community, and existing racial attitudes—as exemplified by such a figure as D. C. Cloud—would achieve a much more elaborate expression in the roll calls and debates of the 1857 constitutional convention.

I

On January 26 the convention delegates—fifteen Democrats and twenty-one Republicans—began their labors in earnest. In numbers they were only half as many as their 1844 predecessors; in composition they differed in certain subtle ways. In 1844 men who termed themselves farmers formed a majority; now, reflecting the pace of Iowa's modernization, the decisive balance had shifted to lawyers. No longer did southern-born delegates form the largest contingent in each party. Although native southerners still dominated the Democrats, men originally from New England, New York, and the Old Northwest comprised the Republican majority. In one important way the convention factions differed demographically: as a group, the Republicans were rather singularly "new" men—not just in the figurative sense of their personal political transformations, but in the literal sense of their recent dates of arrival in the state. Two had been Iowans for only two years, four others for only three. Together these six newcomers made up nearly a third of their party's convention strength.

In political stature the delegates, as in 1844, ranged from the anonymous to the renowned. Penn Clarke was no doubt the best known Republican, although once again some subtle prejudice worked against him. His party colleagues elected Francis Springer, a popular lawyer and sometime legislator, as convention president. Among the Democrats, Jonathan C. Hall's voice proved the most authoritative. Once one of the most active members of the 1844 convention, Hall was the single recidivist present. After his strenuous if out-of-character defense of the Salem nineteen in 1850, he served briefly on the Iowa supreme court before accepting presidency of the Burlington & Missouri River Railroad Company. Had the Democrats held a majority in the convention, Hall would have presided.[8]

Several delegates besides President Springer had been legislators, and five had cast votes on civil equality. Two of them, Springer himself and one Democrat, had registered as progressives; two Republicans had opposed black exclusion; one Democrat had identified himself as an ultra conservative by voting for the Haun bill. Hall still held his racist views. Although he had never participated in an equal-rights roll call, his racism was on the record of the previous constitutional convention, and in remarks recently presented to Iowa's chapter of the American Colonization Society he certified that his outlook had changed not a whit since 1844. Others, he said, might have come to colonization out of a philanthropic anxiety for the lot of African-Americans. Not him; his concern was for the well-being of *white* America. Given blacks' biological inferiority, "it is only from wild and deluded fanaticism that any attempt or any effort to make them morally, socially, and politically equal to the white population, can emanate." To rid the nation of this "unfortunate class of created beings" was to Hall "the greatest and noblest idea of this enlightened, and glorious age."[9]

The need to liberate Iowa's economic growth from its dependence on out-of-state sources of currency and credit had impelled Iowans to call the convention. But about a fifth of the delegates' formal deliberations concerned race, slavery, and—inevitably—the partisan ramifications of these things. Several, indeed, claimed that alterations in Iowa's black code had been very much on constituents' minds. As one Democrat put it, equal rights "is perhaps about the most important question—except it may be, the banking question—that can come before this convention. And I believe the people feel more interest in this question at this time than in any other, except the one I have alluded to."

Prompted by the recent colored convention's resolutions, Muscatine's delegate, John A. Parvin, moved that the committee on schools consider "making provision for the education of the children of blacks and mulattoes." But he postponed presenting the black Iowans' petition requesting the elective franchise until February 4, the day scheduled for the delegates' first formal consideration of the constitution's suffrage clause. In the interim, evidently because the gentleman from Delaware County (a Democrat) refused to do so, the delegate from Henry County presented a petition signed by a future Iowa secretary of state, Dr. James Wright, and fifty-five other citizens of Delaware "without distinction of party," requesting "incorporation into the constitution of a provision that no person should be disfranchised on account of color." And on February 11 Parvin submitted a third civil rights petition, this one signed by Henry O'Connor and 128 other Muscatine citizens—Democrats and Republicans alike—protesting "incorporation in the Constitution of any provision again imposing upon the black population of this State the disabilities in regard to giving evidence in Courts, and the holding of property." Three petitions were not many, but they made up a quarter of those presented to the convention. Most Republicans appear to have treated them as serious expressions of public opinion.[10]

A dozen important roll call votes dealt specifically or implicitly with civil equality. Two arose from Democratic threats to repeal the Act Relating to Evidence should they ever regain control of the legislature. The more progressive Republicans' response, in light of this warning, was to put the McCoy Act beyond repeal by writing it into the new constitution's bill of rights. A Republican minority first helped the Democrats reject a proposal that no person be disqualified as a witness "in consequence of belonging to any particular sect, class or party of men." Three weeks later, however, impressed by Penn Clarke's eloquent argument that its support should be a litmus test of party loyalty, the majority approved a motion that no person "cognizant of any fact material to the case" could normally be disqualified from testifying in court.[11]

With respect to public schools, the Republicans issued a flat rejection of the recent senate amendment urging the continued exclusion of blacks. They first voted favorably on Parvin's resolution that the education committee consider ending this policy. A month later they agreed to make no reference whatsoever to race, rejecting both a specification that the schools "shall be free of charge and open to all" and a proposal that they should be reserved "for the education of all white children of the state." This did not rule out racially segregated facilities, as Penn Clarke noted, but at least the constitution would not require them.

Three roll calls disposed of other race-related amendments to the bill of rights. The first harkened back to the original draft of the Haun Act, which would have disallowed property holding by colored in-migrants. Would a resurgent Democratic party resort again to such a Draconian discouragement of black residency? Eight Republicans thought it possible; they favored an unsuccessful motion that nonwhites "shall enjoy the same rights in respect to the possession, enjoyment and descent of property, as native born citizens." The other two roll calls split the delegates along party lines. Over the opposition of Democrats sensitive to the least hint of racial egalitarianism, the majority Republicans changed the phrase "all men are, by nature, free and independent" to "all men are, by nature, free and equal." And they let stand a section guaranteeing jury trials in all cases "involving the life, or liberty of an individual," both sides viewing this as a nullification of the Fugitive Slave Law's rendition process—an Iowa version, as it were, of the "personal liberty laws" with which several northern states had recently experimented.[12]

The delegates grappled several times with colored suffrage. This issue, as one delegate put it, "entered more largely, perhaps, than any other, in the recent campaign which has resulted in our being assembled here." No Democrat, of course, could stomach the prospect, and J. C. Hall savaged the notion that any substantial body of Iowans—Democrat or Republican—favored a racially impartial franchise. But a few Republicans had pledged themselves to work for a constitutional provision submitting black suffrage to a popular vote. This device—as in Illinois in 1848, Wisconsin in 1849, Michigan in 1850, and Indiana in 1851—promised the only wholly decisive resolution of a grass-roots standoff between a strongly committed civil-libertarian minority and a hostile (or at best apathetic) white majority. Wisconsin, in fact, was in the process of scheduling a second equal rights referendum for late 1857. Iowa's convention delegates decided to follow suit.

When the committee on suffrage recommended leaving the electoral eligibility clause as it had been drafted in 1844, only four Republicans opposed creating a new committee to consider a vote on suffrage reform by the people. But when this committee urged that the referendum propose removing the word "white" from *every* section of the new constitution, all but two Republicans thought this too extreme. Later, in a strict party-line split, the delegates agreed to submit black suffrage to voters on August 3, 1857, in a referendum separate from that concurrently asking approval of the new constitution. But at the instigation of James F. Wilson, a Republican, they burdened the measure with a truly extraordinary handicap. According to Wilson's wording of the proposition, impartial suffrage would pass only if the votes in favor of it exceeded half those cast both for and against the first referendum item on the ballot—the new constitution. This meant that anyone voting on the new constitution (proposition 1) could vote against suffrage reform (proposition 2) simply by ignoring proposition 2 altogether. This peculiar referendum design had been borrowed from Wisconsin. Originating as a careless mistake by civil rights activists in that state's 1848 constitutional convention, it had foredoomed black suffrage in Wisconsin, just as it promised to do in 1857 in the Hawkeye State.[13]

Agreement on the proposed referendum ended action on what remained of the Iowa black code. The new constitution, like the old, would still restrict the franchise to adult white males, and it would exclude blacks from sitting in the legislature, from being included in state census enumerations, from being taken into account when apportioning the legislature, and from serving in the militia.

In the convention's final days, and after plenty of warning from its sponsor, the delegates finally confronted a proposed clause mandating black exclusion. Offered by Amos Harris, an Ohio-born Democrat from southern Iowa, it did not repeat the mysteriously extant law of which Billy G. Haun had been the author. It was instead almost a word-for-word copy of the exclusion clause of Indiana's 1851 constitution. As such, it would ban the in-migration of free blacks, nullify all contracts between citizens and illegal migrants, and subject the employers of such migrants to fines of up to five hundred dollars. These proceeds would be earmarked for the African colonization of blacks legally resident in the state. On none other than J. C. Hall's motion, however, and without so much as a word of debate, the delegates hastily tabled the proposal. No Republican favored it, and for the first time on an important civil rights issue the convention's Democrats split, opposing black exclusion 5–8. The ghost of Justice Story once again worked its spell, fragmenting the Jacksonians while uniting their foes.[14]

II

The convention's multiple roll calls on race-related issues suggest that for the first time in the record of Iowa's lengthy political encounter with white supremacy the behavior of a body of its lawmakers may be elaborated upon in some detail. A technique called "scaling" has helped arrange the 1857 convention's votes on relevant questions in such a way as to locate each delegate's place on a continuum of behaviors from most to least egalitarian; delegates in adjacent locations on this continuum have then been appropriately grouped. The 1857 data suggest the existence of five such groups: progressive Republicans, moderate Republicans, conservative Republicans, conservative Democrats, and ultra conservative Democrats (table 8.1).[15]

It will be noted that no matter how racist, every Republican delegate ranked as more egalitarian than any Democrat. Indeed, the largest gap anywhere on the continuum—the hiatus between scale scores 5 and 2—is a gap that divides the two parties. Little variation characterized the Democrats until the exclusionary vote; up to that moment not a single Democrat had offered any systematic support to equal rights. Black exclusion, as noted, finally split them, the five antiexclusionists ranking as conservative, the eight exclusionists as ultra conservative. The overwhelmingly rightward cast of the Democrats is vividly, even astonishingly, illustrated by the irrepressibly racist J. C. Hall. By virtue of a ballot he cast against closing public schools to black children, Hall ranked as the convention's single most racially progressive Democrat.[16]

The behavior of William Patterson, who came to the convention with a record as a progressive, provides the only other surprise on the Democratic side. Virginia-born and Kentucky-bred, at fifty-four the second oldest delegate in the convention, Patterson had supported a racially impartial welfare system in the 1841/42 legislature—the only Democrat to do so—and had voted against black exclusion four years later. In the 1857 convention he personally revealed nothing of his racial attitudes, but a midlife career change may explain his metamorphosis to ultra conservative. In 1846, tired of agriculture, he moved from his farm near West Point into Keokuk, eventually becoming one of that city's most prosperous businessmen. But with this shift in residence he also escaped the political reach of the New Garden Quakers and the Denmark Congregationalists whose abolitionism he had twice indulged. Now, without two of Iowa's

Table 8.1 Racial egalitarianism scale: the constitutional convention of 1857

	Scale score	Roll calls involving equal rights																					
		1	*2*	*3*	*4*	*5*	*6*	*7*	*8*	*9*	*10*	*11*	*1*	*2*	*3*	*4*	*5*	*6*	*7*	*8*	*9*	*10*	*11*
							Progressive Republicans																
David Bunker	11	+	+	+	+	+	+	+	+	+	+	+											
R. L. B. Clarke	11	+	+	+	+	+	+	+	+	+	+	+											
							Moderate Republicans																
W. Penn Clarke	10		+	+	+	+	+	+	+	+	+	+	–										
George W. Ells	10		+	+	+	+	+	+	+	+	+	+	0										
Hosea W. Gray	10		+	+	+	+	+	+	+	+	+	+	–										
J. C. Traer	10		+	+	+	+	+	+	+	+	+	+	–										
A. H. Marvin	10		+	0		+	+	+	+	+	+	+	–			–							
Robert Gower	9			+	+	+	+	+	+	+	+	+	–	–									
Alpheus Scott	9			+	0	+	+	+	+	+	+	+	–	–									
Thomas Seeley	9			+	+	+	+	+	+	+	+	+	–	–									
Harvey J. Skiff	9			+	+	+	+	+	+	+	+	+	–	–									
John A. Parvin	8		+		+	+	+		+	+	0	+	–		–				–				
John T. Clark	8				+	+	+	+	+	+	+	+	–	–	–								
Lewis Todhunter	8				+	+	+	+	+	+	+	+	–	–	–								
W. A. Warren	8				+	+	+	+	0	+	+	+	–	–	–								
							Conservative Republicans																
John Edwards	7					+	+	+	+	+	+	+	–	–	–	–							
S. G. Winchester	7					+	+	+	+	+	+	0	0	–	–	–							
James F. Wilson	6		+		+		+	+	+	+	+	+	–		–		–						
Francis Springer	6				+		+	+	+	+	+	+	–	–	–		–						
James A. Young	6		+				+	+	+	+	+	+	–		–	–	–						
J. Hollingsworth	5					+		+	+	+	+	+	–	–	0	0		–					

Conservative Democrats												
J. C. Hall	2	+	+	+	−	−	−	−	−	−	−	−
Squire Ayers	1	+	+	0	−	−	−	−	−	−	−	0
Timothy Day	1	+	+	−	−	−	−	−	−	−	−	−
Daniel W. Price	1	+	+	−	0	−	−	−	−	−	−	−
Edward Johnstone	1	+	−	−	−	−	−	−	−	−	−	0
Ultra conservative Democrats												
J. H. Emerson	0	+	−	−	−	−	−	−	−	−	−	−
Amos Harris	0	+	−	−	−	−	−	−	−	−	0	−
H. D. Gibson	0	−	−	−	−	−	−	−	−	−	−	−
George Gillaspy	0	−	−	−	−	−	−	−	−	−	−	−
D. P. Palmer	0	−	−	−	−	−	−	−	−	−	−	−
William Patterson	0	−	−	−	−	−	−	−	−	−	−	−
John H. Peters	0	−	−	−	−	−	−	−	−	−	−	−
D. H. Solomon	0	−	−	−	−	−	−	−	−	−	−	−

Key to symbols: + is egalitarian vote; − is antiegalitarian vote; 0 is absent or not voting, probable vote estimated. Votes lying outside the general pattern are assumed to be either recording errors by the convention clerk or unreflective eccentricities in judgment. All roll calls "scale" with one another better than .50 except for roll call 1, which was nevertheless retained in order to distinguish the progressives from other Republicans. Democrats A. R. Cotton and M. W. Robinson were unclassifiable due to prolonged absences.

Key to roll calls:

Roll call 1: Against Skiff motion amending the resolution of the select committee on suffrage so that the proposed popular referendum would include removing the word "white" only from the suffrage article rather than from the entire constitution (Mar. 2). W. Blair Lord, ed., *The Debates of the Constitutional Convention of the State of Iowa* (Davenport, 1857), 665, 912.

Roll call 2: Against Hall motion to table Marvin substitute specifying that the common schools "shall be free of charge and open to all" (Feb. 27). Ibid., 825, 829–830.

Roll call 3: For R. L. B. Clarke motion amending the proposed bill of rights so that no person would be disqualified from giving evidence "in consequence of belonging to any particular sect, class or party of men" (Feb. 3). Ibid., 172, 180.

Roll call 4: For Skiff motion referring the question of equal suffrage to a select committee in expectation that the committee would recommend a popular referendum on that measure (Feb. 4). Ibid., 217, 219.

Roll call 5: For Penn Clarke motion amending proposed bill of rights so that no knowledgeable person normally would be disqualified from giving evidence (Feb. 24). Ibid., 735.

Roll call 6: For Parvin resolution that the committee on education and school lands considered "making provision for the education of the children of blacks and mulattoes" (Jan. 28). Ibid., 62.

Roll call 7: For recommendation of the select committee on the bill of rights that the phrase "all men are, by nature, free and independent" be changed to "all men are, by nature, free and equal" (Feb. 24). Ibid., 732, 734.

Roll call 8: For amended resolution of the select committee on suffrage providing for a popular referendum on equal suffrage (Mar. 3). Ibid., 913, 917.

Roll call 9: Against Harris motion amending the proposed bill of rights so as to remove an implied negation of the fugitive slave clause of the U.S. Constitution (Feb. 24). Ibid., 736, 741.

Roll call 10: Against Gillaspy motion amending the schools section so that the state board of education "shall provide for the education of all white children of the state" (Feb. 27). Ibid., 832, 837.

Roll call 11: For Hall motion to table Harris substitute mandating a black exclusion clause (Mar. 2). Ibid., 913.

strongest civil rights constituencies to answer to, Patterson could at last express his personal feelings on racial issues—which were those normal to an Old School Presbyterian and southern-born Democrat. By 1857, in any event, he not only favored exclusion but also, like Hall, had become an active colonizationist.[17]

The Republicans exhibited much more behavioral variation. Only two registered as progressives, voting the egalitarian position on every roll call. Their isolated support for a referendum that might have produced a wholly nonracist constitution set them off from the moderates. Not surprisingly, the two had been elected from those old abolitionist and Free Soil enclaves, Henry and Washington counties. The thirteen Republican moderates, men who favored the egalitarian position in at least eight roll calls, represented most of northeastern and east-central Iowa, except for two urbanized enclaves along the Mississippi (Clinton and Dubuque counties) plus a strip of thinly settled territory stretching west from Dubuque. In contrast, save for the gentleman from Henry, none but Democrats or Republican conservatives—the latter including President Springer—represented the lower two tiers of Iowa counties abutting Missouri.

Otherwise, with regard to men of both parties, neither the geographic nor the demographic aspects of the convention's divisions on civil equality seem to have been significant, with one curious exception: the body's four youngest members chose the least egalitarian grouping permitted by their party allegiances, two registering as conservative Republicans, the other two as ultras. Nor do the delegates' scaled positions on banking reform match their scaled attitudes toward blacks, except that three of the convention's four Democrats who proved positively hostile to banks also registered, perhaps significantly, as racial ultra conservatives.[18]

Some two hundred pages of the delegates' remarks on race and slavery punctuate the published convention debates, most of them extended set pieces rehashing the issues of the late presidential campaign. The Democrats' comments are of least interest, as they reiterate with monotonous consistency the timeless clichés of white supremacy. Several of the Republicans, however, talked openly of their feelings about blacks, their thoughts on color prejudice, their readings of public opinion respecting race. These expressions illuminate Republican behavior to an extent rarely permitted in the cases of such second- and third-echelon political figures as made up most of the 1857 contingent.

The elder of the two progressives, David Bunker, was now an old hand at representing his Washington County constituents in matters of race. He had braved the contempt of his fellow legislators back in 1843 by presenting a petition for repeal of the old black regulatory law, and in 1851 he happily cast his vote against the Haun bill. Now forty-six, his scraggly full beard—according to his convention photograph—streaked with grey, he described himself as much less sanguine about eradicating color prejudice than he once had been. It was Bunker who suggested changing "independent" to "equal" in the clause embracing natural rights, but he confessed that he didn't feel as strongly about it as others did. More important, Bunker had come from his farm to the convention doubting the wisdom of writing black suffrage into organic law. The intransigence of the Democrats' racism changed his mind. By retaining the word "white" anywhere in the new constitution the delegates would do more to endanger *all* Iowans' civil liberties, he said, "than we would by allowing the few negroes who may be in the State the privilege of voting at our elections."[19]

If Bunker indulged in little soul-searching, his progressive colleague from Henry County offered a very loquacious contrast. Thirty-seven, Connecticut-born from the same stock that had produced the great revivalist theologian Jonathan Edwards, reared in New York's renowned Burned-Over District, Rufus L. B. Clarke (no kin to Penn Clarke) had been for the past six years a relatively obscure Mount Pleasant lawyer. His most memorable attribute, for those who knew something of him, was that he happened to be the older brother of Grace Greenwood, one of America's most celebrated writers of genteel nonfiction and verse. This kinship may well have influenced many Iowans' measure of R. L. B. Clarke: they found him excessively cultivated. Although "an accomplished, pleasant and genial gentleman," notes a reminiscence, "his manners were too refined to make him popular, and as a result, he did not succeed in acquiring a large general practice."

Slender, dark-haired, fastidious, in his convention portrait he wears the mustacheless "Quaker" whiskers favored by most delegates, his gaze is steady, the fine aquiline nose juts forth, the lower lip is firm. At the 1854 Whig convention Clarke had shaped a condemnation of the Kansas-Nebraska Act that helped bring his party to its merger with the Free Soilers, and in the ensuing fall campaign he came within 214 votes of winning a seat in Congress. But his political prospects rapidly faded. His personal demeanor was one thing; his absolute refusal to be a "party man" probably proved decisive. His one historic moment was his season as the Iowa convention's persistent gadfly on equal rights.

Although he claimed to be no more an abolitionist than any other delegate, R. L. B. Clarke left no doubt as to his stand on color discrimination. "It is unmanly," he said. "It is ungenerous. It is unchristian." And, worst of all, it arose from "mere prejudices," wholly devoid of rationality. Yet—a thing as shamefully inexplicable in himself as in others ("perhaps it arises from education, and is induced by [the] very degradation [of] that injured and degraded race")—Clarke, too, found himself biased against blacks. "I am a friend of the whole human race," he explained, so in the abstract sense also "a friend of the negro." But "there is probably no man who has a greater repugnance naturally to that race than I have; and no man would be more rejoiced than myself if there was not one of that particular race on this continent; and there is no man who would go farther to remove them than I would, if it were practicable"—which of course it was not.

When J. C. Hall reissued, as a committee minority report, his 1844 brief against black equality, Clarke mercilessly ridiculed its awesomely gloomy scenario. Yet Clarke's own bleak prognosis of America's interracial fate differed not at all from Hall's, foreseeing "amalgamation, or perhaps what is worse, the growing antipathy, hating and strife of the races, and the whole body of evils that the most vivid imaginations of gentlemen upon the other side"—that is, the Democrats—"can conceive of." He marveled that "God in his inscrutable providence has permitted this thing—I cannot see why, and I must not ask wherefore. It is here and we must meet it."

A man for whom democracy was literally sacred ("the very spirit and essence of christianity itself") and for whom America's multiracial character was some divinely orchestrated test of the nation's ideological commitment, Clarke saw no option but to "throw aside my own feelings and prejudices, and say, let us unite together and do right, whatever the consequences." Since no one could forecast the long-term result of admitting blacks to full citizenship, it was a moment for unflinching moral courage and absolute trust in God. "We must believe, if the principle be correct, that nobody will be injured."

In the convention bargaining on equal rights R. L. B. Clarke compromised only twice. Until black Iowans gained the vote he was unwilling to impose upon them the obligations of militia service. And he finally conceded on suffrage reform because he shared a universal apprehension that the public would reject the entire constitution were not the franchise—at least initially—restricted to whites. But he joined the Republican majority in insisting on submitting the matter to the people. Not that Iowans would approve black suffrage—no delegate was so sanguine as that. But to Clarke the referendum, no matter what its outcome, would have a consciousness-raising effect. "If the people were correctly educated in this matter; if they would throw aside this childish timidity, this worse than foolish prejudice, that leads them to imagine innumerable evils that might fall upon them," he said, as if forgetting for a moment that he shared the people's fears, "they would go for . . . a constitution free from all invidious personal distinctions, and based upon universal suffrage."

Sooner or later the principle of absolute civil equality would carry Iowa, he said, and in this Clarke was a better prophet than those delegates who smirked at the thought. "We live in an age and in a community [in which] the people think and act for themselves. Their hearts are in the right place, and as soon as they get the idea in their minds that a thing is right they go for it." Wherever lawmakers struggled to dismantle black codes, said Clarke, "the public mind is alive and acting in this matter, and it is nothing but true republican democracy . . . working out its heaven-directed mission."[20]

The gentleman from Johnson County, Iowa City's Penn Clarke, suggested early on that what separated R. L. B. Clarke from moderates like himself was more means than ends: "We do not differ so much in our object, as in our modes of getting at it." For one thing, moderates thought much more in *party* terms than did racial progressives. While this caused them to calibrate their actions to what they thought the voters would bear, it also led them to insist that Republicans had a collective mandate—explicit or implicit—to expand the liberties of blacks. It was one delegate's impression, for example, that some one-third of the Republican party consisted of former Democrats such as himself. Did his fellow Republicans think, he asked, that all had "left the old Democratic party simply on account of banks, railroads and internal improvements?" No, he said; "freedom and equal rights" was the cause.

Penn Clarke agreed. The proposition that "all men are created free and equal [and] have the same natural rights," he said, was the "fundamental principle of the Republican party, the foundation stone upon which the party rests." The moderates thus appealed not only to the eternal verities R. L. B. Clarke invoked, but to the discipline of party ideology as well. They also drew on the new-fangled notion of "progress," and saw their organization as its political manifestation. "The Republican party of this country, sir," said one, "is emphatically a progressive party." And a moderate's stand on race-related issues defined itself by an insistence that the new constitution be "progressive, . . . so that upon examination it will be found that we have made progress in the right direction."

Penn Clarke, the convention's most politically experienced moderate, was a youthful thirty-nine in 1857, with a narrow, clean-shaven face, large, rather protruding eyes under arching black brows, and a boyish mop of dark hair. Baltimore-born and bred, he had internalized conventional southern attitudes toward blacks. But, as he told the delegates, "the world is presumed to be progressive, and it is progressive, and I have progressed somewhat with it, and at my stage of life, I have come to the conclusion that we should look upon these matters as questions of natural right and duty." God created men equal; men alone made racial distinctions. Clarke spoke eloquently of the natural honesty and trustworthiness of blacks, the parity of moral faculties between the races. Color prejudice was, in his judgment, "not becoming this age and generation."[21]

Clarke argued that "the beaming intelligence and onward progress of the age" required that the McCoy Act on racially impartial court testimony be written into the new constitution, and he scorned predictions of a popular backlash. "I believe the people are marching onward," he said, "and progressing upon this doctrine of human rights." But that was in early February. Three weeks later, after the convention's Democrats had threatened to go public in their resistance to black code reform, he sharply modified his confidence in popular opinion, fearing, for instance, that publicity about R. L. B. Clarke's proposed elimination of the word "white" from the entire constitution might be perceived as a Republican consensus. That, he felt, would play directly into the Democrats' hands.

As noted earlier, Penn Clarke drew a careful scholarly distinction between civil rights (rights of residence, property ownership, access to public education, access to the courts) and civil liberties (voting and office holding). But his negative attitude toward suffrage reform seems mainly motivated by a fear of the political cost to his party—the party whose success or failure would so definitively decide his own political future. He was even against a plebiscite on impartial suffrage, pleading that there was no popular groundswell (even among black Iowans) for holding a referendum, and that its own strongest advocates admitted it would fail. He predicted that at least half the state's Republicans would reject black suffrage.

Two of Penn Clarke's fellow moderates personally favored extending the franchise to blacks, a change they thought would be best accomplished by a popular vote; others personally opposed it, but were willing to abide by a public verdict; yet others had promised constituents to work for a suffrage referendum. It finally seemed time to bring some party discipline to bear on Penn Clarke. George W. Ells pointed out that all convention Republicans save the gentleman from Johnson favored a referendum, and a week later the recalcitrant Clarke came around, gracelessly agreeing to vote in favor of the measure—but only because the Democrats had made it a partisan question and were solidly opposed. He would, he said, personally vote against it in August, but Ells took the occasion to announce that Clarke had thoroughly obliterated any "difference of opinion . . . between himself and the republican party."[22]

Republicans who recently had been Democrats exhibited the strongest impulse to express themselves on matters of slavery and race. They had devoted, after all, far more reflection and reappraisal to these matters than those who had made the ideologically easier shift from the Free Soilers or Whigs. Excepting Penn Clarke, the most vocal moderates in the convention proved to be three ex-Democrats.

George Ells was one. Nine years Clarke's senior, Ells evidently felt qualified to remind the younger man of his duty. Thin, beardless, tousle-haired, Ells turned a solemn, even melancholy expression to the camera's eye in 1857. Although a Yankee by birth, he (like Clarke) had grown up in the

South, in this case Virginia, where he had seen enough of "slavery in its mildest forms" to learn to hate it ardently. He later fled to Ohio, where he became a Liberty party activist, taking an important role in the party's national convention in 1847. He had once been an attorney, but after settling in Davenport he turned to a more congenial occupation as a bookseller. From the writings of Thomas Jefferson, Ells said, he came to realize that the term "democracy" meant "equal and exact justice to all men." That had helped him to intellectualize his hatred of slavery, and—although he worried a bit about being *too* far "in advance of public opinion"—to emphasize civil rights. He chided J. C. Hall for denouncing "the whole negro race as immoral." "I have seen, Sir, as much moral worth under a dark, as I have ever seen under a white skin," he said, "and that [too] among that degraded class, called negro slaves." And when a Democrat spoke of his "trust in God" that he would never favor school integration, Ells labeled the gentleman's trust badly misplaced, remarking that if he wished to thank "the author of his implacable and bitter prejudices against color, he should be thankful to the prince of darkness, for he rather than his Maker, was the author of that feeling."

Ells's most interesting observation was his contrast of free-state with slave-state forms of antiblack attitudes. "There is no doubt sir, but what there is a prejudice universally existing here at the north against color. I feel it myself," he admitted, "and so does almost every other man." But he did not stop (as R. L. B. Clarke had done) with this confession; he went on to suggest that such prejudice was actually a kind of abstraction. He hypothesized an encounter with a free black man: "At the first thought, I feel a repugnance to him, but the moment he approaches me as an intelligent being I forget that he is black. I believe that is the experience of most northern men." But something quite different pertained in the South. "Southern men have no prejudice against color; with them it is the condition"—the servile status of most African-Americans—that provoked prejudice. Southerners, in fact, seemed predisposed to grant *free* blacks a kind of rough equality, and on the whole, Ells implied, that was the healthier situation.

"If slavery were abolished in Kentucky, or any other southern state," a northern black had once told Ells, "I would go there at once, because I prefer to live among a people that have no prejudice against my race." That, said Ells, ought to disprove fears that the repeal of Iowa's black code would bring a flood of colored migrants. He consequently viewed the question of suffrage reform not "as a practical one in this State," but rather as a matter of "carrying out a consistent rule of right action." And should Iowans reject it in the forthcoming referendum, "let the decision so remain until we can convince the people that they are wrong." To George Ells it seemed as uncomplicated as that.[23]

A second moderate and ex-Democrat, John T. Clark, also spoke at length. The balding, gaunt Waukon lawyer had spent most of his life in the Burned-Over District, first as a farmer, then reading law part-time for eight years, finally at age forty-two removing himself and family to a village practice just below the Minnesota line. Clark strongly agreed with Ells that color prejudice was not innate. It did not exist, for instance, among Europeans—witness the recent reception abroad given the prominent ex-slave Frederick Douglass. But Clark extrapolated Ells's diagnosis of southern attitudes to all white Americans, North and South, and appended a uniquely historical explanation for its rise.

Although he had been reared a Democrat "of the strictest sect," John Clark had always believed "that the negro by nature is just as good as the white man." He thought it true that "the negro in this country, as a general thing, is degraded," but he held this to be owing "not to any defect in his nature, but to the unnatural position which through generations the negro race has been compelled to occupy in the world." Anticipating the Afrocentric argument of a later era, Clark said his reading had led him to understand that "there was a time when this same race was on a level with the rest of mankind, and when, in fact, [its members] excelled in the arts and sciences." The slave trade, however, had destroyed the indigenous civilization of Africa, and "it is no wonder that you find the African the ignorant and degraded being that he is. But you may take the history of any other people in the world where they have been oppressed and ground down for ages, and you will find the same results will follow." American blacks had been similarly "deprived of the very first attributes of humanity. They have had their manhood torn from them; the image of God in which they were created, has been stripped from them, and they have been dragged to the earth and trampled under the iron heel of slavery."

John Clark deeply regretted the "feeling of revenge, hatred and malice" held by Democrats "against a man because he is colored." Those who would discriminate had surrendered "to a prejudice unfounded in principle, and unfounded in reality except from the fact of its growing out of the unnatural position in which we find a certain class of men." As for black laws, Clark agreed with Ells that "we live in a progressive age" in which such measures everywhere were being overturned. He deplored having voted against amending the bill of rights so that no person would be disqualified from giving evidence. He had been induced to cast that vote, Clark explained, "against my own convictions of what was right," and would not again support any proposal he thought designed to discourage black residency. "I am not in favor as an individual of the emigration of blacks to this State," he confessed, "and I am opposed to it so far as I can do so legitimately and properly." But he explained neither the basis for his position on in-migration nor how he would discourage it.[24]

A third moderate and former Democrat did explain his views. A New Jersey native, John A. Parvin was among the convention's several old-time Iowans; he had crossed the Mississippi in 1839 and had lived in Muscatine ever since. At forty-nine he was still a sternly handsome man. "His tall form, rather clerical dress, grave manner and rigid morals," wrote one who knew him, "always reminded me of a Puritan." A deeply religious Methodist, Parvin had served in the 1850/51 legislature and had voted against black exclusion. But much of his 1857 behavior on race-related issues was a response to the pressure he felt from his town's interracial civil rights lobby. Though personally opposed to black suffrage and unwilling in the convention to alter the suffrage clause, he had nevertheless pledged himself to work for a referendum. Otherwise, Parvin's racial attitudes mainly expressed themselves in terms of the school question, the improvement of public education being—besides temperance—his lifelong concern.[25]

All convention Republicans apparently agreed with Penn Clarke that public education was a civil right, but disagreed on the question of racially integrated schools. For example, A. H. Marvin, a farmer, had been reared in the heart of the Burned-Over District, had attended integrated country schools, and saw no reason to fear them. But Harvey J. Skiff, a banker, also came from the Burned-Over District—and had graduated from Amherst College and then read law with Millard Fillmore as well. Skiff opted strongly for segregated schools.[26]

John Parvin, the convention's expert on educational issues, initially favored Marvin's position. Although he now termed himself a farmer and civil engineer, Parvin until his thirties had been a teacher. It was a matter of some pride that he had once supervised an integrated school: "no person in the neighborhood, in that county, thought it was wrong. The colored children were there; it was necessary to educate them; so they sent them to school; and I, as the teacher, took as much pains with them as with the whites." Parvin's experience in a second community had differed painfully, however. A young mulatto boy requested and was granted admission to Parvin's school, but had attended for only two days before white parents demanded that he be expelled. "As I was a stranger there," Parvin recalled, "and not able to fight the whole neighborhood, I dismissed the young man; told him that he could not come; and I had to tell him the reason. He went away crying." The encounter still haunted him. If he had it to do all over again, "I should stand against the neighborhood. I would teach the boy, and let all the rest leave, if they chose."

The failure of a motion that the public schools be "free of charge and open to all" evidently suggested to Parvin the necessity of compromising with segregationist delegates. He said he had no objection to legislatively mandated separate systems, but did not welcome that option. "We are too sensitive upon this subject. The assumption of prejudices, where they may not exist, I think is wrong." He thereby implied that school integration best be left strictly to local school boards. And it was a good measure of Parvin's influence that, in the end, all Republicans voted against imposing segregation by organic law.

As for racism, Parvin conceded its influence. "I think I have my prejudices against them. . . . My prejudice is such as to lead me to desire that they shall not be left in this country, because I do not think their presence would be advantageous to either of the races. I am, therefore, a colonizationist." But his remarks also reflected the distinction between masses and individuals that George Ells had described: "I will, for myself, judge a man by his head and his heart. . . . If he has 'a heart that can feel for another's woe,' [and] has intelligence, he is a man and a brother. I care not what his color may be."[27]

Finally, there were the six Republican conservatives. Most impressive among them was a fledgling politician whose rising star would—within seven years—light his path all the way to chairmanship of the powerful House Judiciary Committee in Washington, D.C. "That young man is an intellectual giant," one Democratic delegate later observed of James F. Wilson, "and displayed great power in the debates of the convention." Ohio-born, an apprentice harnessmaker turned lawyer, only three years an Iowan, stocky, clean-shaven, with close-cropped hair that made him look even younger than his twenty-eight years, Wilson, despite the convention's mild animus against excessive activism by its junior members, turned out to be its most vocal Republican. His personal feelings toward African-Americans, however, remained hidden, perhaps in deference to his political ambitions vis-à-vis a southern Iowa constituency strongly opposed, he said, to "any change of the old Constitution in relation to the races." His most eloquent statement, in fact, was not anything he said, but was rather his introduction, with virtually no explanation, of the politically unnecessary amendment that would so brutally bias the outcome of the 1857 referendum. James Wilson's positive contribution to the struggle for black equality—his influential words and actions on behalf of the Thirteenth Amendment and of suffrage reform in the District of Columbia and of the Civil Rights Act of 1866—awaited his elevation to Congress.[28]

John Edwards, a Chariton lawyer, was the one conservative Republican moved to expound his racial views. At age forty-two, in his convention portrait he looks open, earnest, eager to please. The offspring of a Louisville slaveholding family, Edwards while still a young man had conceived an obsessive hatred of slavery and had moved across the Ohio River to escape it. On later inheriting slaves from his father's estate, he not only freed them but gave them property with which to start life anew in the

North. In 1853, after serving two terms in the Indiana legislature as a Whig, he came west.

Edwards felt he knew black people. "I have played with them; I worked with them until I was seventeen or eighteen years of age. It was the custom where I was born and reared." And having been "educated with all the prejudices of the slaveholder," he made it clear that antiblack attitudes were "the prejudices resulting from the degraded condition of that race" rather than antipathy to color as such. Even in the North, said Edwards, the association of color with slavery continued to damage the rational perception of blacks. "There is a prejudice in the community against that unfortunate race, from the fact that their brethren have been held in bondage, and scourged, and driven by the lash. . . . And we say they shall not enjoy rights with us here, except just so far and no farther."

A Democrat accused Edwards of sounding much more egalitarian on the convention floor than in committee, and the gentleman from Lucas County did seem ambivalent, content to blame his southern Iowa constituents for aspects of his behavior unacceptable to the Republican moderates he probably deemed in charge of the party. For example, Edwards could "cordially endorse" the principle of nonwhites' giving evidence while yet opposing the proposition itself. "I am not willing, upon the grounds of expediency, . . . to shock the moral sensibilities of those who entertain prejudices against that unfortunate race of people." But three weeks later, in the second roll call on nonwhite testimony, Edwards, like several other Republicans, reversed himself. As to suffrage, however, he pronounced himself "satisfied with that portion of the constitution as it now exists," apparently troubled by the notion that political power might not be good, somehow, for blacks themselves. "I do not know whether it would be an advantage or not to the negro to confer upon him the right of suffrage," he said, and reiterated the sentiment several times.

Edwards, in short, could not escape the genteel paternalism created by his Kentucky upbringing. He seemed unable to conceive of blacks being empowered by absolute civil equality to work out their own destinies; his warmest hope was instead that "means will be devised to ameliorate the condition of this unfortunate class of people." Like John Parvin, he favored colonization, but not because the prospect of a major black presence discomfited him; rather, it was that expatriation to Liberia seemed to him the only politically feasible means of liquidating slavery.[29]

III

It is, of course, impossible to know if this handful of active and vocal convention Republicans typified the state's entire breed. But certain consistencies suggest a consensus on race-related issues that may have extended at least to the party's middle-level leaders who, through the nominating process, had sent the delegates to the Iowa City gathering and to whom the delegates would return, no doubt with an enlarged sense of party solidarity and ideological definition.

No Republican delegate had offered remarks asserting the innate inferiority of blacks. Several may privately have held to that belief, but any impulse to air it appears to have been repressed in deference to an interpretation of black inferiority as socioeconomic, not biological or cultural. Race prejudice was deemed to be fundamentally a negative psychological response to the generally low status of blacks. Those who, like most Democrats, consciously held to the delusion of innate inferiority did so, it was felt, because that is what they had been taught. Therefore, prejudice—or more properly its manifestation in *de jure* racial discrimination—could be politically overcome by strenuous arguments opposing the idea of natural black inferiority and stressing that blacks' status inevitably would rise with the removal of discriminatory restrains. Finally, it was generally thought that a person afflicted by race prejudice should restrain himself from *behaving* as a racist. At the same time, however, so long as one could justify it on other than blatantly prejudicial grounds, colonization was an increasingly respectable solution for those uncomfortable with the potential social complications of a biracial civilization.

On March 5, 1857, the gentlemen of the convention voted on the new constitution as a whole. Four Democrats—George Gillaspy, Edward Johnstone, William Patterson, and Daniel W. Price—sided with the Republicans; Gillaspy and Patterson warned that they yet might oppose the instrument in the forthcoming referendum. J. C. Hall, on the other hand, while voting to reject the new constitution, hinted that he might well support it in August. The ever-articulate R. L. B. Clarke then tested the patience of the delegates until called to order for exceeding his time. Ed Johnstone and Penn Clarke sparred briefly over the state mental hospital's location at Mount Pleasant. Finally, on John Edwards's motion that all personal differences among the gentlemen "be sunk in oblivion and forgotten from and after this date," the delegates rallied to this thought. President Springer reserved the last words for himself, offering a gracious little speech appropriate to the moment of separation. "Our task is done," he said. "The work we have been sent here to perform is completed. The results of our labors and deliberations we commit to the people and to history. The judgment of both we may abide, I think, with undoubting confidence."

A month later, on the first Monday in April, Democratic candidates captured two of the three political offices in dispute that spring—their party's first statewide electoral victories in nearly three years. Had the people, if not history, already spoken in judgment?[30]

Vox Populi

9

Iowa's arctic winter of 1856–57 took its toll in many ways. Early in March, out beyond the line of general population advance, a band of hungry and demoralized Santee Sioux vented its rage on an isolated settlement of Iowans at Spirit Lake, butchering thirty-two hapless children and adults before retreating into Minnesota, terrorized hostages in tow.

But for most Iowans the season's woes had less to do with their safety than with the agricultural fate of what was yet to be named the Corn Belt. Once again nature had demonstrated that no variety of winter wheat known to them—not Mediterranean, not Red or White Chaff Bald, not Red Chaff Bearded, not Black Sea, not Yellow Lamas, not Soft Siberian, not White or Canada Flint, not China, not Early May, not Golden Chaff—would survive Iowa's prairie winters. With autumn's planting gone, farmers itched to get into their fields to sow substitute crops of spring wheat. But spring came late. Ice an inch thick formed in ponds and puddles on the night of April 10. One week later the heavens shed nearly a half a foot of snow. As far south as Muscatine on the first of May not a green thing was yet in sight.

"How are you enjoying these dark cold spring days?" George W. Ells inquired of his late constitutional convention colleague William Penn Clarke. "For myself I . . . hope I have seen the worst specimen of the article or I shall be tempted to seek a warmer climate even at the expense of enduring the sight of the peculiar institution."[1]

I

Politics, to Republican loyalists, seemed as woefully backward as the season. The offices at stake in April's election were nothing most rank-and-file partisans, after Frémont's resounding conquest of Iowa, could get very excited about, and early reports suggested that only about half the state's voters had bothered to turn out. And so lacking in interest did local officials deem the results that three weeks later various county returns still drifted into the secretary of state's office. The precise outcome would not be known until May's official canvass.

James W. Grimes felt entirely optimistic. The governor's principal concern remained the forthcoming referendum on the new constitution. Since adjournment of the convention he'd talked to four of its Democratic stalwarts, all of whom assured him that there would be no organized opposition to ratification in heavily Democratic southeast Iowa. "I am convinced," Grimes wrote Samuel J. Kirkwood, the Iowa City businessman now serving as chairman of the state central committee, "that the new constitution is destined to be popular and that it will be adopted by an overwhelming majority." The Democrats had been boxed in by the nonpartisan nature of the proposition, he thought, and "are too shrewd to be driven into opposition to it." The new constitution should carry in August by twenty to twenty-five thousand votes.

After April's election, which Grimes prematurely reckoned a narrow Republican triumph, the governor felt moved to reassert that "the new constitution will be adopted by an overwhelming majority." But a niggling concern had entered his calculations, and he scaled down his earlier estimate of the ratification majority by five to ten thousand votes. The Democrats, whose constitutional convention delegates had threatened to politicize Republican support of racial impartiality in school funding and in the courts, had indeed availed themselves "of the cry of negro evidence [and] negro equality," Grimes reflected. "The fact is," he wrote Kirkwood, "there was more capital made against us on the score of the new constitution at the recent election, than there ever can, or will be again. We have sustained the shock of their attack & we shall now rally for the victory."

But Grimes spoke much too soon. On May 7 the state canvassing board confirmed that the Democrats had captured the posts of state superintendent of public instruction and register of the state land office, while the Republicans took only the directorship of the Des Moines River Improvement Commission. Pleased Democrats read the official outcome not only as a first step in their political reconquest of the state, but also as validating their strategy of attacking the new constitution on racial grounds. The Democrats in his area, the Republican ex-conventioneer John Edwards complained to Penn Clarke, "have calculated their recent success to be in consequence of the unpopularity of the new Constitution. All their cry is the making of negroes better than white men."[2]

As spring gave way to summer, the Democrats devised a critique of the new constitution that excoriated its provisions on banks, on corporations, and on state debts. But their early mobilization of a white backlash against the constitution and its "codicil," as the black suffrage proposition came to be called, remained their most reliable argument against exchanging the old constitution for the new.

Republicans responded with two arguments. They followed Grimes in insisting that the document had been a bipartisan product and thus deserved the warm support of all right-thinking Iowans regardless of party. And they resolutely distanced themselves from suffrage reform, terming that proposition, in the minutes of one local Republican gathering, "no part or parcel" of the new constitution, "but as a supplement, upon which every man is free to express his own judgment." The Republican editors of the Lyons *Mirror* offered perhaps the clearest expression of the desire to disclaim party responsibility for the measure:

> The opponents of the new Constitution attempt to connect with [it] a proposed amendment to the article on the right of suffrage; but that is clearly unjust and unfair. . . . It does not go with the new Constitution; and was only submitted to the people, on a separate vote, to gratify the wishes of a small, but a respectable portion of our people, who were desirous of recording their votes in favor of admitting the negro to the right of suffrage. No persons expect it to carry: the body of the Republican party, as well as the Democratic party, will vote against it.

A subhead in a Keokuk newspaper tartly emphasized the distinction: "NO NIGGER EQUALITY IN THE CONSTITUTION."

In May a printed circular issued by a committee of black Iowans announced that a colored convention would meet in June "for the purpose of taking into consideration the proposition now before the people, shall the word white be struck from the new Constitution?" According to Muscatine's Republican editor, to whom Alexander Clark handed a copy of the announcement, "It is expected that the convention will appoint speakers of their own number to canvass the State, and address the people in favor of [this] proposition." The editor cautiously approved. "No harm can result from a discussion of this great question of human rights," he wrote. "We hope these advocates for the colored race will not be insulted or derided in any part of the State, but will be listened to with candor. If they can succeed by fair means in convincing a majority to vote for the proposition, we shall cordially acquiesce."[3]

Within a month, however, black suffrage had been defined as a political orphan, the unwanted progeny of Republican indiscretion. No evidence suggests that a special gathering of Iowa's African-Americans convened in June, but if it did the prospects for effectively influencing the forthcoming referendum vote must have appeared so bleak that no black speakers actually took the field. It was not, even Alex Clark might have agreed, the moment for bold strokes that would serve no purpose but to help cripple support for the new constitution and the gains—the very limited gains—it offered blacks.[4]

By July, as the Democratic assault on the new constitution escalated, Governor Grimes detected another crisis: his strategy of characterizing the document as bipartisan had been a serious mistake, unintentionally luring many of the party faithful to assume that Republicans could be as officially neutral on the constitution as on its codicil. In Lee County, for example, delegates to a local convention expressed their determination to vote for the new organic law, but opposed making it a test of loyalty. A resolution that would have done so, their secretary reported, was taken up and "warmly discussed at some length. Several gentlemen opposed [it] on the ground that the Republican party did not wish to make the adoption or rejection of the constitution a party question, but to leave every member free to vote upon it as he pleased. This view prevailed." Grimes estimated that the proposition would receive a thousand-vote majority in Lee County despite this happenstance, but lack of a coordinated party stand left too much to chance. "I think it would be well to have our confidential friends in the several counties written to by the Central Committee," he advised Kirkwood, "urging them to cause *for the constitution,* or whatever the words are, to be printed on all our tickets."

Before the advent of the Australian ballot, with its nonpartisan listing of candidates, in Iowa as elsewhere local political parties printed the election ballots, willingly undertaking this task as a means of encouraging straight-ticket voting. On election day loyal Republicans accepted and dutifully deposited in the official ballot box long, narrow "slip tickets." Such ballots displayed only the names of Republican nominees, ballots that in a national election year might extend over a foot in length and designate up to thirty candidates—from the party's choice for President of the United States down to its selection for township constable, and often followed by one or more referendum propositions. Loyal Democrats deposited similarly contrived tickets.[5]

But referendum propositions could appear on a party-printed ballot in either of two ways—depending on whether or not the party had taken an official stand on the question embraced. What Grimes feared was that in counties such as Lee, where local Republicans had refused to take an official position on the new constitution, proposition 1 would appear at the tail of the Republican ballot in this format:

New Constitution
YES.
NO.

A voter would "scratch" one alternative with a pencil, leaving the remaining option as his choice. But Grimes now wanted the state central committee to insist that county organizations print Republican ballots that included only one choice on proposition 1:

New Constitution—YES.

In this case a Republican loyalist would have no alternative to Yes short of scratching the official option and substituting his own. This ballot form would have to be prepared covertly, however, since the state's Democrats would surely publicize it as proof that proposition 1 was a very partisan measure indeed.[6]

With only two weeks left before the referendum, the Republican central committee responded to Grimes. Over the signature of ex-Congressman James Thorington, the committee's newly appointed secretary, a confidential circular mailed to all county committees laid it on the line. "The adoption of this Constitution is of more importance to the Republican party in Iowa than the members of the party are generally aware of. It is unquestionably a Republican measure—got up by a Republican Legislature—put forth by a Republican Convention. Now it rests with the Republicans of Iowa to . . . act in concert and sustain a measure that will aid to sustain them as a party." Thorington briefly touted the referendum as an opportunity to rid Iowa of an organic law "that has and will ever continue to cramp the energies of a State like ours." But the rest of his message attempted to inject some good old antislavery passion into the ratification campaign, raising an issue on which the party's conservatives and radicals stood in militant accord: the Fugitive Slave Law. Thorington boldly conceded that section 10 of the new constitution's bill of rights, guaranteeing jury trials in all cases involving the "liberty of an individual," contradicted the federal statute. "If we had no other reason for voting for it," he urged, "this section alone should be sufficient to determine our action."[7]

II

Meanwhile, suffrage reform languished. The question most earnestly at issue was not whether the codicil would fail, which nobody doubted, but rather whether the codicil—proposition 2—would take proposition 1 down with it. There proved to be, as August approached, no limits on how low Democratic campaigners seemed willing to stoop. "Do you wish to see your children sit side by side with little *darkies* in our common schools?" asked the editor of the Keokuk *Times*. "If so, vote for the new Constitution. Do you wish to pay taxes to support a mongrel pauper population? . . . Do you wish to amalgamate with negro bucks and wenches? If so, vote for the new Constitution." And a widely disseminated letter by a prominent Fairfield Democrat assured readers that three hundred black Ohioans planned to emigrate to Iowa the instant they learned of the new instrument's ratification.

In the face of such intimidating nonsense, the state's Republican editors showed little appetite for discussing the merits of a racially impartial franchise. That, plus the tactical need to disentangle questions of minority rights from those legitimately raised by the proposed organic law, steered most of them into a strict neutrality on proposition 2. Some fifty Republican newspapers appeared regularly in Iowa in midsummer 1857, of which about half still exist in complete enough runs to allow characterization. The managers of sixteen of the twenty-two surveyed avoided the issue entirely or retained an uneasy neutrality on black suffrage, refusing to specify their personal voting intentions or to prescribe how others should vote. Theirs were some of the most influential urban dailies in the state, including both of Dubuque's Republican papers, the Burlington *Hawk-Eye,* the Muscatine *Journal,* and the Keokuk *Gate City.*[8]

Back in April the Marion *Linn County Register,* edited by a Methodist clergyman of old Yankee lineage, had endorsed suffrage reform, but after an ownership change nothing further was heard from it.[9] By election eve only two Republican editors publicly favored the codicil's passage, although neither announced it with fanfare. James L. Enos published his Cedar Rapids *Times* within a few miles of Marion and may have taken heart from its antislavery constituency. A former Chicagoan, an ex-Know Nothing activist and regionally prominent educational reformer, Enos admitted that "we for one might wish that this proposition could carry." The other, Jacob Rich, a one-time medical student from Philadelphia who had come west for his health, edited the weekly Quasqueton *Guardian* in a strongly antislavery settlement thirty miles north of Cedar Rapids. Rich noted in June that the new constitution, despite what the Democrats were saying of it, did not inaugurate impartial suffrage: "The Constitution may be adopted and yet the negro have no more rights than he has at present. We confess that this is our great objection to it. We wish the Convention had itself struck out the word [white], and left it as it should have been, an unequivocal instrument of freedom." Rich then avoided the subject until three days before the election, when—abruptly and without explanation—he printed his preferred version of the local Republican ticket with the following addenda embracing the two propositions:

New Constitution—YES.

Shall the word "White" be stricken
out of the article on the "Right of
Suffrage?"—YES.[10]

At the other end of the spectrum four newspapers directly or implicitly encouraged Republicans to oppose black suffrage at the polls. The most important was the Davenport *Daily Gazette,* its editors announcing their own strong intentions to vote No. The managers of the Lyons *Mirror* followed suit, rationalizing their hostility with the prediction that 90 percent of the voters would reject the measure. The editor of the Montezuma *Republican* angrily emphasized the same prognosis.

But it was young Wells Spicer of the weekly Tipton *Advertiser* who aired the Republican media's most outspoken opposition to suffrage reform, thereby filling a role on the party's ultra right that Jacob Rich played on its far left. An ex-schoolteacher from Illinois, Spicer had been elected a county judge on the Know Nothing ticket, had participated in both the American and the Republican state conventions in 1856, and had been one of the short-lived party's most important publicists before surrendering to Republicanism. Both he and Rich, at age twenty-four, managed village newspapers in east-central Iowa. There the similarities ended. History, in its capriciousness, would forget the one and grant the other minor immortality. Jacob Rich achieved an imposing if ultimately anonymous identity as dean of his adopted state's political journalists and as a chief strategist of the Republican political elite that ruled Iowa in the Gilded Age. Wells Spicer won imperishable notoriety as the justice of the peace who mysteriously exonerated Wyatt Earp from a murder charge after the gunfight at the O.K. Corral.[11]

But in late July of 1857 what set apart these two youthful editors were polar attitudes on the franchise. Whereas Rich included only a Yes alternative in his version of proposition 2, Spicer published the single ticket offering Republicans only the converse option:

> Shall the word "white" be stricken out of the article on the "Right of Suffrage?" NO.[12]

III

August 3, 1857, broke warm and muggy. James Chamberlin, a native Pennsylvanian who farmed on the Big Bottom floodplain northwest of Iowa City, read the wide morning sky and spent the early hours cutting five acres of grain for a neighbor. "That Finishes his Wheat," he wrote with satisfaction in his diary that night as a steady drizzle pecked at the farmhouse roof. And then he all too laconically summarized the rest of his day: "Went to the election AM. Rained PM."[13]

Nearly eighty thousand Iowans had joined Chamberlin at the polls. There they granted the new constitution a razor-thin majority—51 percent of their ballots—while overwhelmingly rejecting suffrage reform (table 9.1). Thus Iowa's new organic instrument took effect with an unamended, whites-only definition of the electoral franchise. So much for the outcome. To understand the behavioral components of the referendum vote, how-

Table 9.1 Results of the referendum of August 3, 1857[a]

	Proposition 1: New constitution	Proposition 2: Equal suffrage
Yes ballots	40,811	8,479
No ballots	38,686	49,267
Roll-off[b]		21,751

Source: Secretary of State, "Election Records" (microfilm copy, University of Iowa Libraries), reel 1.

a. The statewide totals as given in the original source have been corrected by reaggregating its county returns.

b. The number of ballots for and against the new constitution minus the number of ballots for and against equal suffrage.

ever, we need to know more than James Chamberlin's diary or any other narrative source tells us of the individual choices pondered by rank-and-file voters that day.

Only some two-thirds of all Iowans eligible to vote actually turned out for the referendum. Chamberlin had finished work in time to attend the polls, but the wheat harvest caused hundreds of farmers to shirk civic duties in favor of agricultural imperatives. And, as might have been expected of any off-year electoral proceeding, overall voter turnout fell 17 percentage points from that recorded in Iowa's exciting presidential contest of 1856.[14]

The Iowans who did turn out in August 1857 were probably most interested in the concurrent election of candidates for judge, sheriff, and other courthouse jobs at stake. Local races, after all, would have been the subject of much partisan discourse on streetcorners, over backyard fences and in country lanes, in taverns, in courthouse corridors. The referendum propositions, in contrast, probably aired mainly in the press (of which not every voter was a reader) and in formal appearances by regionally prominent politicos.[15] But the evidence from nearly three hundred townships for which both election and referendum returns are extant indicates that substantially all those voting for county judge—95 percent—also cast ballots on the new constitution. This suggests that local elective offices and proposition 1 were everywhere carried on a unitary ballot. While the election itself, then, may have drawn the typical voter to the polls, once he had supported the nominees of his choice inertia would prompt him also to declare himself opposed to or in favor of the new constitution.

But fewer than three-quarters of those who voted on proposition 1 went on to vote for or against black suffrage. The physical setup of the referendum balloting to some extent accounts for this. The late convention had specified that the second referendum proposition "be separately submitted to the electors of this State for adoption or rejection in the manner following—Namely: A separate ballot . . . to be deposited in a separate box."[16] Unlike proposition 1, therefore, the suffrage codicil could not be printed on the regular election ticket. Thus while it was easy enough for a voter to cast a unitary ballot on party candidates and on the constitution, voting on proposition 2 required that he repeat the process, take a second piece of paper in hand, use a pencil to scratch out either the Yes or No option, and drop it into a supplementary ballot box. Almost twenty-two thousand voters present at the polls did not take the extra trouble, compounding the effect of the low referendum turnout. In all, only half of Iowa's estimated eligible voters actually cast ballots on proposition 2.

Opposition to suffrage reform is the more complicated aspect of the referendum behavior of 1857, since a hostile voter could express himself electorally in more than one way. The most emphatic option was to vote No on the new constitution: its defeat would make the alteration of its whites-only suffrage article a moot point. And, in fact, the postelection comments of some Republicans attributed the closeness of the result on proposition 1 to the frightening success of the Democrats' racist appeal. "One voter to our certain knowledge," fumed Muscatine's Republican editor, "remarked upon depositing his ballot *against* the Constitution that *he* was opposed to educating his children in the same schools with 'little darkies.' " Many others, he said, "actually believed that the question of allowing negroes to vote was involved with that of adopting the Constitution, and voted against the latter on that account." The managers of the Davenport *Gazette* also waxed indignant. "Even in this county," they charged, "certain Democrats, and leading Democrats, stood at the polls, and shamelessly told those Republicans whose close labors in the shop or field had prevented them from fully informing themselves, that if they voted for . . . the new Constitution, they would vote for eating, sleeping and voting with *niggers*—that they would vote for placing the negro on a perfect equality with the white man, for giving him the same rights of citizenship with themselves."

But the insistently racist voter could underscore his opposition to black suffrage by *also* casting a No ballot on the codicil, "voting against the amendment and the Constitution both," as another editor remarked, "so as to be sure to scotch the heresy one way or another."[17] And a good plurality of those voting on the new constitution—about 42 percent—did just that, rejecting both propositions (table 9.2).

It will be recalled that James F. Wilson's convention amendment to the new constitution made it possible to cast a perfectly legal No on suffrage by voting on proposition 1 without voting at all on the codicil—or, in the professional jargon of politics, by "rolling off" on proposition 2. Some

Table 9.2 How voters on the new constitution responded to equal suffrage in August 1857 (estimated percentages)

	Yes	No	Rolled off	
Pro-constitution	9	22	20	
Anti-constitution	2	42	5	
				100

Regressions: 1857 proposition 1 returns × 1857 proposition 2 returns (county N = 77).

25 percent of all who had voted on proposition 1 did avoid black suffrage. But rolling off may not always have been a proxy for straightforwardly voting No, in that the equivalency of the two options had been imperfectly explained. As one badly confused village editor, a Democrat, wrote of Wilson's amendment on the eve of the referendum: "Here is a clause which has late become a subject for discussion in lyceums and no one has as yet been able to give an explanation of its meaning." After the election, in fact, the officials of every county but one tallied up the No votes without first augmenting them with the roll-off. And the state canvassing board later did precisely the same.[18]

The Yes vote on suffrage reform—15 percent of the total if counting only the Yes and No ballots, 11 percent if calculated as intended by the Wilson amendment—is also a bit complex. At most polling places, without benefit of the privacy afforded in modern elections, it must have taken considerable moral courage to disregard the amusement or disgust of onlooking friends and neighbors in depositing Yes ballots in the separate boxes required. In James Chamberlin's township, where a log schoolhouse sheltered the polls, only four men had both the impulse and the gumption to vote Yes. And in nearly one-fifth of the townships for which returns are extant, proposition 2 received no approval at all. Nor did it in one entire county—Montgomery—in the southwest corner of the state. In each of another dozen counties it won less than ten votes. And that it received any support whatever seemed downright astonishing to some. An editor at Bloomfield, in extreme southern Iowa, could not believe his eyes. "For striking out the word 'white,'" he marvelled of the Davis County returns, "there was twenty-eight votes!"[19]

But Iowans' colossal rejection of black suffrage in 1857 is not the whole story. On the Minnesota border 190 miles north of Bloomfield proposition 2 registered its only major victory. Mitchell County's voters cast 264 Yes ballots and 242 No ballots, with eight men rolling off. Impartial suffrage thus won 52 percent of the ballots cast, and it carried 44 percent of the county's estimated electorate.

First settled only five years earlier, Mitchell vibrated to the noise of a land boom. In May 1857 four of its townships being thrown on the market drew some two thousand strangers and one million dollars in gold to the land office at Osage, a bustling townsite its proprietors had named not for the famous Indian tribe but in honor of O. Sage, a Massachusetts banker. That may have been Mitchell County's last flirtation with lower forms of humor. The famous writer Hamlin Garland would spend his adolescence there within the hard rural culture that begot his dour portraits of nineteenth century farm folk. And there the great social inquisitor Thorstein Veblen would gloomily rusticate, academically unemployable, in the seven-year interim between Yale doctorate and matriculation at Cornell. And very much later a Mitchell County school teacher, Jane Elliott, casting about for a pedagogically immediate response to Martin Luther King's assassination, would devise the famous "blue eyes/brown eyes" classroom exercise so that white children might experience to some degree the dehumanizing effect of biologically based prejudice.[20]

But in the 1850s Mitchell's distinctive political feature was the domination of its electorate by three earnestly Republican nativity groups—New Yorkers (31 percent of the total), New Englanders (19 percent), and Scandinavians (11 percent)—in proportions very much larger than in Iowa's electorate at large. And seven church edifices reflected a religious makeup complementing its political demography: three Congregational, two Baptist, one Methodist, one Lutheran. Yankee and Yorker evangelicals had long been vulnerable to antislavery and other programs of social reform. As for Mitchell's Lutherans, these were immigrant Norwegians of the Saint Ansgar settlement who had followed their influential pastor, the Rev. Claus L. Clausen, west from Wisconsin in 1853. A major figure in the establishment of Norwegian Lutheranism in America, the dynamic clergyman was also Iowa's first Scandinavian-born legislator, a racially progressive Republican in the 1856/57 general assembly, and he would soon gain prominence as a fierce critic of temporizing on slavery within the Midwest's politically conservative Norwegian Synod. The evidence suggests, in sum, that Mitchell County was unique in more than its prosuffrage behavior.[21]

Suffrage reform also carried at least twenty-two individual townships (map 9.1).[22] These smaller prosuffrage voting units prove, on examination, to have been somewhat more rural—and thus economically more homogeneous—than the state as a whole, 74 percent of their male residents classifying themselves as farmers as against 57 percent for Iowa at large. They were also much more strenuously Republican: 64 percent of their estimated eligible voters had favored Frémont in 1856 as against 42 percent statewide. And their aggregate voting population diverged most importantly from the electorate at large by harboring a proportional sur-

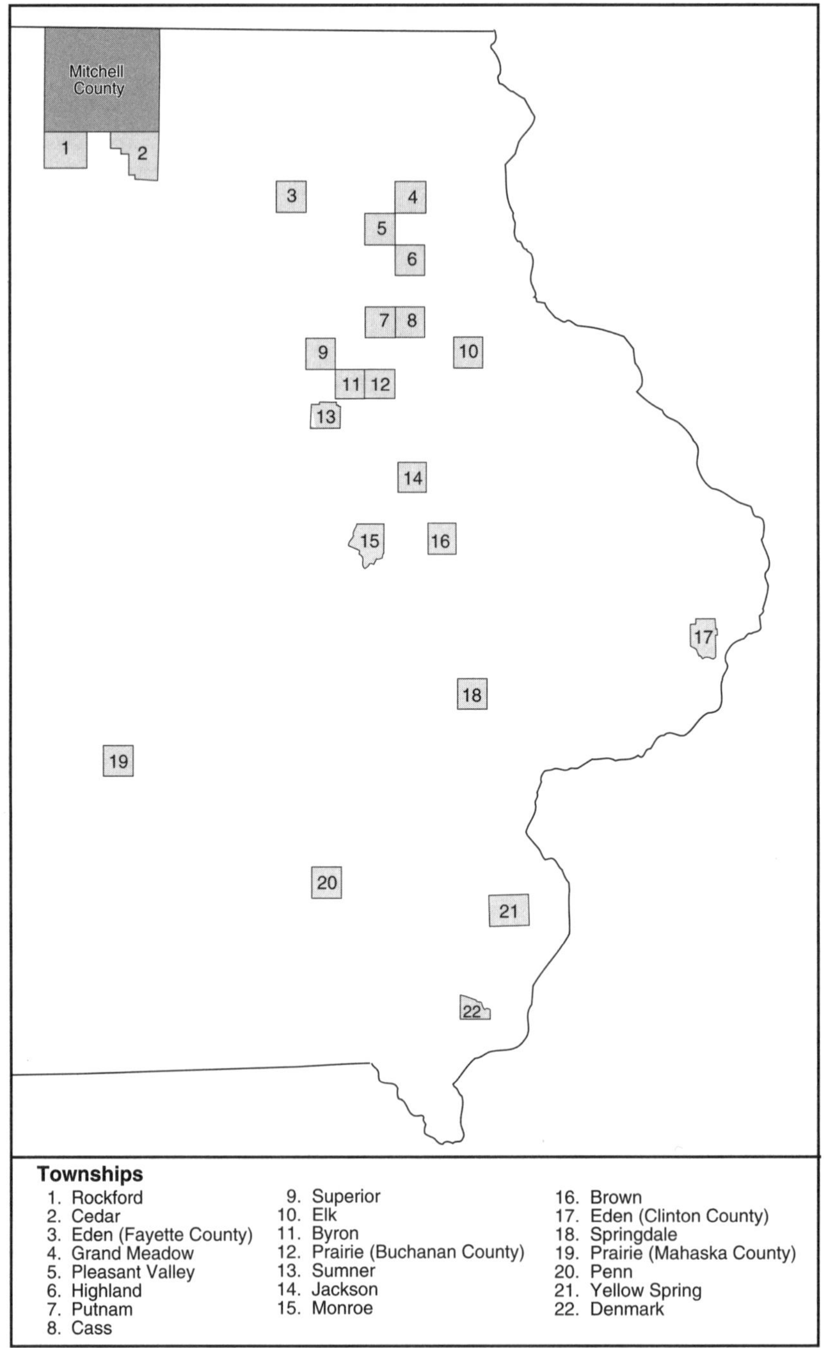
Mitchell County
1
2
3
4
5
6
7
8
9
10
11
12
13
14
15
16
17
18
19
20
21
22
Townships
1. Rockford
2. Cedar
3. Eden (Fayette County)
4. Grand Meadow
5. Pleasant Valley
6. Highland
7. Putnam
8. Cass
9. Superior
10. Elk
11. Byron
12. Prairie (Buchanan County)
13. Sumner
14. Jackson
15. Monroe
16. Brown
17. Eden (Clinton County)
18. Springdale
19. Prairie (Mahaska County)
20. Penn
21. Yellow Spring
22. Denmark

Map 9.1 Prosuffrage voting units in 1857.

plus of New York and Ohio natives at the expense of southerners and Germans.[23]

Half these prosuffrage townships have some additional attribute plausibly associated with racially progressive behavior. Two happened to be the former Liberty party strongholds of Denmark and Yellow Spring (how the other old abolitionist constituencies voted on proposition 2 we do not know). Three others were predominately Quaker communities, one of them, Springdale, soon to be the site of John Brown's new military base. Seven others formed a semicircle around either Marion or Quasqueton, although neither village itself yielded prosuffrage majorities. The other ten progressive townships mainly lay scattered across recently settled northeast Iowa between Floyd and Clinton counties. Native New Yorkers formed voter pluralities in all ten, with transplanted New Englanders making up the second largest contingents in five. But none of the ten seems to have been denominationally homogeneous. Local histories suggest that various mixtures of Baptist, Congregational, Disciples of Christ, Methodist, United Brethren, and Wesleyan Methodist influences predominated, with only the last two sects being uncompromisingly abolitionist.[24]

Interestingly, legislative voting on Thomas Hardie's resolution in the 1856/57 house of representatives had foreshadowed the prosuffrage inclination of these northeastern and east-central regions. Only six men, all Republicans, opposed the Hardie motion censuring civil equality in general and black suffrage in particular. Two of the six represented southeastern Iowa constituencies; one or both were Quakers. Of the other four progressive assemblymen, one represented Linn County, one Delaware, one Clayton, and one a large frontier zone embracing Kossuth, Cerro Gordo, Floyd, and five other northern counties.

In the same vein, the influence of prosuffrage sentiments in James Enos's *Times* and Jacob Rich's *Guardian* appears to be reflected in the Linn and Buchanan county returns. But elsewhere any such direct journalistic relationships are hard to discern. Prosuffrage Mitchell County's only Republican newspaper entirely avoided proposition 2, for example, while in adjacent Floyd County, which contained two prosuffrage townships, the managers of the Republican paper also refused to discuss impartial suffrage—and after the election applauded its statewide defeat. "It will be some time yet," they said, "before a majority of the people will become amalgamationists." Such disjunctive instances caution against overgeneralizing from editorial attitudes.

Although the twenty-two prosuffrage townships lay far from Iowa's centers of urban black population, in the case of rural Fayette County close proximity to the "colored settlement" did not alter racially progressive behavior on the part of unbiased whites. Jacob Wentworth Rogers, one of Fayette's prominent businessmen, campaigned for a county judgeship in August 1857 and, after he was publicly challenged on the point, admitted that he favored proposition 2. Describing local African-Americans as respectable folk who "associated with white people on equal terms," he argued that retaining the color line in the new constitution "would disgrace them—throw them out of the pale of society—which [is] wrong." Rogers won his race, and three local townships granted ballot majorities to proposition 2.[25]

The evidence from these uniquely prosuffrage units is principally of value in suggesting possible determinants of voter responses to proposition 2 statewide. Certainly party affiliation seems to have been the most inclusive indicator, Republicanism forming the broad ideological umbrella under which presumably all prosuffrage voters mustered—even though not all Republicans, of course, supported the codicil. Figure 9.1 plots each county electorate's percentage for Frémont against its percentage of Yes votes on impartial suffrage. A strong positive relationship would have been revealed by a gradually ascending cloud of points, indicating that as support for Frémont increased, so did the Yes vote. But the pattern suggests otherwise: the prosuffrage percentage, except in three instances, could not rise above 25 percent no matter how strong the vote for Frémont. But in progressive Mitchell and two other northern frontier counties, Cerro Gordo and Kossuth, support for black suffrage, in contrast, surpassed 30 percent, rising sharply in conjunction with quite modest increases in Frémont's strength.[26] All honor to the Republicans of these

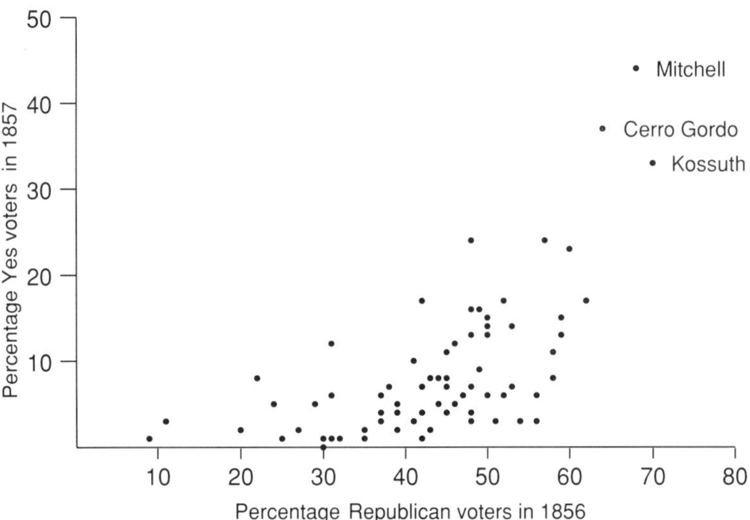

Figure 9.1 Frémont voters and black suffrage in 1857 (percentages are of estimated eligible voters).

Table 9.3 How the 1856 electorate behaved in August 1857 (estimated percentages)

	New constitution			Equal suffrage				
	Yes	No		Yes	No	Rolled off		Not voting
Republicans	26	3		10	5	14		10
Democrats	5	21		−5	31	0		7
Americans	4	3		1	3	3		2
Nonvoters	3	1		0	0	4		9
1856 ineligibles	−1	7		2	6	−2		0
			72				72	28

Regressions: 1856 presidential returns × 1857 proposition 2 returns, with three outliers omitted (county N = 70); a few estimates rounded down in order to equalize subtotals.

three "nonconforming" counties, but we must exclude them from the next analysis. It is Iowa's mainstream behavior that concerns us.

Table 9.3 summarizes the 1856 electorate's response to the 1857 referendum.[27] The breakdown of partisan voting on proposition 1 contains no surprises: Frémont supporters by a large margin favored the new constitution, while the Democrats strongly opposed it and Fillmore's American party voters split. Toward suffrage reform, understandably enough, Democrats registered an overwhelming hostility. But the Republicans' response to proposition 2, also understandably, was ambiguous. Frémont voters yielded twice as many Yes than No ballots, although about as many of them rolled off on proposition 2 as voted. The reason seems the same as historian Phyllis F. Fields gives for the roll-off in New York State's 1860 referendum: "Republicans antagonistic to both equal suffrage and the Democratic Party . . . refused to vote on the question of suffrage at all rather than gratify the Democrats by opposing it."[28] If we take into account the relatively large number of Frémont voters who did not even turn out at the polls in August 1857 the Republican fragmentation is strikingly precise: a quarter of Iowa's Republicans favored black suffrage, half either opposed it forthrightly or declined to cast ballots either way, and another quarter had been too busy—or not sufficiently interested—to turn out.

Few Republicans evidently felt *politically* obligated to vote Yes. Those who did support impartial suffrage, we may surmise, did so because of some additional attribute or impulse. Table 9.4 explores this question by summarizing the manner in which various population groups reacted to

Table 9.4 How various subgroups responded to equal suffrage in August 1857 (estimated percentages)

	Yes	No	Rolled off	Not voting	
The work force					
Farmers:					
Prosperous counties	3	21	3	4	
Middling counties	2	11	2	2	
Poorer counties	2	6	3	1	
Nonfarmers	1	7	11	23	
					102
Moral reformers and nonreformers					
Dry voters	6	−1	4	15	
Wet voters	−3	29	−3	−3	
Uncommitted voters	−2	2	14	12	
1855 ineligibles	6	15	3	5	
					99
Churchgoers					
Methodists (downstate)	0	13	4	3	
Presbyterians	2	1	5	9	
Methodists (upstate)	3	7	2	3	
Roman Catholics	−1	7	−1	8	
Baptists	1	6	4	1	
Congregationalists	2	2	1	3	
Disciples of Christ	0	7	−2	1	
Quakers	1	−1	2	1	
Lutherans	1	1	1	0	
Episcopalians	0	2	1	0	
Miscellaneous	−1	0	2	1	
					102
Voter nativity groups					
New Englanders	3	−3	3	5	
New Yorkers	2	9	1	0	
Pennsylvania	0	10	0	6	
Ohioans	5	0	6	8	
Indianans	1	5	1	−1	
Southerners	−3	14	3	2	
Other native-born	1	2	−2	2	
Britons and Scots	1	2	−1	1	
Irishmen	−1	4	0	5	
Germans	0	7	3	−3	
Other foreign-born	−1	−1	2	2	
					100

Regressions: 1856 occupations × 1857 proposition 2 returns (county N = 70); 1855 liquor referendum returns × 1857 proposition 2 returns (township N = 59); 1860 church seats × 1857 proposition 2 returns (county N = 43), with groups listed in descending order of size in 1860; 1856 voter nativities × 1857 proposition 2 returns (township N = 186).

proposition 2. The breakdown by occupation (first panel of table 9.4) reveals, for one thing, that voter turnout for the referendum was far lower in town than in the countryside, the wheat harvest notwithstanding. Non-farmers who had avoided the polls in the late presidential election made up about 13 percent of the 1856 electorate; in August 1857 this percentage soared to 23. That finding dispels any supposition that town-dwellers might have felt more threatened by the prospect of black equality than Iowa's farmers did: they seem, in fact, to have been little energized by the referendum.[29] Secondly, farmers of all categories opposed proposition 2, although somewhat less vehemently in the state's poorer counties. As noted in chapter 7, the farmers of prosperous and middling areas had supported Buchanan in 1856, while farmers of the poorer frontier counties had given a slight plurality to Frémont—a position congruent with a more moderate stance on the codicil.

Moral reformers, in this case those who had voted dry in the 1855 liquor referendum, differed substantially from their wet opponents on black suffrage (second panel of table 9.4). Iowa's abolitionist and Free Soil visionaries had equated prohibition and civil rights, investing both with a potential for emancipating the human spirit from moral bondage. Their conservative opponents, in dismissing all social reforms as emanating from a misplaced idealism, tended to equate the two as well. But these positions were also closely tied to political partisanship, the drys predominately Republican, the wets Democratic. Therefore, the drys suffered from the same large roll-off and low turnout characteristic of Republicans in 1857; while they cast more Yes than No votes on black suffrage, *most* of them did not vote at all on the issue. Meanwhile, wets predictably rejected suffrage reform in no uncertain terms. Also not surprising is that the uncommitted (those who had not voted in the 1855 referendum) mainly rolled off or did not turn out in 1857. More ominous was that new voters, those who had become members of the electorate between 1855 and 1857, overwhelmingly rejected admitting blacks to the franchise.

As for Iowa's churchgoers, none but the Presbyterians and the Quakers—two thoroughly Republican groups—appear to have cast more Yes than No votes. As we saw earlier, the state's largest denomination, its Methodists, had recently subdivided into downstate and upstate units. The bifurcation was for associational convenience, not because of major internal divisions on slavery or any other issue.[30] Yet the two groups differed importantly in response to proposition 2—just as they had in the 1856 election. Upstate Methodists had almost yielded a Frémont majority, and they rebuffed suffrage reform much less lopsidedly than their downstate brethren. The greatest hostility to proposition 2, indeed, came from Iowa's downstate Methodists, its Catholics, and its Disciples of Christ, who granted the codicil virtually no Yes votes. All had been Democratic in 1856. Among the larger denominations the greatest percentage-point disparities between their levels of support for Frémont and for proposition 2 were to be found among the three groups that had given absolute majorities to Frémont—the Presbyterians, the Baptists, and the Congregationalists.

Voter nativity analyses, taking up where the ethnocultural consideration of specific counties and townships left off, depict estimates derived from a 186-township sample (third panel of table 9.4). Of the sample's larger voter groups native southerners, Pennsylvanians, Irishmen, Germans, and Indianans cast the most emphatic No votes. All but the Germans had registered as Democratic in 1856, so their racially conservative 1857 behavior requires no further explanation. That also holds true for the German-born Democrats.[31] But the similarly unanimous conservatism of German-born Republicans invites special scrutiny. Evidence from the several townships in which Germans made up over a third of the electorate supports the statewide estimates: black suffrage fared only a trifle better among Republican than among Democratic Germans.[32]

The Germans' three Republican newspapers are not extant for 1857. But much may be inferred from the rhetoric of both major parties in the late 1850s, locked as they were in a political struggle—in the Hawkeye State as eastward—for the loyalty of numerically important German-American voters. From Iowa's Democratic newspapers and speakers Germans learned that if Republicans everywhere had their way, as in Massachusetts, blacks would vote while recent immigrants would have to suffer a lengthy probation before being admitted to the electorate. From Republican spokesmen Germans learned that if Democrats everywhere had their way, as in Kansas, immigrants would be relegated to the same low status as blacks: neither group would be permitted to vote. Both arguments thus played to the status anxieties of the ethnically very sensitive Germans, and neither was likely to provoke any sympathy at all for equal rights.[33]

Ohio-born voters, overwhelmingly Republican in 1856, divided. About three-quarters of those voting on proposition 2 cast No ballots. This sharp division reflected the situation of Ohio itself. Unlike New England or the South, each of which can be said to have achieved something of a public consensus on racial issues, the Buckeye State had been agitated for decades without much resolution. Iowa's Ohioans, like their former friends and neighbors back home, might be largely Republican, but their specific attitudes toward blacks would depend on other attributes—whether they hailed from the abolitionist Western Reserve, for example, or from racially distressed Cincinnati and other downstate regions, or whether their denominational preferences were strongly or weakly antislavery.[34]

Only New Yorkers, New Englanders, and Britons and Scots definitely cast more Yes than No ballots. In some respects transplanted Yorkers resembled Ohioans on proposition 2. While, as we have seen, a number of townships dominated by voters of New York birth favored impartial suffrage, the two civil divisions of the township sample *most* heavily populated by native Yorkers rejected proposition 2, albeit by a narrow margin in one case.[35] New York's citizens, like Ohioans, had long experienced the divisive issue of civil rights. They soundly rejected black suffrage in an 1846 referendum, and they would do so again in 1860 and in 1869. But half the counties in the Empire State's Burned-Over District yielded prosuffrage majorities in the second referendum, and nearly all of them in the third, thus justifying the region's reputation as a great reservoir of reformist impulse. Eight "banner" counties, five lying within the District plus three situated in extreme northeastern New York, went prosuffrage in all three referendums.[36] As if to demonstrate the strength of the regional factor, 106 capsule biographies of New York-born men who settled before 1858 in Iowa's several prosuffrage and strongly Yorker voting units reveal that half had been born within the Burned-Over District. But, even more cogently, the native counties of 22 percent had favored suffrage reform in 1846, a percentage that rose to 43 in 1860 and 63 in 1869. Indeed, almost one-third of the biographees originally hailed from New York's egalitarian banner counties.[37]

These findings, tentative as they are, suggest that Iowa's New Yorkers had something of the same capacity for favoring equal rights as the localities from which they had come, although the correlation was by no means perfect. For instance, the settlers of the two antisuffrage Yorker townships also came predominately from the Burned-Over District and from counties that ultimately approved black suffrage, although far fewer had been born in the prosuffrage banner counties. Perhaps the most important point is that few of Iowa's Yorkers apparently originated in relentlessly antisuffrage downstate New York.[38]

That native New Englanders supported impartial suffrage more consistently than any other group is no surprise. Phyllis Field nicely summarizes the scholarly consensus on Yankee attitudes. In New England, she notes, "economic, political, and religious institutions had been structured so as to place primary responsibility on the individual for his personal conduct and economic and political well-being. This emphasis on individualism helped foster an egalitarian ethic, for 'rank' and 'privilege' were the antitheses of individual endeavor." As with rank and privilege, she reasons, so with the color line. Historian Paul Kleppner adds that transplanted New Englanders held most firmly to their ethnocultural behaviors when they felt themselves in conflict with other groups. Presumably there was nothing like an equal rights referendum to bring a sense of embattled righteousness to the typical Yankee, although New Englanders' low 1857 turnout remains unexplained.[39]

Typically present in smaller numbers than their Yorker neighbors, Yankees ranged between 8 and 29 percent of the voters in twenty-seven Iowa townships that Empire State natives dominated by percentages of 31 to 60, and manuscript census schedules document considerable intermarriage between the two groups. This social interpenetration of Iowa's Yankees and Yorkers may have been particularly consequential in 1857: back in the Empire State freshly settled Yankee communities were the most religiously evangelical, the most caught up in social reform, and the most likely to favor equal rights.[40] Thus the Yankee/Yorker combination undoubtedly offered the suffrage codicil its greatest chance for success, but even among such settlers the racially impartial franchise was no more a sure thing than it had been, and was to be, back in New York State. Only when Yorkers and New Englanders together dominated a voting unit by over 60 percent, as they did in nine known cases, did black civil equality have a greater chance of winning than losing. Proposition 2 carried five such townships, lost three, and tied in one.

Just as in New York State native Yankees and immigrant Britons and Scots were the state's leading prosuffrage birthplace groups, so also on the trans-Mississippi frontier. Like the Yankees, Iowa's New British, as they are often referred to by historians, were, in Kleppner's words, "politically cohesive and strongly anti-Democratic." Famous for their deeply held religious beliefs, their strict observance of the Sabbath, their hatred of liquor, and their staunch anti-Catholicism, British immigrants were eager recruits for the crusade against slavery and white supremacy. In neither New York nor Iowa did their prosuffrage behavior depend on the sharp promptings of leaders. Like the Yankees, in both New York and Iowa the British voted for suffrage reform, one might say, long before it became politically respectable to do so.

Of all the variables examined here, which are the most important in explaining the Yes vote on black suffrage in 1857? A statistically generated summary is only partially satisfactory because many probable causes are not easily reducible to machine-readable form, and because, as explained in appendix A, the data employed here are housed in separate county and township files. Nevertheless, of the county-level variables, the most important in accounting for variation in the Yes vote is the Democratic percentage in 1856, the Yes percentage strongly correlating—negatively, of course—with Buchanan's electoral support. The second most important variable is the percentage of northern Iowa Methodists in the population. Third is Frémont's percentage. Together these three variables explain 53 percent of the Yes vote's configuration. Among the township-level variables Frémont's percentage ranks first, the percentage voting Yes on the new constitution second, and the percentage of New York-born voters third. Together they explain 46 percent of the variation.[41]

In both files, therefore, the special saliency of 1856 presidential preferences and of New York-born Methodists is certified. Yet about half the variation in the Yes vote remains unexplained. That is not surprising, given the large latitude for random variation stemming from the unique complexity of the referendum voting process, the apparent dependence on local issues to generate turnout, and the Republican strategy of consigning proposition 2 strictly to the dictates of the individual conscience.

Critically underscoring the Republican elite's larger responsibility for the debacle of August 1857 is what happened three months later, when the voters of neighboring Wisconsin went to the polls and cast ballots on suffrage reform. As in Iowa, the proposition failed—but by a far closer margin of 41 to 59 percent. In contrast to its Iowa counterpart, Wisconsin's Republican party had expressed formal hostility "to the proscription of any man on account of birthplace, religion, or color," and—again in clear contrast—most of its newspaper editors had urged referendum support of the measure. And unlike in Iowa, a strong majority of Wisconsin's rank-and-file Republicans subsequently favored impartial suffrage. Such comparison strongly suggests that a causal relationship between leadership messages and voter responses more than anything else explains the 1857 referendum behavior of Republicans in both states.[42]

IV

But the end was not yet to the season's preoccupation with race: Iowans would go to the polls a third time in 1857 to elect a new governor, a new lieutenant governor, and members of the 1858 general assembly. Gathering in Iowa City two weeks after the August referendum, Republicans honored Governor Grimes's desire for retirement from the state house (and ascension to United States Senate) and nominated the popular Ralph P. Lowe, a lawyer from Ohio who had been a Hawkeye for nearly twenty years, to replace Grimes. To balance the ticket geographically they chose as Lowe's running-mate an unknown newcomer from upstate, a Methodist ex-college professor drawn west because of ill-health. From his farm in Mitchell County, surrounded by fellow New Yorkers, he had responded in August 1857 to proposition 2 in much the same way as had the plurality in Iowa's only prosuffrage county. "ORAN FAVILLE, Republican candidate for Lieut. Governor," wrote a scandalized Democratic editor, "*voted to* **Strike out the word White,** *and glories in it!!!*"[43]

A week later, as if in deliberate reaction, Iowa's Democrats nominated two southern-born ultra conservatives, Ben M. Samuels, who had led the fight against exclusion law repeal in the 1854/55 legislature, and George Gillaspy, who had favored black exclusion in the late constitutional convention. And the Democratic platform sternly criticized the newly approved constitution, labeling it "anti-democratic, unjust, and containing principles that tend to subvert the distinction between the white and black races." While their opponents deemed banking and slavery extension the leading issues, the Democrats, seeking to make the October election yet another showdown on equal rights, concentrated on proving that Iowa's Republicans were hell-bent on school integration. At least one candidate for the state senate, John A. Parvin, appears to have been defeated simply because of the positive statements on black educational aspirations he uttered in the 1857 constitutional convention.[44]

In October Lowe and Faville both gained office, and Republicans retained their command of both houses of the legislature. But the Democrats' assault on school desegregation resonated unpleasantly in the 1858 assembly, which met for the first time at the new state capital, Des Moines. The aborted educational reform bill introduced in the previous legislature and amended to permit the racial integration of a school only with "the unanimous consent of the householders of the district," now reemerged with the amendment in place. Seven senate Republicans sought to alter "unanimous consent" to "consent of a majority," but found themselves badly outnumbered, and four holdovers who had forthrightly opposed the amendment in 1857 now refused even to support its liberalization. In the house a similar effort won the votes of only twelve Republicans, although the majority, as in 1857, refused to mandate absolute segregation.[45]

This local-option veto over racially integrated public schools became the last addition to Iowa's black code. Constructing that code had been the work of twenty years. Destroying it would be a matter of another twenty-two years, decades in which the mighty national experience of war and reconciliation would force Americans everywhere to rethink the significance of civil equality in a multiracial democracy.

POSTBELLUM

II

Battlegrounds

10

At the village of Tabor, Iowa, one late November day in 1857, John Brown calmly unveiled a scheme of frightening portent. To the men of his tight inner circle he disclosed plans for an armed incursion into the Commonwealth of Virginia that would touch off a black revolt and bring America's long-festering slavery issue to a final resolution in fire and blood. A few weeks later he quartered the nucleus of his guerrilla band among the Quakers of Springdale Township, where that winter, as their leader scouted the East for funds, the young men studied army manuals, drilled, and reflected cautiously on their fate.

In 1858 Brown briefly returned to Iowa to lead a diversionary raid into western Missouri. And in 1859, ready at last, he struck. His party, which included four Iowans, captured and briefly held the federal arsenal at Harpers Ferry before it was overpowered by U.S. marines. Two Iowans died fighting, one was hanged with Brown, one escaped and returned home.

Samuel J. Kirkwood, the current governor of the Hawkeye State, delayed the young fugitive's extradition to Virginia until he could disappear again. The governor's calculated inaction, part of a gigantic wave of sympathy toward the martyred abolitionists that swept the North, helped fuel a slave-state hysteria that universally regarded Brown's raid not as an isolated incident, but as the opening round in a secret campaign by which extremists hoped to foment slave uprisings throughout the South.

In 1860 the Republican party's presidential candidate, Abraham Lincoln, won all the electoral votes of all the free states except New Jersey. But, disbelieving Lincoln's promise that his administration would not disturb slavery where it existed "legally"—that is, within the South itself—southern nationalists withdrew their states from the Union and formed the Confederacy. When they fired on Fort Sumter, Lincoln declared them to be in rebellion and requested the activation of militia units to help preserve the Union by force. And so the war came.[1]

Before it was over Iowa had contributed fifty-eight regiments and four artillery batteries to the war for the Union. In the western theater of operations, where the Civil War's outcome was largely decided, some 76,000 Iowans served in every major campaign. Indeed, Iowans came to believe that they had sent more men per capita to the Union army than had the citizens of any other loyal state. This happens to be wrong. Yet 49 percent of Iowa's prewar white military-age population did take up arms, a record outclassed by only four other northern states.

Such a level of participation had its price. Thirteen thousand Iowans—19 percent of those who went off to war—never came home or returned only to die. Besides suffering heavily on southern battlefields (one of every four Union soldiers slaughtered at Shiloh, for instance, was an Iowan), the men and boys of Iowa regiments died from disease in a proportion unequalled by troops from any other northern state. This was because they had been deployed almost exclusively in the West. While Virginia was the Civil War's great killing ground, it was the lower Mississippi Valley that proved so lethal in other respects. However computed, a larger proportion of Iowans in uniform met death than did the fighting men from most loyal states.[2]

Alexander Clark thought it fair that Iowa's black population, increasingly augmented by self-emancipated African-Americans fleeing Missouri, should share the lethal burden of what, by military necessity, was becoming a war to free the slaves. In 1862 he wrote Governor Kirkwood, offering to raise one or more black military companies for service with Iowa's regiments in the field, only to be admonished (by Kirkwood's secretary) that white troops would not tolerate a racially integrated army. Yet the southern-born governor, hamstrung both by prejudice at home and by the timidity of a federal government hesitant to arm blacks, strongly agreed with Clark's intent. "When this war is over & we have summed up the entire loss of life it has imposed on the country," he complained to the War Department, "I shall not have any regrets if it is found that a part of the dead are *niggers* and that *all* are not white men."[3]

In 1863 Washington reluctantly yielded to the routine formation of colored regiments, and black combat troops demonstrated their courage at the battles of Port Hudson, Milliken's Bend, and Fort Wagner. But black recruitment in Missouri presented special difficulties. Because the state was no longer officially in rebellion, Lincoln's Emancipation Proclamation had no application there. And Missouri's Unionist but proslavery governor, attempting against all odds to prop up the old labor system, remained sensitive to the economic interest of "loyal" slaveholders who opposed the military enrollment of their men.

In June 1863 the War Department authorized an antislavery colonel at Saint Louis to enlist Missouri blacks—but only those who had been legally emancipated or who had escaped from disloyal owners. The colonel's attention then strayed to southern Iowa, where considerable numbers of black Missourians had taken refuge. He applied to Kirkwood, overcoming the governor's doubts that a regiment's worth of adult black males could be found within the state, and Kirkwood in turn petitioned the War Department. Permission for a recruiting station at Keokuk immediately followed. From that place enlistment parties ransacked the towns and villages of southern Iowa and, in a clear disregard of instructions, of northern Missouri. The outcry from both Unionist slaveowners and conservative military men ended these activities, but not before its white officer corps had mustered into service six companies of the "1st Iowa Volunteers (African Descent)," later designated the 60th U.S. Colored Infantry Regiment. With its remaining four companies later recruited at Saint Louis, the unit's enlisted personnel mainly admitted to being Missourians by birth or residence. Only 287 (32 percent) claimed to be Iowans.

They did not include the irrepressible Alex Clark. Appointed sergeant-major of the regiment, its top enlisted rank, he flunked the physical exam because of a leg disability. But he was nonetheless asked to present to the regiment its national banner, sewn by the black women of Keokuk and Muscatine. Clark thought it the proudest moment of his life.[4]

Iowa's black regiment served its time in eastern Arkansas, a military backwater where Union troops held a few well-defended urban strongpoints while the countryside belonged to an elusive foe. The 60th Infantry fought only once—on its first time out from base. In July 1864 eighty of its men, two understrength companies originally mustered at Keokuk, formed part of a reconnaissance force of 360 black infantrymen, accompanied by two field guns and their black crews, that suddenly found itself trapped by a thousand of Jo Shelby's Confederates at Wallace's Ferry. Taking cover behind a railroad embankment, they fought desperately amid the suffocating heat and smoke, and the ear-splitting crash of musketry. After a severe four-hour fire fight that killed the commander and three other officers, the detachment was on the brink of being overrun when it was reinforced by Union cavalry. Still grossly outnumbered, the troops executed an orderly withdrawal, alternately marching and skirmishing, carrying the wounded with them, back to Helena. (Three men, too badly injured to move, were left behind and finished off by the rebels.)

"During the whole fight the colored men stood up to their duty like veterans," reported the white battery commander, "and it was owing to their strong arms and cool heads, backed by fearless daring, alone that I was able to get away either of my guns. They marched eighteen miles [without a break], fought five hours, against three to one, and were as eager at the end as at the beginning for the fight. Never did men, under such circumstances, show greater pluck or daring." "Will they fight?" chortled district headquarters. "Ask the enemy." "The colored troops fought like veterans," emphasized the district commandant, "none flinched."[5]

While losing only its white regimental adjutant and 11 of its enlisted personnel in combat, the 60th U.S. Colored Infantry lost no fewer than 332 members—an appalling 29 percent—to disease. But in this, as in their allocation mainly to garrison and fatigue duties, Iowa's African-American regiment replicated the typical black military experience in the Civil War.[6]

I

Billy G. Haun's law also died in the war. In the later antebellum years the exclusion act had attracted little attention. In 1856, possibly at the prompting of Keokuk's growing black community, a Methodist clergyman carried to the southern Iowa conference of his church a resolution unsuccessfully urging his colleagues to seek repeal of the measure. In 1857 Keokuk's city marshal commenced a wholesale expulsion of blacks under the Haun Act's terms. The ensuing notoriety, coming at a moment when the business community was preparing to receive an excursion party made up of eastern dignitaries and railroad investors, forced the marshal's campaign to be quietly shelved.

In 1858 George McCoy, who had failed to obtain a straightforward vote on the Haun Act's repeal in the 1856/57 senate, tried again. And once again most racial progressives preferred that the statute not be publicly challenged lest it provoke a new law of unambiguous legality: five senators who had opposed school segregation joined their conservative colleagues in burying McCoy's effort in committee. Four years later, responding to several petitions, conservative legislators either ignorant of the Haun Act or wary of its legality unsuccessfully sought passage of a new exclusionary measure.[7]

A courtroom test of the exclusion law finally came at the state capital in *Webb* v. *Griffith* (1863). Archie P. Webb, a young Mississippi-born ex-slave, recently had arrived from Arkansas, where, as it happened, Keokuk's Gen. Samuel R. Curtis commanded all Union forces. Although other western generals, writes Ira Berlin, "hoped to win the support of Confederate slaveholders by limiting military interference with slavery, Curtis . . . favored the slaves over their masters." Responding to congressional legislation authorizing commanders to "confiscate" blacks used in aid of the rebellion, Curtis began issuing certificates of emancipation to slaves who had been conscripted by the Confederate army as laborers. This produced a "general stampede" into his lines. Within a year more than one thousand Arkansas freedmen had emigrated to northern states via Saint Louis.

Archie Webb made it all the way to central Iowa, only to encounter the wartime revival (there as in all other midwestern states) of exclusionary angst. In January 1863, arrested for violating the Haun Act, Webb lay behind bars in Des Moines pending his agreement to pay a fine and leave the state. He instead instituted a suit against the county sheriff, and by agreement of attorneys for plaintiff and defendant the cause was continued as a *habeas corpus* hearing at the next term of the Des Moines district court. There Webb's lawyer argued that the 1851 law was nonexistent because it had not been published, as required, in the Mount Pleasant *Iowa True Democrat,* and that in any event the law violated both the state and federal constitutions. Webb's chief witness was Dr. James Wright, now Iowa's secretary of state, a racial progressive who had once organized a petition drive favoring suffrage reform. Wright willingly testified that his official files held no proof that the exclusion law had been legally promulgated. Opposing counsel then debated the other issues at length.

Judge John Henry Gray, a native Marylander, rendered a decision that acknowledged "the very considerable interest manifested by the public and the importance necessarily attached to this case." He explained that just because the law had not been enforced for twelve years did not negate its legality, and he dismissed Samuel L. Howe's refusal to publish the act in his Free Soil weekly as too small a technicality to invalidate it. But Gray did hold that the Haun Act violated provisions of the old Iowa constitution in effect in 1851, most specifically by authorizing unreasonable seizures and by failing to provide jury trials for those accused of illegal entry. And, as Hawkeye critics of exclusionary legislation had long claimed, he held it to violate the privileges and immunities clause of the United States Constitution guaranteeing the interstate movement of "citizens." No blanket interdiction of African-Americans could be legal, he ruled, since in some New England states they were without question full citizens, and as such could not be denied entry into Iowa. And if some free blacks, then all free blacks, since the legalities must weigh equally on all. "The law under which the plaintiff was arrested," Gray said, "is inoperative and void."[8]

Defendant's attorneys served notice of appeal to the Iowa supreme court, but the case was not immediately heard. With the ultimate fate of the Haun Act apparently pending, during the winter of 1863–64 the sheriff's office in Des Moines—and local lawmen elsewhere in Iowa—again began applying its provisions. An excited Secretary of State Wright carried word to the general assembly that a number of blacks had been confined in the Polk County jail for having violated the law. "Noticing that I took an active part in the House proceedings," recalled Samuel McNutt of Muscatine, "he asked that I devise some means to stop those arrests and set free the persons now imprisoned." McNutt introduced House File 19, a bill to repeal Haun's handiwork, the very next day.

A veteran legislator from abolitionist Crawfordsville moved to table, but for most Republicans the time seemed long past when it was best to leave well enough alone. H.F. 19 passed with a preamble acknowledging doubts "on the part of some" as to whether the Haun bill had ever become law, but there was no dispute that its enforcement "has been attempted contrary to the wishes and intentions of a large majority of the people of this State." Repeal would "set all doubts at rest." Even one house Democrat voted in favor of passage. In the senate three additional Democrats voted Yes. "This act," McNutt recollected, "made Iowa, in reality, one of the free states of this Union."[9]

II

By the spring of 1865, as the war ground to its unglamorous close in the Carolina swamps and the trenches circling Petersburg, the question of black suffrage had vexed Congress for over a year. Originally, like the unqualified abolition of slavery, the issue had belonged exclusively to antislavery activists. But now suffrage reform enjoyed friends in Congress. So-called Radical Republicans—only a few of them prewar abolitionists—argued that voting rights for former slaves were the only sure means to avoid a national catastrophe: returning the rebellious states to the complete control of their white populations. Impartial suffrage promised the only plausible defense of black life and property from the vengeance of dispossessed slaveholders, reports of which already had begun appearing in the northern press. It would also help safeguard the freedpersons against their *de facto* reenslavement by a resurgent southern aristocracy. And a southern black electorate would surely vote Republican, which might insure the continued hegemony of the Republican party in Congress. But, misreading President Lincoln as conservative on black enfranchisement, Radicals felt he required convincing that the North wanted suffrage reform as part of any general program of southern "reconstruction."[10]

Certainly the most dramatic means of so convincing Lincoln would be popular repeal of the whites-only voting provisions of most northern state constitutions, including that of Iowa. To this end the editor of the Davenport *Gazette* inaugurated a campaign to overthrow Iowa's 1857 outcome on equal rights. Those who favored a racially impartial franchise, wrote Edward Russell, "have increased to a mighty host. The people of Iowa are now, we doubt not, fully prepared to abolish the odious enactment by which color of the skin is made a test of fitness to exercise the elective franchise."

Born a Londoner of Scots parentage, Ed Russell had learned something of slavery at the age of six, when his father packed him off to a boarding school where the inmates suffered daily floggings by a sadistic headmaster and the random brutality of upperclassmen. Russell, according to his son, never completely recovered from the experience. In America, where the family emigrated in 1845, first to a forest clearing in New York, then to the open horizons of Iowa, young Russell immersed himself in the literature of the nation's leading issue. He became an uncompromising abolitionist, and had probably not yet reached his majority when Professor Howe published his first writings in the *Iowa True Democrat.* Soon he was also contributing occasional pieces to the Free Soil movement's Washington *National Era.*

In 1862 Russell assumed management of the Republican paper in Davenport, one of Iowa's foremost commercial towns. Like all good abolitionists, he urged immediate emancipation, the mobilization of black troops, and other policies far in advance of Lincoln's cautious approach to war. The administration nonetheless appointed him postmaster, a sinecure that helped him make ends meet in a tough river city that did not appreciate his intemperate radicalism. According to his son, "It became a popular outdoor sport to gather about the house at night, hurl stones at the door and imprecations in at the windows and cordially invite the 'damned nigger stealer' to come out and be hanged." Someone took a shot at him; drunken roughnecks twice invaded his editorial office; and a mob once "surged about our house with rope in hand, yelling its purpose to make an end at once of the damned Yankee." But Russell, who had survived the horrors of Hill House Academy, never faltered. Iowa's prominent prewar abolitionists had long since subsided from political roles. A latecomer, Russell successfully reanimated an abolitionist initiative inside Iowa's Republican party.[11]

In April 1865 the Lincoln administration appeared to be coming around. Three days before a white supremacist sent a bullet through the President's brain, Lincoln publicly hoped that the southern ballot could at least be extended to African-American war veterans and "the very intelligent" blacks. But Booth's shot elevated an unalloyed ultra conservative to the White House.

Pres. Andrew Johnson's announcement of a reconstruction policy lacking suffrage reform, together with a lukewarm local response to Russell's initiative, injected a new urgency into the Davenport journalist's demands. The autumn elections would be crucial to the process of amending the Iowa constitution, he noted, since they must result in a prosuffrage assembly majority on whose shoulders initial responsibility for the process would rest. "It is morally certain that the next Legislature will thus refuse or neglect to act," he urged in early June, "unless *previously unequivocally instructed by the people.*" But the people were not likely to pressure their legislative candidates without themselves having been instructed by the forthcoming Republican state convention. That, said Russell, "is the practical question to be decided on the 14th day of the present month at Des Moines."[12]

A week later Russell himself and at least 662 other delegates to Iowa's 1865 Republican convention gathered at the capitol, forming the largest deliberative body ever mustered within the state. Many delegates, according to one insider, had been on hand as early as three days before, so that politicking over nominations had concluded by the time the first gavel fell. A "good sprinkling" of office holders came as delegates: Congressmen Josiah B. Grinnell and Hiram Price, Lieutenant Governor Enoch W. Eastman, Adjutant General (and former New Hampshire governor) Nathaniel B. Baker, and Peter Melendy, United States marshal for the District of Iowa. Ex-governor Samuel J. Kirkwood and ex-Congressman James Thorington were there. Freshly demobilized military officers of high public standing included Gen. Marcellus M. Crocker, a war hero of soaring political prospects, and Col. James B. Weaver, a future Congressman and Greenback and Populist presidential candidate. Henry P. Scholte, patriarch of the Dutch colony at Pella and one of the party's most important ethnic leaders, future governor William Larrabee, and former journalist Jacob Rich also counted as notables. Besides Russell, important editors present as delegates included Frank W. Palmer of the Des Moines *Register,* Clark Dunham of the Burlington *Hawk-Eye,* and Charles Aldrich, lately of the Dubuque *Times*. Benjamin F. Gue of the Fort Dodge *Iowa North West* came as a delegate, but withdrew after agreeing to stand for lieutenant governor.[13]

At least nineteen delegates, among them Grinnell, Price, and Kirkwood, had been present at the creation of Iowa's Republican party in 1856, but only in Kirkwood's Johnson County delegation did such charter Republicans make up as much as a third of the members. At least five former Free Soil activists attended; the most prestigious among them was Muscatine's Henry O'Connor, now a Civil War combat veteran. At least one old Liberty party man, Gen. Hugh T. Reid, a war veteran whom the convention honored as one of its vice presidents, symbolized the Republicans' distant ancestry: the political abolitionism of the 1840s.[14]

Nor was the rank and file unrepresented. Each county had been permitted to send at least one delegate, but the weighting system that defined the size of each delegation gave the advantage to heavily Republican urban counties such as Scott, Lee, and Linn, which had been allotted the largest delegations: 34, 32, and 29 respectively. But distinctly nonurban Henry County—the motherland of Iowa's antislavery politics—followed close behind with 27. The convention's designers had sought to achieve the most scrupulous reflection possible of the state's grass-roots Republican strength. Only seventy-two of Iowa's ninety-nine counties actually sent delegations, however, and many consisted of fewer members than authorized. But whoever represented a county cast that unit's entire vote. Clayton County, allotted 26 delegates, for example, sent only 5. The rules permitted those 5 to cast 5.2 votes each to form Clayton's allocated ballots. Thus the 663 delegates found themselves entitled to a grand total of 879 votes.

A committee on resolutions, consisting of one delegate from each of Iowa's twelve congressional districts, was charged with divising the 1865 platform. Keokuk's George W. McCrary, a future Congressman and Secretary of War, may have been its most conservative member. As a prewar legislator, he had favored the virtual exclusion of black children from the public schools. But journalists Russell, Rich, Gue, and Palmer made up a racially progressive one-third of the committee; apparently some offstage intervention—probably by Congressman Price, Russell's powerful colleague in the Scott County delegation—had insured that these *particular* newspapermen had been named to the panel. Russell, of course, intended to make suffrage reform the most important agendum of the day. Rich, it will be recalled, had been uniquely prosuffrage in 1857. In 1858 Gue had voted in the legislature for integrated schools, and he had recently endorsed Russell's suffrage proposal. Palmer had been Iowa's first editor to suggest the merits of enfranchising black war veterans, and had reflected, if elliptically, on the eventual triumph of impartial suffrage throughout the land.[15]

Gue's withdrawal as a delegate diminished this prosuffrage nucleus, but perhaps not before Russell's plans had already gone awry. At the committee's noon caucus his proposal for an emphatic party endorsement of black suffrage failed to carry even the committee's egalitarians, who grew worried about the possible political costs. Russell would later recall "the tremor of the eleven prudent men in the Committee on Platform, when one Radical member would not abandon his conviction [in deference] to their fears." The progressives apparently abstained in the vote against Russell, but they helped pass a compromise whereby the committee agreed to a resolution 4 that approved black suffrage in principle. "With proper safe-guards to the purity of the ballot-box," it read, "the elective franchise should be based upon loyalty to the Constitution and Union, recognizing and affirming the equality of all men before the law."[16]

For Ed Russell that was not enough. The delegates reconvened at 2:00 P.M. After the nominations had been lustily approved, and the platform read from the podium to "enthusiastic applause," Russell, from the convention floor, proposed an addition to resolution 4: "therefore, we are in favor of amending the Constitution of our State by striking out the word 'white' in the article on suffrage." Someone moved to table. "This motion would have prevailed by a large majority," wrote Frank Palmer, had not the convention chairman ruled that a motion to table Russell's proposal would table the entire resolutions committee report. That forced a floor debate. "Many of the timid delegates were alarmed," Benjamin Gue remembered, "and made strong efforts to persuade Mr. Russell to withdraw his resolution." But Russell refused, making "a vigorous defense of his measure."

Several delegates then rose to challenge it. They included the freshly chosen chairman of the state central committee, Joshua Tracy, a lawyer who had voted against receiving Alex Clark's petition in the 1854/55 legislature. But far and away the most prestigious spokesman for the opposition was Congressman Grinnell, the urbane, nationally prominent clergyman and educator to whom Horace Greeley had given the immortal advice, "Go west, young man, go west." Interestingly enough, J. B. Grinnell was one of Iowa's most distinguished antislavery activists of the late 1850s. As a legislator, he had wavered on the schools question in those same years, first voting for racial integration and then reversing himself. But in the 1864 U.S. House of Representatives, as Iowa's only consistent Radical in Washington, he had led a doomed effort to add black suffrage to the aborted Wade-Davis bill, the Radicals' alternative to presidential reconstruction.[17]

Explains Gue: "Grinnell and many who opposed the Russell amendment were in favor of the principle for which it stood, but opposed a bold declaration for the reform as impolitic and liable to bring party defeat." The Congressman and others argued that many Republican voters, while strongly antislavery, opposed black suffrage, "and it was urged," says Gue, "that they held the balance of power in Iowa politics and that this amendment would drive them from the party." As another editor phrased it, Russell's motion "elicited a warm debate, many of those opposing it saying that the resolution as originally reported covered the whole ground, and it was making the question needlessly prominent to add the amendment." After Edward Stiles, a young attorney from southern Iowa, had reiterated the political peril inhering in Russell's proposal, Congressman Hiram Price could contain himself no longer. He rose to challenge these prognostications.[18]

Price at age fifty-one was the prototypical western Republican, a poor Pennsylvania farm boy who, by his own efforts, had risen to become a leading midwestern banker and railroad capitalist. Stiles terms Price "an old-time radical abolitionist," but this was a misapprehension. In 1846, two years after settling in Davenport, Price signed a petition calling for a "north-western Liberty convention," but that appears to have been his only flirtation with abolition. He remained a Democrat probably until 1854, when the Whig/Free Soil coalition embraced the two programs closest to his heart: resistance to slavery extension and passage of an antiliquor law. As longtime president of the state's foremost temperance group, Price helped draft the 1855 prohibitory law. The following year he was one of the most active members in the meeting that founded Iowa's Republican party. In 1861, as president of the state banking system, he proved instrumental in organizing financial backing for Iowa's early military buildup and became the impromptu paymaster for Hawkeye troops in Missouri. In 1862 the voters of his district elected him to Congress.[19]

Price not only possessed a political stature to be reckoned with, but was also a man not to be trifled with in public debate. "He was both fiery and formidable," says Stiles, "and no man ever left an encounter with him free of scars." Now, on the floor of the 1865 convention, Price unleashed "a very scathing and heated speech," recalled Stiles, "in reply to my own." Benjamin Gue recollected it as no less forceful. The Congressman, he says, "made one of the great speeches of his life. . . . Those who heard it will never forget the fervid eloquence, the sledge-hammer logic, or the powerful and irresistible appeal [that] poured forth in a torrent of righteous indignation that has seldom been surpassed." Although the speech "was entirely impromptu, and never reported or published," Gue remembered it as follows:

> The Republican party is strong enough to dare to do *right,* and cannot afford now, or at any other time, to shirk a duty. The colored men, North and South, were loyal and true to the Government in the days of its greatest peril. There was not a rebel or traitor to be found among them. They ask the privilege of citizenship now that slavery has been forever banished from our country.
>
> Why should the great freedom-loving State of Iowa longer deny them this right? Not one reason can be given that has not been used to bolster up slavery for the past hundred years. The war just closed has swept that relic of barbarism from our land; let the Republican party have the courage to do justice.
>
> I have no fear of the result in a contest of this kind. We shall carry the election and have the satisfaction of wiping out the last vestige of the black code that has long been a disgrace to our State.[20]

Adds Gue: "The timid delegates were shamed into silence." He thereby implies that no further remarks were to be heard from the conservatives. Stiles, on the other hand, says he "rejoined in the same spirit. The result was considerable heat in the convention."[21]

Two other notables also spoke forcefully in the amendment's behalf. One of them, the eloquent Henry O'Connor, "was probably [Iowa's] most popular political orator," says Stiles, but his words on this occasion have not survived. The amendment's other advocate, Lieutenant Governor Eastman, an eccentric ex-Yankee, also happened to be "a speaker of unusual force. . . . He was a master of sarcasm, and no man who knew him well," Stiles testifies, "ventured to invoke its withering shafts." Eastman earlier had amused the delegates by declining renomination in favor of "the next best man." Of his remarks on Russell's amendment we know only that he emphasized the hypocrisy in Iowa's disfranchisement of men who had served honorably with the 60th U.S. Infantry. "How can you insist that loyal negroes shall vote in South Carolina," he asked, "when you refuse to allow the colored soldiers of your own Iowa colored regiment to vote here?"

The delegates at last decided the issue in a roll call vote about which nothing more than the result is known: 513½ votes (58 percent) in favor of the Russell amendment, 242½ votes (28 percent) against, and 123 votes (14 percent) not cast. The political standing and oratorical talents of Price, O'Connor, and Eastman had carried the day against J. B. Grinnell and other patrons of equivocation. It had been one of those moments, as Michael Les Benedict has written of the national encounter with racism, "that . . . once again testifies to the strength rather than the weakness of the American egalitarian tradition."[22]

Gue always remembered it as a straight showdown in which "right prevailed over policy." Editor Palmer offered a somewhat more perceptive conclusion: "The Convention being thus brought to a direct vote upon the amendment, and being unwilling to stand committed even in *appearance* against the principle of negro suffrage, adopted the amendment by a large majority, and the universal expression of the delegates after the adjournment was that inasmuch as the issue must be squarely met, it might as well be met this year as next."[23]

III

In the decade between Bleeding Kansas and Appomattox, Iowa's Democracy had hemorrhaged. First its most angry opponents of slavery extension deserted to the Republicans. Then Fort Sumter and its aftermath split the party into war and peace factions, sheer patriotism and a repugnance for their Copperhead colleagues impelling many War Democrats to the party of Lincoln. Governor Kirkwood, Representative McNutt, Congressman Price, Lieutenant Governor Eastman, Generals Baker and Crocker, Colonel Weaver, Dominie Scholte, Messrs. Tracy and Stiles—to name just a few—had all once been Democrats. Even the politically imposing Jonathan C. Hall—he of the 1844 and 1857 constitutional conventions and the famous *Daggs* case—had finally abandoned ship. Democrats saw their once vigorous domination of the Hawkeye State shrivel to ten seats in the 1864 legislature.[24]

But in 1865 the surviving Jacksonians sensed an impending resurgence. They first pinned their hopes on President Johnson, whose continuing rightward shift had begun to energize state Democratic parties all across the North. Then came the Iowa Republicans' unqualified support of a racially impartial franchise. "It is perfectly idle for us to run a ticket if we cant get some votes off of the Republicans," a party loyalist wrote to the state Democratic chairman. While he considered a Johnson endorsement useful for patronage purposes, "I think the only chance we have is upon the question of Negro suffrage." In July a number of influential Democrats caucused with their state central committee and, eschewing the Democratic label, issued a nonpartisan call for all Iowans opposed to suffrage reform to meet in Des Moines on August 24 to nominate a white-supremacy ticket. Among the five names appended to this document, as if its owner had been awaiting some precisely appropriate moment to emerge from political oblivion, was that of Billy G. Haun.

This Democratic stratagem fooled hardly anyone, and events in Keokuk encouraged a further refinement in the Democrats' campaign. A gateway for Iowa troops returning from the South, the state's southernmost city had already become an arena for the expression of convalescent and demobilized soldiers' racial antagonisms. Despite occasional evidence to the contrary, Iowans of both parties believed that army veterans returning from the South, having seen African-Americans at their most abased and impoverished, harbored strongly hostile attitudes to civil equality of any kind. Without consulting the Democratic high command, editor Thomas W. Claggett of the Keokuk *Constitution* issued a formal invitation to "all soldiers and other loyal citizens opposed to Negro suffrage" to meet in Des Moines on August 23 (the day preceding the thinly disguised Democratic convention) to nominate a "white man's ticket." Claggett's idea for a nonpartisan slate, it appeared, might succeed where that of the Democratic central committee had not.[25]

Out of these maneuverings came the Union Anti-Negro Suffrage party, the candidates and platform of which—condemning equal rights and exalting Andrew Johnson—gained the expected Democratic endorsement the following day. At the head of this fusionist Soldier's Ticket, as it was termed, stood Col. Thomas Hart Benton Jr. A nephew of the famous U.S. Senator from Missouri, Benton had voted for exclusionary legislation in the 1846/47 senate and then, as the state's highest-ranking educator, had presided over the largely white Iowa school system for most of the period up to the outbreak of the war. In response to the nomination of Benton and his running mates, reciprocal "soldiers' conventions" met in several counties to endorse the state ticket and nominate local candidates for office, in at least one case specifically expelling veterans who had no objection to equal rights.

Some Republicans panicked. "The suffrage question will require much labor," a close observer had privately noted in summarizing the June 14 convention, but the first mention of the issue in the extensive correspondence of ex-governor Kirkwood came in late July with a report that a bipartisan antisuffrage alliance had formed in Ottumwa. Other such communications followed. A weakening of party morale showed up in the Republican press. In the month following its convention nearly a quarter of the party's journalists rallied in support of resolution 4, urging immediate black enfranchisement on grounds of justice and natural right. From mid-July to mid-August, as opposition to black suffrage crystallized, that percentage dropped 14 points. In the campaign's final period—from Benton's nomination to the October election—editors strongly supporting suffrage reform dropped to just one: Edward Russell. Over the same weeks the percentage of journals taking refuge in neutrality rose 10 points. Though only one Republican newspaperman overtly rejected the resolution, and the party's editorial center, which supported resolution 4 on largely pragmatic grounds, still held firm, it was clearly time to bring up the big guns—the GOP's major political figures—in support of the embattled proposition.[26]

Judge Chester C. Cole of the Iowa supreme court later identified himself as "probably the first man of influence in the state to put himself . . . publicly on record in favor of this then unpopular measure." In employing these words Cole unconsciously emphasized his own stature as a party insider as against that of an ideological irritant like Russell. Of New England parentage and Burned-Over District birth, a Harvard Law School graduate who first practiced in Kentucky, Cole had migrated northwestward in 1857, uncomfortable with the portents of secession. In Des Moines he quickly became, as E. H. Stiles puts it, "an idol of the Democratic Party," gamely if unsuccessfully running for the supreme court and then for Congress. In 1863, at Governor Kirkwood's request, Cole stumped the counties of southern and southwestern Iowa ("every one of which had given majorities for me"), reassuring the racially conservative citizenry that Lincoln's Emancipation Proclamation was not an occasion for joining rumored Copperhead conspiracies. Cole's reward came in 1864 when the new governor, William M. Stone, named him to fill a seat on the freshly expanded Iowa supreme bench, a position to which Cole, now a Republican, was subsequently elected. In late June 1865 a friend writing on behalf of many of his acquaintances in southwestern Iowa, asked Cole's opinion of resolution 4. Cole answered at some length in the Des Moines *Register*.

He began by flatly asserting that he himself felt strongly in favor of black suffrage. But he reminded Iowans that irresponsibly hasty action was neither contemplated nor possible. Refashioning the suffrage clause of Iowa's constitution could only be done via a three-step sequence: passage of a proposed amendment by two successive assemblies, followed by the amendment's submission as a referendum proposition. The process could not be completed until 1868 at the earliest—more than enough time for sober reflection and debate—after which the people themselves would decide.

Cole then offered a lawyerly four-part rendition of Radical Republican orthodoxy on suffrage reform. First, the national emergency gave the federal government positive authority—"the right of self-defense and self-protection which inheres in every Sovereignty"—to impose black suffrage in the lately rebellious states. Second, only an enfranchised ex-slave population could provide the help needed to control the subjugated but still defiant white majority there, and to insure that unreconstructed Confederates did not regain their prewar influence in national affairs. The "sagacity, wisdom and fidelity of the black race" displayed in aiding escaped Union prisoners of war testified to their reliability, said Cole, and "that skill and bravery which has characterized their use of bullets against our enemies, ought to be received as sufficient proof of their ability thus to use the ballot also." Third, the ex-slaves required political power for their self-protection, without which, at the absolute mercy of vindictive whites, "they would be soon 'apprenticed,' and then would follow a condition not unlike 'Mexican Peonage,' and finally, in spite of Federal constitutional inhibitions, a condition of abject slavery, under some new [and] more euphonious cognomen."

Finally there was the matter of "*God's law of equality,*" said Cole. "It was devolved upon Abraham Lincoln, by his Proclamation of Emancipation, to inaugurate the *Fact* of freedom; and the same Providence has devolved upon us the duty of *completing the fact,* by making all men equal before the law, as they are before their Maker." Abandoning the voice of reasoned pedagogy for the stern idiom of his Puritan forebears, Cole invoked the familiar Protestant belief that the war was divine punishment for America's centuries-long toleration of slavery. That "terrible scourge," he wrote, had "indelibly taught us the Biblical truth that 'Sin is a reproach to any people.' . . . If we shall, however, *refuse justice* to that Race, on whose account, God evidently has scourged us as a Nation, I shall confess to the *fear* that He has in store for our Rulers, and us, as a Nation, further manifestations of His displeasure."

Cole closed by noting that "so far as negro voting in Iowa is concerned, the question amounts here practically to but little." He echoed the hypothesis that once civil equality had been established in the South, most blacks would return to "what they prefer, and by nature seem adapted to—a warmer climate." Yet Iowans had a crucial role to play. "The *moral influence* of correct action in Iowa," he said, "will be potent for good upon the National cause." Just as the Hawkeye State had been in the forefront in the war for the Union, "let her be *first* in the great act of political progress . . . to secure complete victory in the struggle for equality which alone can crown our brilliant triumph in arms and make our Nation practically and really 'the land of the Free and the home of the Brave.' "[27]

As October's election approached, several of Iowa's representatives in Washington offered opinions on resolution 4 in letters widely circulated by the Republican press. None matched Judge Cole's hearty specificity. Congressman John A. Kasson's statement proved less an endorsement of the controversial platform plank than a forecast of his approaching break with Iowa's increasingly Radical House delegation.[28] Candidly admitting his white supremacism, Kasson would limit an expanded franchise—in Iowa as in the South—to black war veterans and property holders, and he lamely argued that "a right interpretation of our State Platform shows nothing in conflict with these views." The statement of Kasson's congressional colleague, J. B. Grinnell, mainly scolded Colonel Benton, a former friend, for becoming the puppet of Copperheads and rebels. The declaration by U.S. Sen. James W. Grimes agreed with Grinnell's convention stand against the Russell amendment, which Grimes termed "uncalled for and impolitic . . . however just I might believe the principle to be." Iowans, added the respected founding father of the state's Republican party, must not be distracted by "any such side issue."[29]

The comments of ex-Senator James Harlan, now President Johnson's Secretary of the Interior, loyally insisted that one could logically support both the administration's emerging southern policy *and* resolution 4. A man with no very high opinion of African-Americans' capacity for citizenship, in May he had counseled Johnson against imposing unqualified suffrage reform on the South. Now, Harlan said, he "would vote to extend the right to all classes of persons possessing the requisite intelligence and patriotism"—that is, to literate black veterans. But, he admitted, "I do not believe that the liberty of any class of people can be considered safe, who are to be permanently deprived of the exercise of this right." A month later, in an autumn visit to his Mount Pleasant home, Harlan became more straightforward. "Why should not all intelligent men be given the ballot?" he asked. In Iowa, with its tiny colored minority, "there can surely be no injury in granting [the black man] that right, even if he is *not* qualified to vote."

Harlan, alone of all the discussants so far described, brought forward the key linkage between suffrage reform in the South and in the Hawkeye State. So far it had been too easily dismissed by northern radicals, but its importance came much more clearly into focus as southerners—including

President Johnson himself—wryly began to make it an integral part of the white supremacist defense against congressional reconstruction. A South Carolinian, Harlan hypothesized, might well inquire of any Iowa Congressman pressing for black suffrage in the South, "How is it that you ask this, while in Iowa, the land of education and refinement, you do not permit even the educated negro to vote? Go first and clean your own skirts ere you attempt to require this of us." Iowa, like most northern states, in other words, should purge itself of its own constitutional shortcomings before presuming to superintend the civic regeneration of the South. That was soon to become President Johnson's public refrain.[30]

Meanwhile, the man at the head of the 1865 Republican state ticket had also been required to define his position on resolution 4. The prosuffrage influences bearing directly on Governor Stone may have been considerable, since two of his three running-mates already had established themselves as racial progressives. Benjamin Gue, candidate for lieutenant governor, had been an early proponent of black suffrage, while Oran Faville, standing for reelection as superintendent of public instruction, had voted for suffrage reform in 1857. The fourth member of the ticket, Chief Justice George G. Wright of the supreme court, although a school segregationist, had opposed the Haun bill in 1851. And of the eight other top officials within Stone's administration at least four were racial progressives: Lieutenant Governor Eastman, so forcefully prosuffrage in the convention; Secretary of State Wright, prosuffrage in 1857 and heavily involved in the *Webb* case and exclusion law repeal; State Treasurer William H. Holmes, a man who had voted to receive Alex Clark's petition in 1855; and of course the supreme court's Judge Cole. A fifth official, State Auditor John A. Elliott, hailed (like Faville) from prosuffrage Mitchell County.[31]

What counsel any of these men might have rendered Governor Stone the record saith not. But it does include the campaign advice offered by the prestigious Gen. M. M. Crocker. Crocker had supported Russell in the late convention, and he now privately responded to Stone's request for his thoughts on handling the suffrage issue. An officer who had been one of Ulysses S. Grant's most respected division commanders, he took a combat soldier's tightly focused view of the matter. "I hold that we are bound by every principle of right and justice, now that we have . . . declared that the negro shall be free and that he shall be regarded as a citizen of the Republic, to extend to him the means by which as a freeman he can protect himself." Crocker harbored no illusions about the South. "Freedom [for southern blacks] can only exist by the bayonet or the ballot. We do not intend to give the negro the bayonet; then we must give him the ballot." The crisis demanded action. "We must meet this question, and that too, in such a manner as will insure the Right to prevail; and the *sooner* we do it, and the *bolder* we do it, the better.—Now is the time, in my opinion, [while] we are not hampered by other issues." That Iowa's Democrats took so violently against resolution 4 simply proved its virtue and would impel Republicans to honor it. "And unless I am very greatly mistaken," he assured Stone, "your majority this fall will fully vindicate the wisdom of the Convention, and will be such an endorsement of the doctrine of Universal Suffrage as will put the question at rest finally as far as the action of this State can do it."[32]

So advised, Governor Stone made his peace with resolution 4. Although born of old Yankee stock in the Burned-Over District and coming of age in the equally abolitionist Western Reserve, Stone, like Judge Cole, had been reared a Democrat. A poor boy, virtually self-educated, he nevertheless gained admission to the bar, married into a local gentry family, and moved to Iowa in 1854. He briefly managed the Knoxville *Journal* as a Know Nothing organ, participated vigorously in the formation of Iowa's Republican party, ran as a Frémont elector, and gained a district judgeship. He served gallantly in the war as a regimental commander, barely surviving Grant's vast frontal assault on Vicksburg. Returned home to recuperate from a shattered forearm, the tall, handsomely bearded colonel agreed to address the 1863 Republican state convention, where the delegates, deadlocked over two leading candidates, impulsively nominated Stone for governor and the voters obliged.[33]

Self-confident, uncommonly gregarious and uninhibited for a public man, Stone early in his reelection campaign adeptly began to defuse Democratic baiting about resolution 4 by laying out the history of his personal feelings on black freedom and civil equality. Regarding Iowa's first suffrage proposition, he recalled: "In 1857 . . . I voted against it, not because I was opposed to it as a question of abstract right, but simply on the ground of expediency. I doubted whether we were ready for it." (Which is to say that he did no more than internalize the prevailing Republican party line.) And when the war came Stone was at first willing that it be won without dislodging slavery. A reporter paraphrased his explanation: "He had been rather slow upon this subject, and had never been regarded as a strong advocate of emancipation. He had been conservative on this question. He had been raised a Democrat, and shared the views of that party." "I was so conservative," added Stone, "[that] I did not endorse Lincoln's preparatory proclamation of emancipation as heartily as many did. I questioned its expediency at the time; although by the time when he issued the final proclamation . . . I was fully prepared to sustain it." (Note the rapid adjustment being described here: in three and a half months Stone's attitude toward emancipation shifted 180 degrees.)

Stone also felt initially uneasy about the idea of enlisting African-Americans as servicemen: "He was not, for some reason, very much in favor of the organization of colored regiments." But it had been ordered. "And [now] he believed if they would take out of the war what the black men had done, in various ways, as guides, teamsters, mechanics, laborers, and soldiers, the war would still be raging." Without the black military contribution "he seriously doubted whether we ever could have conquered the South." About suffrage reform in postwar Iowa, finally, Stone admitted in July 1865 that he had been hesitant on resolution 4 only two weeks before. "It is true he was not in favor of putting that plank in the platform, because he did not think there was any practical necessity for it. He was not a member of the convention, but if he had been he should probably not have favored its adoption." Yet it was now a *fait accompli,* and he willingly accepted the challenge it posed. He declined to say how he would vote on black suffrage three years hence, "but with his present feelings and convictions he was in favor of it."

What one discerns in Stone's attitudinal odyssey is not some deep conversion experience, but simply that the governor read the newspapers, listened to his peers, and reflected on what he had read and heard. And he, in turn, powerfully conveyed his changed views to others. ("Upon the hustings," says Stiles, "he was one of the most effective political orators that the State has ever had.") In later speeches, for example, Stone elaborated, if a bit vaguely, on the contributions of Iowa's own black regiment, and folksily emphasized how those of its members credited to Iowa's wartime manpower quota had exempted over two thousand white Iowans from the 1864 draft.[34]

Governor Stone deftly transposed the logic of suffrage reform, as expounded by Judge Cole and other political intellectuals, into a vernacular appropriate for a listening electorate. In doing so he discovered how effectively the fight for equal rights could be linked to America's cherished egalitarian ideals. In a remarkable platform confrontation between himself and Benton a week before the election, Stone cornered the colonel into answering a series of questions about resolution 4, during which Benton laconically admitted his objection to the phrase "all men are equal before the law." "Well," said Stone, delighted to portray Benton's confession as far to the right of the accepted range of attitudes, "this is the first time I ever heard an American citizen state that he did not believe in the equality of all men before the law!" The audience exploded in applause.

Twenty years earlier, only the most extreme antislavery constitutionalists dared argue that the Founding Fathers and the nation's first state documents had been deliberately abolitionist. Now that notion became the common currency of Stone's discourse. "I say that we [Republicans] carried out the spirit of the Declaration of Independence," Stone insisted, "in that resolution, when we said that 'all men were equal before the law.' (Applause.) We stand where Madison and Franklin and Jefferson stood, when we asserted that 'all men are equal before the law.' We stand where stood the framers of the federal Constitution and where the men stood who fought the battles of the Revolution. (Applause.) I tell you this principle that all men are equal, comes from the Almighty God Himself, and it must and will prevail. (Applause.)"[35]

IV

Two days later the Republican central committee chairman at last offered assurances that there was little cause for alarm. "I have reports from nearly all the counties in the state," he wrote Kirkwood, "and they are much more favorable than I anticipated. Our majority will be about 20,000."

On election day in October this prediction proved entirely accurate—with the exception of Governor Stone himself, who lagged some two thousand votes behind the rest of the ticket, an event to be accounted for less by Stone's stand on resolution 4 than by lingering resentments over certain of his wartime policies as governor.[36] Stone defeated Benton by a comfortable 56 percent; his running mate, Benjamin Gue, won by 58 percent, a somewhat better measure of Republican strength. But even Gue's majority was down 6 points from the enormous percentage tendered Abraham Lincoln in 1864, and the Republican slate lost ten counties that had been carried by the late President. These counties, like most of those carried by Benton, lay along the frontier, where small population movements readily altered outcomes (map 10.1). Four of Benton's other counties lay in southern Iowa, the region most sensitive to the conservative axiom that impartial suffrage would prompt a massive invasion of Missouri blacks. And one of them, Lee, enclosed racially polarized Keokuk. "The burden . . . imposed by the Des Moines Convention," concluded a Lee County editor, "was too heavy to carry."

Otherwise the suffrage issue appears to have had surprisingly little impact on the returns. Excluding soldiers' votes cast from out of state in 1864, statistical analysis suggests that about 15 percent of Lincoln's Iowa supporters did not vote at all in 1865. Instead of its being a case of conservative Republican distaste for both suffrage reform and Benton, however, this percentage was a normal drop-off from a presidential election year—about the same, for example, as that of 1861. Virtually no Lincoln voters defected to the Democrats. Veterans indeed may have responded more dramatically to the suffrage issue than did the electorate at large, but since we have no means to isolate their votes in 1865 we cannot say so for sure.[37]

It was, in short, a remarkably uncomplicated outcome, given the complexities punctuating the campaign. Republican journalists paused to dispute its meaning among themselves before returning their attention to the Democrats. A frothy exchange between the Burlington *Hawk-Eye* and Ed Russell's Davenport *Gazette* enlivened things for readers all across the state. Many Republican campaigners had endlessly iterated that the issue

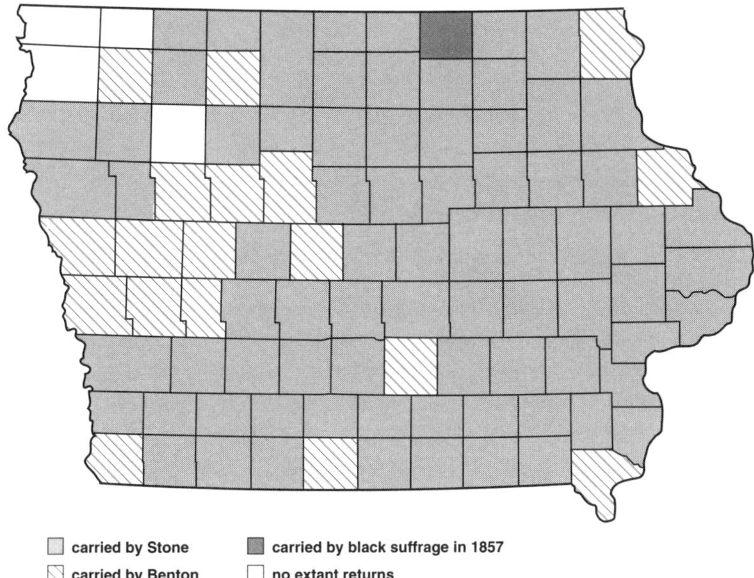

Map 10.1 The "Union Anti-Negro Suffrage" election (for key to county names see map A.1, appendix A).

was only whether or not to hold a referendum, and many postelection editorial commentaries doubted that Stone's victory implied a victory for equal rights. But the redoubtable Russell—the man who in March 1865 had started it all—brought everyone's attention back to the essential truths: in June the Iowa Republican party had explicitly endorsed suffrage reform, in August the Democratic party had made it the leading issue of the campaign, and the October result possessed an irrefutable significance.

"Stone has been elected upon the 'negro suffrage' platform, by a large majority," reflected a Sioux City editor, "and therefore we may regard the popular opinion of the State as expressed in favor of the extension of the rights of citizenship to the black man." No friend of a racially impartial franchise, he had registered as conservative early in the summer, then declined even to discuss the issue. While he agreed with Russell's enemies that resolution 4 had been an unnecessary appendage to the party platform, he now bespoke an assurance that all had been to the good, a notion that he no doubt shared with hundreds of other relieved Republican loyalists.

"The contest is passed, the victory won, notwithstanding the side issues; and today the Republican party is stronger than it would have been had the 'negro suffrage' clause been left out of the platform. We are now out of the woods," he concluded, "let all crow who feel like it."[38]

Bright Radical Star

11

Behind his back some referred to him as "the dapper gentleman" or "the urbane." Others simply mistook him for an aristocratic son of the South. Slender, grey-eyed, sternly handsome, attractive to women, polished of manner and intellect, always fashionably groomed, John A. Kasson impressed many Iowans as an unlikely Yankee. Indeed, his season as tutor to the children of a Virginia planter may have had more effect on his demeanor, perhaps even his character, than the New England village culture that had produced him, or the University of Vermont from which he had graduated second in his class, or the seaport society of New Bedford, Massachusetts, where he had practiced law until decamping west.

Although he had been a delegate to the Free Soilers' famous 1848 convention, Kasson was an antiextension Democrat with no very burning animus against slavery itself. Reestablished in Saint Louis, he promptly purchased a black house servant. But ultimately he turned as grim about his political prospects in Missouri as earlier he had been in Massachusetts. He abandoned a flourishing practice and, having manumitted his slave, in 1857 migrated to Des Moines and rapidly became a power within the Iowa Republican party. After a term in Washington as President Lincoln's First Assistant Postmaster General, which bestowed upon him a sustained influence over the wartime dispensation of federal patronage within his newly adopted state, Kasson in 1862 won election to Congress. Three years later, however, the Iowa party's leftward shift exceeded Kasson's ideological capacity to adjust. The Congressman became a major exception to the rule that Democrats, once loosened from their old political moorings, tended to transmute into the Hawkeye State's most racially progressive Republicans.[1]

In the summer of 1865, Iowa's James Harlan having resigned from the U.S. Senate in order to become Interior Secretary, it became the pleasant option of Gov. William M. Stone to name a replacement. Kasson and ex-governor Samuel J. Kirkwood emerged as the leading aspirants. But Kasson's letter clarifying his conservative views on reconstruction and suffrage reform, and his explicit plea that resolution 4 not be made a test of party loyalty, doomed his senatorial chances by opening his candidacy to a host of patronage grievances. Stone, with his own political fate riding on Iowans' acceptance of colored suffrage, expected anyone who desired his favor to rally to the cause as forcefully as himself. "Gov Stone has said," wrote a local politician of the Harlan vacancy, that "he will appoint no man who is not sound on the 4th Resolution of the state platform." And the campaigning Oran Faville, fresh from a strategy conference with Stone, met with politico Jacob Rich at Independence, the two prosuffrage enthusiasts agreeing that, as Rich put it, "Kasson has, by his letter, . . . thrown away his prospects for the Senatorship or even a reelection as Representative."[2]

If Kasson was the first important political victim of resolution 4, Kirkwood was its second. A man who had opposed school integration in 1858 and two years later still hoped that a revitalized colonization program might resolve the slavery issue, Kirkwood regularly accepted party assignments to canvass conservative southern Iowa, where his Maryland birth and former Democratic affiliation always played to best effect. Stone had promised to appoint the popular ex-governor to the Senate vacancy, but then reneged on the deal, apparently angered by what he interpreted as Kirkwood's insufficient campaign ardor on the controversial platform plank. "You are not sound on that," one of Kirkwood's informants confided after the election, "—consequently you will not be appointed." "You were charged with being opposed to equal suffrage," wrote another, "and of having shirked this question in the last State canvass."

In the end Stone simply let the 1866 general assembly handle the senatorial succession—that is, naming someone to fill the rest of Harlan's unexpired term (the so-called short term) and also electing someone to the regular senatorial vacancy (or long term) that would begin in 1867. The legislators from Kasson's district, as it happened, declined to press his case. Toward Kirkwood the assemblymen, though sensitive to the allegation about his suffrage views, displayed a more forgiving attitude than had Stone. They elected Kirkwood to the short term, naming Harlan himself—who had revealed his dismay as a member of the increasingly unpopular Johnson Administration—to the more desirable long term.[3]

The results of the 1865 election sent a message to Iowa's congressional delegation of 1866. Only the unpredictable Sen. James W. Grimes modulated his radicalism, although he eventually accepted the pragmatic connection between southern reconstruction and black suffrage in the North. He would not fall from grace until, as one of the "seven martyrs," he cast his famous negative vote at President Johnson's impeachment trial. William B. Allison and Josiah B. Grinnell continued to be impeccably radical, while A. W. Hubbard, Hiram Price, and James F. Wilson transformed themselves from centrists into Radicals. That left Kasson and Kirkwood, who loathed each other, as the delegation's conservatives.

And, as Jacob Rich predicted, Kasson's membership in that delegation proved to be as abbreviated as Kirkwood's. In the House, after Hiram Price scathingly rebuked him for ignoring the prosuffrage inclinations of Iowa's electorate, Kasson lapsed into silence on reconstruction issues and modified his voting behavior somewhat, trusting that popularity with his southwest Iowa constituents and his long intimacy with important men like Iowa's Gen. Grenville M. Dodge would save him.

But the officer, unlike the gentleman, had been radicalized. Dodge had been reared, like Kasson, in a Democratic household in New England. His wartime experience with black combat troops, plus his close work as one of General Grant's intelligence chiefs with black informants and line-crossers, had converted him from a youthful racist into a reconstruction hard-liner and firm advocate of suffrage reform. "You know we have got to meet this question," Dodge privately lectured Kirkwood, "and I of course have but one view on it, that is . . . fight for it on the ground of right, justice &c. and educate the people up to it."[4]

In June 1866 Kasson narrowly lost the Republican nomination to Dodge. "A majority of the people here are radical," a voter assured the general, "and have been somewhat dissatisfied with Kasson's course last winter. The most of us are prepared for universal suffrage and we all feel that you would be an advocate for the great principles of human rights."[5]

I

In his 1866 inaugural address Governor Stone movingly pressed suffrage reform on the Iowa legislature, recapitulating the rhetorical distillate of his late gubernatorial campaign. Southern blacks—"under no perceivable obligation to assist in the maintenance of a government from which they have never received either justice or mercy"—nevertheless had offered wartime services of incalculable worth. Enfranchisement would enable them to defend their newly granted freedom, and simultaneously deploy them as "an army of occupation . . . in the yet unquiet regions of the South." But Iowans must do their part. "We cannot ask others to adopt this stern principle . . . if we reject it in our own State. Before we assert that the freedmen of the South should be invested with equality of political rights, let us . . . practically illustrate the sincerity of the convictions we profess to cherish." Upon their demobilization at Davenport, Stone noted, hundreds of surviving members of Iowa's own 60th U.S. Colored Infantry

Regiment had petitioned the legislature to begin the process by which suffrage reform would be secured. "Have we that degree of moral courage which will enable us to recognize the services of these black veterans," asked the governor, "and do them justice?"[6]

The assembly majority responded affirmatively, agreeing that "during the late civil war the colored residents of our State have voluntarily and generously contributed their efforts to the support of the Union cause, and have earned for themselves the right to an equal enjoyment of the liberties which are continued to us through the services of our soldiery." It produced a joint resolution eliminating the word "white" from the suffrage article of the constitution. In the most crucial house roll call only four Republicans, two of them having been elected as antisuffrage "independents," joined the Democrats against franchise extension. The most critical senate vote was on adopting a minority report that would have restricted nonwhite suffrage to war veterans and those able to read and write—a measure that, if seriously considered, Stone wanted applied to naturalized citizens as well as blacks. Seventeen Republicans voted in favor of this conservative option; ironically, only the opposition of die-hards who were against *any* black suffrage kept it from passing. The original measure then passed with the defection of only four Republican senators.[7]

The assembly's joint resolution simultaneously proposed removal of all other racial discriminations from the constitution—except that excluding nonwhites from legislative membership. This was not an oversight, and in the lower house it occasioned, recalled Col. Alonzo Abernethy, "one of the sharpest battles of the session." Abernethy identified the main culprit as "that astute embodiment of legal lore," C. Ben Darwin, a combative, intellectually eccentric ex-New Yorker who provided "the zealous leadership" of a bloc of Republican conservatives. Abernethy offered a rectifying resolution concerning legislative qualifications that went to the committee on constitutional amendments. The committee refused to recommend it. Abernethy once again took the matter to the house floor, and a week later the committee's recommendations *did* concede a racially impartial legislative membership. But of the six specifications voted upon, it was the only one to fail. It did so because thirty-two Republicans joined the Democrats in opposition. They included Samuel McNutt, who only two years before had written the legislation that killed Billy G. Haun's exclusion law. But suffrage reform was as far as McNutt and a third of the Republican house contingent would go; black membership in the general assembly was asking too much.[8]

For Governor Stone, for Henry O'Connor, and for other racially progressive Civil War veterans, Colonel Abernethy was the right kind of man, and they began urging his nomination as secretary of state. But no honors could ease Abernethy's memory of the infamous day when "policy finally prevailed over principle, and for more than twenty years longer the word 'white' must needs blot the constitution of Iowa."[9]

The failed roll call on nonwhite assembly membership permits some insight into the ideological character of legislative Republicanism in 1866. With the exception of ten men who cannot be classified because of failure to vote on the membership question, one can conveniently separate the forty-one Republicans who, like Abernethy, favored eliminating *all* racist distinctions in the organic law of the state, from the thirty-two Republicans who, no matter how they might stand on black suffrage, wished to keep the assembly all-white. The two groups did not differ importantly in terms of birthplace, age, length of residence in Iowa, wartime military status, occupation, or attitude on women's suffrage and corporate regulation. But three categories did distinguish them. The racial progressives were much more likely (as was Colonel Abernethy) to be Baptists—despite their denomination's mixed prewar record on abolition. They were much more likely to have been elected (as was Abernethy) by constituencies that had given at least 15 percent of their ballots to suffrage reform in 1857. And they were much more inclined (as was Abernethy) to be hard-line drys on the liquor question. To seriously reform-minded Republicans black civil equality and temperance retained a fundamental moral analogy from the Iowa party's formative years: both demanded policy implementation in any society that pretended to public virtue, and the same intense impulse toward social perfectionism presumably drove them both.[10]

But sufficient unto the day was the evil thereof. The ensuing political events of 1866 swept aside any lingering doubts about the central ideological role of black suffrage. June's Republican convention featured a determination to excise all intraparty disunity on the question. Delegates approved the platform before selecting candidates, thus minimizing the possibility of a nominee's later repudiating the suffrage plank. The platform caucus fashioned a compromise acceptable to delegates from southern Iowa, among whom, as the Des Moines *Register* reported, "great anxiety was manifested relative to the tone of the Resolutions which should be adopted . . . and while they asked no deviation from the line of policy which was ratified at the polls last fall, they asked that no new test should be introduced into the Resolutions this year."

Adopted in an overpowering display of unanimity, the 1866 suffrage plank simply asserted that the "first and highest duty of our free government is to secure all its citizens, regardless of race, religion, or color, equality before the law, equal protection from it, equal responsibility to it, and to all that have proved their loyalty by their acts, an equal voice in making it." Most of the formulation was by Henry O'Connor, who this year acknowledged the political utility of a less specific statement than 1865's resolution 4. The phrase about proofs of loyalty was not his, however, and from the convention floor he apparently objected to a possible construction that an enlarged franchise belonged only to black veterans. He seems to have been shouted down.

Actually, of course, the added touch reinforced the plank's attraction. It could appeal to Republican conservatives who still hoped for a *qualified* extension of the suffrage to African-Americans. On the other hand, while clearly referring to the late war, the phrase could satisfy those who saw it as acknowledging that the whole black population of Iowa had vicariously proved itself through its sponsorship of a regiment. It could also, finally, serve as an endorsement of congressional Republicans' policy toward the South. The lavish praise Edward Russell, the author of resolution 4, heaped on this statement reinforces the conspiratorial ambience surrounding its lack of specificity. Yet in light of the general retreat from black suffrage by other northern states that year, any endorsement, however ambivalent, was remarkable. "Iowa Republicans alone," writes historian Leslie Fishel of 1866, "came out strongly for enfranchisement."

Reconstruction policy proved to be the main issue that autumn, although the election was in part a replay of the previous year. Convinced that with more time to campaign he could have won on the Soldier's Ticket, Col. Thomas Hart Benton Jr. helped organize a so-called Conservative Republican convention. This body assembled, nominated racist candidates, and approved a platform, penned by Benton himself, opposing suffrage reform. Iowa's Democrats, once again offering no slate of their own, endorsed the Conservative nominees.[11]

This time the fusionists reaped unambiguous disaster. Voter turnout rose by 23,000, the Republican vote by 21,000. It was a remarkable display, a Republican resurgence all across the state. All eight Conservative counties had been carried the year before by Benton, most by larger margins. Benton's other ten counties now went Republican. Virtually all the unhappy Republicans who had gone over to 1865's Anti-Negro Suffrage ticket, plus half those who sat out the 1865 election, came back to the aid of their party. Joining them in the Republican column were some thousands of voters who had avoided the polls in both 1864 and 1865. We cannot know what impelled these voter movements. One good guess is that it was Pres. Andrew Johnson, whose stormy break with Congress and whose acrimonious campaign tour on behalf of a new National Union party had enlivened 1866, Reconstruction's so-called critical year. Racists many Iowans might have been, but they would not acquiesce, any more than their progressive Republican compatriots, in a Johnsonian attitude toward the South of forgive and forget.[12]

Lt. Gov. Benjamin F. Gue concluded that among other things the 1866 election "clearly demonstrated the fact that the people of Iowa, by a large majority, were determined to remove from the organic laws of the State . . . all race discriminations which in early years were enacted against persons of African descent." His colleagues within middle levels of the Republican elite must have agreed with Gue; at least they collectively acted as if they did. There seemed little need to equivocate further. The party platforms of 1867 and 1868—adopted in both instances without important convention dissent—specified that amending the Iowa constitution so as to "secure the rights of the ballot . . . to all men, irrespective of color, race or religion" was now to be considered "a cardinal principle of our political faith." And in both years the assembled delegates enthusiastically nominated Henry O'Connor for attorney general, an honor understood to be a full vindication of the articulate Irishman's fight for black suffrage in the conventions of '65 and '66.

To gratifying applause O'Connor characterized Iowa for the delegates of 1868 as "a frontier State, still rising by honorable action higher, higher, inscribing upon its flag, in words of bright lustre, that 'all men are equal.' " And he gently admonished them, as he chided himself, for positions long outgrown. "Don't you feel," he asked, "as I do, some times, a blush of shame coming to my cheek at the thought that I should ever have hesitated for a moment [to certify] the equal rights of the whole human brotherhood?"[13]

II

In the aftermath of the 1866 debacle an Iowa Democrat warned his state party chairman that "there is a well defined and clear determination among democrats to fight our battles hereafter under the old Democratic banner and *nothing else*." Fusion, he wrote, had not worked because the conservative element of Iowa's Republicans was not numerically strong enough to be worth trifling with. In response to such advice from several quarters, the Democrats, for the first time in three years, fielded their own slate of candidates in 1867. And while their platform denounced suffrage reform (plank 2), it made opposition to the protective tariff and the tax-exempt status of federal bonds (planks 3 and 4) the key questions touching national affairs. But advocating repeal of Iowa's 1855 prohibitory law and the enactment of "a well regulated license law in lieu thereof" (plank 5) reactivated a party position on which Iowa's Democracy would campaign annually until well into the twentieth century. While by no means conceding the suffrage question, it brought another divisive issue effectively into play.

This Democratic tactic served most effectively at Davenport, seat of Iowa's largest and most politicized German community, where normally Republican Germans cooperated in electing four legislative candidates on an antiprohibition People's party ticket. While two additional People's candidates reached the legislature from other constituencies, the Republicans' 1867 gubernatorial nominee, Col. Samuel Merrill, won election by 59 percent of the ballots, a slight falling off from 1866 but attributable to another sharp dip in Republican turnout rather than to any important loss of voters. Yet prohibition spelled trouble. "The Election Lesson," wrote one worried Republican editor, no longer hinged on equal rights (which he did not mention) but rather on "premonitions of weakness growing out of distractions" better left to nonpartisan philanthropists. "The temperance issue has lost us five or six legislators in Iowa this fall," he warned, "and thus are we playing into the hands of the enemy." As a new general assembly convened in January 1868 close observers echoed this disquietude. The leadership's problem, said one, was to avoid jeopardizing "the paramount question of reconstruction & yet something is necessary to quiet the stormy feelings of the temperance men on one side & the license men on the other . . . within the Republican party."[14]

Divided they might be on liquor, but Republican assemblymen toed the line on franchise extension with remarkable unity. The relatively unknown Colonel Merrill had won the Republican gubernatorial nomination against retiring Congressman J. B. Grinnell in part, thinks one authority, because of Grinnell's 1865 opposition to resolution 4. And Merrill went on to win the election at the expense of the Democrats' candidate. Judge Charles Mason, the territorial chief justice who wrote the praiseworthy *Ralph* decision back in 1839, had become in the waning years of his distinguished career not only a notorious Copperhead but a racist of unrivaled ferocity. He had been instrumental in helping forge the quixotic national alliance of Democrats and pro-Johnson Republicans that American voters ravaged in 1866. In 1867 he reluctantly accepted the Iowa party's gubernatorial nomination, announcing his resistance to the "leveling down of the white race" allegedly inherent in suffrage reform. "It is not . . . a mere unfounded prejudice we feel to this social equality & intermarriage with the negro," he assured Iowans. "It is the voice of God speaking through our own instincts. It is a provision of Nature to preserve the purity of the white race." But such rhetoric availed him not.[15]

Once in office Samuel Merrill proved as uncompromising on black suffrage as Stone had been. He urged legislators to ignore the recent failure of equal rights initiatives in Connecticut, Ohio, Wisconsin, Minnesota, Kansas, and Colorado. The Hawkeye State, he said, should neither "emulate their cowardice nor share in their dishonor." And he echoed the words of Hiram Price in the historic 1865 Republican convention, at the same time neatly reversing the political logic that had equated war service with racism. Let its military veterans, said Merrill, "never have cause to charge Iowa with lack of courage to do justice to her colored soldiers and residents."

At this strategic juncture Iowa's black community again spoke up for itself, convening at the state capital "for the purpose of considering the question of our enfranchisement, which is now before the Legislature." With a number of whites present as guests and spectators, over thirty black delegates from thirteen towns and cities gathered on Lincoln's birthday, and that evening heard rousing remarks from the ubiquitous Alexander Clark, followed by "a fine and stirring speech" by Iowa's new attorney general, Henry O'Connor. The following day Clark read the convention's official address "to the People of Iowa," a document composed by himself and subsequently published in several Republican newspapers as well as in pamphlet form. The address emphasized what had emerged by 1868 as the two most appealing prosuffrage arguments not directly keyed to southern reconstruction. It asked enfranchisement "in the honored name of 200,000 colored troops, five hundred of whom were from our own Iowa." And in the grand tradition of antebellum black protest it invoked Thomas Jefferson's famous Preamble: "being men, we claim to be of that number comprehended in the Declaration of Independence, and . . . entitled not only to life, but to equal rights in the pursuit and securing of happiness and in the choice of those who are to rule over us."

Suffrage reform breezed through the Iowa house with only one Republican dissenter—the representative from Fremont in the extreme southwest corner of the state, a normally Democratic county in the late sixties despite its very Republican name. Even racially conservative John Kasson, elected to the general assembly by a portion of his old congressional constituency, found it in himself to join the majority (although he would not return to his party's good graces for another several years). A resolution that would also have eliminated the ban on nonwhite legislators passed the house with much more cohesive Republican support than its champions had been able to muster in 1866.

Table 11.1 displays the markedly leftward behavioral shift in the two-year interim. The number of unclassifiable Republicans remains constant, but the middling position is all but eliminated by the new progressive consensus. Only a dozen Republicans sat in both sessions. All twelve, however, registered as progressive in 1868, although two had been only moderates in the earlier assembly and one had been a conservative. While the nonwhite legislators measure died in a senate committee, the suffrage amendment passed the senate with no Republican opposition at all. Even one heroic *Democratic* senator felt the presumed will of the whole people of Iowa more pressing than that of his ultra conservative Dubuque County constituency, and he cast an unprecedented prosuffrage vote.[16]

Having passed two consecutive assemblies, the five constitutional amendments—striking the word "white" not only from the suffrage clause but also from those covering state census enumerations, senate apportionment, house apportionment, and militia service—finally were ready for referendum approval or disapproval in November 1868. With the popular

Table 11.1 Republican legislative positions on equal rights in the 1860s (percentages)

	1866 session (N = 83)	1868 session (N = 78)
Progressive[a]	49	85
Moderate[b]	34	3
Conservative[c]	5	1
Unclassifiable[d]	12	12
	100	101

Sources: Iowa House Journal (1866), 644–646; ibid. (1868), 402, 514–515, 527, 566.
a. Voted Yes on question of black legislators.
b. Voted No on question of black legislators, Yes on equal suffrage.
c. Voted No on equal suffrage.
d. Did not vote on question of black legislators.

Ulysses S. Grant heading the national Republican ticket that autumn, the Iowa leadership felt little anxiety about the impending presidential race. "The amendment of our State Constitution will be the big fight in our State," the Des Moines *Register*'s editor reminded General Dodge early in June, and he asked the Congressman to send along for his readers any information the federal Freedmen's Bureau might have on black voting in the South. "Iowa is not doubtful on the general issue," Senator Harlan informed the Republican national committee in late July; "but we have the question of colored suffrage submitted to the people and it may require considerable effort to secure its triumph." He begged off a campaign assignment to the West Coast in order to stump southeast Iowa for the cause. Similarly, ex-Senator Kirkwood agreed to take the case for suffrage reform into several questionable counties on the southern border of the state.

Democratic campaign rhetoric on race had shifted subtly as the great postwar financial questions increasingly preoccupied party spokesmen who began mingling economics and racism in specific appeals to heightened working-class anxieties. Vote for "a free white Democratic ticket," thundered a Democratic stump-speaker to an upstate, largely Republican audience. "You freed the negro; you put down that awful curse '*negro* slavery' and fastened eternal white slavery upon yourselves and children by lowering and knuckling to . . . the monied monopolies of the country. Good bye laboring man! The bondocracy of New England have fixed your status." Democratic editors renewed predictions that suffrage impartiality would draw a flood of cheap black labor into the state, "which will be a good thing," said one, "for the wealthy bondholder who is to be their employer." Meanwhile, charged another, the federal government's special solicitude toward southern freedmen was costing taxpayers eleven million dollars annually "for feeding a lot of idle, lazy niggers."[17]

Republican political locution adjusted comfortably, rephrasing suffrage reform according to the muscular vocabulary of competitive achievement that accompanied the expanding free-market economy of postwar America. *"That man is a Coward who fears negro suffrage,"* insisted one Republican editor. "It is not the color of the skin you fear, it is the fear you have, that the negro will outstrip you in the race of life." "A Democratic friend in Edenville," wrote another, "is afraid that 'the nigger' will get the start of him in the race of life and in the struggle for preferment." He rebuked the prejudice that "would hamper the colored man in the pursuit of an industrious livelihood." That "the negro [lags] behind us," Kirkwood told his downstate audiences, was all the more reason for civil equality. "Let us give him a chance," he said, "and if after we have had more than three hundred years the start of him he gets ahead of us, in the name of God let him go."

Republican spokesmen's main effort was not to convert rank-and-file Democrats to equal rights, but simply to keep otherwise loyal Republicans in line. In July the party's central committee chairman, Peter Melendy, included in a published summary of seven Republican priorities the eradication of racial discrimination and the winning of suffrage reform. In August he circulated a confidential memo to editors and party notables. "The Constitutional Amendment will meet with some opposition in our own ranks," he warned. "Labor to make that opposition as small as possible. We cannot afford the defeat of this measure." In September Melendy's executive secretary offered an ambivalent prognostication to national headquarters. "We feel very confident of carrying it," he wrote of the suffrage proposition, "altho many Republicans will oppose it and the maj. for it, if it carries, will be small." Two days later the chairman himself could assure General Dodge that in Iowa "things look bully for Grant," and he redoubled efforts toward rallying a prosuffrage majority.

In October Melendy circulated to local committees a model Republican ballot. A unitary slip ticket headed by Grant for President and descending to a space for the names of township candidates, Melendy's recommended ballot also displayed a format for the five equal rights propositions that permitted only Yes votes:

> On the Amendments to the State Constitution,
> FOR THE FIRST AMENDMENT.
> FOR THE SECOND AMENDMENT.
> FOR THE THIRD AMENDMENT.
> FOR THE FOURTH AMENDMENT.
> FOR THE FIFTH AMENDMENT.

And finally, a few days before the election, Melendy issued a last appeal to the faithful. "You are called upon to say [that] you are willing to give to *all men* the same rights, the same chance in life . . . which you yourselves enjoy. . . . Vote to give other men, as President Lincoln expressed it, a fair start and an equal chance in the race of life." He beseeched Republicans to "vote for the Amendments unanimously."[18]

Decisive emphasis came in the final hour of the campaign, a report that General Grant himself (despite his policy of avoiding comment on the heated question of black enfranchisement) had said that he "hoped the people of Iowa, whose soldiers achieved such immortal renown in the field, would be the first State to carry impartial suffrage through unfalteringly." It had failed elsewhere, he said, "but he trusted that Iowa, the bright Radical star, would proclaim by its action in November that the North is consistent with itself, and willing to voluntarily accept what its Congress had made a necessity in the South."[19]

III

On November 3, 1868, Grant took Iowa handily, winning 62 percent of its ballots and all but six of its ninety-seven organized counties. And as anticipated, black suffrage lagged slightly behind with 57 percent. Proposition 1 lost fourteen counties in addition to the five it and Grant lost in common (map 11.1). Yet about 90 percent of Grant's supporters also voted Yes on suffrage reform. In sum, the party's effort to make civil equality part of a Republican "straight ticket" succeeded exceptionally well. Or, to put it another way, Grant's coattails proved long enough to carry the burden assigned them. None of the counties carried by Grant's opponent approved black suffrage, and in the fifteen counties carried or tied by Grant but in which the amendment failed, the general's majorities were simply too small to lift suffrage reform above 50 percent.

But Grant need not be given all the glory. A good statistical correlation (+.65) between the Yes percentages of 1857 and 1868 reveals that the basic configuration of the prosuffrage vote had taken shape before the Civil War. Stone's 1865 reelection had brought that vote closer to its final form, the governor's support correlating highly (+.79) with that for the Yes ballots of 1868. What had occurred between the 1857 and 1868 referendums was a massive shift all across Iowa wherein the prosuffrage percentage in *every* county rose dramatically, the strength of its final approval very much related to how progressive its vote had been in 1865 and, to a lesser extent, in 1857.[20] Multiple regression analysis, moreover, discloses that Stone's support is nearly four times more useful than the 1857 percentage in predicting the patterns of the prosuffrage vote in 1868. Together, however, the two predict fully 72 percent of that final configu-

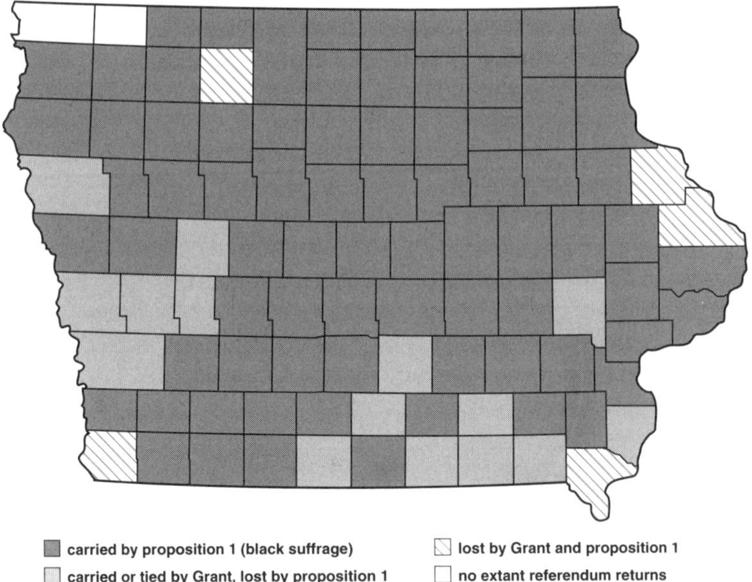

Map 11.1 The 1868 election and referendum (for key to county names see map A.1, appendix A).

ration. Thus the influence of Grant's coattails—as well as any independent effect of the Republican vote in 1866 and 1867—could not have been more than 28 percent.[21]

Over four-fifths of the Republican voters of 1867 supported suffrage reform in 1868, the minority fragmenting between those who voted No, those who rolled off, and those who had not turned out at the polls in the first place (table 11.2). Taken together, no more than fifteen thousand voters—12 or 13 percent of Grant's support—revealed themselves as ultra conservatives by scratching the printed option and casting write-in No votes or by rolling off, most easily accomplished by ripping the end from the Republican ballot before depositing it. As in 1857, those who refused to vote at all may have disdained black equality, but did not wish to gratify the Democrats by putting it on the record.[22] The referendum propositions won no help at all from the Democrats, who, as universally expected, balloted with virtual unanimity for their party's presidential nominee and against equal rights. But almost two-thirds of the previous year's nonvoters, presumably the Republican proportion of that body of temporarily disinterested eligibles, turned out to give their support to reform. About half the state's newly eligible voters followed suit.

Thus Iowa's Republicans redeemed themselves. Eleven years after having collaborated in the disastrous 1857 plebiscite, which came 3 percentage points short of being the worst civil rights referendum defeat on record, they overwhelmingly approved the first equal rights proposition ever to gain a majority in any state where voters knew unequivocally what they were casting ballots for and against.[23]

IV

Iowans approved all five amendments in 1868. And in other ways the state's unique hostility to racial discrimination also revealed itself. In an era in which the "separate-but-equal" doctrine was employed all across America to legitimize racially segregated public facilities, the Iowa supreme court refused to conform. Its 1868 ruling on schools was, writes historian J. Morgan Kousser, "one of the signal black triumphs in court [that] preceded the ratification of the Fourteenth Amendment." Alex Clark brought the landmark case, an action against a Muscatine school board that refused his daughter's admission to an all-white public school. Attorney General O'Connor, acting in his private capacity, enthusiastically served as one of Clark's lawyers. Judge Chester C. Cole, who had joined O'Connor in strenuously urging suffrage reform in 1865, wrote the majority opinion striking down segregated public education within the Hawkeye State. Seven years later the court reaffirmed its *Clark* judgement. And it ruled similarly on public accommodations, specifically in the case of a segregated Mississippi River steamboat, in 1873. In these actions Iowa's high court employed a definition of equal rights that proved far in advance of its time.[24]

But the antebellum term "free white" continued to mandate the makeup

Table 11.2 How the 1867 electorate behaved in November 1868 (estimated percentages)

	President			Equal suffrage				
	Grant (R)	Seymour (D)		Yes	No	Rolled off		Not voting
Republicans	43	0		38	2	3		1
Democrats	−1	31		−2	32	0		0
Nonvoters	10	3		11	3	0		4
1867 ineligibles	6	2		4	3	0		1
			94				94	6

Regressions: 1867 gubernatorial returns × 1868 presidential and 1868 proposition 1 returns (county N = 97).

of the Iowa legislature. In 1870 the general assembly, which also expunged the last racially discriminatory item from Iowa's statute law by opening the legal profession to nonwhites, passed a requisite joint resolution eliminating the racial qualification for legislative membership. (The single nonconformist in a straight party-line vote in both houses was an Iowa City Democrat who defected to equal rights.)[25] But the effort to repeal the clause faltered in 1872, the legislature for some reason failing to complete the necessary repassage of the joint resolution. Since any proposed constitutional amendment was required to carry two successive sessions of the assembly before going to the people as a referendum proposition, the process had to begin all over again.[26]

The cause then found its champion. At the moment of Iowa's first referendum he was, at fifteen, learning to run the family farm in northern Vermont so that his father might indulge a consuming thirst for village politics. By the time of Iowa's second referendum he was a twenty-six-year-old combat veteran who had been mustered out of the Civil War with a captaincy; he had served as an assistant clerk in the Vermont legislature; and he was concluding a course of reading in the law. Then Elden J. Hartshorn headed west in search of opportunity, ultimately settling on the frontier in northwest Iowa and in 1874 commencing a lengthy career representing his region in the general assembly. There ("in order that the Constitution might be consistent with itself," he once explained) he kept the amendment question alive session after session, but with very little fanfare—in part, perhaps, because his immediate political constituency happened to be an immigrant Irish enclave: today the statue on the Palo Alto County courthouse lawn is not that of a Union soldier but of the immortal Irish patriot Robert Emmet. Hartshorn's constituents, who had rejected black suffrage in 1868 by the largest county margin in the state, would love him not for his stand on equal rights but for his having legislatively forced a railroad to build through Emmetsburg.[27]

With Hartshorn chairing the house committee on constitutional amendments, both chambers of the 1874 legislature passed the amendment resolution, and for the first time in Iowa's history a question of black civil equality attracted substantial Democratic support. Nine house Democrats favored the measure, with only one against; in the senate a Democrat actually moved the resolution's passage, which he and all but one Jacksonian then voted for. Thus came the first practical expression locally of the national Democrats' New Departure strategy for the seventies and eighties.[28]

Inaugurated in 1871 and promptly endorsed by Iowa's Democracy, this gambit promised the national Democratic party's acceptance of the three great Civil War amendments to the United States Constitution—the Thirteenth outlawing slavery (1865), the Fourteenth guaranteeing a racially impartial citizenship (1868), the Fifteenth guaranteeing equality of political privileges (1870)—"as no longer issues before the country." To Republicans everywhere the New Departure smacked more of public relations than of a genuine metamorphosis, its most startling effect being the abrupt substitution of "negro" or "colored person" for the formerly ubiquitous "nigger" in the nation's Democratic press.

Yet it was undeniable that thousands of Democrats, at least in the North, welcomed their party's abandonment of "the dead issues of an effete past," as one New York City spokesman put it. Congressional Democrats still opposed measures designated to *enforce* the Fourteenth and Fifteenth amendments in the South, but that, they said, was only a consequence of their party's reemphasis of states' rights, limited government, and fiscal retrenchment. And in time their opponents reciprocated. The 1876 elevation to the White House of Rutherford B. Hayes, a Republican pledged to stop the use of federal troops to uphold civil rights in the South, signalled not only the formal end of Reconstruction but also mainstream Republicans' assent to a nonpartisan policy in matters of race.[29]

Because of a mixup about prior publication of the measure as decreed by the amendment process, Iowa's 1876 general assembly could not follow through on "free white" repeal. The effort began anew in 1878. Under the watchful supervision of E. J. Hartshorn, now a member of the senate, the 1878 and 1880 assemblies finally produced technically perfect as well as remarkably bipartisan amendment legislation.

In the meantime, with race having so abruptly subsided as an issue formally dividing the parties, the reform-minded had moved on to other things, their energies coopted by the bitter antimonopoly and prohibition wars of Iowa's Gilded Age. By 1880 most Iowans—white progressives, white conservatives, even black activists—seem to have forgotten that a vestige of the antebellum black code lurked in the Iowa constitution. At the capital, for example, little publicity attended the final success of the amendment resolution. Undersized headlines on inside pages of the Des Moines *Register* announced its senate passage ("Knocking the Word 'White' out of the Constitution with an Amendment Club") and its quiet triumph in the house ("Passage of the Constitutional Amendment Cleaning Out the Last Remnant of Class Prejudice"). But no follow-up story in Iowa's leading newspaper ever appeared.[30]

In August 1880 the Republican state convention met in Des Moines. The venerable Alex Clark, at fifty-four pondering a career change to the law, attended as a delegate, and Davenport's old radical agitator, Ed Russell, now retired from the stresses of active editorship, chaired the resolutions committee. Yet neither the convention's minutes nor the report of a reception honoring its black delegates, which featured an address by Clark, make reference to the pending referendum. In September blacks from central Iowa met in Des Moines to celebrate the anniversary of the Emancipation Proclamation. None of the speakers mentioned the referendum. Judge C. C. Cole, now in successful private practice, recapitulated his role in the famous *Clark* decision but said nothing about "free white" repeal. Gov. John H. Gear dwelt at length on civil equality, describing Iowa to his largely black audience as a state "where every political right is yours." Incredibly, he had forgotten about the existing ban on nonwhite legislators, about his having approved a rectifying proposition, and about his having signed, not two weeks earlier, an official proclamation (composed by his secretary of state and not yet released) announcing the November election, a document that included no less than four paragraphs on the upcoming amendment.[31]

On September 29, Governor Gear's proclamation began its unsystematic series of appearances as a paid legal notice in selected newspapers throughout the state. It announced that two referendum items would accompany the election. Proposition 1 asked voters whether or not they desired that a constitutional convention be held, a query routinely required by law every ten years. Proposition 2 embraced "free white" repeal. An accompanying statement warned all concerned that a recently passed statute mandated a change in the mechanics of referendum voting on constitutional amendments. Henceforth, proposition ballots must be "separate from the ballots for officers . . . and shall be deposited in [separate] boxes."

That same day a Republican village editor in upstate Hancock County issued Iowa's first media comment about the referendum. He observed that two propositions would be on the ballot in November. "The second question will hardly admit of discussion," he said. "If a colored citizen in any district wishes to go to the legislature and a majority of the voters of his district entertain a similar wish in his behalf, they certainly ought not to be debarred the right to their choice." A week later, with the wider dissemination of the governor's proclamation, a second country journalist at Nevada issued a more elaborate statement. His editorial, "The Free and White Amendment," sought to inject some partisan spirit into the question. The success of proposition 2 would repeal "the last remaining political distinction between the whites and the blacks," he wrote. "Democrats, of course, will be entitled to their constitutional privilege of voting against the amendment, and this will probably be the last chance they have of venting their spleen against the 'damned niggers,' as they still insist on calling them."

But the editors of the first urban daily to respond to proposition 2, the Dubuque *Daily Herald,* long one of Iowa's most prominent Democratic journals, handled the question with lightly sardonic neutrality. And the following day an Iowa City Democratic sheet followed suit more earnestly, briefly explaining the targeted clause as "an inadvertency when the constitution was amended several years ago." Simultaneously a story in Knoxville's Republican weekly implicitly urged a Yes vote on proposition 2 by describing the racial qualifications for legislators as "not in keeping with the sentiments of the people of the State."[32]

On October 15, less than three weeks before election day, the Des Moines *Register* finally carried the governor's proclamation, but postponed comment on the referendum for another week. And in other respects too the state capital's leadership seemed oblivious. The Republican elite had been devoting its energies to meeting the challenge of the Greenback party, the national farmer-labor coalition that in Iowa had steadily risen in strength since the mid-seventies. Top priority was to recover two congressional seats lost to the Greenbackers and to counter the effect of the Greenback presidential candidate's being an Iowan—the prominent antimonopolist and monetary reformer, James B. Weaver. All else got lost in the shuffle.

On October 21, with just a week and a half to go, the Republican state central committee at last perceived that something of an emergency existed: proposition 2 was likely to fail unless election officials awoke to the matter of separate ballots and boxes. Its secretary hastily dispatched a circular to all local committees calling attention to the proposal's special needs, suggesting in addition that each Republican ballot carry proposition 2 "at the bottom of the ticket" with a note telling the voter "to detach and vote it separately."[33] Simultaneously an Associated Press dispatch from Des Moines urged much the same information on "all county committee-men of all parties"—Republican, Democratic, and Greenback.[34]

Since 1880's Republican platform took no note of the proposed amendment, the central committee did not feel absolutely obligated to do very much—even if it had had the time—to create a groundswell of support for proposition 2. Left strictly to their own devices, therefore, only a third of the state's Republican editors urged its passage, while another third displayed an affable neutrality and the remaining third took no notice at all of the proposal beyond the fine print of the governor's proclamation. None encouraged a No vote—but then neither did any Democratic editor, two of whom, in line with New Departure politics, actually recommended "free white" repeal.[35]

Wishing to do nothing to dissipate the nonpartisan ambience surrounding the amendment, the proprietor of the Des Moines *Register* editorialized with caution. But James S. ("Ret") Clarkson could not suppress an anxiety that proposition 2 might miscarry. As its editor from 1869 to 1891, Clarkson transformed the *Register* into the single most important journal in the state, and himself into one of Iowa's three most politically powerful figures and an influential voice within higher national circles of the GOP. Indiana-born, his long-standing commitment to civil rights stemmed from his once having witnessed a Kentucky slave auction. In the late 1870s, to protest President Hayes's policy of sectional reconciliation at the expense of southern blacks, he resigned his Des Moines postmastership and became one of the administration's angriest Republican critics. At the end of the 1880s, once again protesting a Republican administration's neglect of its African-American constituents, he was, in the words of historian Stanley P. Hirshson, "the most outspoken advocate of human rights in the [entire] party."[36]

On October 22, in his first specific story on the measure, Ret Clarkson endorsed the state central committee's idea that the Republican ticket should include proposition 2 at its tail, "with a check rule cut across, so that the same can be easily detached." But the next day he reversed himself, urging that the referendum ballots be printed separately on colored paper so as to be "more clearly distinguished and more certainly counted right." And on October 26, discreetly recommending that it "be adopted by all other committees" in the state, Clarkson reproduced the proposition 2 ballot devised by Polk County's Republican committee. On close examination it could be found offering voters only the Yes alternative:

BALLOT.

PROPOSED AMENDMENT TO CONSTITUTION.

FOR THE AMENDMENT.

Shall the Constitution be amended as follows:

"Strike out the words "free white" from the third line of section four (4) of article three (3) of Constitution, relating to the legislative department."

How influential Ret Clarkson's suggestion proved to be is uncertain: only two other Republican county committees are known to have stacked the cards in the recommended manner.[37] Most 1880 ballots, irrespective of party, probably employed the proposition wording that concluded the fifteen-inch Republican slip ticket adopted at Vinton:[38]

Tear this off and Vote Separately.

"Shall the Constitution be amended as follows?"

"Strike out the words "free white," from the third line of section four (4) of article three (3) of said Constitution, relating to the legislative department."

YES.

NO.

V

Just as the second popular vote on black suffrage in Iowa had coincided, quite by accident, with 1868's presidential election, so Iowans voted once more on a question of civil equality at the presidential election of 1880. James A. Garfield's name headed the Republican ticket, and on November 2 the Ohioan won Iowa almost as handsomely as Grant had taken it twelve years earlier, carrying all but five counties and winning 57 percent of the ballots. Victory was denied him in downstate Davis County only because the Greenback party's candidate happened to be a hometown boy.

In contrast to Garfield's solid Iowa majority, proposition 2 won by a landslide—63 percent of the referendum ballots cast—losing only eleven counties (map 11.2). A 6-point statistical disparity separated the Garfield and the proposition 2 percentages, even though in only one county did the raw number of Yes ballots actually outnumber Garfield votes. And in many a fiercely Democratic enclave the exaggerated voter roll-off allowed "free white" repeal to win by default. The Democratic nominee, Winfield Scott Hancock, carried Liberty Township of Clinton County by 69 percent of the ballots, for example. But so, by 98 percent, did proposition 2. And while Hancock won three of Dubuque's five precincts, "free white" repeal easily carried them all. Such oddities point up an anomaly of very consid-

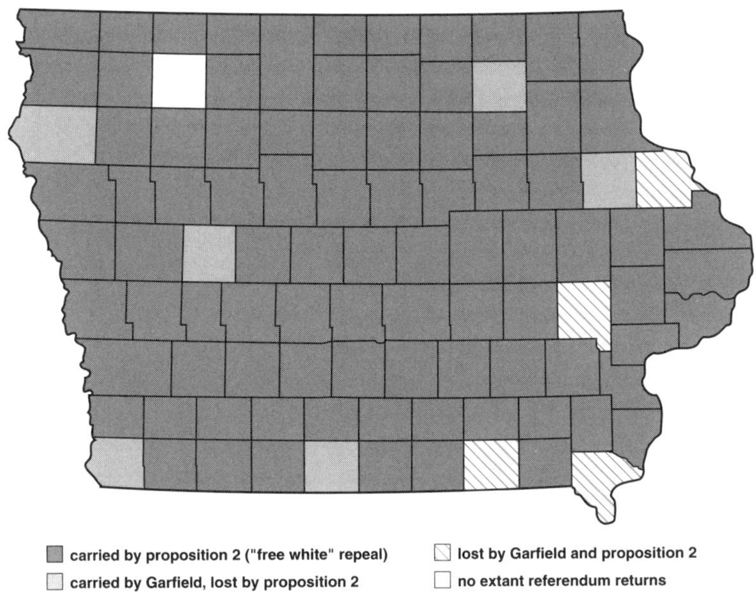

Map 11.2 The 1880 election and referendum (for key to county names see map A.1, appendix A).

Table 11.3 How the 1879 electorate behaved in November 1880 (estimated percentages)

	President				"Free white" repeal				
	Garfield (R)	Hancock (D)	Weaver (GB)		Yes	No	Rolled off		Not voting
Republicans	48	2	−1		28	4	18		−3
Democrats	0	23	2		−2	7	20		−1
Greenbackers	1	3	9		0	4	9		1
Nonvoters	2	1	0		1	1	1		8
1879 ineligibles	3	1	0		−1	−1	5		1
				94				94	6

Regressions: 1879 gubernatorial returns × 1880 presidential and 1880 proposition 2 returns (county N = 98); two estimates rounded up in order to equalize subtotals.

erable import: despite a voter turnout of about 95 percent of the state's estimated eligible voters, only some 50 percent of them cast ballots for or against proposition 2. Half the electorate, in other words, did not vote at all on "free white" repeal.

It appears to have been a classic case of too little voter information offered too late. The newspapers of less than half of Iowa's counties publicized the forthcoming amendment, and in any case their effect on referendum participation appears to have been negligible.[39] Most voters evidently learned of proposition 2 only upon arriving at the polls to cast ballots for national, state, and local candidates. Suddenly somebody was telling them they could also vote, if they wished, on letting blacks into the legislature. Given the impossibility of much reflection, the half who responded with Yes and No ballots must have possessed fairly definite opinions, unequivocally progressive or unmistakably conservative. But tens of thousands begged off, presumably in confusion, especially the newly enfranchised.[40]

"We saw many a stalwart [Republican] walk up to the polls Tuesday and cast his vote against striking out the word 'white,'" wrote a cynical Democratic journalist at Marshalltown. But such remarks exaggerate. In the commentator's own town, for example, only 109 men cast No ballots. Even if all had been Republicans—an assumption contrary to logic—they would amount to but a small minority of Garfield's local support. Statewide (table 11.3), about 60 percent of Iowa's Republicans voted Yes on proposition 2, the rest of them mainly rolling off. Virtually no Democrats cast Yes ballots, and about twice as many of them voted against "free white" repeal than did Republicans. Race prejudice continued to divide the two major parties at the grass roots, New Departure or no New Departure. It was not yet true in Iowa, as historian Lawrence Grossman has written of the early eighties nationally, that "no longer could one generalize about a man's stand on Negro rights simply by examining his party label."[41]

But Iowa's third great referendum stands witness to what contemporaries would have found unthinkable in 1857 or 1868: a solid majority of the state's Democrats rolled off on a proposition involving black civil equality rather than vote No. The times had changed, even though the signs of the times did not point unambiguously to the declining significance of race.

The Egalitarian Moment

12

In the 1870s thousands of settlers overspread the interior of Iowa's far northwest corner, bringing to a close the frontier era of the Hawkeye State some fifty years after it had begun.[1]

The Republican party had ruled Iowa for nearly half that period, and the days when the territory and state had been a reactionary Democratic fief surely seemed, to those who experienced them, oddly remote. Many had played protagonists' roles in Iowa's transformation from perhaps the most racially conservative free state in the Union into one of its most progressive. Some were no longer on hand to savor the fruits of their labors.

The Rev. Asa Turner Jr., Iowa's very first antislavery activist, was still an Iowan in 1880 and witness to what God and man had wrought. But a number of his clerical brethren in the struggle had been no more than trans-Mississippi sojourners. In 1843, as we have seen, the Revs. James H. Dickey and William T. Allan, from opposing schools of abolitionism, collaborated just long enough at Yellow Spring to help launch the Iowa Anti-Slavery Society before returning east. In 1847, also at Yellow Spring, the Rev. Alanson St. Clair presided at the birth of Iowa's Liberty party, then edited its newspaper for a season before following the antislavery lecture circuit to Michigan and settling there. In 1854 the Rev. Simeon Waters had been crucially instrumental in forging the coalition at Crawfordsville that overthrew Iowa's Democracy, but soon afterward he withdrew to an obscure religious vocation in New England. And in the late 1850s the Rev. Richard H. Cain, having served a frontier apprenticeship as Muscatine's AME minister, returned to a wartime pastorate in New York City, then was called to South Carolina. As one of Reconstruction's most prominent African-Americans, he ultimately represented that key southern state in Congress.

A few activists, notably the pioneer abolitionists Aaron Street Jr. and Samuel L. Howe, as well as James W. Grimes, chief architect of the Hawkeye State's Republican movement, had died by 1880. Yet others, their hopes for upward mobility within the party frustrated by vague jealousies and animosities, had moved on. William Penn Clarke, the battle-scarred Free Soiler, and the loquacious civil libertarian Rufus L. B. Clarke, leading figures in the 1857 constitutional convention debates on equal rights, retired to anonymous patronage appointments in Washington, D.C. Also eased out to pasture was the ex-governor to whom the critical ideological triumph of 1865 owed so much. William M. Stone finally sought fresh opportunities in Colorado, only to return home broken in spirit and pocketbook before he, too, gratefully accepted a federal job.

Many others simply found that Iowa no longer offered sufficient challenge to their aspirations. Such was the case with its most persistent civil rights activist, Alexander Clark. Clark's son became the first black to graduate from the University of Iowa law school, whereupon Alex himself decided to become the second. After that he would divide his time between a Muscatine legal practice and the editorship of a Chicago newspaper. In 1891, no doubt farther from home than he could have imagined when setting foot on Iowa soil nearly fifty years before, Clark died while serving as United States special envoy to Liberia.[2]

I

Iowans eliminated the formal color line through an unplanned succession of events. Some black laws expired in the codification of 1851. Others vanished in the 1857 convention, still others in the wartime general assembly and in the state supreme court. But removal of the Democratic party's control of public policy had been the most important single step.

In Iowa that occurred very much according to the two-phase process originally suggested by Michael F. Holt and brilliantly elaborated by William E. Gienapp.[3] First came the apparent resolution of the slavery-extension issue by the Compromise of 1850, leaving a void promptly filled by new issues—liquor, immigration, Catholicism—that cut across existing party lines and dealt a mortal blow to the Whigs while weakening the Democrats. Second came the events of 1854–1856: a reemergent slavery issue, formation of the Whig/Free Soil coalition and its 1854 triumph, the struggle between Anti-Nebraskans and Know Nothings as ethnocultural anxieties continued to vie with slavery for the attention of voters, and the ultimate resolution of that struggle, after the national American party failed to repudiate slavery extension, with the founding of an Iowa Republican organization that contained an important Know Nothing element.

For civil libertarians, practically all of them ensconced within the new party, the next task was to persuade the party's own leadership to take a decisive stand against Iowa's black code. This task had been far from accomplished in 1857, when the state's first suffrage referendum failed by an enormous margin, and little had changed when war erupted in 1861. But one important local result of the Civil War was to consolidate the Iowa Republicans' ascendancy. Among northern states only Rhode Island, Massachusetts, Vermont, and Minnesota outclassed the Hawkeye State in wartime Republican electoral strength. Historian V. Jacque Voegeli suggests the appropriate significance of that fact. "In states such as Iowa," he notes, "where Republicans were distinctly in the majority they tended to be more radical than they were in closely divided states such as Illinois and Ohio."

Rhode Island, Massachusetts, and Vermont had long permitted African-Americans to vote. In 1868 Minnesota and Iowa took this uncommon step, the only states to do so by referendum before approval of the Fifteenth Amendment dissolved the need for an arduous state-by-state campaign. The larger point is that Minnesota's and Iowa's Republican majorities identified those two states as politically safe, where voter reprisals for Republican radicalism might be minimized by effective party leadership. And so it proved. Minnesotans granted black suffrage, after two previous referendum losses, when its Republican-dominated legislature finally submitted the proposition to voters as "an amendment of Section 1, Article 7" of the state constitution—without any direct reference to the elective franchise.[4]

That Iowans, in contrast to their northern neighbors, approved suffrage reform that same year with a compelling candor proves that their political struggle over black suffrage had already been resolved in 1865, when Governor Stone withstood the demagogic assault of Thomas Hart Benton Jr. and his Union Anti-Negro Suffrage party. After that there was no turning back, and the emerging affinity between suffrage reform at home and in the South stiffened Iowans' conviction that they had rightly committed themselves to the civil equality of blacks. Thus 1868's outcome may be seen as mainly a ratification of 1865's result.

In 1880, finally, with southern reconstruction abandoned by the national Republican party and questions involving race shouldered aside by state and regional economic concerns, Iowa's "free white" proposition took both Republicans and Democrats by surprise. A strong majority of the ballots favored proposition 2 at the same time that an almost equally strong majority of the state's eligible voters had declined to commit itself one way or the other.

II

Much depends, in any summary judgment of Iowa's three great plebiscites, on how the outcomes are percentaged. The official tallies (panel one of table 12.1) fail to accommodate the enormous numbers of abstaining voters in 1857 and 1880. By contrast, calculating the ballots for each option as a proportion of the state's estimated voters (panel two) usefully highlights the complicating effect of those who did not vote. But it also implies—incorrectly—an identity of nonvoter behavior in 1857 and 1880. While most of the abstainers from Iowa's 1857 referendum had stayed home, in 1880 most rolled off, turning out to vote in the candidate election but refusing to cast ballots on equal rights. Splitting the abstaining bloc into its component parts (panel three) emphasizes the difference between the two referendums while offering further elaboration. The largest voter grouping of each now aptly characterizes the ruling behavioral theme of that referendum. Iowa's No voters predominated in 1857, its Yes voters in 1868, and those who rolled off in 1880.

It is not clear if similar underlying attitudes governed roll-off behavior in 1857, 1868, and 1880. While refusal to vote on any of these occasions

Table 12.1 Iowa's equal rights referendums percentaged four different ways

The official tallies	Yes	No		
1857	15	85		
1868	57	43		
1880	63	37		
With abstainers included	Yes	No	Abstained	
1857	8	44	48	
1868	51	39	10	
1880	27	15	58	
With roll-off isolated	Yes	No	Rolled off	Not voting
1857	8	44	19	29
1868	51	39	5	5
1880	27	15	53	5
With No ballots and roll-off aggregated	Yes	"Enhanced No"		Not voting
1857	8	63		29
1868	51	44		5
1880	27	68		5

Source: Secretary of State, "Election Records" (microfilm copy, University of Iowa Libraries), reel 1.

may not have been prompted by deep-seated hostilities toward blacks, without any doubt the roll-off identified Iowans who lacked any serious inclination to vote Yes. It is therefore arguable that No voters and rollers-off should be merged to form an "enhanced No" vote for each referendum, applying, in effect, James F. Wilson's disregarded formula for computing the negative vote in 1857. Thus recalculated (panel four), the percentages strongly contradict the impression given by the official tallies that Iowans' racial attitudes steadily improved over time. Instead, the strong similarity between 1857 and 1880 is reemphasized, leaving 1868 to stand alone as the singular moment when Iowans voting Yes outnumbered all eligible voters who did not.

How Republicans and Democrats behaved in the three referendums has been statistically explored in chapters 9 and 11. But the results reported there may be recalculated in a manner that enhances their comparability (table 12.2). Among Republicans, the most notable change between 1857 and 1868 was a dramatic enlargement of the Yes vote. But the Yes percentage slumped in 1880, a downturn matched not by an increased No vote or in more Republicans failing to turn out at the polls, but in a swollen roll-off. Among Democrats, virtually none of whom *ever* voted Yes on equal rights, the most dramatic change was a huge drop in No ballots between 1868 to 1880, a shift that corresponds to an identical rise

Table 12.2 Major-party voter positions on equal rights, 1857–1880 (estimated percentages)

	1857	1868	1880
Republicans			
Voting Yes	25	87	58
Voting No	11	4	7
Rolling off	37	7	35
Not voting	27	2	0[a]
	100	100	100
Democrats			
Voting Yes	0[a]	0	0[a]
Voting No	85	100[b]	25
Rolling off	0[a]	0	75
Not voting	15	0	0[a]
	100	100	100

Regressions: 1856 presidential returns × 1857 proposition 2 returns (county N = 70); 1867 gubernatorial returns × 1868 proposition 1 returns (county N = 97); 1879 gubernatorial returns × 1880 proposition 2 returns (county N = 98).

a. Percentage set at minimum value and others adjusted.

b. Percentage set at maximum value and others adjusted.

in roll-off. The Republican roll-offs of 1857 and 1868, we may guess, were indeed implicit No votes cast by party loyalists opposed to black suffrage but too anti-Democratic to act as Democrats by voting No. Therefore, aggregating No votes and roll-off seems entirely legitimate for 1857 and 1868, but not for 1880, when rolling off was a Democratic as well as a Republican behavior, an outcome largely prompted by neither party's having provided much guidance.

A measure of the significance of such guidance is whether or not important numbers of Iowans changed their minds over time, modifying, if not their underlying racial attitudes, then at least their conceptions of how they should *behave* with respect to equal rights. How many who had voted No in 1857 then voted Yes in 1868? Given the rapid growth typical of a frontier population, Iowa's 1868 electorate was necessarily very different from what it had been in the fifties.[5] It is within the range of statistical possibility, in fact, that 1868's triumphant Yes vote could have been cast solely by new voters (men who had arrived in the state after 1857 or who had come of voting age during the intervening years) without a single Iowan reversing his 1857 position in 1868.[6]

Analysis credibly suggests that a great many Iowans did in fact change their minds on suffrage reform (table 12.3). Frémont men, only a third of whom supported proposition 2 in 1857, cast virtually all their votes against the openly racist Colonel Benton in 1865 and went on to support proposition 1 strongly in 1868. In numerical terms, something like ten thousand antebellum Republicans switched from opposing black suffrage before the war—by voting No or rolling off in 1857—to supporting it afterward.[7] It is also apparent, however, that former Frémont voters alone did not carry proposition 1 to victory in 1868. Old Know Nothings—Fillmore men who had become flaming Republicans by the close of the war—also gave majorities to Stone and to suffrage reform. Yet it was those who had not been eligible to vote, because they had been underage or nonresident before 1868, who gave the largest boost to black suffrage: almost a third of the 1868 electorate consisted of recently enfranchised Yes voters.

But what of 1880? Did any large number of 1868 voters again switch position in the absence of timely party advice concerning "free white" repeal? Indeed they did (table 12.4). Virtually all Governor Stone's supporters cast Yes ballots in 1868. But such was not the case twelve years later, when perhaps as many as forty thousand of them cast No votes.[8] Virtually none, however, rolled off in 1880; perhaps those who had participated in the political excitement of 1865 had no trouble knowing their own minds, pro or con, when it came to the abruptly resuscitated issue of equal rights. Meanwhile, those who made rolling off the most popular voter response to "free white" repeal were mainly old Benton supporters

Table 12.3 How the 1856 electorate voted on equal rights, 1857–1868 (estimated percentages)

	1857				1865			1868			
	Yes	No	Rolled off	Not voting	Stone	Benton	Not voting	Yes	No	Rolled off	Not voting
Frémont voters	10	5	14	10	22	0	8	19	−4	2	6
Buchanan voters	−5	31	0	7	3	25	−5	−4	26	−1	−3
Fillmore voters	1	3	3	2	6	−1	1	4	−1	1	1
Nonvoters	0	0	4	9	2	3	5	3	4	0	0
1856 ineligibles	2	6	−2	0	13	8	10	29	15	1	2
				100			100				100

Regressions: 1856 presidential returns × 1857 proposition 2, 1865 gubernatorial, and 1868 proposition 1 returns (county N = 70).

Table 12.4 How the 1865 electorate voted on equal rights in 1868 and 1880 (estimated percentages)

	1868					1880				
	Yes	No	Rolled off	Not voting		Yes	No	Rolled off	Not voting	
Stone voters	33	−4	3	2		17	6	0	−2	
Benton voters	−5	32	0	−1		−5	5	13	3	
Nonvoters	7	4	0	3		0	0	5	4	
1865 ineligibles	15	8	1	2		15	5	34	0	
					100					100

Regressions: 1865 gubernatorial returns × 1868 proposition 1 and 1880 proposition 2 returns (county N = 94).

plus some 115,000 men (two-thirds of them Republicans) who had only become eligible to vote after 1865.

Voter behavior is also made clearer by comparing successive Democratic and Republican electorates on equal rights over time. To augment comparability, each set of voting returns added horizontally equals 100 percent. No estimates for how the 1856 or 1860 electorates might have voted in 1880 are included because the lengthy time span precludes credible results.

The numbers suggest a great deal of difference between the major parties. Successive Democratic electorates advanced to their destinations in lockstep (table 12.5). Confirming a point made earlier, virtually none of any Jacksonian cohort—from the Buchanan men of '56 to the Hancock men of '80—ever voted Yes on equal rights. And when their collective behavior shifted in the 1870s, it did so with a minimum of disarray. Democrats voting No in 1880 varied by only 18 points from lowest to highest percentage, those rolling off and abstaining by 14 points each. This implies that after 1871 Iowa's Democrats responded with a kind of collective ideological precision to their national party's New Departure platform—the main message of which, it will be recalled, was not that the Democracy embraced the civil equality of African-Americans, but rather that the issue was no longer political. By declining to vote at all on proposition 2 in 1880, the majority of Iowa's Democrats simply expressed their deference to that message.

In contrast, the behavior of successive Republican electorates reveals much more ambiguity (table 12.6). The 1856 and 1866 Republicans favored black suffrage in 1868 less enthusiastically than did the others, but no cohort voted less than 78 percent Yes in 1868. Every GOP electorate later supported "free white" repeal in lower percentages than it had favored suffrage reform in 1868, although the depth of the declension varied. The 1864 and 1865 electorates favored proposition 2 by 70 and 77 percent; the electorate of 1866, as well as every postwar presidential electorate, gave the proposition only about 50 percent of their ballots; and the 1867 electorate's 62 percent looks much like a transition vote.

Turnout data suggest a possible reason for this pattern. Eighteen sixty-five and 1867 were years of low Republican turnout at the polls, while in 1866 and in presidential elections from 1868 through 1880 Republican turnouts surged to new heights. Only the more determinedly ideological—and therefore the more egalitarian—Republicans may have felt compelled to attend the polls in 1865 and 1867. By contrast, we may guess, the high-turnout elections attracted hosts of the less reflective and less issue-oriented Republicans, accounting for those electorates' more conservative behavior in the 1880 referendum.

The Republicans of 1865, 1866, and 1867 also voted No in 1880 in

Table 12.5 How selected Democratic electorates voted on equal rights, 1857–1880 (estimated percentages)

	1857				1868				1880			
	Yes	No	Rolled off	Not voting	Yes	No	Rolled off	Not voting	Yes	No	Rolled off	Not voting
Buchanan voters (1856)	0[a]	85	0[a]	15	0	100[b]	0	0				
Douglas voters (1860)					0	100[b]	0	0				
McClellan voters (1864)					0	100[b]	0	0	0[a]	21	66	13
Benton voters (1865)					0	100[b]	0	0	0[a]	19	73	8
Van Anda voters (1866)					0	100[b]	0	0	0[a]	32	61	7
Mason voters (1867)					0	100[b]	0	0	0[a]	14	65	21
Seymour voters (1868)					0	100[b]	0	0	0[a]	28	59	13
Greeley voters (1872)									0[a]	29	68	3
Tilden voters (1876)									0[a]	27	68	5
Hancock voters (1880)									0[a]	29	71	0

Regressions: 1856–1880 presidential returns and 1865–1867 returns for highest state office at issue × 1857, 1868, and 1880 referendum returns (various county N's).

a. Percentage set at minimum value and others adjusted.

b. Percentage set at maximum value and others adjusted.

Table 12.6 How selected Republican electorates voted on equal rights, 1857–1880 (estimated percentages)

	1857				1868				1880			
	Yes	No	Rolled off	Not voting	Yes	No	Rolled off	Not voting	Yes	No	Rolled off	Not voting
Frémont voters (1856)	25	11	37	27	78	0[a]	4	18				
Lincoln voters (1860)					87	0[a]	1	12				
Lincoln voters (1864)					95	0	1	4	70	12	10	8
Stone voters (1865)					93	0[a]	6	1	77	23	0	0[a]
Wright voters (1866)					80	3	8	9	47	19	28	6
Merrill voters (1867)					87	4	7	2	62	22	16	0[a]
Grant voters (1868)					91	4	5	0	52	9	39	0
Grant voters (1872)									50	12	38	0[a]
Hayes voters (1876)									51	8	41	0[a]
Garfield voters (1880)									54	3	43	0

Regressions: See table 12.5.
a. Percentage set at minimum value and others adjusted.

comparatively large proportions—around 20 percent. One may hypothesize a reason. The members of this important Republican minority, intensely patriotic but also socially conservative, had been persuaded in 1868 that black voting and office-holding were necessary adjuncts to consolidating Union victory over an unrepentant South, a strategy requiring the enfranchisement of Iowa's own blacks. They voted Yes in 1868 despite their misgivings. But, like conservative Republicans elsewhere in America, in the 1870s they grew increasingly uncomfortable with their national party's formal support of southern Republican organizations whose biracial composition and outspoken radicalism so deeply offended the South's "better class" of whites. Elsewhere such dissatisfaction moved Republican conservatives into the Liberal Republican cause of 1872, with its rejection of President Grant and its ill-fated alliance with the Democrats behind Horace Greeley's presidential hopes.[9] But few Iowa Republicans—so the relevant analyses suggest—could bring themselves to repudiate Grant, the great personification of national triumph in the Civil War. Iowa's Liberal movement, in consequence, is most appropriately seen as just another fusion by which the state's Democrats sought to overcome their numerical handicap. And not until the opportunity to reject "free white" repeal came up in 1880 did the lingering racism of Iowa's conservative Republicans find specific political expression.

An important minority of the Republican electorates of 1868 through 1880 rolled off on "free white" repeal. About 40 percent chose to do so—a percentage 25 to 30 points lower than that of their Democratic counterparts. But it can be assumed that they acted from much the same impulses that caused the Democratic roll-off. The advent in 1877 of a conservative Republican administration in Washington, headed by a President pledged to ring down the curtain on Reconstruction, was for masses of Republican loyalists the practical equivalent of the Democrats' New Departure. Those Iowa Republicans who rolled off, like their Democratic opposite numbers, were doing more than silently confessing their need of party guidance. By refusing to vote at all on proposition 2 they, too, testified that the American political universe no longer defined the civil equality of blacks as pertinent.

III

It seems reasonable to suppose, the importance of party loyalties and precise contexts notwithstanding, that some voter groups shifted position on equal rights more readily than others. Postwar Republican efforts to generate support for black civil equality presumably had more effect among some types of Republicans, in other words, than among others. The following pages discuss various tests of this presumption. As before, all tabulations sandwiched between lines equal 100 percent, except that a group's estimated Republican percentage will stand alone as a quick measure of the upper limits of its potential for referendum support.[10]

Iowa's work force of 1856 provides the first set of such groups (table 12.7). Men of all categories shifted position on black suffrage between 1857 and 1868, their Yes percentages reflecting increases of from 32 to 40 points. But what is again emphasized is the overriding salience of party: each group's improved behavior on suffrage parallels its increased Republican vote. Among the farmers of prosperous counties, for example, an approximately 11-point rise in percentage Republican is matched by something like a 37-point rise in percentage Yes, a behavior pattern replicated by each of the other three occupation groups, holding as true for the more Democratic farmers from counties of middling prosperity as for the others. This of course does not prove that a strengthened Republicanism *caused* each group's dramatically enlarged Yes vote, but—given the Iowa party's campaign aims in the late 1860s—that is a fully justifiable inference. Unfortunately, there are no comparable occupation data with which to extend the analysis forward to 1880.

Moral reformers and their opponents make up another set of such groups (table 12.8). The bitterly contending prewar factions, identified by Iowa's 1855 prohibition vote, struck sharply opposite postures on equal rights. But in 1857 and 1868 each was so closely associated with one or the other of the two major parties that its behavior on suffrage reform is little more than a strong partisan conduct: virtually no drys voted against black suffrage, virtually no wets for it. Iowa's second statewide prohibition vote, in 1882, identifies the distribution of moral reformers and their opponents at the close of the era. By the eighties prewar constraints had relaxed to the extent that an important minority of wets could now be found voting Republican. Yet, as in 1857 and 1868, dry voters in 1880 were the much more racially progressive bloc, though not nearly as egalitarian as any of the several Republican electorates of the 1860s and 1870s depicted in table 12.6. For their part, wet voters clearly opposed equality in 1880—although not quite as strongly as any of the Democratic electorates described in table 12.5. Political party in 1880 remained a better predicter of behavior on racial issues than did the hostile array of social outlooks associated with conflicting attitudes about liquor.

Antebellum churchgoers form yet another set of Iowans whose changing behavior toward equal rights can be usefully disaggregated, in this instance by major denomination. In table 12.9 religious bodies are listed in descending order of size, with the state's largest, its Methodists, divided into their original northern and southern Iowa conferences.

In 1856 Iowa's downstate Methodists, its Catholics, its Disciples, and its Episcopalians registered as predominately Democratic. By 1868, how-

Table 12.7 How the 1856 work force voted on equal rights, 1856–1868 (estimated percentages)

	1856	1857				1868	1868			
	Republican	Yes	No	Rolled off	Not voting	Republican	Yes	No	Rolled off	Not voting
Farmers:										
Prosperous counties	42	9	71	8	12	53	46	52	2	0[a]
Middling counties	40	9	67	10	14	46	41	59	0	0[a]
Poorer counties	50	15	57	23	5	60	55	41	0	4
Nonfarmers	40	3	16	27	54	47	39	38	5	18

Regressions: 1856 occupations × 1856 presidential, 1857 proposition 2, 1868 presidential, and 1868 proposition 1 returns (county N = 68).
a. Percentage set at minimum value and others adjusted.

Table 12.8 How moral reformers and nonreformers voted on equal rights, 1856–1880 (estimated percentages)

	1856	1857				1868	1868				1880	1880			
	Republican	Yes	No	Rolled off	Not voting	Republican	Yes	No	Rolled off	Not voting	Republican	Yes	No	Rolled off	Not voting
Prewar drys	86	22	0[a]	14	64	76	74	0[a]	2	24					
Prewar wets	0	0	100[b]	0	0	0	0	100[b]	0	0					
Postwar drys											82	42	8	50	0[a]
Postwar wets											35	15	21	64	0[a]

Regressions: 1855 liquor referendum returns × 1856 presidential, 1857 proposition 2, 1868 presidential, and 1868 proposition 1 returns (county N = 59); 1882 liquor referendum returns × 1880 presidential and 1880 proposition 2 returns (county N = 98).

a. Percentage set at minimum value and others adjusted.

b. Percentage set at maximum value and others adjusted.

Table 12.9 How prewar churchgoers voted on equal rights, 1856–1868 (estimated percentages)

	1856	1857				1868	1868			
	Republican	Yes	No	Rolled off	Not voting	Republican	Yes	No	Rolled off	Not voting
Methodists (downstate)	28	1	65	17	17	54	47	45	3	5
Presbyterians	54	9	4	30	57	70	63	26	4	7
Methodists (upstate)	52	19	46	13	22	69	64	27	4	5
Roman Catholics	18	0[a]	45	0[a]	55	38	33	67	0	0
Baptists	49	8	49	35	8	59	47	37	8	8
Congregationalists	68	24	29	15	32	75	71	19	4	6
Disciples of Christ	6	0	100[b]	0	0	48	46	54	0	0[a]
Quakers	80	18	0[a]	51	31	90	90	0[a]	0	10
Lutherans	61	33	19	35	13	54	52	48	0	0
Episcopalians	17	0[a]	48	45	7	59	56	0	7	37

Regressions: 1860 church seats × 1856 presidential, 1857 proposition 2, 1868 presidential, and 1868 proposition 1 returns (county N = 42), with groups listed in descending order of size in 1860.

a. Percentage set at minimum value and others adjusted.

b. Percentage set at maximum value and others adjusted.

ever, all but the Catholics had grown decisively Republican, while the Disciples and Lutherans each proved to be closely divided in preference. The Lutherans formed Iowa's only major denomination whose early Republican proclivities declined somewhat after the Civil War, a behavior no doubt induced by the revivified liquor issue and the party's inescapable identification among German voters with prohibition.[11]

In any event, the members of all church groups dramatically elevated their support for black suffrage between 1857 and 1868. Iowa's Quakers provided the steepest rise, some 70 points. In 1857 Quakers had been the most Republican of all churchgoers, the only denomination that cast virtually no ballots against equal rights, and the religious body with the highest voter roll-off. Only tepidly egalitarian, rank-and-file Quakers were at least sufficiently embarrassed by proposition 2 that they refused to act like Democrats by straightforwardly opposing it. In 1868 Quakers still formed the most Republican denomination, but now virtually all who turned out at the polls—including the great majority of those who had rolled off in such numbers in 1857—cast unflinching Yes ballots.

Other voter position changes proved almost as dramatic. The Yes vote among Presbyterians and Episcopalians rose by over 50 points, while among Methodists of both Iowa conferences, among Congregationalists, and among Disciples it rose by over 40. Baptists and Catholics improved by at least 30 points, Lutherans by almost 20. Lutherans and downstate Methodists behaved similarly in expressing only precarious Republican majorities in 1868, and in being the only Republican-oriented denominations splitting their referendum votes fairly evenly between Yes and No options. Lutherans aside, the most obvious central tendency is that each church body increased both its Republicanism and its support for equal rights, the first increase presumably prompting the second.

After the Civil War the religious complexion of the Hawkeye State changed only slightly. By the eighties the Methodists, the Presbyterians, the Baptists, and the Catholics still constituted Iowa's largest religious groups, with the five other larger prewar denominations still ranking among its numerically most important. But their politics had continued to evolve (table 12.10). Methodists, Presbyterians, and Congregationalists were about as strong for Garfield in 1880 as they had been for Grant in 1868. But the Republicanism of Baptists, Catholics, Disciples, Quakers, and Episcopalians had declined as issues associated with the Civil War lost their urgency. Only Catholics and Episcopalians appear to have been staunchly Democratic in 1880; Baptists had split between Republican and Democratic loyalties, and Disciples had generated a Greenbacker plurality.

With respect to equal rights, in 1880 rolling off was the behavior of choice among churchgoers as among Iowans generally, although ballot majorities for proposition 2 carried all but the Catholics, Disciples, and

Table 12.10 How post-Reconstruction churchgoers voted on equal rights and on liquor in the 1880s (estimated percentages)

	1880	1880 "Free white" repeal				1882 Prohibition		
	Republican	Yes	No	Rolled off	Not voting	Yes	No	Not voting
Methodists	66	22	11	67	0[a]	64	13	23
Presbyterians	73	47	16	39	0[a]	74	26	0[a]
Roman Catholics	15	0	20	61	19	0[a]	83	17
Baptists	42	39	7	40	14	0[a]	75	25
Congregationalists	80	31	0[a]	55	14	68	12	20
Disciples of Christ	23	23	42	35	0[a]	42	9	49
Quakers	58	43	15	0[a]	42	66	31	3
Lutherans	66	26	8	52	14	43	17	40
Episcopalians	36	0[a]	0[a]	87	13	30	0[a]	70

Regressions: 1885 church seats × 1880 presidential, 1880 proposition 2, and 1882 liquor referendum returns (county N = 72), with groups listed in descending order of size in 1860.

a. Percentage set at minimum value and others adjusted.

Episcopalians. An interesting feature of 1880 is that among Baptists and Disciples a much smaller discrepancy existed between support for Garfield and support for "free white" repeal than was the case among such heavily Republican groups as the Methodists, Congregationalists, and Lutherans—among whom the gap ranged between 40 and 49 points. Republican Baptists and Disciples remained relatively rare. Perhaps because of that very fact these political nonconformists retained an unusually robust sense of their party's traditional commitment to civil rights, and more loyally than other Republicans they expressed that conviction in 1880. Finally, it might be noted that all denominations but the Catholics and Baptists were more enthusiastic about liquor prohibition than black equality.

The behavior of Iowa's major prewar ethnocultural groups is portrayed in table 12.11. Statistically projecting the distributions of smaller aggregations forward in time from 1868 to 1880, however, necessarily reduces their size to the point that plausible results are not forthcoming. Therefore, two groups analyzed elsewhere—the Indianans and the Britons and Scots—have been dropped from the analyses, which employ only nativity groups making up at least 6 percent of all enumerated birthplaces.[12]

Vast numbers of the antebellum cohort changed their politics between the 1850s and the late 1860s. The Republican proclivities of Iowa's Pennsylvanians, strong for the Pennsylvania Democrat James Buchanan in 1856, rose a startling 40 points as the group switched decisively to Grant in 1868. The affiliation of the Ohioans, however, inexplicably plummeted. The perambulations of the other major groups fell between these behavioral extremes. The Republicanism of New Englanders and southerners rose by about 20 points each, although those two voter collectivities were sharply at odds in their attitudes toward Grant. Again, due no doubt to the reemergent liquor issue, the Germans' Republicanism declined by about 25 points. Only among two extreme groups—the solidly Republican New Yorkers and the overwhelmingly Democratic Irish—did the presidential support levels of 1856 duplicate themselves in 1868.

Neither Irishmen nor Germans gave support of any substance to black suffrage in 1857 or in 1868, but the Yes percentages among all other groups rose sharply. Like the Quakers, the New Englanders had been overwhelmingly Republican in 1856, had shied from heartily embracing suffrage reform in 1857, had rolled off rather than vote No. But, again like the Quakers, the Yankees proved themselves hearty egalitarians in 1868, their Yes vote rocketing upward by some 90 points. The Yes percentages of other voters rose more modestly: Pennsylvanians' by some 50 points, New Yorkers' by 40, Ohioans' by 22, southerners' by 14. New Yorkers alone increased their support of black suffrage without any commensurate rise in their Republican percentage between 1856 and 1868.

From 1868 to 1880 these upward trends for the most part reversed

Table 12.11 How prewar ethnocultural groups voted on equal rights, 1856–1868 (estimated percentages)

	1856	1857				1868	1868			
	Republican	Yes	No	Rolled off	Not voting	Republican	Yes	No	Rolled off	Not voting
New Englanders	82	8	0[a]	31	61	100[b]	100[b]	0	0	0
New Yorkers	67	18	63	21	0[a]	70	58	36	6	0[a]
Pennsylvanians	19	0[a]	72	0[a]	28	59	56	38	1	5
Ohioans	94	32	2	12	54	62	54	0[a]	8	38
Southerners	0[a]	0[a]	71	29	0[a]	21	14	86	0[a]	0[a]
Irishmen	5	0[a]	31	0[a]	69	0	0	100[b]	0	0
Germans	35	0[a]	70	30	0[a]	10	5	95	0	0[a]

Regressions: 1856 voter nativities × 1856 presidential returns (township N = 150); 1856 voter nativities × 1857 proposition 2, 1868 presidential, and 1868 proposition 1 returns (township N = 127).

a. Percentage set at minimum value and others adjusted.

b. Percentage set at maximum value and others adjusted.

themselves. Table 12.12 depicts the behavior of the post-Civil War generation of ethnocultural groups. The comparatively small size of the New England contingent dictated its exclusion from the analysis, which with only one exception—the German Catholics—includes groups comprising at least 6 percent of the whole.

The minority Republicanism of voters within Iowa's predominately Democratic groups—southerners, Irishmen, and Germans, both Catholic and Lutheran—proved about as strong in 1880 as in 1868. But that of the firmly pro-Grant aggregations of 1868—New Yorkers, Pennsylvanians, and Ohioans—had declined a good deal as the politics of the seventies shifted to new concerns. And these three groups' Yes percentages on equal rights fell much more drastically than their enthusiasm for Republican presidential nominees. Support declined nearly 70 points among Yorkers, over 40 points among Pennsylvanians, over 30 points among Ohioans. In contrast, the Yes percentage among the mainly Democratic southerners and German Lutherans held steady between 1868 and 1880, that of the former even rising quite a bit—by about the same frequency it had risen from 1857 to 1868. But when it came to black equality, Iowa's Irish and German Catholics proved wholly immune to improvement: virtually no voter of either group cast a Yes ballot in 1868 or 1880. Ballot majorities for "free white" repeal carried only the Pennsylvanians, Ohioans, and German Lutherans, while the New Yorkers and the southerners divided fairly equally on 1880's proposition 2. Great numbers of the postwar voter cohort, like the antebellum generation before it, changed position on equal rights, but this time in a negative rather than a positive direction.

Finally, the ethnocultural cohort of 1880 is behaviorally described in table 12.13. Since the analyses do not require projecting group percentages forward a decade in time, a wider array of birthplaces is feasible. New Englanders, Britons and Scots, and Scandinavians are now represented, and voters of German parentage are again classified as mainly Lutheran or Catholic. The last three columns of the table test each group's behavior on the liquor question, offering a direct comparison between the two great public issues of black equality and prohibition at the end of an era in which they were often associated.

Despite the contextual shift of politics, considerable continuity links the ethnocultural cohorts of 1870 and 1880—the postbellum generation and the post-Reconstruction generation. In 1880 those of New England stock conformed to their enduring historical reputation by being, as in 1868, Iowa's most emphatic Republican voters. Britons and Scots, a group nearly identical in size with the Yankees, were runners-up, followed by the Pennsylvanians and the Ohioans, the New Yorkers, and finally the Scandinavians, whose overwhelmingly Republican ballots were diminished by that group's very poor 1880 turnout.

Table 12.12 How postwar ethnocultural groups voted on equal rights, 1868–1880 (estimated percentages)

	1868	1868				1880	1880			
	Republican	Yes	No	Rolled off	Not voting	Republican	Yes	No	Rolled off	Not voting
New Yorkers	86	86	0[a]	0	14	49	19	19	41	21
Pennsylvanians	71	64	34	2	0[a]	61	23	0[a]	56	21
Ohioans	65	63	0[a]	2	35	42	32	23	35	10
Southerners	38	22	65	13	0[a]	37	37	39	10	14
Irishmen	0[a]	0[a]	89	0[a]	11	0[a]	0[a]	57	10	33
Germans:										
Mainly Lutheran	39	38	53	5	4	44	33	0[a]	45	22
Mainly Roman Catholic	14	0[a]	84	0[a]	16	23	0[a]	84	1	15

Regressions: 1870 voter nativities × 1868 presidential, 1868 proposition 1, 1880 presidential, and 1880 proposition 2 returns (township N = 127); German religious division from German States subfile (township N = 101).

a. Percentage set at minimum value and others adjusted.

Table 12.13 How post-Reconstruction ethnocultural groups voted on equal rights and on liquor in the 1880s (estimated percentages)

	1880	1880 "Free white" repeal				1882 Prohibition		
	Republican	Yes	No	Rolled off	Not voting	Yes	No	Not voting
New Englanders	90	50	0[a]	50	0[a]	94	6	0[a]
New Yorkers	52	0[a]	0[a]	82	18	45	9	46
Pennsylvanians	60	11	0[a]	60	29	68	2	30
Ohioans	63	61	11	0[a]	28	58	0[a]	42
Southerners	28	15	37	48	0[a]	22	58	20
Britons and Scots	70	28	29	13	30	52	16	36
Irishmen	0	7	29	39	25	5	50	45
Scandinavians	44	36	0[a]	4	60	21	0[a]	79
Germans:								
Mainly Lutheran	38	14	25	35	26	0	82	18
Mainly Roman Catholic	8	0	100[b]	0	0	0	100[b]	0

Regressions: 1880 voters' parental nativities × 1880 presidential, 1880 proposition 2, and 1882 liquor referendum returns (township N = 126); German religious division from German States subfile (township N = 70).

a. Percentage set at minimum value and others adjusted.

b. Percentage set at maximum value and others adjusted.

At the other political extreme (again no surprise) Irishmen constituted Iowa's most fervent Democrats in 1880, a distinction they had held twelve years earlier. German Catholics registered as the second most Democratic group, thereby relegating ethnic southerners (something like 20 to 40 percent of whom had permanently deserted to the Republicans in the 1860s) to a poor third. Finally, the exasperated German Lutherans, their normally Republican impulses periodically thwarted by suspicions about Republican liquor reformers, remained as evenly split between the two major parties as they had been in 1868.

On "free white" repeal, New Englanders, New Yorkers, Pennsylvanians, Britons and Scots, and German Lutherans varied in the consistency of their support for Garfield and for proposition 2. Among Republican-oriented groups only the Ohioans and Scandinavians voted Yes at anywhere near the frequency that they embraced their party's presidential candidate, and only those aggregations and the Yankees granted decisive majorities to civil equality. New Yorkers, whose Republican loyalties had declined remarkably between 1868 and 1880, produced the highest voter roll-off on "free white" repeal.

All these behavioral variations are not easily accounted for, and there is no compelling reason to strain for explanations. The general decline of political interest in the once-inflammatory equal rights issue and the lack of specific guidance by the major parties in 1880 clearly maximized the opportunities for random variation in voter responses to "free white" repeal. This seems especially true for larger groups (New Yorkers, Pennsylvanians, Ohioans) with looser cultural identities. A comparison between the same groups' 1880 and 1882 referendum behaviors suggests that this factor, rather than some defect of data or method, is the major culprit.

The second liquor referendum, held in June 1882, did not coincide with any major candidate election. Those who turned out at the polls did so presumably because of their specific desire to cast ballots for or against a proposed statewide ban on strong drink. From this plebiscite historian Paul Kleppner dates the beginnings of Iowa's political "subrealignment" in the eighties and early nineties. But this shift, as his own materials reveal, involved little more than a decisive movement into the Democratic party by the state's politically schizothymic Lutheran Germans.[13] Otherwise, nothing in the 1882 outcome proved unpredictable. Prohibition carried all the predominately Republican groups: New Englanders, Yorkers, Pennsylvanians, Ohioans, Britons and Scots, and Scandinavians. The measure failed among the heavily Democratic groups—southerners, Irishmen, German Catholics—and, of course, among the German Lutherans. Again not surprisingly Iowa's Yankees, the quintessential midwestern reformers, were prohibition's most vigorous champions, while the German Catholics proved its most resolute foes. Such was to be expected when the issue was incisively defined—by voters' religious dictates, by their cultural traditions, or, lacking such deep-seated predispositions, by the political parties through which they confronted questions of public policy.

IV

A long lifetime later, amid the political excitement and intellectual ferment of the 1960s, a fresh generation of American historians—paralleling the rise of similar schools of thought within several academic disciplines—began framing what became known as the "ironic" approach to the record of American race relations.[14] The term rose from historian C. Vann Woodward's influential shift in perspective, as reflected in the fading optimism of successive editions of *The Strange Career of Jim Crow* (1955). This enormously important book, by arguing that southern segregation was neither primordial nor immutable, originally had implied the impermanence of racist attitudes in the South. But Woodward's revised personal viewpoint also reflected a general historiographical change that stemmed from scholars' abruptly elevated social consciousness and their tendency to defer to the escalating cynicism and anger that distinguished the black movement culture of the sixties. Simultaneously, a circle of prominent black Afro-Americanists innovated what historian August Meier has termed "the new paradigm of black history," an extreme form of which embraced the deeply held conviction that white America is—and always has been—hopelessly and unredeemably racist.[15]

It now seemed pedagogically imperative that the historic failures of America's democratic ideals be fully and frankly exposed. In consequence, much of the best scholarship since the sixties has stressed the perceived egalitarian shortcomings of abolitionism and the early Republican party, of emancipation and reconstruction, and of such pivotal figures as Abraham Lincoln, the congressional Radicals, and Ulysses S. Grant. To some extent America's failed egalitarianism came to resemble a thematic orthodoxy, and it proved implicitly more sympathetic than otherwise to the view that true progress toward racial equality in America had been, for all practical purposes, nil.[16]

How frontier Iowans' encounter with the rights of African-Americans is to be brought into a proper relation with this scholarship is clearly problematic: its literature suggests no plausible explanation for the black suffrage victory of 1865–1868. Unless postbellum Iowa is to remain merely (and rather mysteriously) "the exception," in historian Jean H. Baker's phrase, thoughtful validation of its experience must be sought elsewhere.[17] More fully than expected, perhaps, corroboration is to be found in the classic behavioral scholarship on racial attitudes and attitude change, the intellectual product for the most part of the 1940s and 1950s.

From the perspective of today's bitter frustration over persistent residential segregation, continued hostility to busing and affirmative action, and the perplexing role of race in the seeming intractability of black poverty, much of that earlier literature seems quaintly dated.[18] But it had been of critical relevance in the post-World War II years, when America confronted its last powerful vestiges of what sociologist Joe R. Feagin usefully terms "direct institutionalized discrimination," an ample substantiality of law and precedent of which Iowa's black code had once been an unmistakable part.[19] The experience of nineteenth-century Iowans has less affinity with the more recent writing on race relations than with this behavioral literature of an earlier era, a few highlights of which merit review.

Gunnar Myrdal's magisterial survey of racial discrimination in the United States, *An American Dilemma* (1944), conveyed a number of important messages. One of them may be characterized as procedural, and as August Meier and Elliott Rudwick perceptively observe, it "elevated to the level of a scientific theory the strategy that black Americans throughout their history had employed in their struggle for social change." Movement toward racial equality in the United States, argued Myrdal, could be achieved by straightforwardly addressing the collective conscience of its white majority, specifically emphasizing the dissonance between America's universalistic egalitarian values ("all men are created equal") and the widespread denial of those values by black subjugation, segregation, and exclusion.

Myrdal, in short, viewed the incongruities between the nation's elevated ideals and its pervasive racial discrimination—the "American dilemma" of the title—not as an occasion for despair but as a splendid opportunity. Millions of white Americans were troubled, he said, by the internalized conflict of values and behavior, to the repression or rationalization of which they were forced to devote much psychological energy and from which (consciously or unconsciously) they yearned to be freed. Overcoming discrimination, he reasoned, was therefore to a greater degree than was generally realized a matter of deliberate social engineering, the outcome having been biased in favor of equality. Racial progress mainly required a properly enlightened leadership brave enough to make the appropriate argument from scientific fact and official national principle. The rank and file would fall into line much more readily than imagined.[20]

In 1949 Robert K. Merton modified the Myrdal hypothesis by suggesting that any strategy to reduce racial discrimination needed to distinguish among different personality types. White Americans, he noted, included not just outspoken egalitarians and implacable racists, but also "unprejudiced discriminators" and "prejudiced nondiscriminators." The former, despite their own lack of prejudice, supported color discrimination out of deference to the prejudice of others (to hire a black receptionist, for instance, might be bad for business). The latter, in contrast, held in check their own inclination to discriminate in deference to others (to *refuse* to hire a black receptionist might be bad for business). While both types were moved by expediency, the timid egalitarian suffered some degree of guilt for violating his or her conscience and thus was vulnerable to induced behavioral change à la Myrdal. But the inhibited bigot was under strain when he or she *conformed* to America's egalitarian values, so that legal controls, strictly administered, probably would be required to keep their discriminatory impulses suppressed over the long run.[21]

A year after Merton, T. W. Adorno and his associates published their monumental study of the "authoritarian personality," mandating further refinement of the Myrdal hypothesis. The authors demonstrated that among deeply prejudiced persons—a category including hard-core white racists—bigotry rises from the neurotic needs of the bigoted, a psychological plight usually attributable to emotional deprivation in childhood. Healing any such person, they suggested, would require some form of psychotherapy.[22]

Gordon W. Allport's pioneering theoretical work, *The Nature of Prejudice* (1954), acknowledged the value of Adorno's psychodynamic theory in reaching the neurotically bigoted, but its author skillfully reasoned that *most* white prejudice was not deep-seated. It was probable, said Allport, "that about a half of all prejudiced attitudes are based only on the need to conform to custom, to let well enough alone, to maintain the [prevailing] cultural pattern." Later research by Thomas Fraser Pettigrew, one of Allport's most respected students, established this with some precision. Only about 15 percent of white adult Americans are uncompromising racial bigots whose extreme antiblack prejudices rise from authoritarian personality needs, noted Pettigrew. At the other extreme "roughly 25 percent of white adults in the United States consistently support full rights for Blacks, and in most situations will not exhibit antiblack attitudes or behavior." But the large majority, something like 60 percent, hold *no* deeply motivated opinions about African-Americans, and this majority could be expected to exhibit whatever racist—or racially tolerant—psychology their society's institutions and leaders appeared to expect of them. It was this "conforming three-fifths," as Pettigrew called them, who were susceptible to pressure and persuasion, and therefore capable of changing their behavior from discriminatory to egalitarian in fairly short order.[23]

Allport and Pettigrew emphasized the importance of organic and statute law. Just as discriminatory legal codes had served to increase race prejudice, so laws requiring egalitarian behavior tend to decrease prejudice. "Legislation aims not at controlling prejudice, but only its open expression," wrote Allport. "But when expression changes, thoughts too, in the long run, are likely to fall into line. . . . What we are here speaking of is the basic habit of democratic society. After free, and often fierce, debate, citizens bow to the majority will. *They do so with a special kind of willingness if the legislation is in line with their own private consciences.* On this point civil rights legislation has a marked advantage. . . . People need and want their consciences bolstered by law, and this is nowhere more true than in the area of group relations."[24] But the effects are most striking when the legalities come by way of sudden imposition—court decisions, executive orders, administrative rulings. "Strong and forthright action from 'higher up' . . . is, after an initial flurry of excitement, generally accepted," said Allport. "The *fait accompli* is often welcomed if it is in line with one's conscience."[25]

These and numerous ancillary formulations touch the Iowa experience at a number of points. In chapters 9 and 10, for instance, we encountered Merton's nonprejudiced discriminator in the figure of Josiah B. Grinnell, a militant abolitionist who, as an expedient, supported school segregation in the 1858 legislature and opposed suffrage reform on the floor of the 1865 Republican convention. In chapters 2, 3, and 8 we glimpsed William Patterson, an apt illustration of Merton's prejudiced nondiscriminator. A legislator who supported equal rights in 1842 and 1846, most likely in deference to his Congregational and Quaker constituents, he later, while representing racially divided Keokuk in the 1857 constitutional convention, revealed himself as an ultra conservative on matters of race.

But the self-identified prejudiced nondiscriminators in that same convention—George W. Ells, John T. Clark, John A. Parvin, R. L. B. Clarke—seem, on the other hand, to have been well on their way to full-fledged egalitarianism; at the very least they merit historian Michael Les Benedict's praise as men who consciously supported equal rights *despite* their prejudices. And the ruthlessly confessional Clarke may be taken as exemplifying Allport's "fairly common socialized personality pattern," the intropunitive individual who "feels genuine sympathy for the underdog; he himself has deep feelings of inferiority and unworthiness; he is given to self-blame; he empathizes quickly and keenly with the suffering of others, and finds happiness in helping improve the lot of his fellow men."[26] Similarly expressive is Henry O'Connor's professed "blush of shame" (chapter 11) at the thought that he had once denied the innate equality of all human beings, a feeling he was convinced he shared with thousands of his fellow Iowans.

Allport's *fait accompli* principle greatly illuminates Gov. William M. Stone's own series of timely psychological adjustments to the Emancipation Proclamation, to the Lincoln administration's approval of black troop enlistments, and to the Iowa Republican convention's surprise passage of resolution 4 in 1865. And nothing more eloquent than the Myrdal hypothesis explains the applause accorded Stone's bold appeal to the traditional

American sense of equity, justice, and fair play, as well as to the alleged egalitarian intentions of the Declaration of Independence, of James Madison and Benjamin Franklin and Thomas Jefferson, of the framers of the United States Constitution, of the soldiers of the Revolution, and of Almighty God.

Indeed, America's most cherished state paper, the Declaration of Independence, that "inexhaustible arsenal" of egalitarianism as historian Benjamin Quarles has called it, was invoked repeatedly by progressively disposed delegates to the 1857 constitutional convention and the 1865 Republican caucus, as well as by innumerable Republican editors and campaigners of the latter 1860s.[27] But it was not Myrdalian rhetoric alone that made the difference in the mass conversion of Iowa's Republicans to equal rights. As Allport would have appreciated, it was also the stature of those who spoke out. They included such leading civic and party figures as Congressman Hiram Price, Judge Chester C. Cole, most of the state's top elected officials in 1865 and virtually all of the Republicans running to succeed them, both Governors W. M. Stone and Samuel Merrill, top political professionals Jacob Rich and James S. Clarkson, a small host of Civil War military heroes ranging from Maj. Henry O'Connor to Col. Alonzo Abernethy to Generals M. M. Crocker and Grenville M. Dodge, and—by 1868—even such racial conservatives as U.S. Senators James Harlan and Samuel J. Kirkwood. To Iowa's rank-and-file Republicans the egalitarian promptings of such men reverberated with the preemptive authority of Higher Law.

Allport's discussion of "status aspects of contact" decodes an ostensible paradox relating to white Iowans' wartime responses to African-Americans. On the one hand, Iowans soldiering through the South earned a harsh reputation for race prejudice, supposedly generated by their close association with freshly liberated masses of black refugees. It was a racist image plausible enough to tempt postwar Democrats and conservative Republicans into making it the basis for a political movement. On the other hand, Iowans in General Sherman's army grew so enraged by news of the Confederate massacre of nearly two hundred surrendered black artillerymen at Fort Pillow, Kentucky, that they unceremoniously executed a score of rebels captured in a fire fight in Georgia. The difference, as Allport would explain it, is that the southern black masses had formed a destitute peasantry of bottom-of-the-barrel socioeconomic status; casual contact with them predictably increased race prejudice among fascinated midwestern farm boys and artisans. But the blacks slaughtered at Fort Pillow had been fellow-soldiers, colleagues in the transcendent endeavor that was the war to preserve the Union. The power of Iowa's own 60th U.S. Colored Infantry to draw rank-and-file Republicans' opinions toward suffrage reform in 1865 is of much the same character: the Republicans of the Hawkeye State could not conceive of their soldiery, no matter what their color, as anything but their civic equals.[28]

No behavioral configuration is more satisfactory than the Merton-Allport-Pettigrew concept of the conforming majority in accounting for the defining moment of Iowans' equal rights movement, the events of June 14, 1865. In their Des Moines convention 663 Republicans, most of whose attitudes toward African-Americans no doubt ranged from neutral or mildly negative to hostile on the morning of that day, had by evening voted overwhelmingly to bestow the elective franchise on blacks—despite the hotly predicted political costs. Such had been the transforming effect of sheer eloquence upon the conforming majority. And how little the opposition to equal rights among rank-and-file Republicans stemmed from irredeemable racism was detected a few weeks later by a Democratic loyalist near Burlington. "Some of them (say, one third) declare that they never can vote for Negro suffrage," he confided to his state chairman about local Republicans, "[but] my own opinion in regard to this matter is that they dont have so much objection to the *principal* involved as they have to running the risque of coming before the people upon that rather touchy question." Not true prejudice, incredibly enough, but merely politics, he said, underlay lukewarm Republican attitudes toward suffrage reform.[29]

Something like Pettigrewian proportions can be roughly calculated for the division of Iowa's Republican electorate of 1865 into Adornovian racists (perhaps 13 percent), racial egalitarians (another 13 percent), and the superficially racist majority (74 percent) for whom the party's progressive messages would prove decisive by 1868.[30] And neither Allport nor Pettigrew could have been surprised, had they learned of it, by pioneer Iowans' accomplishment: their behavior, although a remarkably early example of successful antidiscriminatory mobilization, lay well within the range of American group behaviors deemed psychologically credible. But neither Iowans' rejection of equal rights in 1857 nor their decidedly equivocal approval in 1880 would be judged peculiar. Each such expression of public choice, to Allport and Pettigrew, would have been determined by the success or failure of the behavioral strategy with which each proposal had been placed before the voters. And the soundness of any such strategy would have depended on how artfully it engaged the well-defined sociocultural imperatives and opportunities available.

Allport wrote in the year of the famous *Brown* v. *Board of Education* decision by the U.S. Supreme Court that began the process of dismantling formal school segregation in America—a decision that would, in his opinion, have been "psychologically sounder" had the court insisted on an immediate, rather than gradual, acquiescence with its ruling. By 1958 he was already deploring the failure of national leadership and "the sorrowful results that have come from indecisiveness and delay." He would be dead by the time his own Boston exploded in violence over the issue of school busing, an experience some behavioralists interpret as a failure of the Allportian approach.[31]

Thus Howard Schuman and his colleagues warn that "it is too extreme . . . to claim that attitudes can be treated as epiphenomena and that determined leadership (as in [Harry Truman's] desegregation of the military) is all that is needed to bring about behavioral change, with attitudes likely to follow thereafter. This point of view tacitly assumes situations in which leaders have their authority protected from serious challenge."[32] Schuman and associates are impeccable sociologists but in this case bad historians: it can hardly be said that President Truman was invulnerable to racist voters in 1948 when—in the midst of a presidential campaign crippled by the revolt of the segregationist Dixiecrats—he issued his famous executive order integrating the armed forces. He was far more politically vulnerable, certainly, than was Governor Stone in 1865, given the strength of Iowa's Republican hegemony. But the civil rights successes of the post-World War II era, in which both Truman and the Myrdal hypothesis played such prominent roles, do invite comparison with the Hawkeye State in the years immediately following Appomattox.

In several respects the situations seem remarkably similar, with Iowa in the late 1860s being asked to play a role vis-à-vis the militarily defeated but politically rebellious South that the South itself in the early Cold War years would be asked to play vis-à-vis Japan and the third world. In 1868 President-to-be Ulysses S. Grant hoped that Iowans would willingly enact black suffrage as a means of helping legitimize its congressional imposition on the ex-Confederate states. The logic of this proposition echoes in President Truman's comment, inelegantly summarizing a point made by Myrdal, on the need for civil equality in the American South. "The top dog in a world which is over half-colored," said Truman, "ought to clean his own house."[33] Perhaps the juxtaposition of the two postwar eras is of use in highlighting the role of political necessity—the need of the federal government to claim high moral purpose for its exertion of power—in generating racial progress. The successes of the years 1865–1870 and 1945–1965 in eliminating direct institutionalized discrimination obviously owe much to larger national agenda.

Allportian social psychology also illuminates the failure of Iowa's egalitarian majority of 1868 to hold form in 1880. As Pettigrew has warned, the relapse of a conforming majority can be expected to occur whenever it receives retrogressive signals from its government and opinion leaders. That, of course, is precisely what occurred in the United States from the late 1880s through World War I, with devastating effects on the limited racial equality achieved in the Civil War era. The 1880 referendum outcome suggests that Iowans simply anticipated this national declension.[34]

V

"The story of our inferiority is an old dodge," Frederick Douglass once remarked, "for wherever men oppress their fellows, wherever they enslave them, they will endeavor to find the needed apology for such enslavement and oppression in the character of the people oppressed and enslaved." Blaming the victims, the victimizers establish their moral innocence. This cause and effect emphasizes an extremely important historical truth: white racism was politically essential to black slavery.[35]

Historians may continue to disagree over which came first to colonial America, race prejudice or black bondage. But much of the original significance of that debate has been diminished by the impressive arguments of such scholars as Frank M. Snowden and St. Clair Drake that systematic antiblack discrimination was not present in the ancient Mediterranean civilizations, and by the evidence presented by Bernard Lewis and others that racism was an innovation by certain Muslim writers at the very moment Muslim kingdoms were busily monopolizing the sub-Saharan slave trade. Within medieval Europe slavery remained as color-blind as it had been in the ancient world, the word "slave" (and its equivalent in Arabic, French, Spanish, Portuguese, Italian, and German) originally denoting a person of Slavic origin. Not until the 1450s, when Turkish capture of Constantinople severed Europe's connection with the great Black Sea slave markets, and Portuguese trading ships reached the Cape Verde coast of Africa, did slavery in the West begin its long association exclusively with blacks. And with this shift came the assemblage of racist folk-myths and fantasies to which the North American experience would give such copious expression.[36]

It seems plausible that white racism was (and is) inherent or innate in neither Western Civilization nor Christianity, in neither capitalism nor any other particular economic system, in neither the Euro-American collective unconsciousness nor its sociobiological genes.[37] And one might further infer that prejudicial behavior and attitudes can indeed be changed—most inclusively by destroying whatever oppressive labor system they had been summoned to protect in the first place.[38] What separated nineteenth-century Iowa from the South in this regard was that in the Hawkeye State there was no *economic* investment in the theory of black inferiority; black Iowans could become equal under law without disturbing the prevailing system of labor. It is perhaps no accident that black southerners would not be truly emancipated until passage and enforcement of the Civil Rights Act of 1964 and the Voting Rights Act of 1965—by which point southern agribusiness was well on its way, through mechanization, to overcoming its traditional need for cheap labor.[39]

Fully comprehending the long and anguished history of white racism in

America means coming to terms with its occasional irregularities as well as acknowledging its dreary uniformity. Such examples as Iowa's, writes historian J. Morgan Kousser, "refute or at least greatly complicate the pessimistic view . . . that white racial opinion in nineteenth-century America was uniformly and deeply racist."[40] That unnecessarily grim perspective obscures or discounts the real gains made. More important, it implicitly demeans the courageous idealism of many individuals, both black and white, who fought for racial justice. And it trivializes the nineteenth century's moral capacity for yielding more substantive equality than it did in fact yield.

Far too much of the inequity to which the idealists addressed themselves so long ago has survived, in one form or another, the years of incredible change from their day to ours. Yet when so many seem unchallenged by what clearly remains America's most important unresolved issue, when new initiatives seem desperately needed, when the complacent suggest that there is no longer a problem and the angry believe that the problem is unresolvable, it is good to have positive examples to prompt us. The circumstances, processes, and strategies that won frontier Iowans to the civil equality of blacks remind us that there are egalitarian precedents as well as a racist tradition in America's past.

Appendixes

Notes · Index

Data and Methods

APPENDIX A

This book's discussions of grass-roots voting derive from analyses of two large machine-readable data bases, a County File and a Township File. Each includes a set of Iowa's mid-nineteenth-century election returns plus one or more subfiles of population data.

The County File covers the period from Iowa's congressional elections of August 1848 through its prohibition referendum of June 1882 and embraces not only the returns from the three great equal rights referendums of 1857, 1868, and 1880, but also, at a minimum, returns from the election at the "top of the ticket" in every year (excepting only 1851 and 1853, two electorally uneventful seasons) within that span. Collecting the original county returns proved relatively simple, the official source being the Iowa Secretary of State's "Election Records" (microfilm copy, University of Iowa Libraries), reel 1.

The main challenge became the calculation of eligible voters for these elections and referendums. The State of Iowa did not allow resident aliens—even those with declared intentions of becoming American citizens—to vote, and in the Civil War era it resolutely enumerated adult males who were so entitled. The discovery that published compilations of Iowa's eligible voters appeared with almost biennial regularity from 1852 through 1875 (conveniently reproduced in John A. T. Hull, ed., *Census of Iowa for 1880* [Des Moines, 1883], 228–235) tempted me to provide more sophisticated estimates than the usual ten-year interpolations between federal census listings of adult males. For the period 1852–1875, therefore, my voter estimates for any given election were painstakingly calibrated. A calculation of the eligible voters in Adair County at the moment of the October 1869 election, for example, involved the June census counts of Adair's electorate in 1869 and 1870 (557 and 963 respectively), and the gain in voters between the two counts (406). How many voters, in addition to June's 557, might have been in residence the following October? Arbitrarily assuming that the addition of new voters was a steady process, my answer was: four months' worth of the twelve months' chronological distance between the first census count and the second, and thus one-third of the 406-voter increase, or 134. This figure, when added to 557, yields an estimated eligible voting population for Adair County in October 1869 of 691.

Post-1875 estimates, however, required more finesse, since not until 1885 would Iowa undertake another voter census. For the elections of 1876 through 1882, therefore, I constructed semi-logarithmic interpolations between 1875 and 1885. For the similarly unreported period before 1852 the resolution proved more complex. Here I had recourse to the 1850 published federal census listings by county of Iowa's white males twenty years of age and older (*The Seventh Census of the United States: 1850* [Washington, 1853], 938–940). I first estimated each county's eligible voters in June 1850 by employing the known percentage of voters to total population in June 1852, plausibly assuming that the same ratio also pertained twenty-four months earlier. I then interpolated semi-logarithmically between these 1850 estimates and the June 1852 listings in order to obtain voter estimates for the August 1850 election. Finally, I projected the 1850–1852 trajectories backward in time (via three-cycle semi-log graph paper) in order to obtain estimates for the August 1849, November 1848, and August 1848 elections.

The County File's nonelectoral data include some variables extracted from published census compilations, even though they pertain to the entire Iowa population and not voters specifically. Variables reflecting the occupational breakdown of the Iowa work force in 1856 came from *The Census Returns of the Different Counties of the State of Iowa for 1856* (Iowa City, 1857). Since 66 percent were listed as farmers, a classification that did not display any intrinsic diversity, I broke this large mass into subdivisions according to agricultural prosperity, aggregating the dollar value of hogs and cattle sold in 1856 to obtain the average value of livestock sold per farmer for each county. I then recoded Iowa's farmers into three groups virtually equal in size—those of prosperous counties, of middling counties, and of poorer counties. The 1856 census's nonagricultural occupations presented the opposite challenge, in that they proved so diverse that even the three largest groupings—laborers, carpenters, and merchants—proved to be too small to yield interpretable results when subjected to statistical analyses. I collapsed the data for all occupations that appeared to be those of nineteenth-century artisans into a single category, relegating the remaining nonlaborer occupations to a business and professional category.

Two other variable sets provided information on religion. For the early part of the era I employed the "church seats" enumerations extracted from the 1860 published federal census (*Eighth Census of the United States, 1860: Mortality and Miscellaneous Statistics* [Washington, 1866], 389–392). Like other historians, I employed these data as a proxy for the religious affiliation of voters, casting them in the form of a denomination's percentage of total church seats within each county in 1860. But because there was in almost every county such a large discrepancy between total church seats and total county population, when analyzing the data I weighted each case by its total population in 1860. I included in the subfile only those denominations present in at least ten counties in 1860, aggregating the remainder into a miscellaneous category. Like farmers, such a disproportionate number of Hawkeyes appear to have been Methodists or Presbyterians that I sought to split these categories into coherent subdivisions.

The Presbyterians proved intractable: the census did not distinguish between

Old and New School congregations, which might have yielded interesting results under analysis, but instead divided Presbyterians into an undifferentiated mass of the main body, on the one hand, and three offshoots (Cumberland, Reformed, and United Presbyterians) on the other, none of the three numerous enough to qualify as a separate variable. At length I simply kept all Presbyterians as a single category. Methodists, however, I split according to that denomination's own northern and southern Iowa subdivisions. (For the boundary between the Iowa and Upper Iowa conferences see Martin L. Greer, ed., *Official Record: Minutes of the Iowa Conference of the Methodist Episcopal Church* [n.p., 1962], 76.) A later reexamination of the data convinced me that those pertaining to sparsely settled western Iowa were seriously incomplete, resulting in distorted percentage relationships between denominations in several counties. In the end I omitted from the analyses all of Iowa west of Worth, Cerro Gordo, Franklin, Hardin, Story, Polk, Warren, Lucas, and Wayne counties.

I discovered a set of church seats data for the later period in Frank D. Jackson, ed., *Census of Iowa for the Year 1885* (Des Moines, 1885), 178–189. This listing proved much more complete than the 1860 compilation. Only two counties lacked data altogether, and convenient notes allowed the calculation of error. I excluded from consideration any county in which 30 percent or more of its church organizations had not reported the seating capacities of their edifices, which left most counties in the sample (N=73). I also furnished *estimates* of church seats in the occasional instances where the listing gave only "1 ch'rh" or "2 ch's," as I did also in cases where seating capacity was unlisted but the dollar value of a structure given. In the first circumstance I allocated one hundred seats per church under the assumption that such edifices were probably on the small side. In the second I calculated the average dollar value of a church seat for each denomination, then employed that average to define the number of seats in cases where I possessed valuations but no seating capacities.

I

The Township File became the main device for statistically measuring the relationship of voters' personal attributes against their politics and their attitudes toward equal rights. There are no extensive published data on voter birthplaces for nineteenth-century Iowa any more than for any other state; as elsewhere, it must be extracted from individual manuscript census entries. To minimize this enormously labor-intensive effort, I shifted the focus to the smallest electoral unit for which both voting and census returns are available; this, in Iowa as elsewhere, was the township. Unfortunately, however, Iowa did not regularly collect and publish township voting returns until 1885, and some earlier data in manuscript form, extant as late as 1940 in the state archives, have been destroyed. Faced with the impossibility of anything but a partial recovery of township data, I concentrated on locating returns for Iowa's three equal rights referendums. I decided that I would let the virtually complete returns of the County File establish the parameters of Iowa's larger political configuration at any given moment in the period 1848–1882, and would use the Township File to offer less systematic—but much more statistically intimate—information on possible associations among local political cultures, ethnic backgrounds, and racial attitudes.

For the 1857 referendum I was able to locate complete township returns for twenty counties, with partial returns for two more. Those for nine counties came from various weekly or daily editions of the Dubuque *Express and Herald* for August 1857. Other local newspapers yielded ten additional compilations of township returns. A search of Iowa courthouses uncovered the existence of manuscript sources for three more counties. In all, I recovered 292 township returns for the 1857 referendum.

Map A.1 indicates the spatial distribution of these 292 townships. Even allowing for the fact that no referendums were held in underpopulated northwest Iowa, nor in six other counties, the extant township data cluster in the eastern third of the state far more than I would have liked. That they compose an almost exclusively eastern Iowa sample seems less important, however, than that the sample extends almost the entire distance from north to south, this axis being a more important geographical feature of early voting variation than the state's east-to-west dimension.

In all instances, the returns for the concurrent referendum to accept or reject the 1857 state constitution came with the equal suffrage returns. I also sought out and recovered as many as I could of my 292 townships' voting returns for the 1856 presidential election. These would provide the partisan context of referendum voting at the local level.

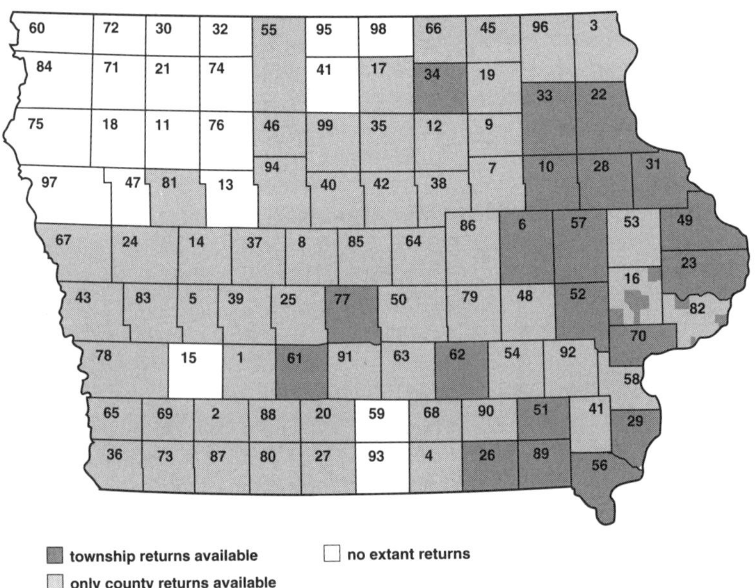

Map A.1 Spatial distribution of extant proposition 2 referendum data for 1857.

KEY TO COUNTY NAMES IN MAP A.1

1. Adair	26. Davis	51. Jefferson	76. Pocahontas
2. Adams	27. Decatur	52. Johnson	77. Polk
3. Allamakee	28. Delaware	53. Jones	78. Pottawattamie
4. Appanoose	29. Des Moines	54. Keokuk	79. Poweshiek
5. Audubon	30. Dickinson	55. Kossuth	80. Ringgold
6. Benton	31. Dubuque	56. Lee	81. Sac
7. Black Hawk	32. Emmet	57. Linn	82. Scott
8. Boone	33. Fayette	58. Louisa	83. Shelby
9. Bremer	34. Floyd	59. Lucas	84. Sioux
10. Buchanan	35. Franklin	60. Lyon	85. Story
11. Buena Vista	36. Fremont	61. Madison	86. Tama
12. Butler	37. Greene	62. Mahaska	87. Taylor
13. Calhoun	38. Grundy	63. Marion	88. Union
14. Carroll	39. Guthrie	64. Marshall	89. Van Buren
15. Cass	40. Hamilton	65. Mills	90. Wapello
16. Cedar	41. Hancock	66. Mitchell	91. Warren
17. Cerro Gordo	42. Hardin	67. Monona	92. Washington
18. Cherokee	43. Harrison	68. Monroe	93. Wayne
19. Chickasaw	44. Henry	69. Montgomery	94. Webster
20. Clarke	45. Howard	70. Muscatine	95. Winnebago
21. Clay	46. Humbolt	71. O'Brien	96. Winneshiek
22. Clayton	47. Ida	72. Osceola	97. Woodbury
23. Clinton	48. Iowa	73. Page	98. Worth
24. Crawford	49. Jackson	74. Palo Alto	99. Wright
25. Dallas	50. Jasper	75. Plymouth	

I next turned to gathering corresponding voter nativity data from the 1856 Iowa manuscript census. A number of the 292 townships had to be excluded from tabulation, since boundary changes associated with creation of new townships between June 1856, when the census had been taken, and August 1857, the date of the referendum, had destroyed the possibility of geographical synchrony between census unit and voting unit. My research assistants and I undertook the recovery of voter nativities for as many of the remaining townships as possible from the microfilm copy of the 1856 census located at the State Historical Society of Iowa in Iowa City, recording the birthplace of every township resident for whom either the "Native voters" or "Naturalized voters" column had been checked by the census taker. Not tabulated at this juncture were the townships found wholly or partially illegible; others tabulated but not added to the Township File were a number I deemed unreliable because our hand tabulations diverged by 10 percent or more from the total township voter figures given in the printed version of the 1856 census. Ultimately, 186 successfully tabulated townships, or a healthy 64 percent of the original 292, became part of the Township File. These embrace a total of 31,677 individual voters—or 31 percent of all Iowa's eligible voters in 1856. Map A.2 locates the spatial distribution of this "186 subfile."

I then devoted myself to the 1868 and 1880 referendums, hoping to find usable returns with which to carry the 1857 analysis forward in time. I discovered that township returns were recoverable for only thirty-six of Iowa's ninety-seven organized counties in 1868, although many county boards of supervisors had begun preserving such voting records in the sixties and seventies. For the 1880 referendum, indeed, the figure slipped to thirty-four.

Because fragmentary voting data presented a continuing problem, there appeared to be no grounds for attempting a systematic sample of townships for any of the three referendums. The only other possibility—collecting the nativity data from a systematic sample of entire counties—I rejected as far too expensive in terms of time and available research aid. Therefore my decision was to select for nativity tabulation only those townships already in the 186 subfile and for which the 1868 and 1880 returns could be found. The resulting database would in effect poll the same voting units three different times on civil rights questions, thus controlling for locality in order to highlight possible behavioral changes in "the same people" over the twenty-four-year period. The existence of the County File encouraged this use of a less-than-perfect Township File in coping with ethnoculturality, since the universal county-level analyses would always serve as a check on conclusions extracted from the township data.

To coincide with the 1868 referendum returns I sought corresponding birthplace data in the 1870 U.S. manuscript census. And for the 1880 referendum the U.S. census of that same year would, of course, serve admirably. But did my townships of 1857 match geographic boundaries with the same townships in 1868 and 1880, as well as correspond to the local census tracts of 1870 and 1880? Not always. In several instances I was able to synchronize boundaries by aggregating townships that had been fragmented after 1857. When this proved impossible, they had to be excluded from the 1868 and 1880 data. Also dropped were townships for which returns for either the second or third referendum were listed as zero Yes and zero No. These proved the lesser problems, however. As it turned out, 55 of the original 186 townships had to be dropped because of the dismaying absence of localized referendum returns for 1868 and 1880.

Based on my experience in organizing the 1856 nativity data, I made some adjustments in collecting new birthplace information. The 1856 effort had involved recording the nativity, as given, of every person designated a voter. But for the much larger—and somewhat more ethnically diverse—township populations of 1870 and 1880, some collapsing of birthplace categories, and the expansion of others, seemed appropriate. The challenge was, of course, to maximize the numerical strength of each category so as to amplify its utility in statistical analysis, yet to have each category, so far as possible, reflect some distinctive political culture or ethnicity. For the foreign-born this was easy, given the separate identities of

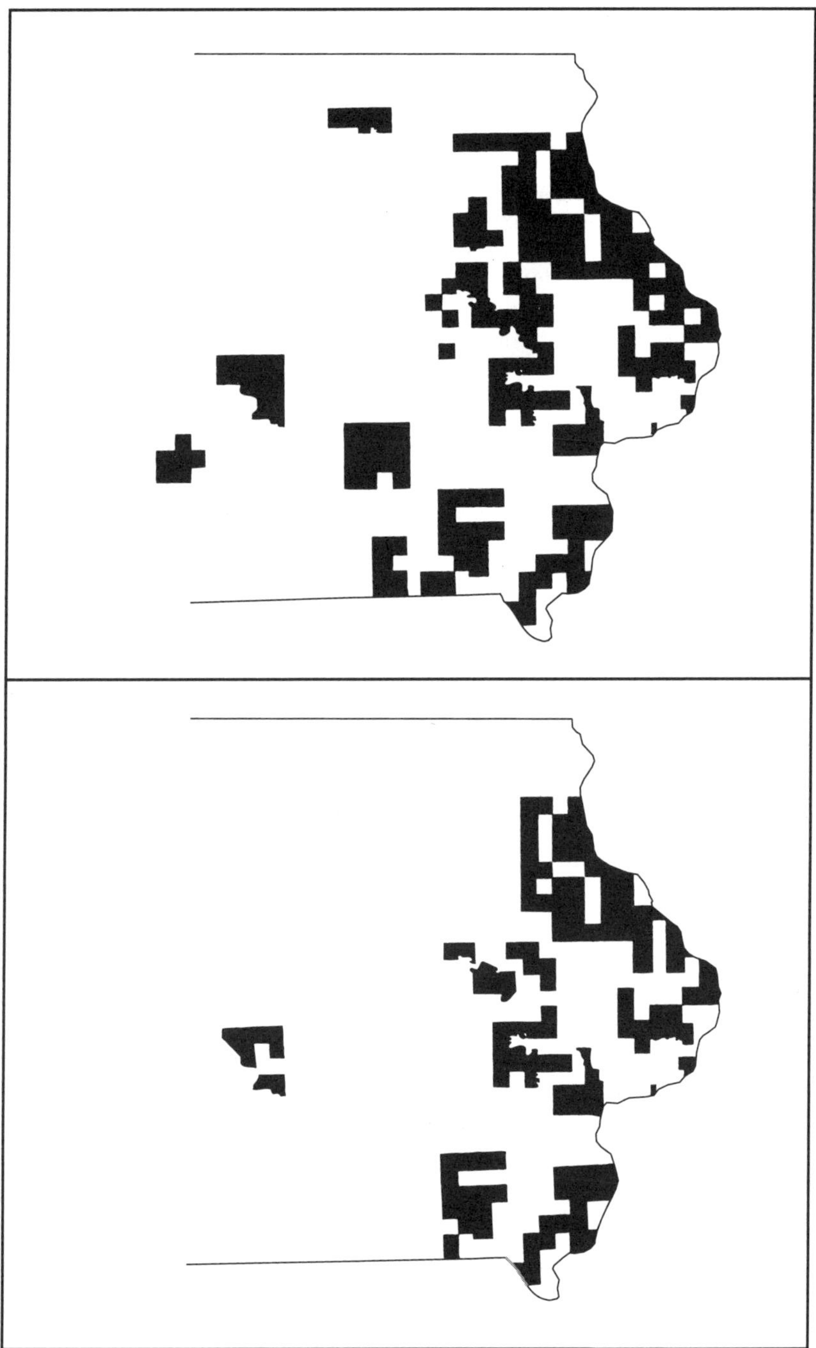

Map A.2 Spatial distributions of 186 subfile (top) and 127 subfile (bottom).

European nations. I merged only the English and Welsh, reserving the option of later having the computer group other categories—the Scandinavians, for example. For the native-born, however, the choices proved more difficult. I retained New York, Pennsylvania, Ohio, and Indiana as discrete nativity categories simply because of the large numbers of voters from these states, without any preconception that they represented distinct cultural units. I retained New Jersey as a separate category merely because of an inability to decide whether to merge it with New York or Pennsylvania. Voters of New England birth, however, I decisively grouped, acknowledging along with other scholars the distinct political culture of that region. I did the same for natives of the South (defined as the slave states of 1860), not out of ignorance of the differences between the upper and lower South, but because all but 2 percent of the native southerners in the 186 subfile had been born in the upper South. Little seemed to be gained from making distinctions.

The question of German-born voters, on the other hand, impelled me to disaggregate where possible. Iowa's 1856 census takers had paid little attention to distinctions between Hessians and Hanoverians, for example, but in 1870 and 1880 the enumerators often had been specific. For these latter censuses, therefore, I created a duplicate "German states subfile." To avoid any possible bias from an unsystematic census mixing of the notations "Germany" and, say, "Bavaria," I included in this subfile only those townships in which at least 90 percent of German-born voters had been categorized by state of birth. The results proved relatively satisfactory: the enumerated townships consisted of 101 for 1870 and 70 for 1880.

From the 1870 federal census manuscript my assistants and I tabulated the birthplaces of all my townships' voters ("Male Citizens of U.S. of 21 years of age and upwards"). But the 1880 census presented a problem, in that no designation of citizenship is anywhere specified. My decision was that, naturally enough, we would tabulate adult males as the closest approximation. But the 1880 census also offered a unique opportunity, in that it recorded the nativities for each enumerated person's parents—thereby adding a better characterization for the now many second-generation Iowans whose instate nativities would be of virtually no analytical use. We therefore collected the *father's* birthplace for each adult male listed as a township resident, assuming this to be the best index to the individual's ethnocultural orientation in 1880, and for the relatively few individuals whose fathers' birthplaces were unknown we substituted mothers' nativities. A test performed with forty-three townships, in which the data had first been collected according to the individuals' own birthplaces, revealed that this strategy would indeed enhance the usefulness of the 1880 data: the Iowa-born contingent fell from second largest to fifteenth, while the southern-born category rose from fifth place to third. Similarly, the German and Irish categories each rose some 4 points in percentile strength.

Some townships had to be eliminated either because of illegibility or some discovered defect in their data. (I dropped the city of Dubuque, for example, after noting that seemingly hundreds of birthplaces in 1880 had been entered not by the census marshals but by a supervisor filling in blanks at some later date.) Such attrition proved relatively minor, however. Ultimately I possessed a subfile consisting of 127 electoral units for which returns for all three referendums, plus corresponding voter nativity data from all three census manuscripts, had been recovered—a sample of 62 percent of the townships for which returns could be located for all three referendums. The individual voters represented included 21,195 for 1856 (or 21 percent of Iowa's total voters); 34,392 for 1870 (or 13 percent of the state total); and 43,441 for 1880 (or 10 percent of all adult male Iowans that year). Map A.2 indicates the spatial distribution of this "127 subfile."

Other than the matter of geography, had any systematic bias been built into the two township subfiles? I tested for this by obtaining from the data of the County File the statewide percentages of the estimated electorate voting Yes in the referendums of 1856, 1868, and 1880 and comparing them with those yielded by each of the township subfiles. As seen in table A.1, the voter attitudes of the Township File in 1856 are virtually identical to those of the state as a whole. For the other two referendums, however, the 127 subfile registered as rather less egalitarian than the state as a whole, in 1868 by 9 percentage points and in 1880 by 5 points. Although this represented more bias in the second and third referendums than I would have liked, at least it was bias in a conservative direction. Because the principal unknown to be addressed by the township analyses would be the possibility of statistical association between racial progressivism and nativity, I felt more comfortable seeking conclusions via conservatively biased data than if they had been skewed in a progressive direction. Nevertheless, the reader is reminded of the Township File's bias where I discuss the township votes of 1868 and 1880 in the text.

A similar assessment of bias in the township *nativity* data proved more problematic. I therefore decided to compare the nativity breakdown of the total population of the 127 subfile with the same data for all Iowans, as a substitute for comparing their political components. This test could be accomplished at only two points in the mid-nineteenth century, but—fortunately for my purposes—they came at the beginning (1856) and shortly after the end (1885) of the referendum sequence, so as to effectively bracket the 127 subfile. For 1885 only the birthplaces of the foreign-born had been tallied by township and published, but a limited comparison seemed better than none at all. Table A.2 displays the results of this exercise.

In most cases the sample percentages do not deviate much from that of the state

Table A.1 File comparisons: the Yes vote on equal rights in 1857, 1868, and 1880 (percentages)[a]

		Township file	
	County file	186 subfile	127 subfile
1857 referendum[b]	7.6	9.4	8.4
1868 referendum	52.5		43.3
1880 referendum	28.3		23.2

a. Specifically, the Yes percentage of total estimated eligible voters at the moment of each referendum.

b. Seven cases from the County file not included (county N = 70); see chapter 9, note 27.

Table A.2 Sample comparisons: residents' birthplaces in 1856 and 1885 (percentages)

	1856		1885	
	All Iowans (N = 508,260)	Sampled Iowans (N = 110,297)	All Iowans (N = 1,753,980)	Sampled Iowans (N = 158,512)
New England	3.6	4.3		
New York	7.0	7.0		
New Jersey	.7	.7		
Pennsylvania	9.0	10.9		
Ohio	17.7	16.3		
Indiana	10.5	6.3		
Other Old Northwest	5.7	4.4		
Iowa	18.4	21.1		
Slave states (1860)	10.9	8.2		
Total native-born	83.5	79.2	82.3	81.0
Canada	1.2	1.5	1.1	.7
England	1.8	2.2	1.5	1.3
Wales	.1	.2	.2	.1
Scotland	.4	.5	.5	.3
Ireland	4.1	5.5	2.4	3.1
France	.4	.6	.1	.2
Germany	5.9	8.7	6.9	9.5
Austria/Bohemia	.3	.5	.6	1.3
Netherlands	.1	.1	.3	.1
Norway	.6	.3	1.4	.7
Sweden	.2	.1	1.5	.7
Denmark	.0	.1	.7	.2
Other/unknown	1.5	.7	.6	.8
Total foreign-born	16.6	21.0	17.8	19.0

Sources: The Census Returns of the Different Counties of the State of Iowa, for 1856 (Iowa City, 1857); Frank D. Jackson, ed., *Census of Iowa for the Year 1885* (Des Moines, 1885).

as a whole, the largest biases being a 4-point deficit of Indianans in 1856, a 3-point surplus of Germans in both 1856 and 1885, and 3- and 2-point deficits of Scandinavians in 1856 and 1885. And note how little the percentage breakdowns, both for all foreign-born Iowans and the sampled foreign-born, changed in the years between the fifties and the eighties. This makes it all the more likely that a comparison of the statewide and sampled native-born in 1885, if permitted, would much resemble the comparison of 1856.

What has been said of the 127 subfile is also true of the 186 subfile, since they are virtually interchangeable with respect to their percentaged 1856 voter nativity breakdowns. Their greatest divergences, the percentages for Pennsylvanians and southerners, amount to less than 2 points in each case.

Despite the good results of these tests, I remained sensitive to matters of size throughout the study, in the actual regression analyses employing only birthplace categories that contained at least six hundred voters each and relegating smaller groups to an "other" catchall.

II

Quantitative methods have advanced considerably since my first encounter with Iowa's civil rights referendums. Political historians appear to agree that the most important methodological advance of recent years has been the introduction of multiple ecological regression, first extensively employed in J. Morgan Kousser's *The Shaping of Southern Politics: Suffrage Restriction and the Establishment of the One-Party South, 1880–1910* (New Haven, 1974). But methodological skeptics continue to suggest that problems in applying the technique severely limit its utility. My own modest contribution to the debate proves that the technique yields much more accurate output than its bitterest critics seem willing to acknowledge (see Robert R. Dykstra, "Ecological Regression Estimates: Alchemist's Gold?" *Social Science History* 10 [1985]: 85–86).

Yet it is always salutary to use caution in interpreting results, especially if they fly in the face of common-sense explanations or contradict good narrative sources. The most satisfying regression outcomes are likely to be those that not only possess the earmarks of intrinsic value—row and column sums of the estimates closely approximating actual residuals, logically impossible estimates being not too extreme and relatively few—but that also comport with other evidence. If I obtained results that showed a large proportion of black voters favoring the 1968 presidential candidacy of George Wallace (to cite an example raised by the critics), I would assume the existence of error. If I could not find and remove that error, I would not use the data. If quantitative historians have learned anything over the years, it is that *no* statistical technique—not even the venerable Pearson's correlation—is so methodologically immaculate that it can be applied with mechanistic abandon. For a sophisticated discussion of ecological regression, including appropriate cautionaries, see William E. Gienapp, *The Origins of the Republican Party, 1852–1856* (New York, 1987), 478–481.

Because regrettably few scholars have had hands-on experience with ecological regression, it can be extremely difficult for the novice to learn the technique, even from those with an excellent knowledge of standard regression procedures. The best description is still, in my opinion, the one by Peyton McCrary, Clark Miller, and Dale Baum, "Class and Party in the Secession Crisis: Voting Behavior in the Deep South, 1856–1861," *Journal of Interdisciplinary History* 8 (1978): 431–435 and notes. But additional remarks by one who has coped with the computational eccentricities will, I hope, make the technique less frustratingly elusive and thus encourage others to apply it to their own political materials. The specific example I employ here involves the regression of one election against another, which is the most common use of the technique in this book and elsewhere.

Perhaps the most complicated aspect of the matter has to do with accommodating net changes in the voting population occurring between the date of election A and the date of election B. The problem is that some men who were ineligible to vote in election A—a few because they had not yet qualified to vote, most because they were not yet residents of the voting unit—later became eligible to cast ballots in election B. This fact requires that for each particular regression a category for "election A ineligibles" be calculated.

In the sample regression setup below (1867 gubernatorial returns × 1868 presidential returns) this is accomplished by the command line beginning "COMPUTE INL67"—that is, compute the number of those ineligible to vote in 1867 who became eligible to vote in 1868. But since these 1867 ineligibles must be expressed in the form of a percentage of all eligible voters in 1868, every other 1867 voter category must be adjusted accordingly. It no longer suffices, in other words, that the Republican voters of 1867 were *47 percent* of all eligible voters *in 1867*. The statistically necessary datum is that the Republican voters of 1867 were *44 percent* of the eligible voters *of 1868*. Thus the need for compute statements for REP67, DEM67, and NONVT67, as well as for INL67.

"Weighting cases" will also be a part of most election regressions; this is necessary in order not to give too much statistical importance to numerically smaller voting units. In the present study, therefore, I weighted each county by its raw number of estimated eligible voters. In the sample regression setup presented below the necessary command line is "WEIGHT BY ESTVTR68"—that is, weight by the figure for estimated voters in 1868. (In obtaining output, I ran each set of data through first *without* weighting, however, in order to obtain the original "N of Cases" count, which is apt to be distorted in the weighted run.)

The specific regression procedures are those embraced by various versions of the "Statistical Package for the Social Sciences" (for the most recent as of this writing see *SPSS/PC+ V2.0: Base Manual* [Chicago, 1988]). In every case I employed the "ENTER" option to force all independent variables into the regression equations, and the "ORIGIN" subcommand to compel the computer to perform some of the simple arithmetic necessary to creating tabular cell entries—that is, aggregating each *B* value with that of its associated constant.

The results of my regression of Iowa's 1867 election against its 1868 election are to be found in the first and third panels of table 11.2. The SPSS command setup for accomplishing that series of regressions is portrayed below. The "G1867" variables represent raw voting data; the figure 99999 designates missing data; the "IF" statements insure that the computer leaves out of the analysis any counties for which election returns are not extant or complete. Anyone reasonably well-versed in SPSS should be able to explain anything else the beginner might find mysterious.

```
COMPUTE REP67=(G1867R/ESTVTR68)*100.
IF (G1867R EQ 99999)REP67=99999.
COMPUTE DEM67=(G1867D/ESTVTR68)*100.
IF (G1867R EQ 99999)DEM67=99999.
COMPUTE NONVT67=(NV67/ESTVTR68)*100.
IF (G1867R EQ 99999)NONVT67=99999.
COMPUTE INL67=((ESTVTR68-ESTVTR67)/ESTVTR68)*100.
IF (G1867R EQ 99999)INL67=99999.
WEIGHT BY ESTVTR68.
REGRESSION DESCRIPTIVES=MEAN.
  /VARIABLES=REP67 DEM67 NONVT67 INL67 R68P D68P
   NVPCT68P
      /ORIGIN
      /DEPENDENT R68P TO NVPCT68P
      /METHOD=ENTER REP67 TO INL67.
FINISH.
```

The rest is easy. The ensuing computer printout yields the information necessary for calculating the individual cell entries of table 11.2. In this instance, listed under Equation Number 1's table of "Variables in the Equation" is a list of the *B* values for each intersection of R68P (Grant's support) with INL67, NONVT67, DEM67, and REP67. The last of these listed values (.98608), for example, reveals that an estimated 98.608 percent of the Republicans of 1867 voted in favor of Grant in 1868. That in itself is useful information, although in these circumstances a more interesting datum (as reported in the top, left-hand cell of table 11.2) is that the 1867 Republicans who favored Grant in 1868 comprised 43 percent of Iowa's total 1868 electorate. This percentage is derived by multiplying REP67's *B* value against the statewide average for REP67 given in the "Mean Label" listing on the printout (43.600). Thus: .98608 × 43.600 = 42.99, or 43 percent.

A similar calculation must then be made for each remaining cell in Grant's column of table 11.2. The printout's Equations Number 2 and 3 offer the respective *B* values for the other two dependent variables, D68P (Seymour's support) and NVPCT68P (the percentage of 1868's eligible voters not voting).

III

In presenting the regression results I included in the text only those tables I deemed immediately necessary, entrusting all others to appendix B. Gienapp's monograph on the early Republican party includes nine tables presenting various regression results on Iowa's voting between 1852 and 1856. Since most of my own regression output did not vary importantly from his, in these instances I saw no reason to duplicate his tables; appendix B therefore contains only results for paired elections not reported by Gienapp. But in two instances I think my own outcomes better than his, and have reported my tabulations rather than refer to his. The interested reader may compare the nativity-group panel of my table B.7, appendix B, with Gienapp, *Origins,* 539, and the work-force panel of table B.7 with his, p. 545.

Supplementary Regression Estimates

APPENDIX B

Table B.1 How the August 1848 electorate behaved in November 1848 (estimated percentages)

	Taylor (Whig)	Van Buren (Fee Soil)	Cass (D)	Scattered votes	Not voting
Whigs	26	3	0	14	−5
Liberty men	1	2	0	−1	0
Democrats	8	−1	40	−13	7
Nonvoters	1	−1	−1	1	16
August ineligibles	0	0	1	3	1
					102

Regressions: 1848 congressional returns × 1848 presidential returns (county N = 32).

Table B.2 How the November 1848 electorate behaved in 1849 (estimated percentages)

	President, public works					Secretary, public works			
	McKean (Whig)	Dayton (Free Soil)	Patterson (D)	Not voting		Allison (W/FS)	Williams (D)	Not voting	
Whigs	29	1	8	−3		33	5	−4	
Free Soilers	2	3	−2	0		4	−1	1	
Democrats	−4	−2	27	17		−9	30	17	
Scattered voters	3	0	1	1		2	1	1	
Nonvoters	2	2	1	12		2	2	12	
1848 ineligibles	1	1	0	1		1	1	1	
					101				99

Regressions: 1848 presidential returns × board of public works returns (county N = 32).

Table B.3 How the 1849 electorate behaved in 1850 (estimated percentages)

	Thompson (Whig)	Clarke (Free Soil)	Hempstead (D)	Not voting	
Whigs	20	1	2	6	
Free Soilers	0	1	0	0	
Democrats	4	−1	27	3	
Nonvoters	4	0	6	17	
1849 ineligibles	2	0	3	2	
					97

Regressions: 1849 board of public works (presidential) returns × 1850 gubernatorial returns (county N = 37).

Table B.4 How the 1850 electorate behaved in 1852 (estimated percentages)

	Scott (Whig)	Hale (Free Soil)	Pierce (D)	Not voting	
Whigs	10	3	−4	17	
Free Soilers	1	1	0	−2	
Democrats	16	0	30	−16	
Nonvoters	3	−1	9	12	
1850 ineligibles	5	0	4	12	
					100

Regressions: 1850 gubernatorial returns × 1852 presidential returns (county N = 42).

Table B.5 How the 1852 electorate behaved in 1854 (estimated percentages)

	McMakin (Free Soil)	Morris (D)	Not voting	
Whigs	5	−3	23	
Free Soilers	4	1	−2	
Democrats	−4	27	6	
Nonvoters	1	6	11	
1852 ineligibles	0	5	20	
				100

Regressions: 1852 presidential returns × 1854 state treasurer returns (county N = 48).

Table B.6 How the 1854 electorate behaved in 1855 (estimated percentages)

	McKay (Anti-Nebraska and Know-Nothing)	Tisdale (D)	Not voting	
Whigs and Free Soilers	25	−4	9	
Democrats	3	25	0	
Nonvoters	2	3	20	
1854 ineligibles	2	3	12	
				100

Regressions: 1854 gubernatorial returns × 1855 commissioner returns (county N = 64).

Table B.7 How various subgroups behaved in 1856 (estimated percentages)

	Frémont (R)	Buchanan (D)	Fillmore (A)	Not voting	
The 1852 electorate					
Whigs	22	−8	5	−2	
Free Soilers	2	−1	0	1	
Democrats	−13	27	1	3	
Nonvoters	4	7	2	−1	
1852 ineligibles	26	12	2	12	
					101
The 1855 electorate					
Anti-Nebraskans and Know Nothings	16	3	5	−1	
Democrats	2	20	2	−5	
Nonvoters	4	9	4	14	
1855 ineligibles	19	3	−2	5	
					98
Voter nativity groups					
New Englanders	7	−1	1	2	
New Yorkers	7	3	1	1	
Pennsylvanians	4	5	5	2	
Ohioans	20	0	−5	4	
Indianans	−1	3	2	2	
Southerners	−2	13	7	−2	
Other native-born	1	1	0	1	
Britons and Scots	4	−1	−1	0	
Irishmen	0	9	0	0	
Germans	3	5	1	0	
Other foreign-born	−2	2	1	1	
					99

Table B.7 (*continued*)

	Frémont (R)	Buchanan (D)	Fillmore (A)	Not voting	
Churchgoers					
Methodists (downstate)	6	10	4	1	
Presbyterians	9	6	2	−1	
Methodists (upstate)	7	4	1	2	
Roman Catholics	2	7	1	2	
Baptists	6	1	0	4	
Congregationalists	6	2	−1	1	
Disciples of Christ	0	3	2	1	
Quakers	3	0	0	0	
Lutherans	2	0	0	2	
Episcopalians	1	1	0	1	
Miscellaneous	1	2	0	0	
					101
The work force					
Farmers:					
Prosperous counties	10	14	6	0	
Middling counties	5	7	3	3	
Poorer counties	4	3	1	2	
Artisans	29	−11	−8	4	
Businessmen/professionals	−8	23	4	−4	
Laborers	2	−1	3	9	
					100

Regressions: 1852 presidential returns × 1856 presidential returns (county N = 49); 1855 commissioner returns × 1856 presidential returns (county N = 65); 1856 voter nativities × 1856 presidential returns (township N = 150); 1860 church seats × 1856 presidential returns (county N = 46), with groups listed in descending order of size in 1860; 1856 occupations × 1856 presidential returns (county N = 76).

Table B.8 How the 1864 electorate behaved in 1865 and 1866 (estimated percentages)

	Governor 1865				Secretary of state 1866			
	Stone (R)	Benton (S/D)[a]	Not voting		Wright (R)	Van Anda (C/D)[b]	Not voting	
Republicans	39	1	8		43	−2	1	
Democrats	4	30	−3		0	29	−2	
Nonvoters	1	3	11		2	3	8	
1864 ineligibles	3	1	3		8	2	6	
				100				98

Regressions: 1864 presidential returns (civilian vote only) × 1865 gubernatorial and 1866 secretary of state returns (county N = 94).
a. Fusion of the Soldier's ticket (Union Anti-Negro Suffrage party) and the Democrats.
b. Fusion of the Conservative Republicans and the Democrats.

Table B.9 How the 1865 electorate behaved in 1866 (estimated percentages)

	Wright (R)	Van Anda (C/D)	Not voting	
Republicans	48	−3	−5	
Democrats	−2	32	0	
Nonvoters	2	2	13	
1865 ineligibles	4	1	6	
				99

Regressions: 1865 gubernatorial returns × 1866 secretary of state returns (county N = 94).

Table B.10 How the 1866 electorate behaved in 1867 (estimated percentages)

	Merrill (R)	Mason (D)	Not voting	
Republicans	32	0	15	
Democrats	7	31	−8	
Nonvoters	0	0	12	
1866 ineligibles	8	2	0	
				99

Regressions: 1866 secretary of state returns × 1867 gubernatorial returns (county N = 95).

Notes

Abbreviations

AI	*Annals of Iowa* (3d series unless otherwise specified)
CWH	*Civil War History*
IHR	*Iowa Historical Record*
IJHP	*Iowa Journal of History and Politics*
JAH	*Journal of American History*
SHSI:DM	State Historical Society of Iowa, Des Moines
SHSI:IC	State Historical Society of Iowa, Iowa City

Generic titles for Iowa legislative minutes and session laws

Council Journal (date of session)
House Journal (date of session)
Senate Journal (date of session)
Laws (date published)

1. Dr. Emerson's Sam

1. Thomas C. Parramore, *Southampton County, Virginia* (Charlottesville, 1978), 76–77; Stephen B. Oates, *The Fires of Jubilee: Nat Turner's Fierce Rebellion* (New York, 1975); Eugene D. Genovese, *Roll, Jordan, Roll: The World the Slaves Made* (New York, 1974), 49–70; James Oakes, *The Ruling Race: A History of American Slaveholders* (New York, 1982), 153–191.
2. Parramore, 72; Vincent C. Hopkins, *Dred Scott's Case* (New York, 1951), 1–5; Don E. Fehrenbacher, *The Dred Scott Case: Its Significance in Law and Politics* (New York, 1978), 239–243, 652–653n.
3. Franc B. Wilkie, *Davenport: Past and Present* (Davenport, 1858), 43; Hopkins, 5; Fehrenbacher, 243–244; Charles E. Snyder, "John Emerson, Owner of Dred Scott," *AI* 21 (1938): 441–442.
4. Wilkie, 27, 167–168; Willard Barrows, "History of Scott County, Iowa," *AI* lst ser. 1 (1863): 14, 44, 58; August Richter, *Geschichte der Stadt Davenport und des County Scott* (Davenport, 1917), 62; Fehrenbacher, 243–244; Snyder, 442–443. Snyder denies that Sam occupied Emerson's claim in 1836, but admits that it could have occurred in 1834 or 1835.

5. Hopkins, 5–7, 9–12; Fehrenbacher, 244–252.
6. Allan G. Bogue, *From Prairie to Corn Belt: Farming on the Illinois and Iowa Prairies in the Nineteenth Century* (Chicago, 1963), 10–13; Malcolm J. Rohrbough, *The Trans-Appalachian Frontier: People, Societies, and Institutions, 1775–1850* (New York, 1978), 321–346; Jean Cutler Prior, *A Regional Guide to Iowa Landforms* (Iowa City, 1976); Thomas E. Fenton and Gerald Miller, "Soils," in *Iowa's Natural Heritage,* ed. Tom C. Cooper (Des Moines, 1982), 81.
7. *History of Johnson County, Iowa* (Iowa City, 1883), 583; A. W. Harlan, "Slavery in Iowa Territory," *AI* 2 (1897): 631–632; *The History of Van Buren County, Iowa* (Chicago, 1878), 489; "The Negro in Iowa" (typescript, SHSI:DM), 22–23, 34–35.
8. Benjamin F. Shambaugh, *The Constitutions of Iowa* (Iowa City, 1934), 83; John Carl Parish, *John Chambers* (Iowa City, 1909), 113, 118, 122, 125, 139, 226, 240; Edward H. Stiles, *Recollections and Sketches of Notable Lawyers and Public Men of Early Iowa* (Des Moines, 1916), 10, 14; Chicago *Western Citizen,* Dec. 7, 1843; *Johnson County,* 463; U.S. Census, 1840, Johnson Co., 245.
9. *The History of Lee County, Iowa* (Chicago, 1879), 729–730; "Negro in Iowa," 34–35; *Sixth Census or Enumeration of the Inhabitants of the United States . . . in 1840* (Washington, 1841), 466–468; *The Seventh Census of the United States: 1850,* 4 vols. (Washington, 1853), 1: 943; Homer L. Calkin, "A Slaveowner in Iowa," *Palimpsest* 22 (1941):344–346; A. T. Andreas, *Illustrated Historical Atlas of the State of Iowa: 1875* reprint ed. (Iowa City, n.d.), 497; J. M. Howell and Heman C. Smith, eds., *History of Decatur County, Iowa,* 2 vols. (Chicago, 1915), 1:184.
10. Andreas, *Iowa,* 423–424; Thomas R. Wessel, "Agriculture, Indians, and American History," *Agricultural History* 50 (1976): 13; Lucius H. Langworthy, "Dubuque: Its History, Mines, Indian Legends, etc.," *IJHP* 8 (1910): 372–373, 377–395.
11. Eliphalet Price, "The Trial and Execution of Patrick O'Connor at the Dubuque Mines in the Summer of 1834," *AI* 1st ser. 3 (1865): 566–574; Andreas, *Iowa,* 424; William Watson et al., eds., *Historical Lectures upon Early Leaders in the Professions in the Territory of Iowa* (Iowa City, 1894), 101–103; "Subscription for a Chapel for the Methodist Episcopal Church, in the Town of Dubuque," MS, SHSI:IC; *Sixth Census,* 466–467. Dubuque's 1840 population was no doubt roughly that of the county's first census district: 1,216. U.S. Census, 1840, Dubuque Co., 58.
12. Dubuque *Daily Times,* July 24, 1870; Richard Acton, "To Go Free," *Palimpsest* 70 (1989): 52–55; T. S. Wilson, "Address of Judge T. S. Wilson at the Opening of the Supreme Court-Room," *IHR* 3 (1887): 460–461; Stiles, 45–52.
13. Stiles, 240–249; William M. Wiecek, *The Sources of Antislavery Constitutionalism in America, 1760–1848* (Ithaca, 1977), 142–143, 194; Helen Tunnicliff Catterall, ed., *Judicial Cases Concerning American Slavery and the Negro,* 5 vols. (Washington, 1926–37), 5:113–117, 139–140.
14. William J. A. Bradford, ed., *Reports of the Decisions of the Supreme Court*

of Iowa (Galena, 1840), 3–7; Eastin Morris, ed., *Reports of Cases Argued and Determined in the Supreme Court of Iowa* 1 (Iowa City, 1847): 1–7.

15. Jean H. Baker, *Affairs of Party: The Political Culture of Northern Democrats in the Mid-Nineteenth Century* (Ithaca, 1983), 64–65; Burlington *Iowa Patriot,* July 11, 18, 1839. Ralph Montgomery took his surname from an indulgent Kentucky owner rather than from Jordan Montgomery. Dubuque *Daily Times,* July 24, 1870.
16. Wilson, 461.
17. Hulda Freeborn to C. Childs, Sept. 23, 1865, William Allen Papers, SHSI:IC; U.S. Census, 1840, Dubuque Co., 71; Galena (Ill.) *North Western Gazette and Advertiser,* Sept. 11, 1840.
18. Dubuque *Iowa News,* Sept. 15, 1838; U.S. Census, 1840, Dubuque Co., 71; U.S. Census, 1850, Dubuque Co., family 990; Cyril B. Upham, "Historical Survey of the Militia in Iowa, 1838–1865," *IJHP* 17 (1919): 319, 336. The Old Testament mandates no more than forty lashes; to insure against a possible violation by miscount, Jewish custom decreed thirty-nine. Deut. 25:3; 2 Cor. 11:24.
19. Galena *North Western Gazette and Advertiser,* Sept. 11, 1840; Freeborn to Childs, Sept. 23, 1865, Allen Papers; Langworthy, 412–413. Morgan's lynching received national attention in antislavery circles. See "Awful Cruelty," *American and Foreign Anti-Slavery Reporter* 1 (1840): 72.
20. *The History of Dubuque County, Iowa* (Chicago, 1880), 395.
21. Andreas, *Iowa,* 404, 423–424; Langworthy, 412–413.
22. *Laws* (1840), 124; *Sixth Census,* 467; U.S Census, 1840, Dubuque Co., 59–60, 67–70, 79–80.
23. John Carl Parish, *George Wallace Jones* (Iowa City, 1912), 127; U.S. Census, 1840, Dubuque Co., 69–70.
24. U.S. Census, 1840, 59–61, 63, 65, 67, 69, 71, 73, 79, 87, 89, 91, 101; Dubuque *Miner's Express,* Nov. 24, 1847.
25. U.S. Census, 1840, Dubuque Co., 79; U.S. Census, 1850, Dubuque Co., families 3, 1424, 1634, 1654, 1664, 1693, 1732, 1733, 1743, 1765, 1827, 1911, 1953.
26. Muscatine *Daily Journal,* Aug. 9, 1856.
27. Andreas, *Iowa,* 449–450; Fred W. Lorch, "Mark Twain in Iowa," *IJHP* 27 (1929): 409, 413–417.
28. U.S. Census, 1840, Muscatine Co., 454, 464, 466, 468, 474, 476; U.S. Census, 1850, Muscatine Co., City of Muscatine, families 24, 29–31, 33, 34, 44, 64, 68, 69, 145, 192, 193, 371, 383, 387, 417, 423. The 1840 population of Muscatine (known until 1849 as Bloomington) was 507. Irving B. Richman, *History of Muscatine County, Iowa,* 2 vols. (Chicago, 1911), 1:448.
29. J. Walton, *Pioneer Papers* (Muscatine, 1899), 332–333; Richman, *History,* 1:260, 285–286; U.S. Census, 1840, Muscatine Co., 476; U.S. Census, 1850, City of Muscatine, families 34, 145, 371, 387; John Mahin, ed., *Muscatine City Directory and Advertiser for 1856* (Muscatine, 1856), 51, 67; entry for "Uncle Ben" Mathews, *Muscatine County, Iowa, Graves Registration* (Des Moines, n.d.); Muscatine *Daily Journal,* Aug. 23, 1856.
30. Bloomington *Herald,* Dec. 4, 1846; Muscatine *Journal,* Mar. 3, 17, 1854;

Muscatine *Daily Journal,* Nov. 23, 1857; U.S. Census, 1850, City of Muscatine, families 24, 30, 31; entry for Lydia Motts, *Graves.*

31. *The United States Biographical Dictionary: Iowa Volume* (Chicago, 1878), 536–541; *History of Muscatine County, Iowa* (Chicago, 1879), 597–598; U.S. Census, 1850, City of Muscatine, family 387.
32. Theodore Hershberg, "Free Blacks in Antebellum Philadelphia," in *The Peoples of Philadelphia: A History of Ethnic Groups and Lower-Class Life, 1790–1940,* ed. Allen F. Davis and Mark H. Haller (Philadelphia, 1973), 111–133; Frank F. Furstenberg Jr., Theodore Hershberg, and John Modell, "The Origins of the Female-Headed Black Family: The Impact of the Urban Experience," *Journal of Interdisciplinary History* 6 (1975): 211–233.
33. *Muscatine County,* 527–528; Muscatine *Journal,* Aug. 4, 1849; Richman, *History,* 1:335.
34. Benjamin Quarles, *Black Abolitionists* (New York, 1970), 116–117, 123–129. Muscatine's 1857 celebration occurred on election day, a traditional festival day among New England blacks. William H. Wiggins Jr., *O Freedom! Afro-American Emancipation Celebrations* (Knoxville, 1987), 28, 31. In 1857, by design or happenstance, that was the day white Iowans first voted on black suffrage.
35. Allen Johnson, ed., *Dictionary of American Biography* 3 (New York, 1929): 403–404; R. R. Wright Jr., *The Encyclopaedia of the African Methodist Episcopal Church,* 2d ed. (Philadelphia, 1947), 568.
36. Muscatine *Daily Journal,* Aug. 3, 4, 1857.
37. Hopkins, 4; entries for Samuel H. Merry and Catherine M. Merry, *Graves;* D. C. Cloud, "A Fugitive Slave Case: 'In re' Jim, or Jim Merry" (typescript, SHSI:DM), 9–10; J. Walton, "Unwritten History of Bloomington (Now Muscatine), in Early Days," *AI* 2d ser. 1 (1882): 47.
38. Cloud, 4–11; Walton, "History," 47–48. Cloud refers to Jim as Jim Merry. Walton, probably more correctly, gives his full name as Jim White.
39. Walton, 48–49; Bloomington *Herald,* Nov. 18, 1848.
40. *Past and Present of Fayette County, Iowa,* 2 vols. (Indianapolis, 1910), 1:131; John Hope Franklin, *The Free Negro in North Carolina, 1790–1860* (Chapel Hill, 1943), 39n, 41; Carter G. Woodson, *Free Negro Heads of Families in the United States in 1830* (Washington, 1925), 26; Emma Lou Thornbrough, *The Negro in Indiana: A Study of a Minority* (Indianapolis, 1957), 32–35; Thomas Draper Peterman, *Historical Sketches of Fayette County, Iowa* (Fort Dodge, n.d.), 77, 79; U.S. Census, 1850, Illinois, Iroquois Co., families 97, 103–107, 364, 386, 388–390, 393.
41. *The History of Fayette County, Iowa* (Chicago, 1878), 688.
42. John R. McKivigan, *The War against Proslavery Religion: Abolitionism and the Northern Churches, 1830–1865* (Ithaca, 1984), 164; Peterman, 77; Iowa Census, 1856, Fayette Co., Westfield Twp., families 4, 20, 21, 167, 170, 219–221, 230, 231.
43. John A. T. Hull, ed., *Census of Iowa for 1880* (Des Moines, 1883), 211; *Fayette County,* 381; Peterman, 77–78; *Past and Present,* 1:131–132; *Plat Book of Fayette County, Iowa* (Philadelphia, 1896), 15.
44. Fehrenbacher, 322–448; Richard H. Sewell, *Ballots for Freedom: Antislavery*

Politics in the United States, 1837–1860 (New York, 1976), 299–301; Samuel J. Kirkwood to Aaron Brown, Mar. 21, 1857, Kirkwood Papers, SHSI:IC.

45. Dan Elbert Clark, *Samuel Jordan Kirkwood* (Iowa City, 1917), 230–246; autobiographical note, Aaron Brown Papers, SHSI:IC; Brown obituary, *AI* 6 (1905): 638–639; *Fayette County,* 419, 428, 449; William H. Thrift, ed., *Roster and Record of Iowa Soldiers in the War of the Rebellion,* 5 vols. (Des Moines, 1908–11), 1:290–291, 294; George W. Crosley, "Lauman's Charge at Jackson," *AI* 1 (1894): 371–381; Iowa Census, 1856, Westfield Twp., family 180.
46. Andreas, *Iowa,* 370; *Biographical Dictionary,* 317–318; Peterman, 78 (italics supplied).

2. Landscape with Black Code

1. Hawkins Taylor, "The First Territorial Legislature of Iowa," *IHR* 6 (1890): 516–517; David Rorer Papers, SHSI:IC; Stiles (see chap. 1, n. 8), 16; John C. Parish, *Robert Lucas* (Iowa City, 1907), 82, 167, 181–182.
2. Charles Negus, "The Early History of Iowa," *AI* 1st ser. 7 (1869): 322–324; Taylor, 522; T. D. Eagal and R. H. Sylvester, eds., *The Iowa State Almanac and Statistical Register for 1860* (Davenport, 1859), 16. This last source seems mainly accurate, though it is partly contradicted by Taylor, who labels Jesse D. Payne and L. B. Hughes as Democrats, and by my judgment that Van B. Delashmutt was a Whig by 1844.
3. Taylor, 519.
4. Leon F. Litwack, *North of Slavery: The Negro in the Free States, 1790–1860* (Chicago, 1961), 16, 31, 35, 60, 75, 85–86, 93–94, 104–106, 114–115; John Codman Hurd, *The Law of Freedom and Bondage in the United States,* 2 vols. (Boston, 1858–1862), 2:29, 34, 128, 135, 140; Jo Ann Manfra, "Northern Exclusionary Measures and the Privileges and Immunities of Free Blacks, 1778–1857: An Unexamined Theme in Antislavery Constitutionalism" (LL.M. thesis, Harvard Law School, 1979), 8–23.
5. Winthrop D. Jordan, *White over Black: American Attitudes toward the Negro, 1550–1812* (Chapel Hill, 1968), xiii, 347–348, 410, 552–553, 559, 562, 564–565, 575; Hurd, 2:5, 15, 18, 20, 77–78, 158; Eugene H. Berwanger, *The Frontier against Slavery: Western Anti-Negro Prejudice and the Slavery Extension Controversy* (Urbana, 1967), 21–23; *Acts of a General Nature . . . of the State of Ohio* (Columbus, 1820), 120–124. Manfra, 25–30, disputes Berwanger's suggestion that Ohio, Indiana, and Illinois seriously considered black exclusion in this period. The only northern state where it did emerge as an important legislative issue between 1800 and 1820 was Pennsylvania.
6. Marcus Wilson Jernegan, *Laboring and Dependent Classes in Colonial America, 1607–1783* (Chicago, 1931), 193–195; Henry Campbell Black, *Black's Law Dictionary,* 4th ed. (Saint Paul, 1968), 1611.
7. Glover Moore, *The Missouri Controversy, 1819–1821* (Lexington, 1953), 135, 142–143, 155, 165–167; Wiecek (see chap. 1, n. 13), 122–124; Manfra, 30–35; E. Charles, ed., *Laws of the State of Missouri; Revised and Digested,* 2 vols. (Saint Louis, 1825), 2:600–602.

8. *Laws* (1839), 180–181, 188, 330, 404; ibid. (1840), 33.
9. Negus, 322–323; *House Journal* (1838/39), 133.
10. *Laws Passed by the First General Assembly of the State of Illinois . . . Second Session* (Kaskaskia, 1819), 354; *Revised Laws of Illinois* (Vandalia, 1833), 463–465; *Laws of the Territory of Michigan* (Detroit, 1827), 484–486; *Revised Laws of Indiana* (Indianapolis, 1831), 375–376; *Laws* (1839), 65–67; *House Journal* (1838/39), 150, 161, 166, 175–176, 191.
11. *Council Journal* (1838/39), 160, 164; Taylor, 522; Negus, 323–324; *Laws* (1839), 67; entry of Jan. 25, 1839, Theodore S. Parvin Diaries, Parvin Papers, Iowa Masonic Library, Cedar Rapids.
12. George M. Fredrickson, *The Black Image in the White Mind: The Debate on Afro-American Character and Destiny, 1817–1914* (New York, 1971), 16–21, 28–29; Lawrence J. Friedman, *Gregarious Saints: Self and Community in American Abolitionism, 1830–1870* (Cambridge, England, 1982), 11–40.
13. George F. Magoun, *Asa Turner: A Home Missionary Patriarch and His Times* (Boston, 1889), 184–190; Fort Madison *Patriot,* July 11, 1838; entry of May 1, 1844, "Journal of Quarterly Reports," Ebenezer Alden Papers, Special Collections, University of Iowa Libraries, Iowa City.
14. Magoun, 191–197, 279–284, 289–290; McKivigan (see chap. 1, n. 42), 219; *Lee County* (see chap. 1, n. 9), 671; Constitution of Denmark Anti-Slavery Society, Jan. 1, 1840, SHSI:IC.
15. Louis Thomas Jones, *The Quakers of Iowa* (Iowa City, 1914), 38–47; Watson et al. (see chap. 1, n. 11), 130; U.S. Census, 1850, Henry Co., Salem Twp., family 1078; Charles Fitzgerald McKiever, *Slavery and the Emigration of North Carolina Friends* (Murfreesboro, 1970), 44–54; Andrew W. Young, *History of Wayne County, Indiana* (Cincinnati, 1872), 295; *History of Wayne County, Indiana,* 2 vols. (Chicago, 1884), 1:626; *Portrait and Biographical Album of Henry County, Iowa* (Chicago, 1888), 683.
16. Thomas E. Drake, *Quakers and Slavery in America* (New Haven, 1950), 133–166; Ruth Ketring Nuermberger, *The Free Produce Movement: A Quaker Protest against Slavery* (Durham, 1942), 30–33; Ruth Anna Ketring, *Charles Osborn in the Anti-Slavery Movement* (Columbus, 1937), 50–56; McKivigan, 105–106; Jean R. Soderlund, *Quakers and Slavery: A Divided Spirit* (Princeton, 1985).
17. Lowell (Ill.) *Genius of Liberty,* Mar. 20, 1841; Philadelphia *Pennsylvania Freeman,* Mar. 24, 1841; New York *Emancipator,* Apr. 2, 1842.
18. Andrew E. Murray, *Presbyterians and the Negro: A History* (Philadelphia, 1966), 127–128; McKivigan, 28–29, 44, 163.
19. Donald E. Zimmerman, *A History of the United Presbyterian Church of Crawfordsville, Iowa* (n.p., 1937), 7–13, 29; Murray, 121; *The History of Washington County, Iowa* (Des Moines, 1880), 432–433, 576–578; *Portrait and Biographical Album of Washington County, Iowa* (Chicago, 1887), 249–250, 294–296; Watson et al., 127–129; Edna L. Jones, ed., *Nathan Littler's History of Washington County, 1835–1875* (Washington, 1977), 8–10, 57, 59–61, 66, 68, 80, 158–159, 196, 209.
20. Chicago *Western Citizen,* Dec. 28, 1843; Murray, 103–113; McKivigan, 82–84, 165–168.

21. J. W. Merrill, *Yellow Spring and Huron: A Local History* (Mediapolis, 1897), 25–30, 45–46, 61; J. W. Merrill and S. C. Merrill, eds., *The Semi-Centennial Celebration of the Organization of the Presbyterian Church, in Yellow Spring Township* (Mediapolis, 1890), 15–18, 49–50; "Minutes of the Session of the Presbyterian Church of Round Prairie, O.S." (Presbyterian Historical Society, Philadelphia, Pa.), 1, 3; "Roll of Members, Yellow Springs Church" (Presbyterian Historical Society), [1]; Murray, 103–104. The names Yellow Spring and Yellow Springs were both employed in the early years of the community.
22. U.S. Census, 1850, Henry Co., Salem Twp., family 1016; Stiles, 120–128; *Pioneer Law-Makers' Association of Iowa Reunion of 1894* (Des Moines, 1894), 57.
23. Petition No. 1, Secretary of State Papers (Legislative Petitions), SHSI:DM; *House Journal* (1840/41), 219, 235, 252, 258; *Reunion of 1894,* 57.
24. Lowell *Genius of Liberty,* July 31, 1841. For the racism of Henry County's representatives L. B. Hughes, John B. Lash, and Simeon Smeed, see *Council Journal* (1838/39), 164; *House Journal* (1840/41), 258; ibid. (1841/42), 159; Petition No. 5, Secretary of State Papers.
25. Magoun, 282; J. B. Chase, ed., *Minutes of the General Association of Congregational Churches and Ministers of the State of Iowa* (Hull, 1888), 9.
26. Petitions No. 3 through 9, Secretary of State Papers; *Council Journal* (1841/42), 61, 85, 130; *House Journal* (1841/42), 119–120, 156–157, 185; Jones, *History,* 139, 146, and passim.
27. *House Journal* (1841/42), 159; *Laws* (1842), 58.
28. *House Journal* (1841/42), 224.
29. Jones, *History,* 80–81. Nathan Littler dated the incident as "June of 1841 or '42." The latter is correct, since Howe arrived in Iowa in late 1841. *The History of Henry County, Iowa* (Chicago, 1879), 569.
30. *House Journal* (1842/43), 126, 224; *Washington County,* 685–686; Bunker obituary, *AI* 3 (1898): 316; Cincinnati *Philanthropist,* Mar. 1, 1843.
31. Chase, 19, 22. At its next annual meeting the association repealed the 1843 resolution. Ibid., 25.
32. "Minutes of the Salem Monthly Meeting of Friends, 1838 to 1846," Men's Meeting (Archives of the Iowa Yearly Meeting, Society of Friends, College Ave. Meetinghouse, Oskaloosa), book A:73, 75, 79; Ketring, 56–62; Jones, *Quakers,* 135–136; Drake, 162–164.
33. Ketring, 63–70; Drake, 164–165; Jones, *Quakers,* 136; Chicago *Western Citizen,* Sept. 21, 1843; "Minutes of the Salem Meeting," book A:149 ff.
34. Chicago *Western Citizen,* Apr. 27, May 18, Aug. 17, Oct. 12, 1843; Betty Fladeland, *James Gillespie Birney: Slaveholder to Abolitionist* (Ithaca, 1955), 225–226; Ward Robert Barnes, "Anti-Slavery Politics in Iowa, 1840–1856" (M.A. thesis, University of Iowa, 1968), 68–69; O. A. Garretson, "Travelling on the Underground Railroad in Iowa," *IJHP* 22 (1924): 425.
35. Murray, 113; Fladeland, 227–228; *Minutes of the General Assembly of the Presbyterian Church in the United States (N.S.)* (Philadelphia, 1839), 104; Merrill and Merrill, 26–27; "Roll of Yellow Springs," [3–4].
36. Chicago *Western Citizen,* Nov. 23, Dec. 28, 1843, Jan. 18, 1844; Merrill and Merrill, 21; Frank E. Shedd, *Daniel Shed Genealogy: Ancestry and Descendants of Daniel Shed of Braintree, Massachusetts* (Boston, 1921), 307; Tru-

man O. Douglass, *The Pilgrims of Iowa* (Boston, 1911), 34, 46; Merrill, 61, 334, 336; Nuermberger, 51.

37. Gilbert H. Barnes and Dwight L. Dumond, eds., *Letters of Theodore Dwight Weld, Angelina Grimké Weld, and Sarah Grimké,* 2 vols. (New York, 1934), 1:272n; Murray, 94; R. C. Galbraith Jr., *The History of Chillicothe Presbytery* (Chillicothe, 1889), 139–140; Norman Dwight Harris, *History of Negro Slavery in Illinois and of the Slavery Agitation of that State* (Chicago, 1906), 131, 139, 142; Chicago *Western Citizen,* Dec. 28, 1843.
38. Barnes and Dumond, 1:90–91n; Robert Samuel Fletcher, *A History of Oberlin College from Its Foundation through the Civil War,* 2 vols. (Oberlin, 1943), 1:242–243; Fladeland, 41–42, 109, 144, 146; Harris, 136, 139, 142, 152; William Ansel Mitchell, *Linn County, Kansas: A History* (Kansas City, 1928), 135, 139–140. In January 1843 Street had invited black artisans and their families from Cincinnati to settle at Salem. This could hardly have escaped Wattles's attention. Cincinnati *Philanthropist,* Mar. 1, 1843.
39. Ronald G. Walters, *The Antislavery Appeal: American Abolitionism after 1830* (Baltimore, 1976), 3–18; Walters, "The Boundaries of Abolitionism," in *Antislavery Reconsidered: New Perspectives on the Abolitionists,* ed. Lewis Perry and Michael Fellman (Baton Rouge, 1979), 13–19; Douglas A. Gamble, "Garrisonian Abolitionists in the West: Some Suggestions for Study," *CWH* 23 (1977): 52–68; Friedman, 68–126; Stanley Harrold, *Gamaliel Bailey and Antislavery Union* (Kent, 1986), 12–54; Lowell *Genius of Liberty,* Mar. 20, May 15, 1841, Apr. 2, 1842.
40. Boston *Liberator,* Aug. 25, 1843; Chicago *Western Citizen,* Nov. 2, 23, 1843.
41. Chicago *Western Citizen,* Dec. 28, 1843, Jan. 18, 1844; Merrill and Merrill, 21.
42. Chicago *Western Citizen,* Jan. 18, 1844; Wiecek, 202–210; Harrold, 37–38; Merrill and Merrill, 21.
43. Chicago *Western Citizen,* Nov. 23, 1843; Harris, 152.

3. The Ghost of Justice Story

1. "Negro in Iowa" (see chap. 1, n. 7), 26–28; Francis Reno, Maria Reno, and Walter Butler, Bond [for] $500, Oct. 9, 1841, Johnson Co. MSS (Miscellaneous), SHSI:IC.
2. "Negro in Iowa," 23; William M. Donnel, "Pioneers of Marion County," *AI* 1st ser. 8 (1870): 224–229 (italics supplied).
3. Leland L. Sage, *A History of Iowa* (Ames, 1974), 80–82; Sewell (see chap. 1, n. 47), 107–130; James L. Sundquist, *Dynamics of the Party System: Alignment and Realignment of Political Parties in the United States* (Washington, 1973), 46–47. For delegates' personal characteristics see Benjamin F. Shambaugh, ed., *Fragments of the Debates of the Constitutional Conventions of 1844 and 1846* (Iowa City, 1900), 408–410 (but party affiliations for several are wrong). Only twenty Whigs were present, of whom all except Joseph D. Hoag (who did not take his seat until October 14) were identified in the local Whig newspaper. Ibid., 21–22, 94, 167. Also not always reliable

is Eagal and Sylvester (see chap. 2, n. 2), 18. Erling A. Erickson, *Banking in Frontier Iowa, 1830–1865* (Ames, 1971), 130–131, errs only in terming John Taylor a Whig.

4. The racist former legislators were Henry Felkner, Stephen Hempstead, George Hepner, Edward Langworthy, Richard Quinton, and William L. Toole. On Hoag and Hobson see Shambaugh, *Fragments,* 409; "Salem Monthly Meeting" (see chap. 2, n. 32), book A:15, 154; Watson et al. (see chap. 1, n. 11), 130–131; Garretson (see chap. 2, n. 34), 427–429; Petitions No. 1 and 7, Secretary of State Papers (Legislative Petitions), SHSI:DM.
5. Philip D. Jordan, ed., "William Salter's 'My Ministry in Iowa, 1843–1846,'" *AI* 20 (1935): 39–40; Jesse Williams, ed., *Journal of the Convention for the Formation of a Constitution for the State of Iowa* (Iowa City, 1845), 32–33; Chase (see chap. 2, n. 25), 24–25.
6. Wiecek (see chap. 1, n. 13), 156; Williams, 32–33.
7. Williams, 33–34; Shambaugh, *Fragments,* 26–29, 155.
8. 1857 constitutional convention portrait album (SHSI:IC), 13; Samuel Wallace Durham, memoir of the 1844 convention, later draft (Durham Papers, SHSI:IC), 11–12; Durham, "Reminiscences of the First Constitutional Convention of Iowa," *Proceedings of the Historical Society of Linn County, Iowa* 1 (1904–1905): 119–120; Stiles (see chap. 1, n. 8), 250–259; Jordan, "Salter," 39; O. Turner, *Pioneer History of the Holland Purchase of Western New York* (Buffalo, 1850), 459; Kathleen Smith Kutolowski, "Antimasonry Reexamined: Social Bases of the Grass-Roots Party," *JAH* 71 (1984): 269–293; Petition No. 5, Secretary of State Papers.
9. Shambaugh, *Fragments,* 27–29; Thomas D. Morris, *Free Men All: The Personal Liberty Laws of the North, 1790–1861* (Baltimore, 1974), 107–129; W. Blair Lord, ed., *The Debates of the Constitutional Convention of the State of Iowa . . . 1857* (Davenport, 1857), 650. Employment of the familiar *Webster's* definition of "citizen" occurred in such widely separated events as Connecticut's famous *Crandall* case (1834) and Iowa's 1857 constitutional convention.
10. Manfra (see chap. 2, n. 4), 12–23.
11. Stiles, 612; Shambaugh, *Fragments,* 33, 409; Williams, 43–44; Berwanger (see chap. 2, n. 5), 43; Manfra, 36–38.
12. Parish (see chap. 2, n. 1), 267–269; Shambaugh, *Fragments,* 33, 42; Williams, 44, 50.
13. Hall's report eventually appeared in three publications: Williams, 52–54; Lord, 650–651; John Mahin, ed., *Journal of the Constitutional Convention of the State of Iowa* (Muscatine, 1857), 241–243. My quotes follow Lord's text and punctuation.
14. William Goodell, *Views of American Constitutional Law in Its Bearing upon American Slavery,* 2d ed. (Utica, 1845), 147; Sheldon S. Wollin, *Politics and Vision: Continuity and Innovation in Western Political Thought* (Boston, 1960), 305–313; John Locke, *Two Treatises of Government,* ed. Peter Laslett, 2d ed. (Cambridge, England, 1967), 112–113; John Dunn, *The Political Thought of John Locke: An Historical Account of the Argument of the "Two Treatises of Government"* (London, 1969), chaps. 9–10; Merle Curti, "The

Great Mr. Locke: America's Philosopher, 1783–1861," *Huntington Library Bulletin* 11 (1937): 140–141.

15. James H. Kettner, *The Development of American Citizenship, 1608–1870* (Chapel Hill, 1978), 322–323; John Fox, *Opinion . . . against the Exercise of Negro Suffrage in Pennsylvania* (Harrisburg, 1838), 11; Frederick Watts, ed., *Reports of Cases Argued and Determined in the Supreme Court of Pennsylvania* (Pittsburgh, 1850), 558.
16. Hall offered no definition of citizenship either in his 1844 report or in his remarks on civil liberties in the 1857 constitutional convention. The latter, however, usefully illuminate the former. Evidently native or naturalized white residents were *citizens,* adult males of this description were *citizens with political privileges,* and nonwhite residents were *noncitizens.* Lord, 176, 692–693.
17. William Blackstone, *Commentaries on the Laws of England,* 2d ed., 1 (Oxford, 1766): 123–125.
18. Thomas Jefferson, *Notes on the State of Virginia,* ed. William Peden (Chapel Hill, 1955), 138; Alexis de Tocqueville, *Democracy in America,* ed. Phillips Bradley, 2 vols. (New York, 1945), 1:375–381; J. K. Paulding, *Slavery in the United States* (New York, 1836), 78–94.
19. Jordan, *White* (see chap. 2, n. 5), especially 150–163, 542–545; Jefferson, 138; Paulding, 271.
20. Williams, 54–55; Shambaugh, *Fragments,* 42–43.
21. Shambaugh, *Fragments,* 220–221; David C. Mott, "Early Iowa Newspapers," *AI* 16 (1928): 190.
22. James Connor, "The Antislavery Movement in Iowa," *AI* 40 (1970): 343–376; Richard B. Latner, "A New Look at Jacksonian Politics," *JAH* 61 (1975): 943–969.
23. Leonard L. Richards, "The Jacksonians and Slavery," in Perry and Fellman (see chap. 2, n. 39), 105; Sundquist, 43–44; Richard L. McCormick, *The Party Period and Public Policy: American Politics from the Age of Jackson to the Progressive Era* (New York, 1986), 167.
24. *Pioneer Law-Makers' Association of Iowa Reunion of 1892* (Des Moines, 1893), 150; Durham, "Reminiscences," 120; Shambaugh, *Fragments,* 66, 409; Williams, 82.
25. Williams, 110–111, 121; Shambaugh, *Fragments,* 109, 123, 409.
26. Shambaugh, *Fragments,* 155–156; Williams, 163–165; Willis Bruce Dowd, *James Grant: A Model American* (Boston, 1909), 10–14; Durham, "Reminiscences," 118.
27. Joseph Story, *Commentaries on the Constitution of the United States* (Boston, 1833), 674; Richard Peters, ed., *Reports of Cases Argued and Adjudged in the Supreme Court of the United States* 11 (Washington, 1837): 154, 159. Manfra, 47, 54, documents the subsequent employment of Story's *Mayor* dissent by enemies of black exclusion in the Florida statehood debates (1845) and in the California constitutional convention of 1849.
28. Charles (see chap. 2, n. 7), 2:600; Shambaugh, *Fragments,* 156; Williams, 165. Both Shambaugh and Williams incorrectly total the vote.
29. Williams, 189–191, 194, 198, 203; Sage, *History,* 84–88.
30. Iowa City *Iowa Standard,* Dec. 24, 1845; *House Journal* (1845/46), 42, 158,

169–170, 178–179; Stiles, 834–836. My judgment that the Wilson bill was an exclusion measure must remain conjectural, but Barnes, 73, at least agrees that H.F. 82 was "an effort to stiffen the [1839] law."

31. Sage, *History,* 88–91. The 1844 and 1846 constitutions may be compared in Benjamin F. Shambaugh, *The Constitutions of Iowa* (Iowa City, 1934).
32. Chicago *Western Citizen,* Dec. 29, 1846; Washington (D.C.) *National Era,* Feb. 4, 1847; *House Journal* (1846/47), 215–216, 235, 341, 352–353; *Senate Journal* (1846/47), 25, 194–195, 250–251; Taylor (see chap. 2, n. 1), 519–520.
33. Those of table 3.1 who supported both exclusion and ordinary racist legislation: Henry Felkner, Stephen Hempstead, George Hepner, Edward Langworthy, and Richard Quinton. The antiexclusion racists: Samuel W. Bissell, David E. Blair, Robert Brown, Jesse B. Browne, Alfred Hebard, Jacob Huner, and William L. Toole. William Patterson opposed both exclusion and ordinary racist legislation.
34. The divisions for all but banking are from Williams, 31, 50, 59, 64, 165, 174. The banking division summarizes eighteen scaled roll calls in which delegates earning scores of 0 or 1 were designated "antibank Democrats." Erickson, 130–134. Respecting daily prayer, the test of Democrats versus Whigs yielded a *phi* coefficient of −.73.
35. Exclusionists who remained Democrats after 1856: Gideon S. Bailey, Theophilus Crawford, Samuel W. Durham, David Ferguson, Joseph Flint, Stephen Hempstead, William E. Leffingwell, John Taylor, David S. Wilson, and Richard B. Wyckoff. Antiexclusionists doing so: James Grant, Dudley Hardy, Sheppard Leffler, Calvin J. Price, and William Patterson. Of those who turned Republican three were exclusion Democrats (Elisha Cutler Jr., William Mordan, and Samuel Murdock), one was an exclusion Whig (Hugh D. Downey), was one an antiexclusion Democrat (Frederick Hancock), and seven were antiexclusion Whigs (Charles Clifton, Stewart Goodrell, Alfred Hebard, Joseph D. Hoag, Samuel H. McCrory, Elijah Sells, and Stephen B. Shelleday). The later affiliations of thirteen men emanate from the records of the post-1856 legislatures in which they served; those of the others were gleaned from various local histories and secondary works.
36. Barnes (see chap. 2, n. 34), 299.

4. Fires of Liberty

1. *Sixth Annual Report of the Executive Committee of the American Anti-Slavery Society* (New York, 1839), 15; Sewell (see chap. 1, n. 46), 37–41.
2. New York *National Anti-Slavery Standard,* Dec. 5, 1844; Cincinnati *Herald and Philanthropist,* Nov. 27, 1844; Harrold (see chap. 2, n. 39), 67–68.
3. Ketring (see chap. 2, n. 16), 71–77; New York *National Anti-Slavery Standard,* Dec. 18, 1845; *Fourteenth Annual Report of the Massachusetts Anti-Slavery Society* (Boston, 1846), 73; Boston *Liberator,* Mar. 19, 1847; *The Liberty Almanac for 1848* (New York, 1847), table titled "Statistics of the Liberty Party."
4. Chicago *Western Citizen,* Apr. 24, 1845.

5. Theodore Clarke Smith, *The Liberty and Free Soil Parties in the Northwest* (New York, 1897), 75, 87, 96–97, 131, 137, 145, 157, 216–219, 231–233, 266, 296–297, 305, 321, 325, 328–332; Barnes (see chap. 2, n. 34); Sewell (see chap. 1, n. 44), 215, 252. Only twenty-eight issues of Iowa's variously titled abolitionist publication are extant. The originals reside at the SHSI:DM, the Cornell University Library, Ithaca, N.Y., and the American Antiquarian Society, Worcester, Mass.
6. Friedman (see chap. 2, n. 12), 1; Chaplain W. Morrison, *Democratic Politics and Sectionalism: The Wilmot Proviso Controversy* (Chapel Hill, 1967); Joseph G. Rayback, *Free Soil: The Election of 1848* (Lexington, 1970); Frederick J. Blue, *The Free Soilers: Third Party Politics, 1848–1854* (Urbana, 1973); John Mayfield, *Rehearsal for Republicanism: Free Soil and the Politics of Antislavery* (Port Washington, 1980); Sundquist (see chap. 3, n. 3), 39–62; Michael F. Holt, *The Political Crisis of the 1850s* (New York, 1978).
7. Chicago *Western Citizen,* Mar. 11, Apr. 1, May 6, Dec. 29, 1846; Barnes, 66–69, 72–81.
8. Rayback, 26–27, 34–55; Barnes, 76–77; Wiecek (see chap. 1, n. 13), 220; Sewell, 170–201.
9. For the quoted descriptions of Alanson St. Clair see L. Hawley to William Lloyd Garrison, Jan. 21, 1840, Antislavery Collection, Boston Public Library, Boston, Mass.; Concord (N.H.) *Herald of Freedom,* Dec. 22, 1843. The bare biographical facts are in Walter M. Merrill and Louis Ruchames, eds., *The Letters of William Lloyd Garrison,* 6 vols. (Cambridge, 1971–1981), 2:210n, 3:26n; Walter M. Merrill to Robert R. Dykstra, Mar. 30, 1979, in author's possession. For St. Clair's religious Odyssey see Richard Eddy, *Universalism in America: A History,* 2 vols. (Boston, 1886), 2:256, 334; *An Inventory of Universalist Archives in Massachusetts* (Boston, 1942), 128, 251, 238; John M. Putnam to A. A. Phelps, Oct. 16, 1840, Antislavery Collection, Boston. For the Tappenite comparison see Friedman, 88–89. For the allegation that St. Clair was perhaps the most devious and unsavory of the anti-Garrison conspirators see "D. W." to Anne W. Weston, Apr. 16, 1839, Antislavery Collection, Boston; Rodney French to Maria W. Chapman, June 17, 1839, ibid.; Maria Weston Chapman, *Right and Wrong in Massachusetts* (Boston, 1839). For the end of his career in New England and his migration to Illinois see Concord *Herald of Freedom,* Dec. 29, 1843; St. Clair to A. A. Phelps, Feb. 10, 1844, Antislavery Collection, Boston; St. Clair to Catherine M. Morse, Dec. 7, 1844, Anti-Slavery Collection, William L. Clements Library, University of Michigan, Ann Arbor; St. Clair to Eliza S. St. Clair, July 30–Aug. 4, 1845, in ibid.; A. T. Andreas, *History of Cook County, Illinois* (Chicago, 1884), 826. Although Garrisonian references discount the quality of St. Clair's mind, Dwight Lowell Dumond approvingly quotes him on the symbolic importance of antislavery petitioning. Dumond, *Antislavery: The Crusade for Freedom in America* (Ann Arbor, 1961), 243.
10. Chicago *Western Citizen,* Aug. 17, Nov. 2, Dec. 7, 1847; Burlington *Hawk-Eye,* Nov. 18, 25, Dec. 23, 1847; Washington (D.C.) *National Era,* Oct. 28, 1847.
11. Washington *National Era,* Feb. 10, 1848; Chicago *Western Citizen,* Jan. 25,

1848; Chapman, 75–77, 80, 98, 114–115; Boston *Massachusetts Abolitionist,* Feb. 7, 1839; Otis G. Hammond, *Bibliography of the Newspapers and Periodicals of Concord, N.H., 1790–1898* (Concord, 1902), 27.

12. The doctrinal dispute between western and eastern factions was very important because it encapsulated alternative theories of the power of Congress and the federal courts to act against slavery. For the "radical antislavery constitutionalism" of the Smith circle see Wiecek, 249–275; Friedman, 96–126.
13. Washington *National Era,* Oct. 28, 1847; Keokuk *Register,* Dec. 9, 1847; Chicago *Western Citizen,* Jan. 25, 1848. James G. Birney may have suggested the Iowans' formulation, having asserted in a recent letter to the *National Era* that "slavery in all the 'new' States—States made and admitted into the Union by Congress—is merely a condition of force, of unlawful force. It has no sanction whatever." As the newspaper's editor commented on the letter, "Its argument, if we understand it, is this: Slavery, down to the moment when the Territory is admitted as a State, is unconstitutional. It [then] continues to be unconstitutional in the State." Dwight L. Dumond, ed., *Letters of James Gillespie Birney, 1831–1857,* 2 vols. (New York, 1938), 2:1081; Washington *National Era,* Oct. 21, 1847.
14. St. Clair to Morse, Feb. 12, 1848, Anti-Slavery Collection, Ann Arbor; Chicago *Western Citizen,* Feb. 22, 1848; Keokuk *Register,* Mar. 9, Oct. 19, 1848.
15. Barnes, 86–87; Keokuk *Register,* May 11, 1848 (italics supplied).
16. Davenport *Gazette,* June 1, 1848; Chicago *Western Citizen,* June 20, 1848; Iowa City *Capital Reporter,* June 21, 1848; Washington *National Era,* July 13, 1848.
17. Rayback, 186–214; Sewell, 146–156; Mayfield, 101–111.
18. Barnes, 89–92; Iowa City *Capital Reporter,* June 21, 1848; Washington *National Era,* Aug. 10, 17, 1848.
19. St. Clair to Morse, Sept. 25, 1848, Anti-Slavery Collection, Ann Arbor; Barnes, 93–95.
20. Rayback, 218–230; Blue, *Free Soilers,* 44–80; Sewell, 156–165; Mayfield, 111–119; U.S. Census, 1850, Van Buren Co., Village of Birmingham, family 38; Oliver Dyer, *Phonographic Report of the Proceedings of the National Free Soil Convention at Buffalo, N.Y.* (Buffalo, 1848), 5, 6, 12, 32; Barnes, 111; Washington *National Era,* Aug. 17, 31, 1848.
21. Sewell, 173–175, 180–181; Mayfield, 116–117, 132, 135, 138–139; Frederick J. Blue, *Salmon P. Chase: A Life in Politics* (Kent, 1987), 68, 71–72.
22. Edward A. Claypool et al., eds., *A Genealogy of the Descendants of William Kelsey,* 3 vols. (New Haven, 1928–1947), 2:321; Franklin William Scott, ed., *Newspapers and Periodicals of Illinois, 1814–1879* (Springfield, 1910), 308; Alanson St. Clair to C. M. Ingraham, Jan. 16, 1852, Anti-Slavery Collection, Ann Arbor; Chicago *Western Citizen,* Nov. 2, 1847, July 4, Aug. 1, Oct. 10, 1848. In his published letters to ibid. Kelsey employed the *nom de plume* "KLC."
23. Iowa City *Capital Reporter,* Sept. 27, 1848; Erik McKinley Eriksson, "William Penn Clarke," *IJHP* 25 (1927): 4–9; 1857 convention album (see chap. 3, n. 8), 21; Iowa City *Iowa Standard,* Nov. 12, Dec. 21, 1845, Jan. 7, 1846.

24. Iowa City *Iowa Standard,* Sept. 10, Oct. 1, 1845; I. W. Lugenbeel to Clarke, May 17, 1851, William Penn Clarke Papers, SHSI:DM; W. McLain to Clarke, Nov. 6, 1851, in ibid.; Lord (see chap. 3, n. 9), 178–179, 196, 198, 826, 833–834, 889; Eriksson, "Clarke," 24–25.
25. Clarke to Dr. Sir, Dec. 4, 1845, Clarke Papers; John Chambers to Clarke, Aug. 19, 1846, in ibid.; Eriksson, "Clarke," 9–10; Iowa City *Capital Reporter,* Sept. 27, 1848.
26. Iowa City *Capital Reporter,* Sept. 27, 1848; Keokuk *Telegraphic Weekly Dispatch,* Sept. 30, 1848; Garretson (see chap. 2, n. 34), 426; Mount Pleasant *Iowa Freeman,* June 19, 1849.
27. John H. Dayton to Clarke, Sept. 27, 1848, Clarke Papers; U.S. Census, 1850, Muscatine Co., City of Muscatine, family 57; Mount Pleasant *Iowa Freeman,* July 10, 1849.
28. Dayton to Clarke, Oct. 20, 1848, Clarke Papers; Mount Pleasant *Iowa Freeman,* July 10, 1849. Pottawattamie County's heavily Whig vote was thrown out on grounds that it reflected an illegal political mobilization of Mormon migrants temporarily settled there following their expulsion from Illinois. The figures employed here, therefore, represent the official count minus the Pottawattamie vote. Louis Pelzer, "The History and Principles of the Democratic Party of Iowa, 1846–1857," *IJHP* 6 (1908): 182–183; "Election Records" (microfilm copy, University of Iowa Libraries, Iowa City).
29. Table B.1, appendix B.
30. Sewell, 202–230; Mayfield, 126–147; Barnes, 124–141; Washington *National Era,* Apr. 26, Aug. 16, 1849.
31. Barnes, 141–144; G. W. Bowie to Clarke, July 16, 1849, Clarke Papers; Burlington *Hawk-Eye,* Aug. 16, 1849; Dayton to Clarke, Jan. l, Mar. 20, 1849, May 17, 1850, Clarke Papers.
32. Burlington *Hawk-Eye,* Aug. 30, 1849; Centreville (Ind.), *Free Territory Sentinel,* Sept. 19, 1849; table B.2, appendix B.
33. Barnes, 164–176; table B.4, appendix B.
34. Smith, 219; Nathan Littler to Clarke, Aug. 12, 1850, Clarke Papers.
35. Chicago *Western Citizen,* Jan. 9, 1849; *House Journal* (1848/49), 155; Bloomington *Journal,* July 7, 1849; John Dorland Cremer, *Records of the Dorland Family in America* (Washington, 1898), 123; Mount Pleasant *Iowa True Democrat,* July 23, Dec. 18, 1850.

5. The Salem Nineteen

1. Wiecek (see chap. 1, n. 13), 62–83; Morris (see chap. 3, n. 9), 1–22; Paul Finkelman, "*Prigg v. Pennsylvania* and Northern State Courts: Anti-Slavery Use of a Pro-Slavery Decision," *CWH* 25 (1979): 5–35.
2. *Laws* (1839), 66, 404.
3. Morris, 107–109; Finkelman, "*Prigg,*" 11–13.
4. Burlington *Iowa Territorial Gazette and Advertiser,* Mar. 23, 1839; Jones, *History* (see chap. 2, n. 19), 87. Nathan Littler's informant misdated the escape by a year; otherwise her recollections dovetail with the 1839 account.
5. "Salem Monthly Meeting" (see chap. 2, n. 32), book A:61, 72–73, 83, 91,

98; Lowell (Ill.), *Genius of Liberty,* July 31, 1841; Jones (see chap. 2, n. 15), 189.

6. Walter Edgerton, *A History of the Separation in Indiana Yearly Meeting of Friends* (Cincinnati, 1856), 134, 138, 184, 239–241, 295–296; Chicago *Western Citizen,* Aug. 3, 1843.
7. *History of Knox County, Illinois* (Chicago, 1878), 210. A Galesburg couple was housesitting for their absent landlord one October day when two Iowa Quakers arrived with a fugitive slave in tow. Since the couple had apparently come to Galesburg in 1842, and shortly after encountering the Iowans the husband voted the Liberty ticket in a November election, the incident must have occurred in 1844. Galesburg (Ill.) *Republican-Register,* Mar. 5, 1887. For Yellow Spring reports of the connection see Morris W. Blair to W. H. Siebert, Jan. 28, 1896, "The 'Underground Railroad' in Iowa," scrapbook, Wilbur Henry Seibert Collection, Houghton Library, Harvard University, Cambridge, Mass.; Edward Heizer to L. O. Leonard, Jan. 20, 1928, Underground Railroad Collection, SHSI:IC.
8. "Salem Quarterly Meeting in Iowa," *Friends' Review: A Religious and Literary Journal* 1 (1848): 675–676; Chicago *Western Citizen,* June 20, 1848.
9. George Frazee, "An Iowa Fugitive Slave Case—1850," *AI* 6 (1903): 9; U.S. Census, 1850, Missouri, Clark Co., family 531; Clark Co. Deeds (Office of the Circuit Clerk and Recorder, Kahoka, Mo.), book C:12, book D:480, book E:39; Garretson (see chap. 2, n. 35), 430; U.S. Census, 1850, Missouri, Clark Co., family 521; ibid., Lewis Co., family 111; *History of Lewis, Clark, Knox and Scotland Counties, Missouri* (Saint Louis, 1887), 304.
10. Garretson, 430–431; Keokuk *Telegraphic Weekly Dispatch,* June 8, 15, 22, 1848.
11. Frazee, "1850," 9–10; "Daggs v. Fraz[i]er et al.," *The Federal Cases,* 30 vols. (Saint Paul, 1894–1897), 6:1112–1113; Garretson, 431–432; Burlington *Hawk-Eye,* June 15, 1848; U.S. Census, 1850, Missouri, Clark Co., family 697; ibid., Slave Schedule, 395.
12. Frazee, "1850," 10, 12–13, 20; *Lewis, Clark, Knox and Scotland Counties,* 252; U.S. Census, 1850, Lee Co., 28th div., family 1392; A. T. Andreas, *An Illustrated Historical Atlas of Lee County, Iowa* (Chicago, 1874), 23, 64.
13. Cincinnati *Philanthropist,* Mar. 1, 1843. Those ultimately convicted included four members of the regular body: John Comer, Thomas Clarkson Frazier, William Johnson, and John H. Pickering.
14. *Henry County* (see chap. 2, n. 29), 542; Frazee, "1850," 12.
15. Frazee, "1850," 13–14, 18–19.
16. Finkelman, "*Prigg,*" 22–23; Frazee, "1850," 11–14, 17–20; *Revised Statutes of the Territory of Iowa* (Iowa City, 1843), 179.
17. Frazee, "1850," 11, 14–17, 19–20; Garretson, 434; U.S. Census, 1850, Henry Co., Salem Twp., family 1161.
18. Keokuk *Telegraphic Weekly Dispatch,* June 8, 1848; Keokuk *Register,* June 8, 1848; Saint Louis *Tri-Weekly Missouri Republican,* June 9, 1848.
19. Keokuk *Register,* June 8, 1848; Saint Louis *Tri-Weekly Missouri Republican,* June 9, 1848; Burlington *Hawk-Eye,* June 15, 1848; Keokuk *Telegraphic Weekly Dispatch,* June 15, 22, 1848; Rachel Kellum, "Reminiscence," *Western Work* 12 (1908): 5.

20. Burlington *Hawk-Eye,* June 15, 1848; Keokuk *Telegraphic Weekly Dispatch,* June 22, 1848.
21. *Henry County,* 543; Garretson, 435–436.
22. U.S. Census, 1850, Henry Co., Mount Pleasant, family 257; Petition No. 5, Secretary of State Papers (Legislative Petitions), SHSI:DM; Keokuk *Telegraphic Weekly Dispatch,* June 22, 1848; "Salem Monthly Meeting," book B:109, 139; entries of June 8–9, 1848, Nathan Isbell Jr. Diary, SHSI:IC.
23. Kellum, 5; Frazee, "1850," 10; Blair to Siebert, Jan. 28, 1896, Siebert Collection; Chicago *Western Citizen,* July 11, 1848.
24. Frazee, "1850," 9; "Daggs v. Fraz[i]er," 1112. For the original report of the proceeding see W. Penn Clarke, "Ruel Daggs *v.* Elihu Fraz[i]er *et al.,*" *Western Legal Observer* 1 (1849): 212–216. Daggs's neighbors apparently took up a collection to help with the costs of the litigation. Keokuk *Telegraphic Weekly Dispatch,* July 13, 1848.
25. Keokuk *Telegraphic Weekly Dispatch,* Jan. 11, 1849; Keokuk *Register,* Jan. 18, 1849; Iowa City *Capital Reporter,* Jan. 24, 1849; Stiles (see chap. 1, n. 8), 161–163, 844–845; "Daggs v. Fraz[i]er," 1113.
26. "Daggs v. Fraz[i]er," 1113; Keokuk *Register,* Jan. 18, 1849. Dyer ignored as redundant the defendants' argument that Daggs was not allowed redress under trover, but was required to seek relief in the Fugitive Slave Law. The plaintiff's lawyers, however, acknowledged this in amending their declaration accordingly.
27. "Daggs v. Fraz[i]er," 1114; Frazee, "1850," 9; Burlington *Hawk-Eye,* June 13, 1850; Stiles, 428–430.
28. Holman Hamilton, *Prologue to Conflict: The Crisis and Compromise of 1850* (Lexington, 1964); Morris, 107–147; Holt, *Crisis* (see chap. 4, n. 6), 67–99; Morton M. Rosenberg, *Iowa on the Eve of the Civil War: A Decade of Frontier Politics* (Norman, 1972), 35–54.
29. Burlington *Hawk-Eye,* June 6, 8, 13, 1850; Paul Finkelman, ed., *Slavery in the Courtroom: An Annotated Bibliography of American Cases* (Washington, 1985), 80. The original report of the trial appeared as George Frazee, *Fugitive Slave Case: Ruel Daggs vs. Elihu Frazier et al.* (Burlington, 1850).
30. Frazee, "1850," 9–21; Finkelman, *Slavery,* 80; Garretson, 432, 437. Interestingly enough, local tradition, while implicating several members of the community in harboring and concealing the fugitives, never confirmed anyone's involvement in transporting them.
31. Frazee, "1850," 21–38.
32. Richard Peters, ed., *The Public Statutes at Large of the United States of America* 1 (Boston, 1845): 302–305; Frazee, "1850," 10, 38–44; Burlington *Hawk-Eye,* June 8, 1850.
33. Frazee, "1850," 44–45; Burlington *Hawk-Eye,* July 11, 1850.
34. Frazee, "1850," 45; "Slaves in Iowa," *AI* 6 (1903): 67; U.S. Census, 1850, Henry Co., Salem Twp., families 1010, 1085, 1134, 1144, 1166; U.S. Census, Agriculture Schedule, 1850, Henry Co., Salem Twp., 267, 269, 271. Kellum, 5, writes that *Daggs* "was not taken out of court until after the [Civil War], and then was compromised."
35. Keokuk *Valley Whig and Register,* June 13, 1850; Burlington *Hawk-Eye,* June 13, July 11, 1850.

36. U.S. Senate, *Appendix to the Congressional Globe,* 31st Cong., lst sess. (Aug. 23, 1850), 22, pt. 2:1623.
37. Louis Pelzer, *Augustus Caesar Dodge* (Iowa City, 1908), 139–152; Rosenberg, 46–47; Hamilton, 191–192.

6. Billy Haun's Law

1. Morris (see chap. 3, n. 9), 130–147; Washington (D.C.) *National Era,* Jan. 23, 1851; Benjamin F. Shambaugh, ed., *Messages and Proclamations of the Governors of Iowa,* 7 vols. (Iowa City, 1903–1905), 1:409–410, 427–428; *Laws* (1851), 244; George Shedd to William Penn Clarke, Feb. 11, 1851, Clarke Papers, SHSI:DM.
2. Burlington *Hawk-Eye,* Nov. 14, 21, 1850, Mar. 3, June 26, 1851.
3. Barnes (see chap. 2, n. 34), 167; Chicago *Western Citizen,* Mar. 26, 1850; Mount Pleasant *Iowa True Democrat,* Apr. 16, July 16, Nov. 14, Dec. 18, 1850, Mar. 26, 1851.
4. Shedd to Clarke, Feb. 11, 1851, Clarke Papers; Mount Pleasant *Iowa True Democrat,* Oct. 31, 1850, Apr. 16, 1851, Mar. 3, 1852; Washington (D.C.) *National Era,* Nov. 21, 1850, Jan. 30, 1851.
5. Fort Madison *Iowa Statesman,* Nov. 16, 1850; *House Journal* (1850/51), 88.
6. Manfra (see chap. 2, n. 4), 46–69; Berwanger (see chap. 2, n. 5), 83.
7. Eagal and Sylvester (see chap. 2, n. 2), 21; Harold M. Hyman and William M. Wiecek, *Equal Justice under Law: Constitutional Development, 1835–1875* (New York, 1982), 44–48; *Reunion of 1894* (see chap. 2, n. 22), 11.
8. Clifford Powell, "History of the Codes of Iowa Law, II—The Code of 1851," *IJHP* 10 (1912): 8–19; Stiles (see chap. 1, n. 8), 19–24, 56–58, 385–388; Emlin M'Clain, "Charles Mason—Iowa's First Jurist," *AI* 4 (1901): 606–607. That the commissioners divided up the work is apparent in a bracketed comment in Mason's draft of the "justices of the peace" section. See Charles Mason Papers (Miscellaneous, box 33), SHSI:DM.
9. H. H. Wubben, "Copperhead Charles Mason: A Question of Loyalty," *CWH* 24 (1978): 46–65; Charles Mason, "Negro equality & its consequences," undated postwar draft, Mason Papers (Miscellaneous, box 44). Black law repeal was accomplished by a section of the code specifying that "all public and general acts passed prior to the present session of the general assembly, and all public and special acts the subjects of which are repugnant to the provisions thereof, are hereby repealed." *Code of Iowa* (1851), 8. Absolute certainty about what was in the commission's final draft is hindered by the disappearance of all copies of the *Report of the Code Commissioners* (Iowa City, 1850).
10. Drafts in Mason Papers (Miscellaneous, box 33); *House Journal* (1850/51), 118, 219; *Senate Journal* (1850/51), 213, 215–216; Powell, 44, 51–53. How the racial clauses came to be written into the "legal settlements" and "attorneys and counsellors" sections of the 1851 code remains unclear.
11. Census of Iowa, 1856, Clinton Co., Elk River Twp., family 5; *The History of Clinton County, Iowa* (Chicago, 1879), 618–620; Andrew *Western Democrat,* Aug. 23, 1850. Employment of the diminutive "Billy G."—evidently by Haun himself—was a southern cultural usage that fell so quaintly on the ears

of Haun's east-central Iowa neighbors that it is specifically noted in the county history cited above.

12. *House Journal* (1850/51), 145, 276, 297–298; Manfra, 61, 63.
13. Iowa City *Iowa Capital Reporter,* Jan. 8, 1851. The eight recidivist ultra conservatives, all Democrats, were Theophilus Crawford, Joseph Flint, R. R. Harbour, George Hepner, William E. Leffingwell, E. S. McCulloch, Laurel Summers, and Richard B. Wyckoff. A ninth Democrat, Henry B. Hendershott, had signed an 1842 petition against repealing the 1839 regulatory law. Petition No. 5, Secretary of State Papers (Legislative Petitions), SHSI:DM.
14. Political affiliations are from Eagal and Sylvester, 21, although the reversed party memberships of Paton Wilson and Andrew Gamble have been corrected.
15. *House Journal* (1850/51), 182, 275–276, 297–300. Some of Haun's opponents attempted to amend his bill so as to include an annual appropriation to the American Colonization Society. Almost half the antiexclusionists (Bunker and six Democrats) joined the exclusionists in voting down this ploy, which appears to have been an angry attempt to irritate rather than a true expression of attitudes toward colonization. Ibid., 298–299.
16. *Laws* (1851), 173 (italics supplied); *Senate Journal* (1850/51), 267, 295; Centreville (Ind.) *Indiana True Democrat,* Mar. 27, 1851. The quote from the Morton rider is from the published text of the law itself rather than from the less accurate wording in the *Senate Journal.*
17. *House Journal* (1850/51), 366–368; Burlington *Hawk-Eye,* Feb. 13, 1851; *Laws* (1851), 172–173.
18. Centreville *Indiana True Democrat,* Mar. 27, 1851; Andrew *Western Democrat,* Feb. 12, 1851; Burlington *Hawk-Eye,* Feb. 13, 1851; Fort Madison *Iowa Statesman,* Feb. 15, 1851; Keokuk *Valley Whig and Register,* Feb. 13, 1851.
19. Nathan Littler to William Penn Clarke, Aug. 3, 1850, Clarke Papers; Eriksson, "Clarke" (see chap. 4, n. 23), 10, 39; George Shedd to William Penn Clarke, Mar. 26, 1851, Clarke Papers; Barnes, 196–198.
20. Sewell (see chap. 1, n. 44), 249–250; table B.4, appendix B; Barnes, 198–206; Sundquist (see chap. 3, n. 3), 57–62; Holt, *Crisis* (see chap. 4, n. 6), 89–130.
21. Whitney R. Cross, *The Burned-Over District: The Social and Intellectual History of Enthusiastic Religion in Western New York, 1800–1850* (Ithaca, 1950), 130–131; Norman H. Clark, *Deliver Us from Evil: An Interpretation of American Prohibition* (New York, 1976), 22–44; Ronald Formisano, *The Birth of Mass Political Parties: Michigan, 1827–1861* (Princeton, 1971), 229–230; Holt, *Crisis,* 121–123; Paul Kleppner, *The Third Electoral System, 1853–1892: Parties, Voters, and Political Cultures* (Chapel Hill, 1979), 63–67. The connection between antislavery and antiliquor movements was as close among Iowa's abolitionists as elsewhere. But not until 1851 did the Iowans insert a temperance plank into their platform, and then only somewhat circumspectly. Mount Pleasant *Iowa True Democrat,* July 2, 1851.
22. Formisano, 219–220, 232–235; Holt, *Crisis,* 131–132; Kleppner, 68–70.
23. Michael Fitzgibbon Holt, *Forging a Majority: The Formation of the Republican Party in Pittsburgh, 1848–1860* (New Haven, 1969), 106–151; Formisano, 218–238; Ronald F. Matthias, "The Know-Nothing Movement in

Iowa" (Ph.D. dissertation, University of Chicago, 1965), 6–7, 73, 76n; Dan Elbert Clark, "The History of Liquor Legislation in Iowa, 1846–1861," *IJHP* 6 (1908): 60–65; Barnes, 203–204, 207–208.

24. Clark, "Liquor," 65–68; Holt, *Crisis,* 144–148; Barnes, 224–225.
25. Harold F. Worthley to Robert R. Dykstra, Sept. 4, 1985, in author's possession; U.S. Census, 1850, Henry Co., Mount Pleasant, div. 2, family 284; John Scholte Nollen, *Grinnell College* (Iowa City, 1953), 69–70.
26. Barnes, 225–228; William Salter, *The Life of James W. Grimes* (New York, 1876), 115; Magoun (see chap. 2, n. 13), 286. The Whig delegate to whom Magoun suggested Grimes's name was William Henry Starr, cousin of Grimes's law partner. *Catalogue of the Officers and Graduates of Yale University, 1701–1924* (New Haven, 1924), 166; Stiles, 292–295.
27. Muscatine *Journal,* Mar. 10, 1854; Magoun, 288; Simeon Waters to Julius A. Reed, Oct. 3, 1854, American Home Missionary Society Papers, Grinnell College Library, Grinnell, Iowa; Barnes, 231–234, 325; Salter, 34–50; Mount Pleasant *Weekly Observer,* Apr. 6, 1854; Chicago *Daily Journal,* June 13, 1854.
28. Eliphalet Price to William Penn Clarke, Mar. 26, 1851, Clarke Papers; Leola Nelson Bergmann, *The Negro in Iowa* (Iowa City, 1969), 15, 28–30; Petition No. 2, Secretary of State Papers. Besides Bunker, the recidivists included Norman Everson, Gilman Folsom, Isaac M. Preston, and Nathanial G. Sales. The cited petition, while undated, is signed by two men, S. L. Vest and Samuel Wright, who did not arrive in Iowa until 1855. Andreas, *Iowa* (see chap. 1, n. 9), 522.
29. Washington (D.C.) *National Era,* July 24, 1851; *Senate Journal* (1854/55), 82, 122; *House Journal* (1854/55), 398. An Anti-Nebraskan effort to repeal the law forbidding blacks to testify in cases involving whites died in committee. Ibid., 17, 74, 87, 121.
30. Fragment (apparently in Alexander Clark's handwriting) erroneously clipped to Petition No. 10, Secretary of State Papers; Petition No. 11, in ibid. That Clark initiated the petition is suggested by his having been its first signatory and by his having appended to the document a signed postscript certifying that the six signatories of the second page "are all colord citizens of Muscatine." Information on twenty of the petitioners can be found in U.S. Census, 1850, Muscatine Co., City of Muscatine; Mahin, *Muscatine* (see chap. 1, n. 29); *Williams' Muscatine Directory, City Guide, and Business Mirror* (Muscatine, 1859).
31. *House Journal* (1854/55), 319; J. W. Cheney, "Glimpses of Henry Clay Dean, a Unique Individual," *AI* 10 (1912): 320–330; Stiles, 573–585; Muscatine *Tri-Weekly Journal,* Jan. 19, 1855.
32. Eagal and Sylvester, 22, mislabel George N. Rosser a Democrat. More importantly, they list all non-Democrats as Whigs. Precisely separating the old-line Whigs from the more numerous Anti-Nebraskans can be done on the basis of the successive ballots to elect a U.S. Senator. I counted as old-line Whigs those who supported Ebenezer Cook over James Harlan in at least two of the three ballots of December 21, 1854: John T. Baldwin, Joseph A. Brown, John Conkey, Allen D. Graham, Andrew J. Hyde, Rolla Johnson, and Samuel H.

McCrory. Dan Elbert Clark, *History of Senatorial Elections in Iowa* (Iowa City, 1912), 59–87; *House Journal* (1854/55), 102–103, 106–107, 109.

33. *Senate Journal* (1854/55), 319, 327, 331, 341, 381. The roll call on Samuels's motion to postpone was inadvertently not included in the printed minutes.
34. It is useful to keep in mind that these occupations probably described what men felt themselves to be in some "essential" sense, rather than how they earned their incomes at the moment. Many who chose to describe themselves as farmers in 1854, for instance, actually pursued other careers. I have employed occupations as given in the belief that their owners at least *identified with* the economic groups of which they described themselves as being members.
35. John L. Hammond, *The Politics of Benevolence: Revival Religion and American Voting Behavior* (Norwood, N.J., 1979), 1–19. See also Kleppner, 63–64.
36. For the Washington County natives see *House Journal* (1854/55), appendix, 246–248. The western New York natives: Lafayette Bigelow, William H. Holmes, James D. McKay, Jairus E. Neal, and O. D. Tisdale. Andreas, *Iowa,* 376; Stiles, 524, 692; W. E. Alexander, *History of Winneshiek and Allamakee Counties, Iowa* (Sioux City, 1882), 197; Genealogical Query No. 6494, Boston *Transcript,* May 24, 1933. I have followed Cross, 85, in defining the Burned-Over District as everything west of the eastern boundaries of Jefferson, Oswego, Oneida, Madison, Chenango, and Broome counties.
37. Cross, 135–136, 252–267; *House Journal* (1854/55), 229–230, 319.
38. McKivigan (see chap. 1, n. 42), 165–167, 170–172.
39. Ibid., 163. The ultra conservative Quaker was Samuel Coffin, a dry Anti-Nebraskan and southern-born farmer of Mahaska County about whom no additional information is readily available. *Senate Journal* (1854/55), appendix, 247.
40. McKivigan, 172–174, 176–178; *History of Buchanan County, Iowa* (Cleveland, 1881), 219; Lewis Cass Aldrich, ed., *History of Yates County, N.Y.* (Syracuse, 1892), 228–229; Barnes, 297.
41. Mount Pleasant *Iowa True Democrat,* Feb. 26, 1851.

7. Present at the Creation

1. Benjamin F. Gue, *History of Iowa,* 4 vols. (New York, 1903), facing 1:275; Salter (see chap. 6, n. 26), frontispiece, 33, 390; Augustine M. Antrobus, *History of Des Moines County, Iowa,* 2 vols. (Chicago, 1915), 1:401–402; John Lauritz Larson, *Bonds of Enterprise: John Murray Forbes and Western Development in America's Railway Age* (Cambridge, 1984), 54, 58–60.
2. Salter, 26, 37, 71; Barnes (see chap. 2, n. 34), 228–230; F. I. Herriott, "A Neglected Factor in the Anti-Slavery Triumph in Iowa in 1854," *Deutsch-Amerikanische Geschichtsblätter: Jahrbuch der Deutsch-Amerikanischen Historischen Gesellschaft von Illinois* 18–19 (1918–1919): 327–335; Fred B. Lewellen, "Political Ideas of James W. Grimes," *IJHP* 42 (1944): 339–404.
3. Barnes, 235–236; table B.5, appendix B; William E. Gienapp, *The Origins of the Republican Party, 1852–1856* (New York, 1987), 121–122, 502. For Whig disloyalty to the coalition compare Gienapp's table 4.7 on 1852 Whigs' support for Grimes with my table B.5 on their support for McMakin.

4. Shambaugh, *Messages* (see chap. 6, n. 1), 2:10, 12–14; Salter, 62–65; *House Journal* (1854/55), 185–187, 229–230, 244–245, 358–359; *Senate Journal* (1854/55), 196, 201, 208; *Laws* (1855), 47–48, 58–70, 114–116.
5. Burlington *Tri-Weekly Hawk-Eye,* June 25, 1855; George Frazee, "The Iowa Fugitive Slave Case," *AI* 4 (1899): 118, 125–129, 135; Salter, 72–73. Grimes's handwriting is normally very hard to decipher, and in Salter's transcription the letter (the original is lost) is made to say that the governor sent word "to David's, *via* Yellow Spring and Huron." My speculative reading accommodates, as Salter's does not, the fact that a delegation was dispatched from Denmark to the hearing. Burlington *Daily Hawk-Eye and Telegraph,* June 30, 1855.
6. Frazee, "Slave Case," 129–134; Salter, 47, 73.
7. Allan Nevins, *The Ordeal of the Union,* 2 vols. (New York, 1947), 2:380–411; Gienapp, 164–166, 168–172, 179–180; Matthias, "Movement" (see chap. 6, n. 23), 1–16, 22–23, 27–28.
8. Mattias, "Movement," 29–43; Gienapp, 278, 520; table B.6, appendix B. On the possibility that some Iowa Democrats were unaware of the Know Nothing endorsement of candidates see Washington (D.C.) *National Era,* Aug. 30, 1855.
9. Salter, 69–70; Washington *National Era,* June 7, 1855.
10. Barnes, 290–306; Ronald F. Matthias, Biographical File, in possession of the compiler, Wartburg College, Waverly, Iowa. The implausibly accused Free Soilers were Samuel L. Howe, Daniel F. Miller, Henry O'Connor, and George Shedd. The plausibly accused was one E. Kilpatrick. Burlington *Daily Iowa State Gazette,* Aug. 4, 1855.
11. Matthias, "Movement," 123. The sixteen were Henry J. Campbell, Ebenezer Cook, John Cook, Thomas Hughes, John C. Lockwood, James Marsh, George W. McCleary, Daniel F. Miller, William Mordan, James M. Morgan, Reuben Noble, John A. Parvin, Elijah Sells, John J. Selman, Francis Springer, and William L. Toole.
12. Gienapp, 181–187, 236; Salter, 71–72, 78–79; Matthias, "Movement," 91–120; Louis Pelzer, "The Origin and Organization of the Republican Party in Iowa," *IJHP* 4 (1906): 499–500.
13. Washington *National Era,* May 12, June 7, Aug. 30, Oct. 4, 1855.
14. Salter, 79; New York *Weekly Tribune,* Mar. 1, 1856. Clarke, ex-state auditor A. J. Stevens, and one C. G. Hawthorne made up Iowa's delegation to the Republican gathering (February 22 and 23). Meanwhile, the American party convention preliminaries were attended by two Iowans, L. H. Webster, a Cedar Rapids lawyer, and Iowa's Know Nothing Congressman, James Thorington. The Americans, after a Sabbath break, resumed their contentious deliberations on February 25, by which time Clarke had arrived from Pittsburgh.
15. Pelzer, "Origin," 521–525. The figure 290 results from eliminating duplications in Pelzer's various listings.
16. Matthias, "Movement," 130–132. The figure forty-two results from comparing the names of Matthias's Biographical File against those listed by Pelzer.
17. The figure twenty-three results from comparing Barnes's list against Pelzer's. I have assumed that the A. Brownville of the latter is the Alex Brownlie of the former. Barnes also obtains a total of twenty-three, but only by adding

the name of Joseph D. Hoag, whom I find in neither his own list nor Pelzer's. Barnes, 281.

18. Barnes, 291. In November 1856 Howe ran unsuccessfully for a seat in the impending state constitutional convention, but that was his last political effort.
19. Barnes, 212, 270–271; Stiles (see chap. 1, n. 8), 120–128, 405–406; Irving B. Richman, "Congregational Life in Muscatine, 1843–1893," *IJHP* 21 (1923): 362. O'Connor, educated in his native Dublin by a monastic teaching order, was identified as a Catholic in the Muscatine *Daily Evening Journal,* Oct. 14, 1856.
20. Pelzer, "Origin," 507–517; Matthias, "Movement," 130–138; Holt, *Majority* (see chap. 6, n. 23), 176. When Gienapp argues that friction over the Iowa nominations was nonexistent because "all officers to be elected in [August] were of limited importance," he fails to appreciate the lubrication provided by the shrewd selection of candidates. Gienapp, *Origins,* 279.
21. Clarke's 1856 ambitions are revealed in a post-convention letter from Grimes to Clarke. That Clarke coveted the attorney general's post is suggested by the governor's remark, "I know nothing of the qualifications of the present nominee." This would seem to apply to Samuel A. Rice rather than to the other candidates. "Letters of James W. Grimes," *AI* 22 (1940–41): 474; Stiles, 276. Rice, alone of the nominees, publicly asserted his opposition to Fillmore's presidential candidacy. Matthias, "Movement," 155–157.
22. Matthias, "Movement," 136–137; Matthias, Biographical File, entries for Sells, Martin Morris, and John Pattee.
23. Matthias, Biographical File, entries for Needham, Noble, Mayne, and Stone. In Pelzer's material Mayne is listed as L. Mayne, but this is corrected in another source. Pelzer, "Origin," 525; Washington *National Era,* Mar. 20, 1856.
24. The racial conservatives: Hugh D. Downey, Thomas Hughes, Samuel H. McCrory, William Mordan, John H. Pigman. The antiexclusionists: Frederick Hancock, Abner H. McCrary, Thomas J. McKean, John A. Parvin. The progressives: James Edie, Robert Holmes, Samuel McFarland, Daniel F. Miller, Reuben Noble, Samuel A. Russell, Francis Springer, James N. Young.
25. Muscatine *Journal,* May 9, 1868; Iowa City *State Reporter and National Crescent,* Aug. 26, 1857; Muscatine *Iowa Democratic Enquirer,* Oct. 7, 1858.
26. Gienapp, 259–263; New York *Weekly Tribune,* Mar. 1, 1856; "Letters of Grimes," 475; Matthias, "Movement," 142–150.
27. Gienapp, 297–303; Nevins, 2:428–437, 471–476; F. D. Kimball to Eli Thayer, May 30, 1856, Thayer Papers, Kansas State Historical Society, Topeka; Ralph Volney Harlow, "The Rise and Fall of the Kansas Aid Movement," *American Historical Review* 41 (1935): 1–10; James W. Grimes to Franklin Pierce, Aug. 30, 1856, Executive Journal: 1855–1858 (SHSI:DM), 237–239; Salter, 84–86; Shambaugh, *Messages,* 2:38–39.
28. Nevins, 2:429, 481–482; *Johnson County* (see chap. 1, n. 7), 263; Iowa City *Daily Republican,* June 9, 12, 16, 1856; *The History of Marion County, Iowa* (Des Moines, 1881), 458; Iowa City *Daily Evening Reporter,* June 23, 1856; Tilden G. Edelstein, *Strange Enthusiasm: A Life of Thomas Wentworth Hig-*

ginson (New Haven, 1968), 182–184; Mary Thatcher Higginson, ed., *Letters and Journals of Thomas Wentworth Higginson, 1846–1906* (Boston, 1921), 137–138; William Elsey Connelley, "The Lane Trail," *Collections of the Kansas State Historical Society* 13 (1913–14): 268–269; James A. Rawley, *Race and Politics: "Bleeding Kansas" and the Coming of the Civil War* (Philadelphia, 1969), 2.

29. Iowa City *Daily Republican,* June 25, 1856; *Marion County,* 459; Connelley, 268; James H. Lane to William Penn Clarke, June 30, 1856, Clarke Papers; entry of July 2, 1856, Richard J. Hinton Journal, Hinton Papers, Kansas State Historical Society; Iowa City *Daily Evening Reporter,* June 23, 1856.
30. Harlow, 14–16; Wendell Holmes Stephenson, "The Political Career of General James H. Lane," *Publications of the Kansas State Historical Society* 3 (1930): 74–75; New York *Daily Times,* June 23, July 11, 1856; New York *Daily Tribune,* Aug. 13, 1856.
31. Leverett W. Spring, *Kansas: The Prelude to the War for the Union* (Boston, 1885), 172.
32. George Minot, ed., *Statutes at Large and Treaties of the United States of America* 10 (Boston, 1855): 639; James W. Grimes to H. K. Craig, May 14, 1856, Executive Journal: 1855–1858, 234; H. K. Craig to James W. Grimes, May 22, 1856, Governors' Correspondence (Militia, 1839–1875), SHSI:DM; Iowa City *Daily Republican,* July 1, 1856; Saint Louis *Daily Missouri Democrat,* June 30, July 8, 10, 1856; Robert E. Shalhope, *Sterling Price: Portrait of a Southerner* (Columbia, 1971), 129; James W. Grimes to William Penn Clarke, n.d. (letter no. 47), Clarke Papers.
33. Muscatine *Daily Journal,* July 1, 1856; entry of July 1, 1856, Hinton Journal; James W. Grimes to George W. McCleary, July 3, 1856 (photocopy), Grimes Papers, SHSI:DM; Shambaugh, *Messages,* 2:21–22; *Laws* (Special Session, 1856), 89; *House Journal* (Special Session, 1856), 39.
34. Richard J. Hinton, *John Brown and His Men* (New York, 1894), 55–56; Hinton, "Making Kansas a Free State," *Chautauquan* 31 (1900): 349.
35. Hinton, *Brown,* 55, 59; entries of July 3, 18, 1856, Hinton Journal; Worcester (Mass.) *Spy,* Aug. 30, 1856. Pardee Butler, a former Iowan and a Disciples of Christ clergyman, was an important opponent of his denomination's conservatism on slavery. David Edwin Harrell Jr., *Quest for a Christian America: The Disciples of Christ and American Society to 1866* (Nashville, 1966), 115–121; Lester G. McAllister and William E. Tucker, *Journey in Faith: A History of the Christian Church (Disciples of Christ)* (Saint Louis, 1975), 198–200.
36. F. B. Sanborn, "The Early History of Kansas, 1854–1861," *Proceedings of the Massachusetts Historical Society* 3d ser. 1 (1908): 344; Sanborn, *Recollections of Seventy Years,* 2 vols. (Boston, 1909), 1:52–53, 62; Connelley, 272–275; John Todd, *Early Settlement and Growth of Western Iowa* (Des Moines, 1906), 115–116, 120–128, 130–133; Burlington *Daily Hawk-Eye and Telegraph,* June 28, 1856; Iowa City *Daily Republican,* Aug. 30, 1856; Robert Morrow, "Emigration to Kansas in 1856," *Transactions of the Kansas State Historical Society* 8 (1904): 304–305; Joseph Logsdon, *Horace White: Nineteenth Century Liberal* (Westport, 1971), 29–30.

37. John E. Briggs, "The Enlistment of Iowa Troops during the Civil War," *IJHP* 15 (1917): 324–329; Shambaugh, *Messages,* 2:201–202; Des Moines *Iowa State Journal,* Mar. 6, 1858; "Letters of Grimes," 494.
38. Nevins, 2:484–486; Todd, 121–122, 133; Harlow, 21–22; Rosenberg (see chap. 5, n. 28), 135–136, 138–139, 141–142; Stephenson, 74; Laura E. Richards, ed., *Letters and Journals of Samuel Gridley Howe,* 2 vols. (Boston, 1906–1909), 2:423; New York *Daily Tribune,* July 23, 1856; Burlington *Daily Hawk-Eye and Telegraph,* Aug. 18, 1856; Salter, 53; Matthias, "Movement," 158–180. With respect to Iowa, it would be hard to argue with William E. Gienapp's conclusion that the switch from an American allegiance to Republicanism required little soul-searching. Gienapp, "Nativism and the Creation of a Republican Majority in the North before the Civil War," *JAH* 72 (1985): 547.
39. Gienapp, 350–353, 378; James Harlan to William Penn Clarke, Sept. 13, 1856, Clarke Papers; Pelzer, "Origin," 517; table B.7, appendix B. It is not possible to obtain any reasonably precise measurement of former Know Nothing behavior in 1856 because American candidates for state office only ran on fusion tickets before that date.
40. These estimated turnouts differ from those prepared by Walter Dean Burnham and published in *Historical Statistics of the United States: Colonial Times to 1970,* 2 vols. (Washington, 1975), 2:1072. He gives the 1852 figure as 80.2 percent and that of 1856 as 87.0. The latter is in perfect agreement with my own estimate, but the 1852 estimate seems way over the mark, probably due to a substantial voter undercount by the compiler. For an exchange on the accuracy of Burnham's calculations see Gerald Ginsburg, "Computing Antebellum Turnout: Methods and Models," *Journal of Interdisciplinary History* 16 (1986): 579–611; Burnham, "Those High Nineteenth-Century American Voting Turnouts: Fact or Fiction?" ibid., 613–644.
41. Rosenberg, 13–14, 25–27, 142–144; table B.7, appendix B; Gienapp, 434, 537, 543; Matthias, "Movement," 170–173, 195–197, 201. Gienapp employs data ingeniously derived from printed census materials for Iowa's Yankees, southerners, Germans, Britons and Scots, Irishmen, and Scandinavians. While my regression estimates of Yankee behavior closely parallel his, mine appear somewhat better with respect to the other groups mentioned, except that my 1856 data do not allow reasonable estimates of Scandinavian behavior. Gienapp, *Origins,* 425n, 539.
42. Ibid., 394–405, 413–414. Gienapp offers no data beyond Yankees and southerners that would provide other examples of the "political identification" phenomenon glimpsed here.
43. What is employed here as a surrogate variable are "church seats" data extracted from the published U.S. census for 1860. My usage of them, including the omission of suspect data for western Iowa, is discussed in appendix A.
44. Gienapp, 423, 426, 431–434, 540–542; table B.7, appendix B; Martin L. Greer, ed., *Official Records: Minutes of the Iowa Conference of the Methodist Episcopal Church* (n.p., 1962), 83, 88, 90, 104, 106, 110–111; Stephen Norris Fellows, *History of the Upper Iowa Conference of the Methodist Episcopal Church, 1856–1906* (Cedar Rapids, 1907), 86–87. A few caveats respecting

the religious panel of table B.7: the percentage of Baptists not voting is probably exaggerated, and one doubts that Fillmore attracted support from Catholics or Buchanan from Congregationalists.

45. Gienapp, 434. See also the cautionary in Formisano (see chap. 6, n. 21), 312–314.
46. My estimates agree fairly well with those presented by Gienapp for farmers in the aggregate, except that in my opinion he somewhat overestimates Republican strength among them. Compare table B.7, appendix B, with Gienapp, *Origins,* 545. For the method by which I divided rural Iowa according to prosperity see appendix A. Farm values in Iowa's regions in the twentieth century are discussed in Sage, *History* (see chap. 3, n. 3), 13–15.
47. Table B.7, appendix B; E. F. Ware, *The Lyon Campaign in Missouri* (Topeka, 1907), 38, 45. My regression estimates again generally agree with Gienapp's, except that his "unskilled workers" are rather more Democratic than my laborers. Gienapp, *Origins,* 545.
48. Gienapp notes that Iowa was the one state for which he was able to measure the relative influence in 1856 of wealth, occupation, ethnicity, and religion. "Occupation had only a small effect on the Republican vote," he reports, "once these other variables are controlled." Gienapp, *Origins,* 357, 439n.
49. Eric Foner, *Free Soil, Free Labor, Free Men: The Ideology of the Republican Party before the Civil War* (New York, 1970), 21–22, 59, 61.
50. Stephen B. Oates, *To Purge This Land with Blood: A Biography of John Brown,* 2d ed. (Amherst, 1970), 177, 223, 242–243; Frederick Lloyd, "John Brown among the Pedee Quakers," *AI* 1st ser. 4 (1866): 668–669.

8. Progress and Prejudice

1. C. C. Cole, ed., *Reports of Cases at Law and in Equity Argued and Determined in the Supreme Court of the State of Iowa* 2 (Des Moines, 1874): 82–83. Usher & Thayer assumed management of the hotel shortly after Motts installed his City Barbering Saloon there; otherwise, the facts of the dispute are obscure. Muscatine *Journal,* Mar. 3, 17, 1854. Hinton is identified in Mahin, *Muscatine* (see chap. 1, n. 30), 63.
2. Andreas, *Iowa* (see chap. 1, n. 9), 392; *Biographical Dictionary* (see chap. 1, n. 31), 582–584; *Debates and Speeches, in the Legislature of Iowa, during the Session of 1856–7* (Iowa City, 1857), 9, 14.
3. *House Journal* (1856/57), 127, 148–149, 157; *Senate Journal* (1856/57), 53, 93–94, 107–108, 593; *The History of Benton County, Iowa* (Chicago, 1878), 311, 367; Lord (chap. 3, n. 9), 195; Ottumwa *Weekly Courier,* Jan. 29, 1857.
4. Muscatine *Daily Journal,* Dec. 10, 1856; *House Journal* (1856/57), 182; *Senate Journal,* 232. That whites as well as blacks signed the memorial is suggested by two things: Muscatine's Republican editor apparently endorsed the signature drive (by terming Iowa's black laws a "disgrace"), and a later Muscatine petition known to have been signed by men of both races included 129 signatures. Muscatine *Daily Journal,* Dec. 10, 1856.
5. Muscatine *Daily Journal,* Dec. 10, 1856, Feb. 6, 1857. Although the proceedings of the 1857 colored convention were issued in pamphlet form, no copies

appear to be extant. B. Bowser, a Mount Pleasant barber, presided and Charles Jackson, a Muscatine clerk, served as secretary. The number of delegates is inferred from the petition's signatures of "Chas. Jackson, and 32 other colored men." Watson Bowron, ed., *Henry County Directory, for 1859-'60* (Burlington, n.d.), 37; Mahin, *Muscatine,* 4; Lord, 216; Mahin, *Journal* (see chap. 3, n. 13), 119.

6. Robert Robinson to Laurel Summers, Jan. 19, 1857, Summers Papers, SHSI:DM; Iowa City *Republican,* Jan. 17, 1857; Keokuk *Daily Gate City,* Jan. 26, 31, 1857; Rosenberg (see chap. 5, n. 28), 152–154.
7. *House Journal* (1856/57), 464–466; *Senate Journal* (1856/57), 444–447, 592. There is some confusion about the vote on the unsuccessful senate amendment: McCoy is listed as favoring it and Charles Foster, another Republican progressive, is recorded as voting both Yes and No. The senators also voted to exempt blacks from paying school taxes, and to have the names of black youngsters omitted from local enumerations of school-age children. *Senate Journal* (1856/57), 445–447.
8. Eagal and Sylvester (see chap. 2, n. 2), 23; Lord, 4; Stiles (see chap. 1, n. 8), 250–259, 532–538.
9. Besides Springer, the other pre-convention progressive was William Patterson; the antiexclusionists were David Bunker and John A. Parvin; the conservative was Moses W. Robinson. For Hall's speech see *The Annual Report of the Colonization Society of the State of Iowa* (Iowa City, 1857), 9–12. Judging from its paid-up dues, membership in Iowa's ACS chapter was no more than thirty-two. Seven were former lawmakers: three racial conservatives (Milton D. Browning, J. B. Lash, Ben M. Samuels), three antiexclusionists (Stewart Goodrell, George W. McCleary, Elijah Sells), and the above-mentioned Patterson, soon to qualify as an ultra conservative.
10. Erickson (see chap. 3, n. 3), 84–85; Lord, 62, 115, 140, 216, 657. Lord gives James Rice as the first name on the Delaware petition, and 199 as the number of Muscatine signatories. These errors are corrected in Mahin, *Journal,* 96, 140. For Wright see *History of Delaware County, Iowa* (Chicago, 1878), 400, 418, 475, 519.
11. Lord, 172, 180, 196–198, 735. Springer voted against both measures, but—most interestingly—strongly applauded the convention's action on black testimony in later years. "The Constitutional Convention of 1857," *IHR* 11 (1896): 490.
12. Lord, 62, 129, 138, 732, 734, 736, 741, 825–826, 829–830, 832, 837; Morris (see chap. 3, n. 9), 166–185. The vote on black property holding, which was not a roll call, is of course excluded from the scalogram of my table 8.1.
13. Lord, 217, 219, 222, 665, 692–693, 912–913, 917; Tom L. McLaughlin, "Grass-Roots Attitudes toward Black Rights in Twelve Nonslaveholding States, 1846–1869," *Mid-America* 56 (1974): 176; Leslie H. Fishel Jr., "Wisconsin and Negro Suffrage," *Wisconsin Magazine of History* 46 (1963): 184–188, 194–195; Michael J. McManus, "Wisconsin Republicans and Negro Suffrage: Attitudes and Behavior, 1857," *CWH* 25 (1979): 38–39. Wilson's amendment did not simply replicate the equivocal wording of the Wis-

consin instrument; the pertinent portion of Iowa's resolution left nothing to chance. Wilson's only justification for offering it was "so that persons who do not choose to vote either way can let it alone, and still their votes would count." Lord, 912.

14. Shambaugh, *Constitutions* (see chap. 1, n. 8), 305, 307–308, 314–315, 325; Stiles, 694–696; Lord, 130, 913. Harris's proposition differed from the Indiana measure only in eliminating the words "and may be willing to emigrate," and in adding the phrase "and to make provisions for the colonization of the negroes and mulattoes, and their descendants who shall at the time of the adoption of this constitution have a legal residence in the State." Compare Lord, 913; *The Constitutions of the Several States of the Union and United States* (New York, 1852), 421.
15. For various methodological aspects of scaling in roll call analysis see Allan G. Bogue, *The Earnest Men: Republicans of the Civil War Senate* (Ithaca, 1981), 345–352.
16. Lord, 837. "However desirable it is to have them educated separately," Hall said, he could not support the continued exclusion of nonwhites from the public schools. "If the negroes . . . are permitted to live and settle in Iowa, the first thing I want to have done is to take them and educate them. I would force education upon them; because they are not fit to be here without some education." A few egalitarian Republicans pointedly congratulated Hall for being at heart less racist than such Democrats as Gillaspy or Harris. And R. L. B. Clarke gave Hall the credit of "struggling with his prejudices as a buffalo would struggle within the folds of the anaconda." Indeed, at one point Hall described himself, perhaps significantly, as being bound by "shackles of prejudice." Ibid., 177, 828, 835.
17. *Biographical Dictionary,* 550–551; *Lee County* (see chap. 1, n. 9), 708; *House Journal* (1841/42), 159; ibid. (1845/46), 179; Lord, 837; *Colonization Society,* 4.
18. Missouri-border constituencies are defined as lying in the two southernmost tiers of Iowa counties. See delegate constituencies in Gue, *Iowa* (see chap. 7, n. 1), 3:468–469. The youngest Republicans were Wilson, 28, and Winchester, 26. The youngest Democrats were Peters, 28, and Solomon, 27. Delegate attitudes toward banks are from Erickson, 138–139, 159n. The antibank ultra conservative Democrats were Emerson, Peters, and Solomon.
19. *House Journal* (1842/43), 126, 224; ibid. (1850/51), 299; *Washington County* (see chap. 2, n. 19), 685–686; 1857 convention album (see chap. 3, n. 8), 18; Lord, 733, 909–911.
20. Nathaniel Goodwin, *Genealogical Notes, or Contributions to the Family History of Some of the First Settlers of Connecticut and Massachusetts* (Hartford, 1856), 27, 31; William W. Van Brocklin, ed., *Re-Union of the Sons and Daughters of the Old Town of Pompey* (Pompey, N.Y., 1875), 292; Dumas Malone, ed., *Dictionary of American Biography* 11 (New York, 1933): 288–289; Stiles, 672–673; 1857 convention album, 15; Lord, 173, 181–182, 641–642, 667, 669–670, 678, 829, 908.
21. Lord, 4, 134, 179, 196, 672; Eriksson, "Clarke" (see chap. 4, n. 23), 4–9; 1857 convention album, 21.

22. Lord, 197, 654, 660, 673, 675–676, 680, 889, 908. Clarke had earlier promised that "when I vote to submit a [black suffrage] proposition to the people, I shall be willing to vote for the proposition itself." Ibid., 676.
23. 1857 convention album, 22; Washington (D.C.) *National Era,* Nov. 11, 1847; Lord, 4, 175, 673–675, 905–907.
24. 1857 convention album, 28; Alexander (see chap. 6, n. 36), 481–482; Lord, 191–192, 194, 709, 716.
25. Stiles, 409; 1857 convention album, 21; *House Journal* (1850/51), 299; Muscatine *Daily Journal,* Oct. 28, 1856; Lord, 699.
26. Lord, 826–828; *The History of Jones County, Iowa* (Chicago, 1879), 674–675; Stiles, 554.
27. Lord, 4, 700, 825, 829–830, 832, 836–837.
28. Stiles, 112–115; 1857 convention album, 14; Erik McKinley Eriksson, "The Framers of the Constitution of 1857," *IJHP* 22 (1924): 80–81; Lord, 186, 912; W. R. Brock, *An American Crisis: Congress and Reconstruction, 1865–1867* (New York, 1963), 90; Michael Les Benedict, *The Impeachment and Trial of Andrew Johnson* (New York, 1973); Hyman and Wiecek (see chap. 6, n. 7), 384–385, 404, 406, 456.
29. Gue, *Iowa,* 4:85–86; 1857 convention album, 16; Lord, 187, 218, 681–683, 686, 735, 883.
30. Lord, 1025–1066; Rosenberg, 152–154.

9. Vox Populi

1. Roy W. Meyer, *History of the Santee Sioux: United States Indian Policy on Trial* (Lincoln, 1967), 97–101; Thomas Teakle, *The Spirit Lake Massacre* (Iowa City, 1918), 94–121; Bogue, *Prairie* (see chap. 1, n. 6), 124–125, 127; Muscatine *Daily Journal,* Apr. 11, 18, 1857; *Muscatine County* (see chap. 1, n. 31), 342; George W. Ells to William Penn Clarke, Apr. 17, 1857, Clarke Papers, SHSI:DM.
2. Muscatine *Daily Journal,* Apr. 11, 22, 1857; Iowa City *Republican,* Apr. 27, 1857; "Letters of Grimes" (see chap. 7, n. 21), 477, 480–481; Rosenberg (see chap. 5, n. 28), 154; John Edwards to William Penn Clarke, May 17–18, 1857, Clarke Papers.
3. Oskaloosa *Weekly Herald,* July 10, 1857; Lyons *Mirror,* July 16, 1857; Keokuk *Des Moines Valley Whig,* July 15, 1857; Muscatine *Daily Journal,* May 4, 1857. The *Journal*'s editor described the sponsoring body of the planned June 2 convention as "the executive committee appointed by the convention of colored people of Iowa" that had met in Muscatine on January 5. No organizer other than Alexander Clark was identified.
4. By mid-May, for example, the Muscatine *Enquirer,* a Democratic sheet, was already strenuously objecting both to the education clause and to the bill of rights of the new constitution as requiring school integration and otherwise encouraging black migration into the state. See quotations in Muscatine *Daily Journal,* May 19, 28, 1857. No follow-up story appeared on the planned colored convention.
5. Keokuk *Daily Gate City,* July 16, 1857; "Letters of Grimes," 483 (italics

supplied); Dale Baum, *The Civil War Party System: The Case of Massachusetts, 1848–1876* (Chapel Hill, 1984), 15–16; Morton Keller, *Affairs of State: Public Life in Late Nineteenth Century America* (Cambridge, 1977), 242.

6. There is no extensive collection of mid-nineteenth century election ballots for Iowa, but facsimile reproductions sometimes appeared in local newspapers of the period. For a good example see Montezuma *Republican,* Aug. 1, 1857.
7. The pro-constitution Republican editors of the Davenport *Daily Gazette,* July 22, 1857, indiscreetly reprinted Thorington's circular in its entirety on their front page, thereby providing the only extant copy of its text.
8. Muscatine *Daily Journal,* Aug. 11, Nov. 17, 1857. For Republican newspapers published in the summer of 1857 see Mott (see chap. 3, n. 21), 161–221. Whether or not a paper is extant can be determined from Alan Schroder, ed., *A Bibliography of Iowa Newspapers, 1836–1976* (Iowa City, 1979). A few papers described by Mott as Republican were discovered to be politically nonpartisan in mid-1857 and were dropped from consideration. Daily newspapers appearing between July 27 and August 12 were examined; similarly scrutinized were the last two July issues and first two August issues of weeklies in the sample.
9. The Marion *Register* is not extant for 1857, but its early stand on suffrage reform was noted, as was the editorship of Rev. George Hubbard Jennison, in the Muscatine *Daily Journal,* Nov. 26, 1856, Apr. 17, May 28, 1857. For Jennison see John Adams Vinton, *The Giles Memorial: Genealogical Memoirs* (Boston, 1864), 265.
10. Cedar Rapids *Cedar Valley Times,* July 30, 1857; Oran Faville, "Educational Journals," *AI* 1st ser. 3 (1865): 457–458; *The History of Linn County, Iowa* (Chicago, 1878), 449–451; Mott, 195–196; Quasqueton *Guardian,* June 13, Aug. 1, 1857; C. S. Percival and Elizabeth Percival, eds., *History of Buchanan County, Iowa* (Cleveland, 1881), 218; George E. Roberts, "The Career of Jacob Rich," *IJHP* 13 (1915): 165–167; Leland L. Sage, *William Boyd Allison: A Study in Practical Politics* (Iowa City, 1956), 50, 63, 72–73, 75. Whether the ticket as printed by Rich was the official Republican ballot is not explained; in the absence of other information, one assumes that it was Rich's own version.
11. Davenport *Daily Gazette,* July 18, 1857; Lyons *Mirror,* July 30, 1857; Montezuma *Republican,* Aug. 1, 1857; Tipton *Advertiser,* July 19, Aug. 15, 1855, Mar. 8, 1856; B. F. Gue, "Early Iowa Reminiscences," *IHR* 16 (1900): 111; Gary L. Roberts, "The Gunfight at O.K. Corral: The Wells Spicer Decision, 1881," *Montana: The Magazine of Western History* 20 (1970): 62–74.
12. Tipton *Advertiser,* July 25, Aug. 1, 1857.
13. Entries for Aug. 3, 1857, "Abstract of Meteorological Observations," vol. 3 (1857–1860), J. P. Walton Papers, Special Collections, University of Iowa Libraries, Iowa City; entry of Aug. 3, 1857, James Chamberlin Day Book, 1852–1862, Chamberlin Papers, in ibid.; *Johnson County* (see chap. 1, n. 7), 795.
14. Burlington *Daily Hawk-Eye,* Aug. 5, 1857; Fairfield *Ledger,* Aug. 13, 1857; Keokuk *Daily Gate City,* Aug. 5, 1857; Knoxville *Weekly Journal,* Aug. 11, 1857; Muscatine *Daily Journal,* Aug. 10, 1857; Ottumwa *Weekly Courier,*

Aug. 13, 1857. The November 1856 turnout was 92,450 (87 percent of estimated eligible voters); the 1857 referendum turnout was 79,497 (69 percent). For the sources of all electoral results discussed in this portion of the text see appendix A.

15. Some insight into these matters is provided by the diary of Jacob Wentworth Rogers, the Republican nominee for Fayette County judge in 1857. Although the diary is not a systematic daily record, it does offer a running account of the campaign by a racially progressive insider. Attitudes toward temperance and slavery, plus the personal character of local candidates as revealed by gossip, appear to have been the issues preoccupying Rogers and those with whom he interacted. No mention of the new constitution appears, and none of black suffrage until two days before the election. Entries of June 23–Aug. 3, 1857, Jacob Wentworth Rogers Diary, Rogers Papers, SHSI:IC.
16. Shambaugh, *Constitutions* (see chap. 1, n. 8), 342.
17. Muscatine *Daily Journal,* Aug. 14, 1857; Davenport *Daily Gazette,* Aug. 12, 1857; Burlington *Daily Hawk-Eye,* Aug. 11, 1857.
18. Vinton *Benton County Democrat,* July 25, 1857. The officials of Cedar County, however, comprehended the Wilson amendment so perfectly that they did not bother to furnish Iowa's secretary of state with a local tally of No ballots, content to let the state board of canvassers do the necessary arithmetic. But the board was no more disposed to cope with the technicalities than anyone else, so they relied on a simple computation of counties' Yes against No ballots in calculating the state outcome on proposition 2. Consequently, Cedar incorrectly entered the record as the only county registering a unanimous vote—284 to 0—in favor of suffrage reform, although technically the proposition *lost* that jurisdiction by 284 to 1,234.
19. *Johnson County,* 193, 748; Bloomfield *Ward's Own,* Aug. 13, 1857.
20. Andreas, *Iowa* (see chap. 1, n. 9), 472; *History of Mitchell and Worth Counties, Iowa* (Springfield, Ill., 1884), 396; Thomas G. Schuppe, "Hamlin Garland of Iowa," *AI* 41 (1972): 843–867; Joseph Dorfman, *Thorstein Veblen and His America* (New York, 1947), 66–67, 77–79; William Peters, *A Class Divided: Then and Now* (New Haven, 1987).
21. *Eighth Census of the United States, 1860: Mortality and Miscellaneous Statistics* (Washington, 1866), 389–392; Leola Nelson Bergmann, "The Norwegians in Iowa," *Palimpsest* 40 (1959): 298–299, 361–363, 366–368; Arlow W. Andersen, *The Norwegian-Americans* (Boston, 1975), 51–52, 61–62, 69–70, 104–108. In the recent legislative session Clausen had supported the McCoy bill. For all sources of voter birthplace data see appendix A.
22. Specifically, these were townships (from the 292 for which referendum returns are extant) in which more than 50 percent of the ballots cast, and at least 20 percent of estimated eligible voters favored, black suffrage. They consisted of Byron, Prairie (name changed to Fremont in 1859), Sumner, and Superior (name changed to Hazelton in 1862) of Buchanan County; Springdale of Cedar County; Cass, Grand Meadow, and Highland of Clayton County; Eden of Clinton County; Elk of Delaware County; Yellow Spring of Des Moines County; Eden, Pleasant Valley, and Putnam of Fayette County; Cedar and Rockford of Floyd County; Penn of Jefferson County; Denmark of Lee

County; Brown, Jackson, and Monroe of Linn County; and Prairie of Mahaska County.

23. This comparison between prosuffrage townships and the entire state was made via 1856 percentage categories embracing occupational structure (farmers, laborers, carpenters, merchants, miscellaneous), political preferences (Republicans, Democrats, Americans, nonvoters), and voter nativities (New Englanders, New Yorkers, Pennsylvanians, Ohioans, Indianans, southerners, other native-born, Britons and Scots, Irishmen, Germans, other foreign-born). The source for occupations was Iowa's published census of 1856, that for political preferences was the County File and the 186 subfile of the Township File, that for township nativities was the 186 subfile and that for statewide nativities was the 1856 published census. For further details see appendix A. The 1857 gubernatorial election results were substituted for missing 1856 election data for the townships of Sumner, Springdale, and Rockford, and neither body of returns was available for Elk. Voter nativities for Prairie, Sumner, and Rockford, all of which were created after the 1856 census had been taken, were extracted from the 1860 federal manuscript census.

24. McKivigan (see chap. 1, n. 42), 85, 96–99, 164. The predominately Quaker townships were Springdale, Penn, and Prairie of Mahaska. Townships adjacent to Marion or Quasqueton were those in Linn and Buchanan counties. The ten townships with native Yorker voter pluralities were Cass, Cedar, Eden of Fayette, Grand Meadow, Highland, Pleasant Valley, Putnam, Rockford, Eden of Clinton, and Elk. The five where native Yankees were the second-largest voter group were Cass, Cedar, Eden of Fayette, Putnam, and Rockford. Elsewhere, Prairie and Superior also had Yorker pluralities, and Jackson, Sumner, and Denmark had Yankee pluralities.

25. *House Journal* (1856/57), 466; Gue, *Iowa* (see chap. 7, n. 1), 3:468; Charles City *Republican Intelligencer,* Aug. 13, 1857; *Portrait and Biographical Album of Fayette County, Iowa* (Chicago, 1891), 181–183; entries of Aug. 1, 3, 1857, Rogers Diary. Rogers earlier had qualified as a racial progressive by voting against tabling the Clark petition in the 1854/55 legislature.

26. The combined voting population of Mitchell, Cerro Gordo, and Kossuth counties in 1856 (N=722) breaks down into the following nativity groups by percentage: New Englanders, 18; New Yorkers, 31; Pennsylvanians, 8; Ohioans, 13; Indianans, 4; southerners, 5; other native-born, 4; Britons and Scots, 2; Irishmen, 3; Germans, 2; other foreign-born (mainly Scandinavians), 9.

27. Of Iowa's ninety-nine counties, twenty-two (most of them thinly settled or unsettled frontier counties) returned no ballots at all for either the 1856 presidential election or the 1857 referendum. Three additional counties (Calhoun, Cass, Cedar) were excluded from table 9.3 because they recorded zero No ballots, which is known to be an error in Cedar's case and presumably also for the other two. Howard County was omitted because its voter turnout grossly exceeded its estimated eligible voters for both 1856 and 1857, suggesting serious errors in the data. Finally, as explained in the text, three "nonconforming" counties were excluded as outliers.

28. Phyllis F. Field, *The Politics of Race in New York: The Struggle for Black Suffrage in the Civil War Era* (Ithaca, 1982), 132.

29. The breakdown of Iowa's nonfarm sector by artisans, businessmen and professionals, and laborers (as was done in the regressions of the 1856 presidential vote) did not yield interpretable results, even when weighted in various ways.
30. This division had nothing to do with the great 1844 schism in which the national Methodist church had split over slavery. Both the downstate Iowa Conference and the upstate Upper Iowa Conference adhered to the northern Methodist church. Since the Methodist conferences in three slave states had been persuaded to join the northern rather than the southern church, the northern branch, in deference, tried to pursue a policy of strict silence on slavery. But by 1856 both Hawkeye conferences were speaking out on the issue. Donald G. Mathews, *Slavery and Methodism: A Chapter in American Morality, 1780–1845* (Princeton, 1965), 246–282; McKivigan, 84–87, 90–92; Greer (see chap. 7, n. 44), 83, 88, 90, 104, 106, 110–111; Fellows (see chap. 7, n. 44), 86–87.
31. Field's 1860 findings for New York comport entirely well with these Iowa results: native Pennsylvanians, native Irishmen, and native Germans were anti-suffrage. Field, 135–138.
32. German Republican townships: Garnavillo (9 percent Yes) and Jefferson (13 percent Yes) of Clayton County. German Democratic townships: Franklin (4 percent Yes) and West Point (1 percent Yes) of Lee County, Jefferson of Dubuque County (0 percent Yes), and Tete des Morts of Jackson County (0 percent Yes).
33. Matthias, "Movement" (see chap. 6, n. 23), 172; Schroder, 39, 90, 131. For Democratic rhetoric see F. I. Herriott, "Iowa and the First Nomination of Abraham Lincoln," *AI* 8 (1907): 204–205, 210n; for Republican (or more properly, Anti-Nebraskan) rhetoric see Herriott, "Neglected Factor" (see chap. 7, n. 2), 261–263, 271, 330.
34. Ohio did not hold an antebellum referendum on equal rights that would clearly designate early sources of progressive strength and opposition in the 1850s. But see Stephen E. Maizlish, *The Triumph of Sectionalism: The Transformation of Ohio Politics, 1844–1856* (Kent, 1983), 16–17.
35. Delaware and Coldwater townships of Delaware County, the latter known as the "Yankee Settlement." *Delaware County* (see chap. 8, n. 10), 556–557.
36. Field, 63, 127, 202. For Burned-Over District boundaries see chap. 6, n. 36 above.
37. *Mitchell and Worth Counties,* 281–288, 296–309, 313–319, 330–343, 345–358, 362–367, 380–383, 386–391, 401–423, 434–437, 448–453, 457, 463–478, 488–501, 505–515, 518–533, 535–536; Percival and Percival, 340–354, 372–376, 378–384, 391–396; *History of Clayton County, Iowa* (Chicago, 1882), 689–706, 826–837, 839–850; *Clinton County* (see chap. 6, n. 11), 754–758; *Delaware County,* 625–630; *Fayette County* (see chap. 1, n. 41), 616–635, 718–732; *Linn County,* 681–686.
38. *Delaware County,* 565–595, 649–660. The biographies are for Delaware Township and for Honey Creek Township, the latter formed in 1858 by combining Coldwater and York townships. To compare this with a centrally located control group, see the same preponderance of Burned-Over District natives among New Yorkers in *Johnson County,* 775–966.
39. Field, 69; Kleppner (see chap. 6, n. 21), 61–62. A passage in J. W. Rogers's

diary suggests that migrant New Englanders were as self-consciously ethnocultural in Iowa as in other regions. "Ezekiel White came up to me in the street," reports the native New Hampshireman, a strong Republican, "and said he should vote for me for County Judge—he was in [the] Democratic Convention & took part—but . . . he would vote for me as a yankee." Entry of July 18, 1857, Rogers Diary.

40. Kleppner, 48, 59, 77–79, 90–91, 172–173; Field, 69–70, 75, 78, 133, 206–207; Hammond (see chap. 6, n. 35), 51, 91n.

41. Field, 71–72, 134, 206–207; Kleppner, 61, 163–165. All independent variables selected for entry into the regression equations correlated at least +.30 with the Yes percentage on black suffrage in 1857, but none correlated +.70 or over with any other independent variable selected. When two otherwise qualifying independent variables correlated +.70 or more, I excluded the variable possessing the weakest correlation with the Yes percentage. All "church seats" percentages were employed in unweighted form. Variables entered into the County File equation (all as percentages) were: vote for Whig candidate for Congressman (1848), vote for Free Soil candidate for President (1848), vote for Democratic candidate for treasurer (1854), vote for Whig candidate for Congressman (1854), Yes vote on prohibition (1855), vote for Republican candidate for President (1856), vote for Democratic candidate for President (1856), farmers in poorer counties, northern Iowa Methodists, Congregationalists, and miscellaneous denominations. Those similarly entered into the Township File equation were: vote for Republican candidate for President (1856), vote for Democratic candidate for President (1856), vote for Republican candidate for county judge (1857), Yes vote on new constitution (1857), New England-born voters, and New York-born voters. The resulting county-level *beta* coefficients were: Buchanan support, −.57; northern Iowa Methodists, +.34; Frémont support, +.36 (fraction of explained variance, 52.7 percent). The township-level *beta* coefficients were: Frémont support, +.60; for the new constitution, +.34; New York-born voters, +.20 (fraction of explained variance, 46.1 percent).

42. McManus (see chap. 8, n. 13), 36–54. Wisconsin's Republican editors on black suffrage: for, 29; against, 3; neutral, 2. Iowa's Republican editors: for, 2; against, 4; neutral, 16. Wisconsin's Republican voters on suffrage reform (as percentage of total estimated electorate): Yes, 20; No, 3; not voting, 9. Iowa's Republican voters: Yes, 10; No, 5; not voting, 24 (for both states, the nonvoter category aggregates roll-off with those not at the polls). McManus, 42–43n, provides the Wisconsin editorial data. That state's election breakdown has been obtained by recalculating McManus's table (ibid., 47), while the Iowa data are those of my table 9.3, as adjusted to McManus's categories.

43. Rosenberg, 155–156; Stiles (chap. 1, n. 8), 64–67; Andreas, *Iowa,* 383; "List of Members and Officers of the [1858] Senate of the State of Iowa," General Assembly Papers, SHSI:IC; Iowa City *State Reporter and National Crescent,* Sept. 23, 1857.

44. Rosenberg, 156–158; Louis Pelzer, "The History of Political Parties in Iowa from 1857 to 1860," *IJHP* 7 (1909): 181–183; Muscatine *Daily Morning Enquirer,* Oct. 3, 1857; Muscatine *Daily Journal,* Oct. 5, 12, 16, 1857.

45. *Senate Journal* (1856/57), 444–445; ibid. (1858), 98, 246, 296; *House Jour-*

nal (1858), 558–559; *Laws* (1858), 65. The four backsliding recidivists, oddly enough, represented racially progressive constituencies: J. W. Cattell, a Quaker from Springdale Township; H. B. Carter from Clayton County; Charles Foster from Washington village; and Josiah B. Grinnell, proprietor of the self-consciously abolitionist townsite that bore his name. "List of Members and Officers"; Nollen (see chap. 6, n. 25), 55–56.

10. Battlegrounds

1. Oswald Garrison Villard, *John Brown, 1800–1859: A Biography Fifty Years After* (Boston, 1910), 308–316, 343; Oates (see chap. 7, n. 50), 221–302; Clark, *Kirkwood* (see chap. 1, n. 45), 155–162; James M. McPherson, *Battle Cry of Freedom: The Civil War Era* (New York, 1988), 202–213.
2. James I. Robertson Jr., *Iowa in the Civil War: A Reference Guide* (Iowa City, 1961), 2; Robert R. Dykstra, "Iowa: 'Bright Radical Star,' " in *Radical Republicans in the North: State Politics during Reconstruction,* ed. James C. Mohr (Baltimore, 1976), 170–172.
3. Hubert H. Wubben, "The Uncertain Trumpet: Iowa Republicans and Black Suffrage, 1860–1868," *AI* 47 (1984): 413; Clark, *Kirkwood,* 294. Kirkwood's later admiration for the fighting abilities of African-Americans as demonstrated at Milliken's Bend (where he toured the battlefield shortly after the bloody encounter) only increased his ardor for a black military presence in the war. H. W. Lathrop, *The Life and Times of Samuel J. Kirkwood* (Iowa City, 1893), 258–259.
4. Ira Berlin, ed., *The Black Military Experience* (Cambridge, England, 1982), 5–11, 187–188; *War of the Rebellion: A Compilation of the Official Records of the Union and Confederate Armies* (Washington, 1880–1901), 3d ser. 3:563, 576, 993; Thrift (see chap. 1, n. 45), 5:1585–1586; *Report of the Adjutant General and Acting Quartermaster General of the State of Iowa [for 1863]* (Des Moines, 1864), appendix, 198–227; *Biographical Dictionary* (see chap. 1, n. 31), 539; Muscatine *Journal,* Nov. 6, 1865. A plurality (one-third) of the regiment's self-identified Iowans gave their residences as Keokuk or its outlying villages, but substantial numbers also came from Davenport, Des Moines, Newton, Iowa City, and Keosauqua. About half had been living in Missouri-border counties, hailing from settlements as far west as Amity in Page County.
5. Thrift, 5:1586, 1590, 1599, 1625, 1628; Charles G. Williams, "The Action at Wallace's Ferry, Big Creek, Arkansas, July 26, 1864," *Phillips County Historical Quarterly* 25 (1987): 46–55; *War of the Rebellion,* 1st ser. 16:12–13, 16–23, 27, 190–191. That the men were those mustered at Keokuk is implied by the mention in dispatches of Capts. Eli Ramsey and Henry C. Brown, who commanded C and F companies of the 60th. Also, the abbreviated regimental personnel records yield the names of four enlisted casualties from the action at Wallace's Ferry. One man belonged to C Company, the other three to F. Ibid., 20, 22; *Adjutant General,* 204, 212; Thrift, 5:1590, 1599, 1625, 1628.
6. Thrift, 5:1587; Dudley T. Cornish, *The Sable Arm: Negro Troops in the*

Union Army (New York, 1956), 285–287; Joseph T. Glatthaar, *Forged in Battle: The Civil War Alliance of Black Soldiers and White Officers* (New York, 1990), 182–185.

7. Greer (see chap. 7, n. 44), 90, 114; Keokuk *Daily Gate City,* May 25, 27, 29, 30, June 4, 5, 6, 1857; *Senate Journal* (1858), 429–430; Olynthus B. Clark, *The Politics of Iowa during the Civil War [through 1863]* (Iowa City, 1911), 167–168; Hubert H. Wubben, *Civil War Iowa and the Copperhead Movement* (Ames, 1980), 77.
8. Nathan E. Coffin, "The Case of Archie P. Webb, a Free Negro," *AI* 11 (1913): 200–201, 204–214; Ira Berlin, ed., *The Destruction of Slavery* 1 (Cambridge, England, 1985): 259–260; Stiles (see chap. 1, n. 8), 130–132; Bergmann, *Negro* (see chap. 6, n. 28), 28–29.
9. Coffin, 204; V. Jacque Voegeli, *Free but Not Equal: The Midwest and the Negro during the Civil War* (Chicago, 1967), 89; Wubben, *Iowa,* 79, 132–133; *Reunion of 1894* (see chap. 2, n. 22), 40–41; *House Journal* (1864), 86–87, 151, 184–185; *Senate Journal* (1864), 176; *Laws* (1864), 6. This legislature also repealed Iowa's ban on black welfare benefits. *House Journal* (1864), 246–247; *Senate Journal* (1864), 408.
10. See especially Herman Belz, *Reconstructing the Union: Theory and Policy during the Civil War* (Ithaca, 1969), 201–202, 217, 251–255, 263–266; Belz, *A New Birth of Freedom: The Republican Party and Freedmen's Rights, 1861–1866* (Westport, 1976), 53–54, 58, 61, 63, 98, 121, 134n, 144–145; Bogue, *Earnest Men* (see chap. 8, n. 15), 205–212, 241–242, 256–257; La-Wanda Cox, *Lincoln and Black Freedom: A Study in Presidential Leadership* (Columbia, 1981), 38, 76–81, 93–98, 111–113, 117–131, 145, 172.
11. Davenport *Daily Gazette,* Mar. 15, 1865; *History of Scott County, Iowa* (Chicago, 1882), 578–582; Charles Edward Russell, "An Anti-Slavery Editor in a Pro-Slavery Town: The Record of One Man's Experiences with the Slave Power before and in the Civil War," *Bulletin [of the] Society for Correct Civil War Information* nos. 56–58 (1940), 53–58, 65–69.
12. Stephen B. Oates, *With Malice toward None: The Life of Abraham Lincoln* (New York, 1977), 460–461; Peyton McCrary, *Abraham Lincoln and Reconstruction: The Louisiana Experiment* (Princeton, 1978), 9, 351; Cox, 146–151; Hans L. Trefousse, *Andrew Johnson: A Biography* (New York, 1989), 214–218; Wubben, "Trumpet," 417–418; Davenport *Daily Gazette,* June 7, 1865.
13. M. B. Hoxie to Grenville M. Dodge and George Tichenor, June 16, 1865, Dodge Papers, SHSI:DM; Des Moines *Daily State Register,* June 14, 15, 1865.
14. For charter Republicans and old Liberty and Free Soil activists present compare delegate listings with Pelzer, "Origin" (see chap. 7, n. 12), 521–525; Barnes (see chap. 2, n. 34), 290–306. For Reid see Nelson C. Roberts and S. W. Moorhead, *Story of Lee County, Iowa* 2 vols. (Chicago, 1914), 1: 302–303.
15. Des Moines *Daily State Register,* June 13, 15, 1865; Stiles, 211–213; *House Journal* (1858), 559; G. Galin Berrier, "The Negro Suffrage Issue in Iowa—1865–1868," *AI* 39 (1968): 244; Wubben, "Trumpet," 416–417.
16. Berrier, 260; Des Moines *Daily State Register,* June 15, 1865. Unless cited

differently, all information on proceedings within the convention has been extracted from the official minutes in this issue of the *Register*.

17. Des Moines *Daily State Register,* June 16, 1865; Benjamin Gue, "The Public Services of Hiram Price," *AI* 1 (1895): 598; *House Journal* (1854/55), 319; Stiles, 306–308; Charles E. Payne, *Josiah Bushnell Grinnell* (Iowa City, 1938); *Senate Journal* (1856/57), 444–445; ibid. (1858), 296; Michael Les Benedict, *A Compromise of Principle: Congressional Republicans and Reconstruction, 1863–1869* (New York, 1974), 27; James M. McPherson, *The Struggle for Equality: Abolitionists and the Negro in the Civil War and Reconstruction* (Princeton, 1964), 246.
18. Gue, *Iowa* (see chap. 7, n. 1), 3:1; Gue, "Price," 598; Iowa City *Republican,* June 21, 1865; Stiles, 63. Stiles confuses the Russell amendment with the original resolution 4, and asserts Price's authorship of the amendment.
19. Gue, "Price," 585–588, 592; Stiles, 63; Chicago *Western Citizen,* Apr. 1, 1846; Pelzer, "Origin," 508, 510n, 512–513; David S. Sparks, "The Birth of the Republican Party in Iowa, 1854–1856," *IJHP* 54 (1956): 26–28.
20. Gue, "Price," 594–599; Stiles, 63, 135. Gue twice published this speech, the two versions differing only slightly. Compare Gue, "Price," 598, with his *Iowa,* 3:1–2.
21. Gue, "Price," 599; Stiles, 63. Ironically, in Benedict's painstaking analyses of roll-call voting in the 38th Congress, the pragmatically antisuffrage Grinnell ranks as an "extreme radical" in 1864 and a "radical" in 1865, while the ideologically prosuffrage Price registers as more conservative—"radical" in 1864 and "centrist" in 1865. Benedict, *Compromise,* 342, 346.
22. Gue, *Iowa,* 3:1–2; Stiles, 405, 710; Davenport *Weekly Gazette,* Apr. 17, 1867; Michael Les Benedict, "Racism and Equality in America," *Reviews in American History* 6 (1978): 19. The figure for votes not cast was derived by subtracting the 756 ballots for and against the Russell amendment from the 879 allocated to the delegates.
23. Gue, "Price," 599; Des Moines *Daily State Register,* June 16, 1865.
24. Wubben, *Iowa,* 145. For Scholte see Robert P. Swierenga, "The Ethnic Voter and the First Lincoln Election," *CWH* 11 (1965): 27–43; for the others see Stiles, passim.
25. Wubben, *Iowa,* 199–201; Joel Silbey, *A Respectable Minority: The Democratic Party in the Civil War Era, 1860–1868* (New York, 1977), 177–181; J. C. Knapp to Laurel Summers, June 30, 1865, Summers Papers, SHSI:DM; J. C. Knapp and J. M. Love to Laurel Summers, June 6, 1865, Summers Collection, Putnam Museum, Davenport; Davenport *Weekly Democrat,* July 20, 1865; Berrier, "Suffrage," 247.
26. Wubben, *Iowa,* 201–202; *Senate Journal* (1846/47), 194; Theodore S. Parvin, "Thomas Hart Benton, Jr.," *IHR* 16 (1900): 1–14; Arthur Springer, *History of Louisa County, Iowa,* 2 vols. (Chicago, 1912), 1:121; M. B. Hoxie to Dodge and Tichenor, June 16, 1865, Dodge Papers; Thomas C. Woodward to Samuel J. Kirkwood, July 25, 1865, Kirkwood Papers, SHSI:DM; Dykstra, "Iowa," 174–176.
27. Andreas, *Iowa* (see chap. 1, n. 9), 363; Stiles, 472–481; Clark, *Politics,* 34n, 127–128, 147, 155–156, 176–177, 196; Des Moines *Daily State Register,*

Aug. 10, 1865; James H. Moorhead, *American Apocalypse: Yankee Protestants and the Civil War, 1860–1869* (New Haven, 1978), 42–47, 96–104, 109–112.

28. Edward Younger, *John A. Kasson: Politics and Diplomacy from Lincoln to McKinley* (Iowa City, 1955), 183–184. The Radical inclination of Iowa's wholly Republican congressional delegation, 1864–65, was not as smooth as necessarily summarized here. According to Benedict, William B. Allison and Grinnell were "radical" in 1865 and "prosuffrage radical" in 1866; Price and James F. Wilson rose from "centrist" to "prosuffrage radical"; A. W. Hubbard rose from "centrist" to "radical"; Grimes declined from "radical" to "radical centrist"; Kasson, unclassifiable in 1864, registered "conservative" in 1865; Harlan was "conservative" in 1864, and his successor, Kirkwood, was "conservative centrist" in 1865. Bogue's similar scaling of Senate roll calls, 1861–1866, ranks Grimes an "unaligned Republican," a label confirming Benedict's characterization of him as "erratic." Harlan registers as a "Republican centrist," although steadily moving in a conservative direction. Kirkwood is not formally ranked but is classified as slightly more radical than Grimes in 1866. Benedict, *Compromise,* 33, 341–353; Bogue, *Earnest Men,* 104–105, 108, 110–112.
29. Des Moines *Daily State Register,* Aug. 17, Sept. 23, 1865; Council Bluffs *Nonpareil,* Sept. 30, 1865; Stiles, 63–64.
30. Des Moines *Daily State Register,* Sept. 12, Oct. 8, 1865 (italics supplied); Bogue, *Earnest Men,* 159, 211; Trefousse, 216; Johnson Brigham, *James Harlan* (Iowa City, 1913), 199–201. Boston's leading Radical Republican newspaper felt obliged to rebut the clean-your-own-skirts argument as early as June 1865. The argument appeared in Johnson's annual message to Congress in December, then became a regular feature of his rhetoric. Boston *Commonwealth,* June 17, 1865; Patrick W. Riddleberger, *1866: The Critical Year Revisited* (Lanham, 1979), 30; George Sinkler, *The Racial Attitudes of American Presidents* (New York, 1971), 125–126.
31. J. Morgan Kousser, *Dead End: The Development of Nineteenth-Century Litigation on Racial Discrimination in Schools* (Oxford, 1986), 18; *Senate Journal* (1850/51), 295; *House Journal* (1854/55), 319; Andreas, *Iowa,* 415.
32. Des Moines *Daily State Register,* Sept. 27, 1865; Stiles, 494–497. Crocker suffered from an advanced case of tuberculosis, from which he died that summer; his letter to Stone was published posthumously.
33. Stiles, 75–76, 78; William E. Hunt, *Historical Collections of Coshocton County (Ohio)* (Cincinnati, 1876), 71, 77, 90, 115; Swierenga, 34; Matthias, "Movement" (see chap. 6, n. 26), 131n; Clark, *Politics,* 180–181; Josiah Bushnell Grinnell, *Men and Events of Forty Years: Autobiographical Reminiscences* (Boston 1891), 125.
34. Des Moines *Daily State Register,* July 12, Sept. 15, Oct. 5, 1865; Stiles, 73. Missouri managed to get 200 members of the 60th U.S. Colored Infantry credited to its own manpower quota, but Iowa retained credit for the rest. Stone parlayed these 700 three-year enlistments into credit for 2,100 one-year enlistments, thereby reducing Iowa's 1864 draft call for one-year men. *Adjutant General,* iv–v.

35. Des Moines *Daily State Register,* Oct. 5, 1865.
36. Joshua Tracy to Kirkwood, Oct. 4, 1865, Kirkwood Papers. Stone had proved a hard-liner on wartime dissent, suspected subversion, and draft evasion; he and Adjutant General Baker issued pronouncements about these matters that alienated numbers of normally Republican voters. Wubben, *Iowa*, 120, 128, 145, 158, 162–164, 198; Eliphalet Price to Kirkwood, Oct. 15, 1865, Kirkwood Papers; Stiles, 875.
37. Fort Madison *Plain Dealer,* Oct. 19, 1865; table B.8, appendix B. Employing the increase in estimated eligible voters between 1864 and 1865 as a surrogate for returned soldiers yields implausible results. The only county-by-county listing of soldiers furnished is also unsatisfactory, since the compilation includes only enlistments for the first half of the war. *Report of the Adjutant General and Acting Quartermaster General of the State of Iowa [for 1865]* (Des Moines, 1866), appendix, 460–462.
38. Berrier, 255–256; Davenport *Weekly Gazette,* Oct. 25, Nov. 8, 1865; Sioux City *Journal,* Oct. 28, 1865.

11. Bright Radical Star

1. Younger (see chap. 10, n. 33), 1–176, 180, 197, 230, 417n; S. R. Ingham to Samuel J. Kirkwood, Aug. 4, 1865, Kirkwood Papers, SHSI:DM.
2. Younger, 178–181; Clark, *Kirkwood* (see chap. 1, n. 48), 145, 303–306; L. W. Hart to Kirkwood, Nov. 15, 1865, Kirkwood Papers; Jacob Rich to Kirkwood, Sept. 23, 1865, in ibid.
3. L. W. Hart to Kirkwood, Nov. 15, 1865, Kirkwood Papers; H. A. Wiltse to Kirkwood, Jan. 13, 1866, in ibid.; *Senate Journal* (1858), 296; Clark, *History* (see chap. 6, n. 32), 133–141; Clark, *Kirkwood,* 308–311; Younger, 196; Brigham, *Harlan* (see chap. 10, n. 35), 211–212. How seriously the antisuffrage charges against Kirkwood were taken by anybody but Stone is problematical. One politico described them as "sometimes of a serious and sometimes of a bantering character, depending upon the circumstances under and the persons in whose presence they were made." But late in his subsequent senatorial term Kirkwood was willing that Nebraska be admitted to the Union with a whites-only suffrage article in its constitution, and he refused to condemn the similar clause still in Iowa's organic law. Adverse press comment ensued, and an agitated General Dodge wrote to sound out Kirkwood's commitment to 1865's resolution 4: "If I remember right on this negro question you openly & boldly met the question on its merits and said from every stump that [the word 'white'] should be stricken from our Constitution while many of the papers & politicians who now censure you hedged the question or said it was not before the people." In reply, Kirkwood admitted that he had presented suffrage reform in Iowa as not "the direct issue. . . . I argued the question of Negro suffrage incidentally in connection with the question of reconstruction, and in favor of Negro suffrage [in the South]." As for his innermost feelings, "I am and have been for some years decidedly in favor of striking that word out of our constitution and when that question shall be before our people [in 1868] I shall, if my health & strength will permit, use whatever power of

argument I may have to persuade them to do that thing." Clark, *Kirkwood,* 306, 314–317; H. A. Wiltse to Kirkwood, Jan. 13, 1866, Kirkwood Papers; Grenville M. Dodge to Kirkwood, Jan. 7, 1866 (*sic* 1867), in ibid.; Kirkwood to Grenville M. Dodge, Jan. 15, 1867, Dodge Papers, SHSI:DM.

4. Salter (see chap. 6, n. 29), 287; Benedict, *Impeachment* (see chap. 8, n. 30), 127, 131–132, 137–138, 143, 168–171, 173–174, 179, 182; Younger, 192–197, 200–203; Stanley P. Hirshson, *Grenville M. Dodge: Soldier, Politician, Railroad Pioneer* (Bloomington, 1967), 4, 67–75; Dodge to Kirkwood, Jan. 7, 1866 (*sic* 1867), Kirkwood Papers. As a student, Dodge had provoked a dustup with a black waiter in a Boston restaurant and had helped heckle a black abolitionist lecturer. But from his base command in Mississippi twelve years later he wrote that "I have some very fine negro troops, well drilled and doing the same [combat] duty as the white troops." And much later he reminisced of his intelligence role that "Negroes were also of great aid to us as messengers and [by] coming into our lines with valuable information and I never heard of a negro giving up a Union Soldier, spy or scout who trusted him." Entries of Jan. 9, 18, 1851, Dodge Diary, Dodge Papers; "Dodge Records," 23 vols. (typescript, SHSI:DM), 3:379, 21:47.
5. Younger, 205–206; George W. Harlan to Dodge, May 23, 1866, Dodge Papers. Dodge apparently won the nomination by bribing a local power broker to favor him with a deciding bloc of votes. But in the larger sense what cost Kasson the nomination was his pro-Johnson behavior in Congress. Once he had fallen out with the rest of Iowa's delegation, of course, he became fair game for some politically ambitious man with racially progressive credentials. It was not until the 1870s, and Kasson's important role in the anti-Greenback effort in Iowa, that he returned to the good graces of its Republican leadership. Younger, *Kasson,* 300–303.
6. Shambaugh, *Messages* (see chap. 6, n. 1), 3:80–87; *Senate Journal* (1866), 67; Muscatine *Journal,* Nov. 6, 1865. The legislators received three petitions asking "the repeal of all laws making distinctions on account of color." One was from 237 white citizens of Muscatine, a second came from Alexander Clark and 60 other "colored people of Muscatine county," and the third was the petition of the noncommissioned officers and men of the 60th U.S. Colored Infantry.
7. *House Journal* (1866), 57, 644–645; *Senate Journal* (1866), 574, 635–636; Des Moines *Weekly Register,* Jan. 10, 1866.
8. *Reunion of 1894* (see chap. 2, n. 23), 65, 68; *House Journal* (1866), 227, 545, 643, 645–646; Andreas, *Iowa* (chap. 1, n. 9), 363; *Rules and Statistics of the Senate and House of Representatives* (Des Moines, 1866), 13; Stiles (see chap. 1, n. 8), 299–300. Reps. M. M. Walden and John N. Rogers were erroneously listed as voting.
9. William M. Stone to Alonzo Abernethy, May 18, 1866, Abernethy Papers, SHSI:DM; Henry O'Connor to Abernethy, May 21, 1866, in ibid.; *Reunion of 1894,* 68. Abernethy did not win the nomination only because the incumbent ultimately rejected a federal appointment from the Johnson Administration. Ed Wright to Abernethy, June 4, 1866, Abernethy Papers.
10. The details appear in Dykstra, "Iowa" (see chap. 10, n. 2), 179, where racial

progressives are referred to in the table and accompanying text as "ultra radicals." Iowa's upstate Baptists had gone on record against slavery as early as 1849, but during the Civil War at least one downstate association refused even to condemn Secession. S. H. Mitchell, *Historical Sketches of Iowa Baptists* (Burlington, 1886), 116, 162–163.

11. Des Moines *Weekly Register,* June 27, 1866; Herbert S. Fairall, ed., *The Iowa City Republican Manual of Iowa Politics* (Iowa City, 1881), 72–73, 75–76; Davenport *Weekly Gazette,* June 27, 1866; Leslie H. Fishel Jr., "Northern Prejudice and Negro Suffrage, 1865–1870," *Journal of Negro History* 39 (1954): 17; William Delbert Heinzig, "Iowa's Response to Reconstruction: 1865–1868" (M.A. thesis, Iowa State University, 1971), 32–47; Thomas Hart Benton Jr. to John F. Lacey, Oct. 14, 1865, Lacey Papers, SHSI:DM; Gue, *Iowa* (see chap. 7, n. 1), 3:12–14.
12. Tables B.8 and B.9, appendix B; Trefousse (see chap. 10, n. 14), 262–267; Riddleberger (see chap. 10, n. 35), 202–229. This paragraph of the text corrects an analysis of the 1866 election given in Dykstra, "Iowa," 181.
13. Gue, *Iowa,* 3:15; Fairall, 77–79; Davenport *Weekly Gazette,* June 26, 1867, May 13, 1868; Muscatine *Journal,* May 9, 1868.
14. J. H. Wallace to Laurel Summers, Oct. 1866, Summers Papers, SHSI:DM; Clark, "Liquor" (see chap. 6, n. 26), 343–344; George H. Henderson to Summers, Sept. 18, 1867, Summers Papers; table B.10, appendix B; Iowa Falls *Sentinel,* Oct. 23, 1867; Charles Stanley to Lacey, Jan. 22, 1868, Lacey Papers. For identification of the successful People's candidates see Davenport *Weekly Democrat,* Oct. 31, 1867; Des Moines *Weekly Register,* Jan. 15, 1868.
15. Mildred Throne, *Cyrus Clay Carpenter and Iowa Politics, 1854–1898* (Iowa City, 1974), 92; Edward L. Gambill, *Conservative Ordeal: Northern Democrats and Reconstruction, 1865–1869* (Ames, 1981), 29–30, 56, 64, 72–74; Charles Mason, "Negro equality & its Consequences," undated postwar draft, Mason Papers (Miscellaneous, box 44), SHSI:DM. Whether or not the Mason manuscript represents an 1867 campaign speech or newspaper article, it clearly postdates mid-1866 in its reference to the Grand Army of the Republic.
16. McLaughlin (see chap. 8, n. 16), 176; Shambaugh, *Messages,* 3:256–259; *Proceedings of the Iowa State Colored Convention Held in the City of Des Moines . . . February 12th and 13th, 1868* (Muscatine, 1868); *House Journal* (1866), 644–646; ibid. (1868), 402, 514–515, 527, 566; *Senate Journal* (1868), 385; Davenport *Weekly Gazette,* Apr. 8, 1868. The 1868 house actually held two roll calls on black suffrage, one to approve a joint resolution embracing impartial suffrage and five other proposed rights amendments, the second to vote on S.F. 186, which provided for submission of the six amendments to the people as referendum propositions. The only apparent difference between the two roll calls are the names of those absent or not voting. I therefore considered a Yes vote on either of them an approval of black suffrage, which allowed me to remove several names from the unclassifiable category. Two Republicans who served in both the 1866 and 1868 sessions, Charles Dudley and P. C. Wilcox, voted Yes on the black legislators question

in 1866, but failed to vote in 1868. I classified them as progressives in both sessions. Mathias J. Rohlfs served as a Republican member in 1866 and returned two years later as an independent. He was progressive in 1866, and but for his party change would have been so designated in the second session.

17. Frank W. Palmer to Dodge, June 1, 1868, Dodge Papers; James Harlan to William E. Chandler, July 28, 1868, Chandler Papers, Library of Congress, Washington, D.C.; Brigham, *Harlan,* 235–236; Lathrop (see chap. 10, n. 3), 394; McGregor *North Iowa Times,* Sept. 30, 1868; Maquoketa *Excelsior,* Oct. 15, 1868; Marshalltown *Marshall County Times,* Sept. 5, 1868.
18. Davenport *Western Soldier's Friend,* Oct. 24, 1868; Marshalltown *Marshall County Times,* Sept. 26, 1868; Lathrop, 395; Luella M. Wright, *Peter Melendy: The Mind and the Soil* (Iowa City, 1943), 268–271; Melendy to Dear Sir, Aug. 12, 1868, Kirkwood Papers; John S. Runnels to Chandler, Sept. 14, 1868, Chandler Papers; Melendy to Dodge, Sept. 16, 1868, Dodge Papers; Des Moines *Daily Register,* Nov. 1, 1868. Presumably most of the Republican tickets were formatted according to Melendy's model. How the Democratic ballots presented the question is not clear.
19. William S. McFeely, *Grant: A Biography* (New York, 1981), 258, 278–279; Des Moines *Weekly Register,* Nov. 4, 1868. The quotes are from a paraphrase of Grant's remarks to "one of the most prominent politicians of this state."
20. For the complete correlation matrix see Dykstra, "Iowa," 185, wherein the coefficient linking the Yes votes of 1868 and 1857 was erroneously rounded to +.64.
21. Technically, what is predicted is the statistical variance in county-level ballot percentages in support of the 1868 suffrage proposition. The relative importance of the 1865 and 1857 Yes ballots is based on *beta* coefficients of +.715 and +.193 respectively. The Wright, Merrill, and Grant elections were not entered into the regression because all intercorrelate with one another in excess of +.70, aggravating the problem of multicollinearity to the point of making it impossible to distinguish between their individual effects on 1868's Yes vote.
22. The assumption underlying my calculation is that virtually all those who voted Yes in 1868 had also voted for Grant—in other words, that virtually no 1868 Democrats knowingly cast prosuffrage ballots.
23. Only Colorado's 1865 black suffrage referendum yielded greater hostility to equal rights (89.8 percent) than Iowa's 1857 No vote (technically 89.6 percent). McLaughlin, 176.
24. Kousser, *Dead End* (see chap. 10, n. 36), 16–18; Bergmann, *Negro* (see chap. 6, n. 31), 53–54; Donald G. Nieman, *Promises to Keep: African-Americans and the Constitutional Order, 1776 to the Present* (New York, 1991), 50–53; Robert J. Kaczorowski to Robert R. Dykstra, Dec. 6, 1973, in author's possession.
25. *House Journal* (1870), 94, 108, 120, 128, 136, 289–290, 296, 480–481, 483, 487; *Senate Journal* (1870), 82, 85, 132–133, 216–217, 230, 414, 434, 521; *Laws* (1870), 21; Des Moines *Weekly Register,* Nov. 3, 1869.
26. *House Journal* (1872), 253, 530. No action occurred in the senate.
27. Elden B. Hartshorn, *Some Hartshorn Families of Lunenburg, Vermont* (Lu-

nenburg, 1959), H7-H8a; Dwight G. McCarty, *History of Palo Alto County, Iowa* (Cedar Rapids, 1910), 115, 120, 128, 141–142; Des Moines *Daily Register,* Feb. 23, 1878. In 1868 only 20 percent of Palo Alto County's estimated eligible voters cast Yes ballots on proposition 1.

28. *Senate Journal* (1874), 290, 313; *House Journal* (1874), 376, 423–424, 429–430. A rare petition favoring "free white" repeal, signed by one G. H. Crowley "and others," was forwarded to Hartshorn's committee. Ibid., 175. For party identifications complicated by an influx of fusionist Anti-Monopoly Democrats and Republicans see Davenport *Weekly Gazette,* Oct. 29, 1873; Muscatine *Weekly Journal,* Oct. 31, 1873; Des Moines *Daily Register,* Feb. 26, 1874.

29. Lawrence Grossman, *The Democratic Party and the Negro: Northern and National Politics, 1868–92* (Urbana, 1976), 15–59; Throne, *Carpenter* (see chap. 11, n. 16), 122–123; Eric Foner, *Reconstruction: America's Unfinished Revolution, 1863–1877* (New York, 1988), 412–425, 506, 567, 581–583; Keller (see chap. 9, n. 5), 252–255, 262–264.

30. *Senate Journal* (1876), 35, 80, 85; ibid. (1878), 33, 116, 135, 183–184; ibid. (1880), 74–75, 155, 171–172; *House Journal* (1876), 139, 210, 288, 390–391, 498, 527–528; ibid. (1878), 251, 260, 307, 383; ibid. (1880), 295, 430; *Laws* (1880), 214; Des Moines *Daily Register,* Feb. 22, Mar. 11, 1880.

31. Des Moines *Daily Register,* Aug. 26, Sept. 23, 1880; Shambaugh, *Messages,* 5:210–213. Edward Russell, who is not listed as the resolution committee's chairman in the *Register,* is so designated in the Davenport *Gazette,* Aug. 26, 1880.

32. Atlantic *Telegraph,* Sept. 29, 1880; Marengo *Republican,* Sept. 29, 1880; Garner *Hancock County Signal,* Sept. 29, 1880; Boone *Standard,* Oct. 23, 1880; Dubuque *Daily Herald,* Oct. 12, 1880; Iowa City *Iowa State Press,* Oct. 13, 1880; Knoxville *Journal,* Oct. 13, 1880.

33. Fred E. Haynes, *James Baird Weaver* (Iowa City, 1919), 102–105, 155–173; Irwin Unger, *The Greenback Era: A Social and Political History of American Finance, 1865–1879* (Princeton, 1964), 393; Younger, 298–303; Kleppner (see chap. 6, n. 24), 267–273. For what was evidently the complete text of the Republican central committee circular see Ottumwa *Weekly Courier,* Oct. 29, 1880.

34. The story is identified as an AP dispatch in Burlington *Daily Hawk-Eye,* Oct. 22, 1880. For what was apparently its complete text see Keota *Eagle,* Oct. 30, 1880.

35. Cedar Rapids *Standard,* Oct. 28, 1880; Burlington *Daily Gazette,* Oct. 27, 1880. My survey included almost 100 extant newspapers for 1880 in the SHSI:DM and SHSI:IC. Editors considered favorable were those who carried supportive comments about proposition 2 (in some cases simply lifted from other journals) or who displayed "sample ballots" with only the Yes option included. Favorable notice: 25 Republican editors; 2 Democratic editors; 2 independent editors. Neutral: 18 Republican editors; 11 Democratic editors; 1 independent editor. No notice: 25 Republican editors; 11 Democratic editors; 1 Greenback editor; 1 independent editor.

36. Leland L. Sage, "The Clarksons of Indiana and Iowa," *Indiana Magazine of*

History 50 (1954): 429–446; Albert Fried, "J. S. Clarkson Letter on Civil Rights," *AI* 35 (1960): 216–225; Stanley P. Hirshson, *Farewell to the Bloody Shirt: Northern Republicans and the Southern Negro, 1877–1893* (Bloomington, 1962), 37, 235, 246–249, 254. Embarrassingly, Clarkson's father had voted against black suffrage in the Iowa senate. *Senate Journal* (1866), 636. For Clarkson as the national innovator of the issue-oriented "educational" approach to presidential campaigning see Michael E. McGerr, *The Decline of Popular Politics: The American North, 1865–1928* (New York, 1986), 79–82, 90–96.

37. Davenport *Daily Gazette,* Nov. 2, 1880; Bloomfield *Davis County Republican,* Oct. 28, 1880. The *Gazette* proclaimed its sample Davenport Township ballot to be "An Exact Copy of the One to be Voted To-Day." Unlike the Polk County ticket, which was designed to be printed separately, Davenport's Yes ballot is described as "placed on the bottom, so that it can be torn off and deposited, as it must be, in a separate ballot box." The same would seem to be the case with the ballot printed in the Bloomfield paper, although it is hard to see how it would be conveniently torn off, since it is followed by the names of candidates for local office.
38. Vinton *Eagle,* Oct. 27, 1880. Although the editor does not label it a facsimile of the official Vinton Township ballot, the item appears to be exactly that. The only other extant examples of sample Republican ballots that include proposition 2 resemble the Vinton ticket. The same is true of the only sample Democratic ballot, also carried by a Vinton journal. Traer *Clipper,* Oct. 29, 1880; Sheldon *Mail,* Oct. 30, 1880; Sanborn *O'Brien Pioneer,* Oct. 29, 1880; Vinton *Benton County Herald,* Nov. 2, 1880.
39. Haynes, 3–10, 162; Supervisors' Minutes (Clinton Co. Courthouse, Clinton), 10:302–307; Dubuque *Daily Times,* Nov. 11, 1880. Referendum participation in the forty-three counties with newspapers that gave publicity to proposition 2 averaged 44 percent of the estimated eligible voters. The statewide average was 41 percent.
40. It was not a case, as in 1868, of racist Republicans rolling off because they feared their No votes would please the Democrats; majorities of the Democrats and Greenbackers *also* rolled off. The ecological regression estimates underlying table 11.3 yielded the following roll-off frequencies: Republicans, 39; Democrats, 80; Greenbackers, 66.
41. Marshalltown *Marshall Statesman,* Nov. 6, 1880; Election Record (Marshall Co. Courthouse, Marshalltown), 389, 393; Grossman, 102.

12. The Egalitarian Moment

1. Robert C. Ostergren, "Geographic Perspectives on the History of Settlement in the Upper Middle West," *Upper Midwest History* 1 (1981): 31–33; Andreas, *Iowa* (see chap. 1, n. 9), 98–99, 466–467, 470–471.
2. Magoun (see chap. 2, n. 14), 318; Walter M. Merrill to Robert R. Dykstra, Mar. 30, 1979, in author's possession; Harold F. Worthley to Robert R. Dykstra, Sept. 4, 1985, in ibid.; Joel Williamson, *After Slavery: The Negro*

in South Carolina during Reconstruction, 1861–1877 (Chapel Hill, 1965), 190–191, 206–207, 324, 368; Henry A. Street and Mary A. Street, *The Street Genealogy* (Exeter, N.H., 1895), 348; *Henry County* (see chap. 5, n. 14), 569; Salter (see chap. 6, n. 29), 387; Eriksson, "Clarke" (see chap. 4, n. 24), 60–61; Stiles (see chap. 1, n. 8), 76, 673; Marilyn Jackson, "Alexander Clark: A Rediscovered Black Leader," *Iowan* 23 (1975): 43–52.

3. Holt, *Crisis* (see chap. 4, n. 6), especially 139–181; Gienapp (see chap. 7, n. 3).
4. Dykstra, "Iowa" (see chap. 10, n. 2), 170; Voegeli (see chap. 10, n. 10), 127; William Gillette, *The Right to Vote: Politics and the Passage of the Fifteenth Amendment* (Baltimore, 1965), 26–28. Wisconsin's black community also obtained the elective franchise in this period, but as a result of an extremely dubious state supreme court decision rather than a ratification by voters. Richard N. Current, "Wisconsin: Shifting Strategies to Stay on Top," in Mohr (see chap. 10, n. 2), 147, 149.
5. For a painstaking quantitative exploration of all aspects of mid-nineteenth century voter mobility see Kenneth J. Winkle, *The Politics of Community: Migration and Politics in Antebellum Ohio* (New York, 1988). The author suggests that political historians have failed to take voter turnover sufficiently into account, but he is not clear as to just how they err. As in this book, those who statistically regress one set of election returns against another commonly include the estimated number of citizens ineligible to vote in the first election but eligible in the second. This at least accommodates *net* voter gain or decline in any given voting unit. In any event, Winkle himself emphasizes the commanding political roles of local elites in providing electorate stability: far from being of little consequence vis-à-vis the churning masses, the elites actually maintained an exaggerated influence precisely because of the geographical impermanence of the majority.
6. Those who voted Yes increased from 8,479 to 105,384 between 1857 and 1868. Entirely new voters could have cast the additional 96,905 Yes ballots in 1868 if (a) all 1857 Yes voters were still in place in 1868 and all of them cast Yes ballots, and (b) the net gain of new voters had been higher by just 5,000 than estimated.
7. The figure 10,000 was obtained from the ecological regressions in the following way: an estimated 38.3 percent of Frémont supporters (N=45,213) voted No or rolled off in 1857, equalling 17,317 voters. Similarly calculated, an estimated 7,279 Frémont supporters voted No, rolled off, or did not vote at all in 1868. Therefore, Frémont supporters who *could have* changed their minds on black suffrage between 1857 and 1868 can be calculated as: 17,317–7,279=10,038.
8. The 40,000 figure was obtained by multiplying Stone supporters (N=152,472) by 27.1 percent, the estimated percentage of Stone supporters voting No in 1880.
9. Foner, *Reconstruction* (see chap. 10, n. 31), 497–511. Foner argues that many northern Liberal leaders were Republicans who felt themselves to have been shunted aside by their various state parties. This was certainly true in Iowa, whose leading Liberals, Josiah B. Grinnell and FitzHenry Warren, were both

disappointed gubernatorial aspirants disillusioned about their political futures. Foner, 500–501; Mildred Throne, "The Liberal Republican Party in Iowa, 1872," *IJHP* 53 (1955): 122, 135–136; Payne (see chap. 10, n. 21), 256–259; Johnson Brigham, *Iowa: Its History and Its Foremost Citizens,* 3 vols. (Chicago, 1918), 1:370–371.

10. For the character and specific sources of the various group variables discussed in this section see appendix A.

11. The German Lutherans' tendency to desert the Republican party every time it too obviously embraced liquor reform was acknowledged by leaders of both Iowa parties. The 1867 campaign, for example, stimulated a considerable interest in repealing Iowa's existing liquor law. In some places Germans bolted the GOP and joined local Democrats in fielding nonpartisan slates, but the alliance was an uneasy one. "For myself I am suspicious of our 'radical loyal German allies,'" asserted one Democrat. "I know that they love a *'copperhead'* verry much like the 'Devil loves holy water' and are still strongly imbued with that rank, sower and stinking herecy of negro equality." A year later the secretary of Iowa's Republican central committee offered a similar assessment: "The German vote which was very generally against us [in 1867] in consequence of the prohibition law question will be with us in the next." George H. Henderson to Laurel Summers, Sept. 18, 1867, Summers Papers, SHSI:DM; John S. Runnels to William E. Chandler, Sept. 14, 1868, Chandler Papers, Library of Congress, Washington, D.C.

12. When one uses voter birthplace data for ecological regressions in which some group results will not be specifically reported, it sometimes makes a difference if such unreported groups are either represented in the analyses in their original percentaged forms or merged into a single catch-all category. Therefore, in the interests of analytical consistency, the regressions reported in tables 12.11 through 12.13 always included an "other" birthplace category for groups too small to merit independent treatment.

13. Kleppner (see chap. 6, n. 24), 313–326.

14. With respect to race relations in America, the legacy of the 1960s in the behavioral sciences, as sociologist Howard Schuman and his associates observe, has been the development of two conflicting, fairly well defined outlooks. The first emphasizes positive white attitude change since the 1940s and is optimistic about further change, the second pessimistically discounts positive change and emphasizes the intractability of discriminatory attitudes. The resolution of this scholarly debate, say the authors, requires acknowledging that progress and resistance to progress have occurred simultaneously. Howard Schuman, Charlotte Steeh, and Lawrence Bobo, *Racial Attitudes in America: Trends and Interpretations* (Cambridge, 1985), 1–8, 163–192.

15. David W. Southern, *Gunnar Myrdal and Black-White Relations: The Use and Abuse of an American Dilemma, 1944–1969* (Baton Rouge, 1987), 166–167, 169–170; August Meier and Elliott Rudwick, *Black History and the Historical Profession, 1915–1980* (Urbana, 1986), 111–112, 148, 168–169, 203–212; J. Morgan Kousser and James M. McPherson, "C. Vann Woodward: An Assessment of His Work and Influence," in *Region, Race, and Reconstruction: Essays in Honor of C. Vann Woodward,* ed. Kousser and McPherson (New

York, 1982), xxv–xxvii, xxxv; August Meier, "Introduction," in Benjamin Quarles, *Black Mosaic: Essays in Afro-American History and Historiography* (Amherst, 1988), 19, 20n.

16. Meier and Rudwick, 167–171. For a rare protest against the negative drift of the historical scholarship see Benedict, "Racism" (see chap. 10, n. 26), 13–20.
17. Baker (see chap. 1, n. 15), 244n. C. Vann Woodward also dismissed the 1868 triumph of black suffrage in Iowa, attributing that success to the state's having sheltered "only a handful of Negroes." But he later discarded the population-ratio argument as explaining neither progressive nor conservative behavior. Compare Woodward, "Seeds of Failure in Radical Race Policy," *Proceedings of the American Philosophical Society* 110 (1966): 7, with his *American Counterpoint: Slavery and Racism in the North/South Dialog* (Boston, 1971), 9.
18. An exhaustive survey of all aspects of African-Americans' status since the 1930s is provided by Gerald David Jaynes and Robin M. Williams Jr., eds., *A Common Destiny: Blacks and American Society* (Washington, 1989). How a subtle appeal to white racism continued to play a role in American politics in the 1980s is statistically explored in Thomas F. Pettigrew and Denise A. Alston, *Tom Bradley's Campaigns for Governor: The Dilemma of Race and Political Strategies* (Washington, 1988). That appeal, of course, became a notorious feature of the 1988 presidential campaign.
19. Joe R. Feagin, *Racial and Ethnic Relations,* 3d ed. (Englewood Cliffs, 1989), 14–15.
20. Gunnar Myrdal, *An American Dilemma: The Negro Problem and Modern Democracy* (New York, 1944), especially xli–lv, 3–25, 997–1034; Meier and Rudwick, *Black History,* 122. Without reference to Myrdal, James Oliver Horton cogently summarizes the Myrdalian thrust of the "traditional" black civil rights movement in *The State of Afro-American History: Past, Present, and Future,* ed. Darlene Clark Hine (Baton Rouge, 1986), 134–135. For the fate of the Myrdal hypothesis within the American academy see Southern, 187–292; Walter A. Jackson, *Gunnar Myrdal and America's Conscience: Social Engineering and Racial Liberalism, 1938–1987* (Chapel Hill, 1990), 231–311.
21. Robert K. Merton, "Discrimination and the American Creed," in *Discrimination and National Welfare,* ed. Robert M. MacIver (New York, 1949), 99–126.
22. T. W. Adorno et al., *The Authoritarian Personality* (New York, 1950), especially 823–830. For a thoughtful assessment of this famous study and its critics see Thomas F. Pettigrew, "The Mental Health Impact," in *Impacts of Racism on White Americans,* ed. Benjamin P. Bowser and Raymond G. Hunt (Beverly Hills, 1981), 97–118.
23. Gordon W. Allport, *The Nature of Prejudice,* 25th anniversary ed. (Reading, 1979), 286; Pettigrew, "Impact," 116.
24. Allport, 469–471. See also Thomas F. Pettigrew et al., *Prejudice* (Cambridge, 1982), 29.
25. Allport, 276. The *fait accompli* phenomenon underlying dramatic changes in

white racial attitudes is suggested in the sequence of public responses to interracial marriage: (a) in 1963 almost half the states had laws that forbade marriages between whites and nonwhites, and 64 percent of white Americans favored such laws; (b) in 1967 the Supreme Court declared such laws unconstitutional; (c) in 1976 only 34 percent of white Americans favored such laws. The Gallup Poll complemented these data by finding that the number of Americans positively approving racial intermarriage rose from 20 percent in 1968 to 40 percent in 1983. Pettigrew, "Impact," 115; George Eaton Simpson and J. Milton Yinger, *Racial and Cultural Minorities: An Analysis of Prejudice and Discrimination,* 4th ed. (New York, 1972), 502–504; D. Garth Taylor, Paul B. Sheatsley, and Andrew M. Greeley, "Attitudes toward Racial Integration," *Scientific American* 238 (1978): 43. But see also Jaynes and Williams, 152.

26. Benedict, "Racism," 19; Allport, 438.
27. Quarles, 107.
28. John Cimprich and Robert C. Mainfort Jr., "The Fort Pillow Massacre: A Statistical Note," *JAH* 76 (1989): 830–837; Margaret Brobst Roth, ed., *Well, Mary: Civil War Letters of a Wisconsin Volunteer* (Madison, 1960), 56–57; Allport, especially 262–264, 276–278. Interestingly enough, the wartime increase in antiblack attitudes by northern soldiers campaigning through the South in the Civil War was replicated during World War II, when thousands of servicemen received their training in the South. Thomas F. Pettigrew, "Regional Differences in Anti-Negro Prejudice," *Journal of Abnormal and Social Psychology* 59 (1959): 31, 35.
29. Robert Robinson to Laurel Summers, July 17, 1865, Summers Papers, SHSI:DM (italics supplied).
30. Robert R. Dykstra, "The Issue Squarely Met: Toward an Explanation of Iowans' Racial Attitudes, 1865–1868," *AI* 47 (1984): 447–450.
31. Allport, xxi–xxii; Ronald P. Formisano, *Boston against Bussing: Race, Class, and Ethnicity in the 1960s and 1970s* (Chapel Hill, 1991); David J. Armor, "The Evidence on Busing," *Public Interest* 28 (1972): especially 93, 110–113; Thomas F. Pettigrew et al., "Busing: A Review of 'The Evidence,'" ibid. 30 (1973): especially 91–93; Armor, "The Double Double Standard: A Reply," ibid., especially 128–129; James Q. Wilson, "On Pettigrew and Armor: An Afterward," ibid., 132–134.
32. Schuman, Steeh, and Bobo, 207.
33. Southern, 123.
34. Thomas F. Pettigrew, "Racial Change and Social Policy," *Annals of the American Academy of Political and Social Science* 441 (1979): 118–120; C. Vann Woodward, *The Strange Career of Jim Crow,* 3d ed. (New York, 1974), 67–109.
35. George L. Stearns, ed., *The Equality of All Men before the Law Claimed and Defended* (Boston, 1865), 38. For the classic assertions that antiblack prejudice was the consequence rather than the precursor of black slavery see Eric E. Williams, *Capitalism and Slavery* (Chapel Hill, 1944); Oliver C. Cox, *Caste, Class, and Race: A Study in Social Dynamics* (Garden City, 1948).
36. Alden T. Vaughan, "The Origins Debate: Slavery and Racism in Seventeenth-

Century Virginia," *Virginia Magazine of History and Biography* 97 (1989): 311–354; Frank M. Snowden Jr., *Before Color Prejudice: The Ancient View of Blacks* (Cambridge, 1983); St. Clair Drake, *Black Folk Here and There: An Essay in History and Anthropology* 1 (Los Angeles, 1987); Bernard Lewis, *Race and Color in Islam* (New York, 1971); David Brion Davis, *Slavery and Human Progress* (New York, 1984), 32–33, 56–57; William D. Phillips Jr., *Slavery from Roman Times to the Early Transatlantic Trade* (Minneapolis, 1985), 57, 69, 140.

37. John Stone, *Racial Conflict in Contemporary Society* (Cambridge, 1985).
38. In the American South, of course, abolition of slavery did not lessen antiblack prejudice. "Racism," writes historian George M. Fredrickson, "although the child of slavery, not only outlived its parent but grew stronger and more independent after slavery's demise," its existence importantly reenergized to justify debt peonage. Fredrickson, *The Arrogance of Race: Historical Perspectives on Slavery, Racism, and Social Inequality* (Middletown, 1988), 3.
39. Gavin Wright, *Old South, New South: Revolutions in the Southern Economy since the Civil War* (New York, 1986), 241–244.
40. J. Morgan Kousser, "Before *Plessy,* before *Brown:* The Development of the Law of Racial Integration in Louisiana and Kansas," in *Toward a Usable Past: Liberty under State Constitutions,* ed. Paul Finkelman and Stephen E. Gottlieb (Athens, 1991), 218.

Index